Social Work Practice in Mental Health

This new edition of *Social Work Practice in Mental Health* builds on the underpinning principles of the previous editions whilst reflecting how the context for practice has steadily evolved.

Organised into two parts and 11 chapters, the book focuses on recovery theory, the importance of relationship and examining the social context and the consequences of illness. It explores the perspectives of consumers and family carers in shaping practice together with a focus on skills including assessment and risk assessment, working in a multidisciplinary team, working with trauma, working within a legal framework and spirituality in practice. The book also maintains the key themes from previous editions of valuing lived experience and the importance of relationships.

This book will be essential reading for social work students and an invaluable resource for practitioners in social work and mental health.

Robert Bland is Adjunct Professor of Social Work at the Australian Catholic University and the University of Queensland, Australia.

Gabrielle Drake is Associate Professor of Social Work in the School of Social Sciences at Western Sydney University, Australia.

John Drayton is Lecturer, School of Nursing, Midwifery and Social Work at the University of Queensland, Australia.

Social Work Practice in Mental Health

An Introduction

3rd edition

Robert Bland, Gabrielle Drake and John Drayton

Routledge
Taylor & Francis Group
LONDON AND NEW YORK

Third edition published 2021
by Routledge
2 Park Square, Milton Park, Abingdon, Oxon, OX14 4RN

and by Routledge
52 Vanderbilt Avenue, New York, NY 10017

Routledge is an imprint of the Taylor & Francis Group, an informa business

First edition published by Allen & Unwin 2009
Second edition published by Allen & Unwin 2015

British Library Cataloguing-in-Publication Data
A catalogue record for this book is available from the British Library

Library of Congress Cataloging-in-Publication Data
A catalog record for this book has been requested

ISBN: 978-0-367-71004-0 (hbk)
ISBN: 978-1-760-52949-9 (pbk)
ISBN: 978-1-003-14891-3 (ebk)

DOI: 10.4324/9781003148913

Contents

Preface to the third edition

This third edition of the text *Social Work and Mental Health Practice* adopts a similar structure to the earlier editions, and while the context for practice has steadily evolved, we have maintained the key themes of valuing lived experience and the importance of relationship.

While Noel Renouf and Ann Tullgren are no longer listed as primary authors, their contributions to the text are significant and enduring. Both have been able to set clearer boundaries around their retirement from employment than I have. Much of the academic groundwork that Noel contributed to the earlier editions remains in this edition, and he has generously encouraged us to use his work here. Noel has made a unique contribution to mental health social work in Australia as a teacher, researcher, practitioner and colleague. He is also a good friend. Ann Tullgren generously agreed to review her contributions and we have used these here too. Student feedback consistently rates the *From Ann* contributions as the most accessible and engaging parts of the text. Ann is a skilled and effective social worker, and I continue to use her stories and example in my own teaching.

My colleagues Gabrielle Drake and John Drayton have both embraced the challenge of reworking the text with energy and commitment. They are both fine academics – the best kind, actually, with lots of experience as practitioners as a starting point for their research and teaching and with a commitment to the discipline of social work and the consumers and families with whom we work.

At some point in the long discussions we had about the chapters we had worked on, Gabrielle said that what she liked about the book was that it had 'a lot of heart'. I think she's right. Perhaps this explains the success of the text book and why students and practitioners like it. Noel, Ann, Gabrielle, John and I have all brought that 'heart' to our writing. We agree that social workers need knowledge and skills for practice, but the real magic of our work only happens when we care deeply about people, share their distress and choose to journey with them towards better times.

Robert Bland
5 September 2020

Part I

The context for practice

1 A starting point

Understanding social work in mental health

Knowledge about mental health and the skills to work effectively with people who have mental health problems are basic to contemporary social work practice. Social workers have been employed in mental health settings for many years now, and mental health has been a traditional field of specialist social work practice. Learning about mental illness and treatment approaches, and critiquing the various medical and social models to explain mental illness and its impacts, have traditionally been core elements of the social work curriculum. Social work's interest in family, community, social welfare and social justice has contributed significantly to the broad knowledge base for policy and practice in mental health. However, beyond the hospital and community mental health treatment settings are a range of recovery-based support services that also employ social workers. As well as working in adult mental health, social workers are employed in areas of child and adolescent mental health, forensic mental health, specialised aged-care settings and with specific population groups such as Indigenous Australians and culturally and linguistically diverse communities.

Understanding the challenge

Despite this long and positive connection between social work and mental health, significant challenges continue to confront the profession in responding to the rapidly changing work environment. In later chapters of this book, we will look at changes to the knowledge base for mental health practice, changes to mental health policy, workforce issues and the challenges to practice arising from the emergence of the consumer and family movements in mental health. Analysis of the highly complex context for contemporary social work practice suggests a number of major challenges for social work. These include:

the highly contested workplace – in multidisciplinary teams, social workers face unrelenting competition for authority and expertise from other disciplines;
the need for a workable paradigm for practice – social workers need to be able to define clearly the distinctive domain for social work practice;
connecting social work practice to a theory or knowledge base;
working collaboratively with consumers and family carers;

DOI: 10.4324/9781003148913-2

the education and training of social workers – what knowledge, skills and values do social workers need for practice, and how might they best acquire these?

Developments in policy, services and education offer opportunities for social work to contribute to the reform process as a vital and relevant discipline. The profession needs to be able to assert with confidence that the core concerns of social work – human rights, self-determination, family relationships and welfare, employment, housing, community, life chances – are central to mental health. We need to continue to argue for a broader agenda in mental health, beyond narrow clinical concepts of illness and treatment. At the same time, we need to demonstrate the range of core knowledge and skills that underpin generic mental health competencies. In the current context of valorising the evidence base for practice and the specificity of interventions, we are challenged to be clear about what we do, and to be able to demonstrate the effectiveness of our actions.

In this book, we take up the challenge to find some directions for the profession. We believe that these directions will be relevant internationally, but we begin by setting out the Australian situation, as this is the specific context from which we are writing.

Social work in the Australian mental health workforce

There are more than 13 000 social workers in Australia. One in six members of the Australian Association of Social Workers (AASW) identifies with the mental health field because of their employment and/or expertise. Others work in human services such as child and family welfare, child protection, acute health, rehabilitation, income security, corrections and juvenile justice, and aged care, which are all fields that require knowledge and skills in supporting people with mental health problems (AASW, 2007). Social workers comprise nearly 10 per cent of the Australian mental health workforce but are active participants in hospital and community mental health services, non-government agencies and private practice. Most social workers are employed in direct service positions, but a significant number work as team leaders and program managers and in policy and program development. Allied health professionals are the fastest growing professional group in state and territory mental health services, and social workers have become the largest single allied health profession (Department of Health and Ageing, 2013).

The Australian National Mental Health Strategy from 1990 to the present day has been based on a multidisciplinary workforce, and social work is identified as one of the five key mental health disciplines (Australian Health Ministers, 1992b). The various policy and workforce initiatives developed through the strategy have included social workers (for example, Deakin Human Services Australia, 1999; National Mental Health Commission, 2013; Victorian Government Department of Health, 2013) and detail the standards of knowledge, skills and values that all mental health professionals – social workers included – should meet. Social work was a contributor to the Mental Health Council of Australia (now known as Mental Health Australia) from its inception in 1996 and as such has had the opportunity to participate in the development and review of national mental health policy.

A project of major significance for the profession was the Commonwealth-funded Development of Competency Standards for Mental Health Social Workers (AASW, 1999). This project was funded as part of the education and training agenda in the National Mental Health Strategy. The AASW tendered the project to a team of social workers, educators and consumers who conducted an extensive national consultation with social workers, consumers and families to develop a comprehensive description of social work practice in mental health. The final product has proven useful as a guide to the accreditation of specialist mental health social workers in Australia and as a basis for educators to develop a curriculum for social work education and training. It has also served as a guide for the accreditation of social workers as approved mental health workers under the recent Commonwealth arrangements to provide some limited Medicare funding for specific mental health interventions provided by social workers in private practice. This document has more recently been revised and republished (AASW, 2008b).

We will discuss many of the policy and practice issues that arise from the strategy in later chapters of this book. At this stage it is important to understand the central place that social work has enjoyed in the history of policy and service developments in Australian mental health.

The ubiquity of mental illness

Recent revisions to the education standards that govern the curriculum in Australian schools of social work (Australian Association of Social Workers, 2020) include psychosocial health and wellbeing across the lifespan as a core component of social work curricula. The argument is that 'mental illness is ubiquitous'. Put simply, this means that no matter where social workers choose to practise they will invariably work with people who have mental health problems.

For example, many people who receive Centrelink benefits will have mental health problems, and those problems will impact on the life experiences of those clients. Clients may be confused and isolated or fearful and angry because of their mental illness. The Centrelink social worker needs to understand how mental illness impacts on the way the client presents and uses services and must work to ensure that the client's entitlements to income support are maintained. The worker needs to be able to engage positively and respectfully with the client, whom other agency staff may perceive as different or even dangerous.

There are a number of such areas of interface between mental health and other social problems, and it is in these areas that much of the creative practice of social workers can be found. Child protection and family welfare is clearly such an area. Mental illness in a parent might impact upon their capacity to provide the necessary care for dependent children. There is a strong need for child protection workers to have a basic understanding of the nature of mental illness and to be able to work effectively with mental health services to benefit children and families. Other areas of interface include mental illness and family violence, disability, health and illness, housing, and schools. We will address some of these specific areas in detail in Chapter 8, and we hope that this book as a whole can be useful for social workers in all settings.

Key themes

Two key themes emerging from the developments in mental health in recent years are central to the way we have conceptualised social work practice in this book. These themes are the importance of the lived experience of mental illness and the importance of relationships as a basis for change. These ideas emerged most strongly in the Deakin Human Services Project (Deakin Human Services Australia, 1999), a highly creative and radical approach to changing the education and training agenda for the professions in mental health. The project was committed to a process of decision-making through partnership among professionals, consumers, family and carers. It brought together eight representatives from each of the five major mental health disciplines (psychiatry, psychology, nursing, occupational therapy and social work) with an equal number of consumers and carers for a series of weekend workshops in Canberra. Each of the disciplines worked on its own agenda to guide professional development (Harries, 1999). Whole-group discussions generated a consensus about an agenda for reform of education and training, which included a commitment of all parties to two central principles identified by the consumers and family carers:

Mental health professionals need to learn about and value the lived experience of consumers and carers.

Mental health professionals should recognise and value the healing potential in the relationships between consumers and service providers and carers and service providers.

These simple but radical principles emphasise a set of values that define practice in mental health in terms of human encounter, rather than as the technical application of skills and knowledge. As we will argue later in the book, relationships are the basis of recovery and hope. They are central to specific interventions such as case management or family work. By giving priority to the lived experience of consumers and families, as defined by consumers and families, we ensure that our work will be guided by principles of partnership, mutuality and empowerment.

Towards a definition of social work in mental health

We have found in our practice across various settings and over many years that the capacity to articulate the social work role in the agency is a necessary condition for effective practice. This is particularly the case in the multidisciplinary workplace, where there is an emphasis on teamwork and the need for each of the disciplines to define their area of competence. There is an irony in this challenge of needing to be clear about the skills, knowledge and values shared by all members of the team (what we have in common) while being able to articulate what is special about social work. Each of the disciplines faces this challenge, but the generic nature of social work education has meant that many social work graduates are not well prepared for practice in mental health.

Review of the teaching of mental health content in schools of social work (AASW Project Team, 2003) showed that, while some schools offer students a solid basis for mental health practice, many offer very little course content on mental health. The review found that students were often exposed to a critique of psychiatry as part of a critical theory approach but were given very little positive direction about the scope and nature of mental health practice. Not surprisingly, these students graduated without a solid understanding of mental health theory and skills and were ill-prepared for practice in the mental health workforce. They needed to gain these skills and knowledge on the job, often with little support or direction. To remedy this variability in professional preparation for practice in mental health, the AASW has set clear guidelines for mental health content in social work curricula as a condition of program accreditation (AASW, 2012).

In our practice, we have noticed a wide range of approaches to defining the role and scope of social work practice in mental health settings. In those agencies where there has been a strong tradition of good professional social work leadership and social workers have been able to assert their role confidently, there has been a high level of agreement among team members about what social workers do, and that role has been valued highly. Just as frequently, however, social workers have appeared confused and defensive about their role, their knowledge base and their effectiveness. In these agencies, social workers have struggled to find a place and a valued role and often report feeling marginalised. They complain that their role is not understood and that they aren't appreciated. The workplace is a site of unrelenting professional contestation. As well as each of the disciplines competing for authority and respect, there are policy and management pressures to promote a view of mental health professionals sharing a knowledge, skills and values base.

We believe that the unique focus of social work is vital and necessary. The work of social work is central to the range of services provided in mental health agencies. Consumers and families need the services of competent social workers. Our argument has consistently been that effective teamwork and best services are delivered to consumers when mental health professionals can meet the twin challenges of shared professional approaches together with high-quality, discipline-specific approaches. For services to work best, the social workers need to be the best mental health social workers they can be, not amateur psychiatrists. Confidence in the social work role and a capacity to articulate the role to other team members, managers, and consumers and families, are central to this challenge.

The unique contribution of social work in mental health

The domain of social work in mental health is defined in *The Practice Standards for Mental Health Social Workers* (AASW, 2008b). It is this domain definition that has largely been adopted in the Australian social work and mental health literature. It may be useful to quote this definition in some detail:

> The domain of social work in mental health is that of the **social context** and **social consequences** of mental illness. The purpose of practice is to promote recovery; to restore individual, family and community wellbeing; to enhance development of each individual's power and control over their lives; and to advance principles of **social justice**. Social work practice occurs at the interface between the individual and the environment: social work activity begins with the individual and extends to the contexts of family, social networks, community and the broader society.
>
> *Social context*
>
> At the level of 'social context', social work is concerned with the way each individual's social environment shapes their experience of mental illness and mental health problems. Its concerns include issues of individual personality, vulnerability and resilience, family functioning, strengths and stressors, support networks, culture, community, class, ethnicity and gender. In addition to the intrapsychic aspects of ego functioning, self-esteem and spirituality and the interpersonal aspects of family functioning and personal relationships, its concerns include broader social issues of economic wellbeing, employment and housing.
>
> *Social consequences*
>
> At the level of 'social consequences', social work is concerned with the impact of mental illness and mental health problems on the individual, the family and personal relationships, as well as on the broader community, including the impact on sense of self; life chances; family wellbeing; and economic security, employment and housing. Social work is concerned with the interface between mental illness and broader health and welfare issues such as child protection and domestic violence.
>
> *Social justice*
>
> At the level of 'social justice', social work is concerned with issues of stigma and discrimination, political freedoms and civil rights, promoting access to necessary treatment and support services, and promoting consumer and carer rights to participation and choice in mental health services. It is concerned with making all human services more accessible and responsive to the specific needs and wishes of people with mental illness and their family and carers (AASW, 2008b, pp. 8–9).

The AASW document also identifies core knowledge, skills and values that underpin social work practice in mental health, and we will be covering many of these in this book. It may be useful at this point, however, to list some of the specific principles that underpin social work practice. These principles reflect the key themes of the lived experience of mental illness and the importance of relationship as central to practice.

Emphasising personhood. Social workers recognise the complexity of human experience and try to see beyond the limits of illness, diagnosis and treatment labels. Accordingly, social workers recognise that people are much more than an illness or diagnostic label and that individuals have broad human needs beyond specific treatment needs. Social workers recognise the importance of family and friendship relationships beyond concepts of 'carer'.

Valuing the lived experience of individual consumers and family members and carers. A guiding principle for practice is a respect for the lived experience of mental illness and consequences for individual consumers, families and other carers.

Affirming the importance of partnership and mutuality. Social workers recognise the importance of working in respectful partnerships with consumers and family carers. These respectful partnerships are marked by efforts to ensure consumer/carer participation and choice in decision-making and self-determination (empowerment) as well as mutuality in assessment and action planning. Partnership and mutuality are values that extend to working with professional colleagues.

Addressing powerlessness, marginality, stigma and disadvantage. Social workers recognise the impact of illness, treatment and stigma on the experience of people with mental illness and their family carers. Social worker practice promotes equity, access and participation, as well as the recognition of all civil and human rights.

Conveying empathy, compassion and hope. Social workers seek to bring human qualities of empathy, compassion and hopefulness to their work (AASW, 2008b, p. 12).

Review of the descriptions of mental health social work in North America and Britain reveals distinct differences in the way that the domain of social work practice is defined. North American social work literature has taken a largely uncritical, clinical focus on practice which has emphasised the therapeutic roles of social work in clinical settings. This reflects, perhaps, the greater number of US social workers in private practice reliant on funding for individual services through third-party health insurance. Social work texts such as Bentley (2003) and Sands (2001) identify a series of key social work activities around such areas as crisis counselling, diagnosis, therapy, mediation, education and even 'medication facilitation'. Social workers are trained in the use of the DSM (American Psychiatric Association,

2013), and there is a strong emphasis on diagnosis and the evidence base for therapeutic interventions (Dziegielewski, 2010).

The review of British models for practice and social work education by Tew and Anderson (2004) reveals a strong similarity with the Australian experience. Their analysis highlights a period of national policy reform and subsequent challenge to the British mental health workforce, in which social work has struggled to meet national practice standards and has been unsure of how to address mental health content in social work curricula. Colin Pritchard's text *Mental Health Social Work* (Pritchard, 2006) is rich in detail in its description of both the range of mental health disorders and the nature of social work practice with specific diagnostic groups. The emphasis in the book is on a biopsychosocial model for practice which incorporates knowledge from diverse discipline areas to inform practice. The approach is eclectic and pragmatic. Two key themes of the book are the importance of relationship (p. xii) and evidence-based practice, themes that will emerge clearly in our analysis. There is less attention however, to developing an overall conceptual framework for social work in mental health. A recent publication by a group of mental health social workers in Northern Ireland develops a number of themes which closely reflect contemporary Australian experience and which are evident in our text. These include an emphasis on relationship-based approaches to work, a focus on systemic practice which locates individuals within a social context, social wellbeing based on dimensions of recovery, social justice and human rights (Office of Social Services Department of Health, *2019*).

We find the AASW definition of the domain of social work and its associated skills, knowledge and values a useful way of understanding social work practice in the contemporary mental health context. It is inclusive and pragmatic, yet there are a number of tensions, or binaries, inherent in the definition. We will describe these next.

Unhelpful binaries

This section will consider a number of unhelpful binaries that bedevil the practice of social workers. We will discuss them as binaries or opposites because that is how they are often presented, but the resolution of each competing binary is invariably about holding the truths of each end of the binary together.

Binary 1: same vs different

We have already encountered this binary. The competing arguments are based on claims about social work being the same as other mental health disciplines, or somehow very different. The National Practice Standards for the Mental Health Workforce, 2013 (Victorian Government Department of Health, 2013) are based on an assumption that the social workers, nurses, psychologists, occupational therapists and psychiatrists who work in mental health share a body of knowledge, skills and values. Each discipline has, in addition, its own special knowledge and skills, and these augment, rather than conflict with, the shared knowledge and skills.

The alternative argument is that somehow social work is fundamentally different from the other disciplines. Social work has, perhaps, been more influenced by sociological theories of social control, deviance and labelling than the other disciplines. Sometimes this argument concerning social work's difference is expressed in the claim that social work is a values-driven profession or that our values are unique. Sometimes it is claimed that social workers are more respectful of consumers and families, less likely to assert power over the consumer or family and more sensitive to issues of confidentiality and self-determination. If social work is fundamentally different from the others, then this difference is not supported in any of the consumer research.

The resolution of this binary is to accept that in some ways social workers are like the other disciplines, and in some ways they are different. There may be shared tasks in the multidisciplinary workforce. All disciplines will share the same knowledge base for practice, and a large part of the values and ethics of the five discipline groups is shared. At the same time, there are significant differences in training, emphasis and world view. As a discipline, we are probably more influenced by sociology and concepts of social justice than the others. Our primary area of expertise is in the social context and consequences of mental illness.

In the end, turf wars are unlikely to be helpful to our work. Trying to show how social work is different is less important, perhaps, than being clear about what it is that we do; about our domain; and about the knowledge, skills and values we draw on to do our work. In this book, we set out to define, describe and defend this social work domain, confident in the importance of social work practice to the outcomes for our client groups, and determined that social workers should have the skills, knowledge and values to practise well.

Binary two: critical vs clinical models of social work practice

Tensions within the practice of social work in mental health settings are sometimes framed around whether social workers should be working from a clinical model or critical model, as if these two models are incompatible and mutually exclusive. The critical/clinical binary is an issue in practice (How do I do social work in mental health?) and in teaching social work practice (How do we teach social work in mental health?). Sometimes the question is asked like this: How can I apply a social justice or anti-oppressive framework to practice in mental health?

The terms *clinical* and *critical* are problematic in their imprecise and value-laden meanings. *Clinical* can simply refer to the site for activity (the clinic), or it can refer to treatment or rehabilitation generally, or treatment in a medical framework. It is often associated with risk management and evidence-based approaches. Typically it relates to a model for practice based on the diagnosis and treatment of mental disorders. *Critical* refers to practice that is associated with a structural understanding of causes of mental health problems and responses, a critique of psychiatry, institutional practices and power imbalances (in both hospital and community settings), and an emphasis on rights. It is concerned with the connections between mental illness and inequality (Rogers & Pilgrim, 2003). For some social workers and academics, *clinical* is close to a curse word, and *critical* is imbued with virtue.

Such is the confusion surrounding this binary that many newly graduating social workers find the transition from university to workplace very difficult. We know that critical theories are central to the teaching of social work practice in most schools and that few schools prepare their graduates for the range of clinical skills they will need in the contemporary mental health workplace. Without the core clinical skills at graduation, the newly appointed social worker either struggles to acquire skills and knowledge quickly and often uncritically or seeks to define their work from a trite if familiar critique of psychiatry which may marginalise their position in the mental health team and, more significantly, compromise their capacity to provide effective support. For many social workers, then, it becomes a choice between being relevant or being critical. The challenge for the profession as a whole, of course, is how to be both relevant and critical.

Renouf (2020) offers a helpful analysis of the nature and importance of the critical perspective in social work practice in mental health. His arguments are central to the themes developed in this text. They include:

- *Working beyond the constraints of the dominant discourse.* He rejects the naïve diagnostic reductionism of seeking to define people by their disorders. The focus has to be on the person's lived experience of their mental health problems, an experience that includes personal distress, meaning-making and the compounding unhelpful responses of people and institutions in the broader social context.
- *The importance of language.* As Ann argues throughout the text, the words we use to describe the experiences of others can be empowering or disempowering. Renouf argues that we have to treat the language of psychiatry as a 'different language' – we have to understand it and be able to engage with it fluently, but we need to be aware of its limits. Our focus is always on a person, not an illness.
- *The coercive nature of involuntary treatment.* Renouf presents a careful analysis of both the dangers and potential of enforcing involuntary treatment. This remains a highly contested dimension of mental health care. As we argue in later chapters of this text, social workers need to approach their work in this area with an awareness of the complexities of the ethical dilemmas inherent in the work.
- *Recovery theory.* Central to critical social work is an awareness of the broader contextual issues that impact on the lived experience of mental health problems. Recovery theory encourages us to focus not just on an illness and treatment but on those aspects of the individual's life where real change is welcome. These include confronting loneliness, having a job, having a home and living a

> life of meaning and purpose. Working with people to develop a sense of power and agency in these important life domains is a core goal of critical social work practice. As such, we recognise the power of structural disadvantage, stigma and discrimination and work to confront these with individuals and in the community.

We acknowledge the specific cultural context of the Indigenous people of Australia and the Torres Strait. Critical social work starts with an awareness and sensitivity to the ongoing impact of colonisation and dispossession together with the complex trauma of generations of oppression and violence.

Through this text, we argue for the importance of maintaining a strong critical social work focus for our work. Social work practice is always going to be more than the narrow application of defined psychological or social interventions. Part of the resolution of the critical/clinical binary is to refuse to treat the two concepts as binary opposites. A more helpful way to present the dimensions might be as follows.

Critical (Concerned with inequality and powerlessness)	vs	**Non-critical** (Unconcerned with inequality and powerlessness)
	and	
Clinical (Concerned with symptoms and disorder)	vs	**Non-clinical** (Unconcerned with symptoms and disorder)

This position treats *critical* and *clinical* as separate concepts with their own dimensions, which can be used as a framework to show how social work practice might focus on one or other of these dimensions, and probably needs to consider both.

We have applied this framework to two examples – housing needs of people with mental health problems and working with families in mental health.

Example A – housing needs of people with mental health problems

A ***critical*** perspective would emphasise:

- access to housing as a common human need;
- advocacy, tenants' rights, housing co-ops, subsidies for low-income tenants / home buyers;
- macro issues such as the development of sufficient housing stock to ensure access to all.

A ***clinical*** perspective would emphasise:

- controlling symptoms that would interfere with secure housing,
- personal support,
- problem-solving,
- learning living skills to support independence in housing.

A comprehensive social work approach would emphasise both perspectives. It is possible to work in a way that ignores either the critical or the clinical dimensions of the problem, but a focus on both dimensions will produce the most effective practice and offers alternative sites for social work activity.

In the second example we apply the framework to another common area of practice, working with family and friendship networks.

A ***critical*** perspective would emphasise:

- a focus on family/friendship networks as a dimension of social inclusion;
- working at the program level to enhance opportunities for developing family and friendship networks;
- advocacy to improve family carer access to resources and legal rights.

A ***clinical*** perspective would emphasise:

- a focus on controlling symptoms that would interfere with family/friendship networks;
- counselling, coaching, psychoeducation and family therapy.

Effective practice with families also clearly involves a focus on both clinical and critical perspectives. We believe that social work needs to work hard to be both critical and clinical in mental health, and it is only when we are able to apply the competing concepts in the real world of the workplace that the potential to resolve the binary becomes obvious. In this book we will focus on both as complementary rather than competing dimensions of practice.

Binary 3: consumer vs family vs worker

This is a 'trinary', perhaps, rather than a binary. It is based on seeing the mental health world as comprising these three distinct groups: consumers, families and workers. As we will show in Chapter 4, the language of the National Mental Health Strategy provides strong recognition of the rights and aspirations of consumers and family carers. These documents are careful to acknowledge that the concerns of consumers may be different from those of family carers. At other times, the phrase 'consumer and family carers' is used more loosely, suggesting that these needs and interests are, if not identical, then at least reconcilable. For example, workers would be expected to consult with consumers and families in planning a new service. At a more subtle level, it is possible for workers to talk about consumers and families and even to talk *to* consumers and families in a way that reflects traditional power imbalances in the giving and receiving of treatment.

At one level, this is about failing to show appropriate respect, as in the case of the elderly mother of a man with long-term schizophrenia, who said that her son's psychiatrist treated her 'like dust beneath his chariot wheel'. At a more subtle level, it is about the ability of relatively powerful people to devalue less powerful people. It is about workers failing to acknowledge a shared humanity with consumers and families. This happens when people with serious illness are reduced to diagnoses, and the complexity of family experience is reduced to the concept of 'carer'. At a pragmatic level, many family carers are also consumers, and many mental health workers are also consumers and family members. There is considerable overlap among the three groups. By emphasising relationship and the lived experience of mental illness as starting points for practice, we resolve this unhelpful trinary.

Valuing the lived experience

Throughout this book, we intersperse text with commentary, reflections and personal experiences of people with mental illnesses. Ann, whose contributions you will find in each chapter, uses her own journey and those of other consumers to provide unique perspectives. Deep listening to the lived experience, in ways that respect, value and empower, is essential to the development of the therapeutic relationship.

People with mental illness often live lives of parallel exclusion in the community. Assigning labels of madness underpins a process of 'othering', when people with mental illnesses are shamed and stigmatised, thought to be different, dangerous and unpredictable. Marginalisation, poverty, despair and suicide often result.

Mental illness can expose the dark underbelly of society. This underbelly is framed by an uncritical adoption of the virtues of competition, individual responsibility, aspiration and hard work (always rewarded by success). The lure of material success is often at the expense of the call to community and relationships. While society espouses the virtues of social inclusion, participation and empowerment, these often sit uneasily alongside other values of economic growth and the creation of the wealth of nations. But the experience of mental illness may also expose narratives of resistance, inclusion and heroism from consumers, family members and professionals. Comments from Ann throughout the book provide perspectives on policies, practices and values which elucidate the contradictions, tensions, binaries and silences that impede the journey to inclusive relationship and valued partnership.

Language

Throughout the book we have tried to use appropriate language to describe the people we're talking about. All the terms to describe the person with the mental health problem are inadequate when used in some ways. We generally use the term *consumer* as most people involved in giving or receiving care and treatment understand and use this term. In Britain and elsewhere the term *service user* is applied. We are aware, however, of situations where a person might have a mental health problem but not be a consumer of any services. They are neither a consumer or service user. We avoided the terms *patient, client* and *sufferer* because they can convey expectations of dependence or control. Similarly, we prefer to use the term *family* as distinct from *carer*, and choose to apply a broad definition of what constitutes *family*. We acknowledge that for some people, friendship networks are more important and intimate than formal family connections. So family for us means those closest to the person. We have restricted the term *carer* to those situations where a person, family or otherwise, provides care and so occupies a caregiving role.

Confusion also surrounds the use of terms like *mental illness*, *mental disorder*, *mental health problem* and *mental distress*. There is no consensus about what these terms mean or the extent of overlap in meaning. There is no agreement about which disorders are illnesses and which label carries the most stigma. We will discuss this problem in greater detail in most of the chapters through the book but particularly in Chapter 5 in our outline of the more common disorders encountered in social work practice.

Structure of the book

We have designed the book to be a useful guide both for social work practice in mental health settings and also for generic practice for which an understanding of mental health issues is needed. We want to convey the challenge and excitement of working with people with mental health problems and their families. There are, of course, many difficulties associated with working in multidisciplinary settings, but the challenges of working in mental health and the joys of sharing those challenges with consumers, colleagues and families make the work uniquely and powerfully rewarding. We want to demystify this work and give it the human face that the best work always has.

Each of us has seen mental illness in its capacity to wound and destroy individuals and families. It can be a cruel and unforgiving enemy. We have also seen wounded individuals and families find the strength and courage to recover and to encourage others in their recovery. Social work with deeply wounded people demands a mature capacity to engage around painful feelings, to be compassionate and hopeful. We value these human qualities in the social worker and encourage you to value them too. We know the importance of social work in supporting people on their recovery journeys. We know that social workers sometimes have to make very hard decisions about their work and struggle with the ethics of being a supporter and an agent of social control. We know the potential of social work to make a difference in people's lives.

Part I: the context for practice

Chapter 2 deals with the lived experience of mental illness. Ann uses her own experience and that of other consumers to describe what it is like from the inside to become ill, to be treated and to work towards recovery. This is an important starting point for us in the book. We have used consumer perspectives regularly throughout the book to emphasise the different ways of thinking about important issues in mental health.

Chapter 3 introduces a number of important principles that underpin social work and mental health practice. These include evidence-based practice, recovery, participation, social inclusion / social exclusion, stigma and discrimination, and spirituality. These are important concepts that social work practitioners will encounter on a daily basis, so the intention here is to help readers to understand the ideas that form a context for practice.

Chapter 4 reviews the mental health policy framework for service delivery and practice in Australia. These policy developments provide a context for service development and practice and reflect the ideas and principles developed in the earlier chapters. This chapter also covers mental health law.

Chapter 5 presents an overview of five of the major mental health disorders – common disorders such as anxiety and depression, as well as schizophrenia, bipolar disorders and borderline personality disorder (BPD). This overview is, of necessity, brief and selective, but we wanted to introduce the reader to the very basic information about these disorders that will inform practice. We have identified a wide range of websites and other resources that will direct the reader towards more detailed information in these and related areas.

Part II: social work practice

In the second part of the book, we provide an overview of key areas of social work practice.

Chapter 6 is about the process of assessment in social work. It provides a useful framework for this most important beginning stage of intervention.

Chapter 7 deals with social casework in mental health settings.

Chapter 8 is about social work practice across service settings, recognising that people with mental health problems come into contact with social workers outside the mental health system.

Chapter 9 addresses the important area of working with families of people with mental disorders.

Chapter 10 is about social work practice in community settings, based on a recognition that much of social work practice involves more systemic approaches to addressing mental illness, particularly in the areas of mental health prevention and promotion.

Chapter 11 is concerned with the organisational aspects of social work practice – working in agencies and teams.

QUESTIONS FOR PRACTICE

1 How can professional expertise be valued while working respectfully and in partnership with experts-by-lived-experience (consumers, families and others)? What are the potential sites for conflict and cooperation?
2 What is social work's unique contribution to professional practice in mental health? What do we share in common with other mental health professionals?
3 What can individuals and families coping with mental health problems reasonably expect the government to provide for them?

Websites

AASW

Includes information about Accredited Mental Health Social Work standards for practice and codes of ethics.
www.aasw.asn.au

Department of Health (Commonwealth Government)

Includes National Practice Standards for the Mental Health Workforce; reports; policies; information.
www.health.gov.au

Mental Health Commission of Australia

The Commission is charged with improving the mental health system through improved planning, coordinating and monitoring.
www.mentalhealthcommission.gov.au

Mental Health Australia

The peak, national body representing and promoting the interests of the Australian mental health sector, formerly known as the Mental Health Council of Australia.
www.mhaustralia.org

Mental Health Foundation of New Zealand

Concerned with mental health promotion, providing resources, innovative stigma and discrimination campaigns, suicide prevention work; offers resources and information.
www.mentalhealth.org.nz

Our Consumer Place

'The Company We Keep: A users' guide to mental health clinicians', a free download. Other publications available.
www.ourconsumerplace.com.au

Psychiatric Disability Services of Victoria

Includes: publications, resources, training, policy documents, links to libraries, clearinghouses, publications and other organisations. Free online magazine/journal, *Newparadigm*.
www.mhvic.org.au

2 The lived experience of mental illness

In recent years, there has been an explosion of accounts of the lived experience of mental illness, that is, views from the inside looking out. Poetry, prose, drama and art tell of suffering, alienation and shame, as well as hopefulness, humour and dignity. These accounts also comment on the services people encounter and how the attitudes of family, friends, professionals and the wider community may either wound and impair or encourage and empower. The narratives may carry the deeply personal into the political sphere, challenging existing orthodoxies around organisational and political policies and practices.

Mental illness may be described from a variety of viewpoints, based on experience, opinion and understanding. Consumers, families, friends and other social groups have their own lived experiences that inform their viewing points and positionality. Importantly, social workers and mental health professionals have opinions, learning and experiences. Indeed there is a multiplicity of possible viewing points, not all of them helpful. How can social workers make sense of this and develop compassion, skill, curiosity and a determination to make a difference?

The first key theme of this book is that learning about and valuing the lived experience of mental illness should be the starting point for professional practice. This is a radical and transformative proposition; it situates the person at the heart of social work, acknowledging that there are experts-by-experience as well as experts-by-training. The second key theme is that social work practice in mental health takes place within the context of relationships. We are all social beings and each life is embedded in that of others. Human existence is situated in relation to society, history, culture, the economy, the political landscape and the ecology of our constructed and natural environments. Whatever the impact of biology, there is rarely a psychiatric crisis without a wider context. Social work, with its unique focus, has always acknowledged this, recognising that recovery takes place within supportive relationships and environments.

In this chapter, the text will be counterbalanced by Ann's account of her own experience and that of other people with mental illness. These narratives illustrate how change occurs through the telling of, and attending to, stories of illness and recovery.

DOI: 10.4324/9781003148913-3

From Ann: becoming ill – the shock of the new

When I was 19 I was diagnosed with endogenous depression. (*Endogenous* means 'coming from within', or 'biochemical', compared with *exogenous*, meaning 'coming from difficulties in living'.) I'd been unsettled over the previous couple of years: moody, withdrawn, unable to stick at work or study. Finally suicidal, walking and walking until my feet blistered. While I knew something was wrong, the diagnosis came as a shock, and I didn't know what it meant. The only depression I'd heard about was economic depression. When I was growing up there were no community education campaigns about mental illness, no tell-it-all TV and radio shows, no internet either. No Beyond Blue. Women's magazines provided limited mental health information (along the lines of how to knit socks, wash socks and pull up your socks).

Get used to the unexpected!

I was hospitalised. The admitting nurse asked me to put on my PJs; I found this strange because it was the middle of the day. She gave me some red pills – I later discovered they were antidepressants. The side effects were just awful – dry mouth, blurred vision, confusion and agitation. Perhaps the most noxious side effect was the one I couldn't have predicted at the time – actually, not many professionals realised it then either – that for people with a predisposition to bipolar disorder, antidepressants can precipitate the illness. My brain seemed to be no longer my own, thanks to depression and the side effects of the tablets. I became alienated from myself and the predictable rhythms of my old life.

Privacy? What privacy?

The hospital had daily group therapy for young patients. While I had been brought up to be emotionally self-controlled and reticent about discussing private experiences, the therapists encouraged venting, emoting, letting-it-hang-out. This easily became emotional incontinence. I'm not sure it was helpful.

You ain't seen nothing yet!

Thinking of that first episode: it was as if I had been stripped bare of the essence of myself. Who was I? How did I come to this point in my life? What on earth was to become of me? I no longer knew, or cared. I learned to distrust emotion, perception and cognition. Add mood swings to the existential despair and ennui felt by many young adults and the outcome was a toxic swill of nothingness. Shortly after the onset of serious mental illness, my mood swings became like the shifting and grating of deep tectonic plates. The waves of despair had the effect of a tsunami on the shores of my life and they became desolate frontiers that even I did not want to inhabit. Is it any wonder that I began to think of suicide?

Lived experience and mental illness

Mental illness doesn't occur in splendid biological or genetic isolation; it evolves out of, and is sustained by, the messy reality of life. The knock-on effects of mental illness – housing insecurity, poverty, estrangement from family and friends, high rates of imprisonment, welfare dependency, casual and unstable employment, loneliness and a myriad of other experiences – speak of our marginalisation. In such ways we become the other, the not-us, the losers, the nutters, the undeserving and the misfits. Thus mental illness becomes a disorder of citizenship and a disorder of otherness.

Thinking about lived experience

It is profoundly personal.

It is the view from the inside, looking out.

It is deeply contextual.

Experience is embodied: pain, hurt, shame, anger and joy are held in the body and are felt viscerally.

Sometimes embodied madness becomes visible in scars and the external markers of difference and poverty.

Merinda Epstein from Our Consumer Place talks about our 'livid experiences' (those that lead to loss of dignity, stigma and shame).

For respectful and lasting change to occur, our lived experiences cannot be compartmentalised, where services/professionals segment our various problems into discrete units that are parcelled out to various agencies to 'fix' (also known as 'referral').

Things that are important to consumers may be less important to services/professionals.

Just as there are commonalities of experience, there are also differences; each person's journey is unique. Reflecting this, consumers talk about consumer viewing points, a term that reflects the diversity and richness of experience.

Viewing points evolve.

How we reflect on our experiences also changes over time.

Consumer thinkers also talk about 'consumer perspective'; this is a commentary voice, creating meaning and theory from experience.

Within the academy, just as there are queer theorists and crip (disability) theorists, some consumer thinkers and academics call themselves mad theorists. Thus thinking about the lived experience of mental illness moves beyond concern with clinical concerns and individual recovery to considerations of politics, power, human rights and alternative ways of providing services.

Sticks and stones may hurt my bones and words can hurt me (deeply)

The words used to describe those who live with mental illness change over time, reflecting historical service delivery frameworks and wider social change. Not so long ago we were called *lunatics*, then we became *patients*, then *clients*, then *consumers*, and more recently *persons-in-recovery*, *peers* and *people with lived experience*. In the UK, the term *service user* is employed. Many of these terms are coined by services, professionals and policies, and many people who live with mental illness are uncomfortable with these descriptors. Thus some prefer to think of themselves as *psychiatric survivors*, a term that reflects the trauma of treatment and human rights abuses. To keep things simple, this chapter will talk about *consumers*; it isn't the best word, but it is the one most recognised at present. Don't forget, each time the label changes so do the stationery, the mission statements and the other documents used by policy wonks and services. And . . . each iteration, each change, takes money away from service delivery, from helping us become who we want to be.

From Ann: the Mad Hatter's tea party – winning ways with peer support!

Against the advice of my doctor, some 12 years after my initial breakdown, I joined the Manic and Depressive Self-Help Group, which met monthly in a suburban home. I met many people, some newly diagnosed, others battling recurrent depression and mania. I went to my first meeting thinking that I'd reached the point where I had nothing more to lose, not realising that I had a great deal to gain. So, what happened there?

We lubricated our interactions with good food, good coffee and even alcohol. We met in Meg's home and spilled out into the sun in the backyard, where we sought shade under a dysfunctional mango tree that never bore fruit, whatever the qualities of foliage, blossom or weather! All were welcome. We treated each other with care and humour. We encouraged each other; believed in each other. I forged a role for myself as a waitress and welcomer, handing around plates of food and drink; that way I got to talk to a lot of people without taking too many risks or appearing too socially inept. Can you even begin to understand what it is like for someone who is still in hospital and who comes to their first meeting, with echoes of the delusion that they are the Virgin Mary ricocheting around their mind, only to be introduced to four other virgins sitting under the dappled shade of the mango tree?

And so we shared stories with tears, anger, humour and hope. We published our own newsletter and compilations of poems, personal accounts, information, advice and art. Our stories became transformational, in large part because we had shared them but also because the words we wrote filled in the silences in the narratives written about us by professionals. Our lived experiences, understandings and insights reduced the isolation of the experience of the other.

We decided whom we would invite to educate or entertain us. Requests for research participants required a quid pro quo: tell us what you are investigating, let us comment on your research design and come back to tell us about the progress of your investigations and receive feedback. And don't bother nipping off after the presentation before people can corner you over a cuppa!

You may be suffering from . . .

There are times when diagnosis is empowering and liberating. It can make sense of something that appears senseless; it may signpost helpful treatments. However, diagnosis can metamorphose into labelling, and treatment can become the dehumanising application of technologies of care and/or containment. As we progress in our mental illness 'career' as passive 'patients' or 'clients', we learn to talk about symptoms and experiences using psychiatric and service-centric jargon. Thus certain discourses are reinforced, while other knowledge or insights are seen as unimportant, eventually disappearing from the way we think about ourselves.

From Ann: life after diagnosis

Once diagnosed, I believed that with treatment (hospitalisation, medication, therapy) I would completely recover. I would get my life back on track and 'prove' my worth to my family through my accomplishments. I anticipated a three-month turnaround. Such was the promise of science. But it did not happen according to the script.

I saw a psychiatrist twice a week. At first, I was highly sceptical about his diagnosis. My experience seemed far more amorphous and chaotic than could be summed up with just one term. Initially during these consultations, I would talk about how I felt, my thoughts and perceptions using everyday language. But his interviewing repertoire was predictable, as he explored my symptoms according to the formula of the diagnostic manual at the time.

I didn't realise that this was what he was doing, but I quickly learned to report my 'lived experience' using his language and cognitive frameworks. I reported some things and ignored others. And so my world shrank . . .

Diagnosis, once liberating, came to mark shameful difference. At first it was empowering ('At last I know what is wrong; there are even treatments'), but after the first flush of hope and expectancy, it became limiting, suffused with deficits, predictive of behaviour, belief and experience – the future.

Instead of hope of recovery, I acquired a new discipline of mind that contained me just as effectively as the walls of old asylums. I became attuned to stigmatising practices (those backward glances, the conversations that limped into nothingness, the visits from the nurse just before ward report so they could have something to talk about during handover to the next shift). Diagnosis became about relapse, sometimes dramatic and at other times halting and insidious. I learned what was expected of someone with my 'problem' (endless hospitalisations, life on income support, medication . . .). For years, everything I owned fit into a suitcase that could be stored in a locked hospital cupboard, and my connections to friends, family and community were gradually whittled away. I was no longer a university student hanging out with friends. I had lost my accommodation and couldn't afford to leave hospital and rent a flat. My family lived in a distant rural area, so I couldn't be discharged there.

I had become a moral failure. All around me, friends were studying hard, graduating from university, travelling overseas, having intimate relationships and working in interesting jobs. I just couldn't seem to try hard enough, for long enough, or in the right way in order to get back on track.

Diagnostic hierarchies

Not all diagnoses are equal. Within the diagnostic lexicon, some labels are seen as more acceptable, more deserving, more serious and enduring, more burdensome for families or more tragic. There are some interesting binaries worth exploring:

mad/bad
neurotic/psychotic
acute/chronic
serious/trivial
public/private
hospital/community
real/imagined

Some diagnoses are thought of pejoratively, perhaps in response to stories in the media, or gossip around the agency water cooler. For example, people with personality disorders may be seen as 'untreatable', 'difficult' or 'manipulative' and may be denied services. People with drug-induced psychoses may be seen as intractable and violent and may be blamed for failure to recover. Older consumers find themselves labelled 'palliative' (obviously by people who have not heard of the importance of hope or the recovery paradigm). Let's call this labelling what it is: vilification.

Policy initiatives and service priorities are prescribed by particular diagnoses, age groups or genders. This may result in well-intentioned rivalry about which practices achieve the best outcomes or where scarce resources should be spent. Frequently, need does not match help available. Falling through the cracks becomes more about service availability than compliance.

From Ann: poverty

This is what more than 20 years of living on social security payments is like: after the bills are paid, no money left for food for three days before payment day; the last pair of shoes gives out and I don't know how I will manage as I walk everywhere because I don't have money for fares; I'm sleeping on a mattress on the floor – that's the limit of my furniture; I can't always afford medication; I keep getting infections – oranges are too expensive to eat every day; the phone booth two streets away is vandalised again and I can't ring my mental health service provider to make appointments. My options keep getting narrower.

The corruption of identity

If our life project is to develop a sense of coherence and meaning about our identity and purpose in life, it follows that for those with mental illness this is a more fraught endeavour. Mental illness may compromise the construction of a rich and valued narrative about personal identity because of distortions in thinking, feeling and perception. Mental illness changes our experience of self and compromises the ways we negotiate the world. It also changes the ways other people think about and relate to us.

Many of us develop mental illness during our late adolescence or early adulthood, which hijacks the usual tasks associated with growing up. There may emerge a huge disconnection between who we thought we were, the hopes we had for the future and the flawed identity that emerges due to the illness and the ways society responds to us. As this chasm deepens, we may sink into chaos, despair, anger, fragmentation, silence and shame. Our experience of stigma, discrimination, powerlessness and pointlessness that attend the processes surrounding diagnosis, treatment, care and management may further propel us on this downwards trajectory. Mental health and other human services can be mentally ill services.

From Ann: seeking God

What follows is not an easy paragraph to read, so fast forward if you're at all squeamish.

The time came when I felt life was not worth living. So, I took a very large overdose and sat underneath a tree waiting to die. Some days later I awoke in intensive care. When I opened my eyes I couldn't see, everything was black. I thought I was blind. I tried to talk but I was connected to a respirator. I flailed around and found that I was naked with ice packed around me. I had double pneumonia. At one point I had died and they had worked hard to bring me back.

A bedside voice introduced himself as Father X, a Catholic priest. He told me that it was OK, that God knew I hadn't meant it and that I was forgiven. The trouble was I had meant it and the fact that not even God had wanted me by taking me to heaven confirmed my abject nature. I flailed around a bit more and the voice went away.

Some days later it was decided I could get out of bed to have a shower. A nurse brought me some of her own shampoo, conditioner and scented soap from her home; she gently helped me to wash away the sticky, smelly, stale residue of hospital. I have never forgotten her compassion and the gentle dignity with which she touched me and spoke to me. It was a brief relationship but a pivotal moment in my recovery journey.

Salience of the inside-outside perspective

Because madness is repeatedly described, theorised and treated by those who haven't experienced it, and because these processes have society's official ticks of approval, the knowledge and insights gained during consumers' day-to-day lived experiences are often overlooked, disrespected, neglected or trivialised. The meanings ascribed to various labels are integral to the process of othering, where the recipient of mental health services is seen as different and inferior to normal people (whom I shall refer to as 'normals'). This is not always a malevolent process; othering may arise from benevolence, when people think they are being caring or 'acting in our best interests', while in fact they are being condescending, infantilising and paternalistic (Epstein et al., 2012).

If you are a student, or you are in the early years of practice, you may think that this will not become your way of working. I invite you to maintain critical reflection on your practice, asking consumers to critically reflect with you to develop shared understandings. I also invite you to heed the tiny voice inside you that says, 'Am I sure this is how I want to think or act?' The theory of cognitive dissonance suggests that when people think and behave in ways that are inconsistent with their values, they experience a sense of disquiet or unease. If this discomfort is ignored, it will fade and the opportunity to develop as a worker in ways that are consistent with deeply held values will be lost. The potential for values conflict is ubiquitous in all psychiatric practice, and it is for this reason that social work in mental health can be intellectually tough and challenging, frustrating and, in equal measure, exciting and inspiring.

In recent years, increasing numbers of those with lived experience have moved into the academy, and the lived experience is informing their theorising, research, lecturing and interactions with others in academia and the mental health sector. Dr Sarah Gordon in NZ was instrumental in the formation of the International Association of Service User Academia; at Kings College London in the UK, Dr Diana Rose was the first professor in user-led research. She established SURE, a globally unique research group that focuses on mental health services and treatments from consumer and carer perspectives.

From Ann: finding meaning

When I was in senior school and during my prodromal period – a time of increasing but ill-defined un-wellness – a teacher gave me a copy of Viktor Frankl's *Man's Search for Meaning* (Frankl, 1984). The Holocaust became a powerful symbol for me in my struggles, although I was uncomfortable using it as a metaphor for my life in case that diminished its meaning for others. The salience of the Final Solution for me was that, just as Nazis stripped Jews, gypsies, gays, the mentally ill, the disabled and those with certain political views of their identity and place in society (shaving their hair; taking away their clothes, wedding rings and other markers of personhood and relationships; and ultimately killing them by the millions), so too did mood disorder and repeated hospitalisations rob me of these things. Frankl helped me to understand that my innate worth as a human being did not depend on whether I worked, or owned a home, or had lots of friends, or took holidays to fashionable resorts. It showed me that the meaning I constructed around my experiences would help me survive mental illness.

Viktor Frankl was important for me when I was young because there were no first-person accounts from people who had experienced madness and recovered, no Beyond Blue, no Black Dog Institute. Some sensationalist novels were passed around the ward, as was a battered copy of *The Divided Self: An Existential Study in Sanity and Madness*, which we all pretended to understand (Laing, 1960). Instead, Viktor Frankl became my companion.

Lived experience and social work practice

The processes and values that underpin much mental health work are constructed using scientific and professional discourses that invite workers to demonstrate practice competency, intentionality and objectivity. There follows a paradox that, while current practice in mental health has never been so well supported through research, supervision, management systems, codes of practice and continuing professional education, there continue to be scandals, reports and inquiries that expose professional worst practice, and there are policies and political practices that discriminate, violate basic human rights or even involve criminal behaviour.

Successive reports note that Australia's mental health systems are in crisis. Between 2006 and 2012, there have been around 50 separate enquiries into different aspects of systemic failure (Rosenberg & Hickie, 2013). The solution usually entails more professional education, increased fidelity to evidence-based treatment protocols, rigorous risk assessment, improved outcome measures, key performance indicators, different models of supervision and accountability. In reality, however, recommendations are rarely put into effect, leading to the cascade of well-meant intentions. Each new enquiry entails more trauma for those with lived experience who recount their experiences.

But is there another way? Perhaps a deeper understanding of lived experience (mine, yours and ours) and a focus on relationship can enhance professional practice and result in improved outcomes.

By giving pre-eminence to the lived experience, human service workers acknowledge that we are more than our faulty neural firings, thus privileging the person and the relationship rather than the problem (our diagnoses, our failures to thrive, to recover). By your curiosity and compassion for the ever-unfolding narrative of my life, you will change me, and I you, and so change will continue long after our appointment is completed.

Most social workers embark on professional studies and the early years of practice with cherished ideals about helping people; they want to make a difference, to empower the disempowered and to challenge disabling orthodoxies. In a nutshell, they want to become change agents. The next step is more challenging; it is to gain a deeper appreciation of statements such as 'although different, all are equal', or 'all should be treated with dignity and respect'. For such statements to be enduring and meaningful they must be based on sound intellectual footings, critically reflected on and incorporated into daily life; that is, the challenge for all is to find a rich conception of what it means to be a human being.

In this book we take the view that a philosophy of care is as important as a technology of care. This is a bold statement. It places ethical curiosity and a willingness to learn, reflect and act on changed understandings at the centre of professional practice.

The next section of this chapter will elucidate a lived experience ethic of practice that is both relational and contextual. Philosophical constructions about the nature and worth of each life, and related issues such as free will, moral responsibility, personal agency and authentic existence, all explicitly and implicitly inform workers' professional relationships and practices. It is proposed that a rich understanding of dignity provides an overarching framework for understanding and responding to a lived experience of mental illness.

From Ann: missing children

A friend was a social worker in a government agency providing financial assistance. A young woman of 16 told her that she and her younger sister had run out of food and had no money to catch the bus to school. Their rent was in arrears. The social worker asked about her parents. She and her sister lived with their mother who had been admitted to a mental health facility six weeks earlier. Their mother did not leave any money for them and would not allow her daughters to access her bank account so that they could buy food, pay rent and catch buses. My friend rang the hospital and discovered that the staff there were unaware that their patient had any children, that the children were living without adult care or that they were hungry.

On human dignity

Nora Jacobson (2009) argues that a focus on bio-ethics is critical in human services; she calls it the new metanarrative of care. Within this framework she identifies dignity as the pre-eminent concept. In placing dignity at the heart of social work in mental health, special attention is given to understanding the nature and meaning of human existence, and to the processes that enhance or violate dignity in worker-consumer interactions. Dignity is essentially a relational and contextual concept. Drawing on narrative therapy, it is about how lives are co-authored as each person exists within the stories of others, a web of narratives and discourses that connect or disconnect, enable or disable. It can bind the teller of the narrative (those in pain and distress) to those who listen and bear witness. It is how we accompany each other that matters.

Unlike many terms used in human service work, *dignity* has not yet become jargonised and politicised. Additionally, everyday understandings – definitions-in-use – are similar to theoretical and empirical definitions (Jacobson, 2009). Contrast this with terms used in mental health such as *recovery*, *participation*, *empowerment*, *contributing life*, all of which have metamorphosed from their everyday definitions to incorporate troubling nuances informed by neo-liberalism about personal responsibility. Dignity means having grace under fire, keeping a sense of humour, finding a way to come out into the sunlight from a time spent on the sidelines, being a person rather than a diagnosis, accompanying each other with respect and understanding.

From Ann: doing recovery

I was referred to a rehabilitation service (the term *recovery* had not then been invented). During the first week I was 'assessed'. I was asked questions about my 'activities of daily life', and some basic psychometric tests quantified my functional intelligence. It seemed to me that far more interest was shown in assessing my disorder and disability than my abilities and hopes.

The resultant individual service plan (ISP) identified possibilities for me in future clerical work, but for this to happen I would need to improve my spelling. So, I sat at a table with a how-to-spell-book. Four years previously, I had come in near to the top in the state in several subjects in my leaving certificate and had gained admission to a law degree at a prestigious university.

The disconnection between my past and present seemed now clear-cut, and my dreams for the future were dimmer than ever. I didn't want to become a clerical worker, so learning how to improve my spelling seemed a pointless endeavour and soon I stopped attending the service. In any case, the more I read over time and the more I wrote, the better my spelling became. And . . . isn't 'spell-check' a wonderful thing!!

Personhood, relationship and language

Desmond Tutu notes that none of us comes into the world fully formed and that we need others in order to become ourselves, fully human. For Tutu (2004, p. 25), 'The first law of our being is that we are set in a delicate network of interdependence with our fellow human beings'. In Africa this is known as *Ubuntu*, and it means that our humanity is inextricably bound to the humanity of others so that when one person is diminished, humiliated or oppressed, then all others are too. *Ubuntu* gives people resilience and the strength and courage to survive and grow (Tutu, 2004).

Since we are embedded in the human world, we share in the possibilities or limitations of language. Language is a vehicle for understanding others, for describing how each person is situated in their environment. It underpins a rich and nuanced understanding of personal identity and connectedness to others – our lived experiences. The trajectories of wellness and relapse are partially mediated by how each person thinks about and talks about the experience of being human and how this changes over time. Stigmatising beliefs and practices, including self-stigma, chip away at human dignity and the possibilities of being alive. 'Deep listening' may be an antidote to this. The Daly River community in the Northern Territory have a notion of 'Dadarri', a kind of deep inner listening, and still awareness (ABC Radio, 2007). Other Indigenous cultures in Australia talk about listening and thinking at the same time, as an act of inner reflection. Dadarri and Ubuntu are beliefs and practices from ancient cultures that provide a fresh perspective on the bio-ethics of mental health practice.

From Ann: my story, myself – a narrative in permanent draft format

When I was born, I was whole and full of promise; a Rubik's Cube still packaged for sale, before anyone twists, turns and distorts the colour pattern only to find it near impossible to get it back to 'normal'. At least that's what I thought.

Looking back, the stories I told myself as a child resembled fairy tales: I was Sleeping Beauty, or Snow White, or the Ugly Duckling. It was no great leap of imagination to think I was the eighth member of Enid Blyton's Secret Seven, always ready for adventure. Whatever trials and tribulations of the journey, the ending always came good.

In a similar manner, as I grew older, I embraced the plot lines others had for me: work hard at school, be good, keep the Catholic faith, go to uni, travel, find meaningful work. Then, get married, have kids and raise them to be all of the above! . . . But when I was in my mid- to late teens, the storylines became fractured, and I no longer had words for the evolving plot where the key protagonist was mental illness.

I embarked on conventional treatment: I consulted a psychiatrist and spent a lot of time in hospital. I learned a new language to describe this radically reshaped life; it was the language of diagnosis and treatment. It was useful to have words and concepts to make some sense out of my experience and to help me explain it to others. At the same time, I felt rather clever that I had learned quickly (and could spell and pronounce) the labels and concepts underpinning a medical understanding of madness, the names of the medications and the sad prognoses. Embracing science, I cast aside those quaint and comfortable colloquialisms: 'A touch of the vapours', 'A sausage short of a picnic', 'A kangaroo loose in my top paddock', 'A bit cracked', 'A walk with the black dog', or 'Fairies at the bottom of my garden'. Instead, I had endogenous depression, and later on, manic depressive illness. These were later known by other titles: major depression, unipolar depression, bipolar disorder.

Looking back, I was imprisoned by a web of jargon and ideas. The post-modern use of power isn't about manacles or walls. Instead, we learn to become our own jailors by using the official discourses of failure and brokenness that provide a far more effective confinement. In the end, the language of medicine was the language of disease and deficit, not the language of strengths, possibilities and transformation. Yet, to think about it another way: did the dog (myself) wag the tail, or did the tail (this madness constrained, contained and replicated by the jargon and ideas of medicine and science) wag the dog?

It was much later in life that I learned other ways to story my life; ways informed by literature, poetry, sociology, religion and philosophy. These can layer and enrich the narrative, making it subtler, opening up possibilities that underpin a dignified and meaningful life. But in the end, the language and stories of the possibility of redemption and change come most poignantly from poetry and art.

I have moved beyond the facile fairy book construction of life where I thought that I could only reach 'heaven' (a better place) by keeping the Rubik's Cube of self unsullied. I am content to keep the books of science and psychiatry on a shelf, where I can consult them when I need to. My pills are in the dosette box next to a glass for water (they help). But I have learned that my route to 'heaven' (what is possible) is through the back door to that road less travelled. There are no scientific cures for me, just good enough treatments that provide space to live a good life.

What really matters is how I story my suffering, my heroism and my humour. My narrative quest takes me towards a life of grace and dignity. It can heal the wounds left by reason.

Developing narrative competency

Relationship and language, both verbal and non-verbal, are reciprocally bound together. Once you, the healer, form a relationship with us, people with mental illnesses, you become part of our lived experience, and we become part of yours. We co-construct each other. How language is used may enhance or restrict our relationships. Language informs how we think and act, and it also limits or enhances how others hear us, enhancing or violating the essential dignity of existence and connection with others.

Language is laden with implicit and explicit values. The languages of diagnosis and 'helping' are extremely powerful. They are used to formulate the 'case history', which is elaborated in reports, referral documents and the multitudinous files you construct about us, usually without our knowledge or contribution. Such cascading descriptions can become the dominant stories told about us, entrapping us in our problem-saturated lives and future prospects.

Signposts: language

Here are some signposts to help you on your journey; why not pin them up near the water cooler or on the tea-room noticeboard?

Use person-first language that privileges our personhood, rather than our disabilities, illnesses and related conditions or characteristics.

Use terms that indicate that our diagnosis is just one part of us: a person with lived experience rather than a schizophrenic, or a depressive.

Beware of 'hot-button phrases' and derogatory codes: we are people first and last (Jane or John), not a diagnosis. How often have you seen in case files such shorthands as '25yo F (schiz) or client (c), or patient (pt), or consumer (con), or someone with personality disorder (PD)'?

When you focus on what's wrong, what's right is often ignored. This ensnares us in the problem and is another violation of dignity.

Persons/professionals/agencies that control language through use of jargon and rarefied concepts and terms inevitably exercise power over others.

Privileging professional and scientific discourses can lead us to unnecessarily rely on experts – perhaps your expertise, rather than our own.

Using worn-out, service-centric language confines you to old ways of seeing and thinking and interacting (God save us from more acronyms).

Communication may be made up of silent gestures, small noises, queries, glances and shifts in body position, as well as words and silences.

When you say that you are my case manager, or worker, and that I am your client, you imply possession or control.

Each time you write or talk about us, are you demonstrating respectful curiosity and a hopeful attitude, or are you demonstrating your professional expertise by comprehensively assessing and describing our problems in ways that will lead to being praised for your competency?

Choose language with care, and be aware of its negative and positive possibilities.

Help us deconstruct the truisms of Western society: that the virtues of individualism, stoicism and hard work will bring material rewards (the so-called prosperity gospel).

Facilitate the development of alternative/possible metaphors and stories that open up possibilities and make sense of chaos and despair. This is how hope is storied and imagined and tried on for size. These are the first steps in developing a sense of agency.

Make meaning with us. Together, how can we interrogate the questions, *Why me? Why my family? How will I survive this?*

Explore and resist binaries: for example, professional/consumer, expert/ignorant.

Listen with patience to silences and seemingly confused narratives.

Listening is different from assessing.

From Ann: through the retro-spectroscope

We live in a society that esteems robust individualism and self-help, that rewards hard work and initiative with success and status. Thus, a person's value is consequent to our do-ings (employment, education, income, homes acquired, holidays taken), rather than our human be-ings (who we are deep within ourselves, our inherent worth and dignity of being).

Looking back, there were some pivotal turning points in my recovery, involving both do-ings and be-ings.

Do-ings

After many false starts I finally completed university studies. My first degree in education took six years to complete. I did the first year from my hospital room and was helped with developing academic skills and confidence by a room-mate who was a university research assistant. The second degree, social work, I completed on time. I value an education that recognises that all knowledge and experience are historically, contextually and linguistically constructed. I learned to check out the binaries, to look for transactions of power, to observe the possibilities of language. I have fought for social justice, to accompany others in need. Most important of all are the friendships I have made and the people who changed my life (and perhaps the people whose lives I changed, sometimes for the best, sometimes not).

Be-ings

Early on I spent a lot of time angrily and hopelessly convinced that my situation was utterly unfair, thinking about the meaning of life, protesting against my suffering. I then progressed to my saintly phase: I would learn to live with suffering; I would offer it up to make reparation for the world's pain. Then there was my feel-the-pain-and-be-damned period – 'I will bloody well get on with things; I will discipline myself, even if it means I crash through and burn!' Somewhere along the line I learned to put the 'I' to one side, to focus on the 'we', the 'us', the 'our'. The Manic and Depressive Self-Help Group was pivotal in these changes. And I learned to listen and to hope.

Of late I am using the Acceptance and Commitment Therapy (ACT) model. It acknowledges that suffering happens but that there are techniques to minimise its hold so that life can be lived purposefully, according to the values or ethics that we hold deep within us and which inform life's journey. I recently discovered a journal I kept at school and have found that my intellectual interests, my moral compass and my values have remained fairly constant throughout my life. Despite everything, the essence of myself endured. This means that I don't have to wait for the mood disorder to abate in order to live purposefully, although this is easier said than accomplished. I can take my experience of mental illness along with me, sometimes as a heavy suitcase, at other times as a cumbersome shoulder bag, or even as a glitzy 'look-at-me' clutch purse! But always something that invites possibilities.

QUESTIONS FOR PRACTICE

1 How can appreciation of lived experience change professional practice?
2 How is power being used when you see clients, or write up notes, or talk about them in case conferences?
3 What does the agency expect of you? What does the client expect of you? What about the family? How does it feel to be torn between competing needs and agendas?
4 Where do you usually 'see' clients? How does that place influence the encounter?
5 How do you demonstrate to other staff / your supervisor / the family / your client that you are competent? What is competency in mental health work?
6 How do you use professional distance and professional authority? How is this different from having boundaries?

Websites

ACT Mindfully

Resources, training and information on Acceptance and Commitment Therapy for consumers and professionals.

www.actmindfully.com.au

Service Users Academia Symposiums

Develop and promote the work of consumers in the academy. Held yearly.

No website; Google 'Service Users Academia Symposiums' for further details about past and future symposiums.

Our Consumer Place

A groundbreaking organisation that presents a thoughtful and radical consumer voice. No longer operating but web site will take you to lots of thought-provoking past publications.

www.ourconsumerplace.com.au

Service User Research Enterprise

Conducts research into mental health services and treatments from consumer and carer perspectives.

www.kcl.ac.uk

3 Concepts and issues in mental health

Social work practice in the mental health area operates within a changing context of concepts and values. This represents a theoretical basis for practice that shapes the way policy and services are developed. In this chapter, we identify and define some of these concepts and show how they shape social work practice. The concepts are relevant to social work in all settings but are most important in practice in multidisciplinary settings where social workers have to manage the competing practice paradigms of other disciplines. As we argued in Chapter 1, we want social workers to be clear and confident about what they do and to be able to articulate the theoretical basis for their work. We want social workers to be able to connect their practice to a knowledge and value base. Each of the concepts discussed in this chapter provides theoretical direction for practice and a language to describe the work. The concepts provide consistent themes for the articulation of social work practice that are described in later chapters.

Key concepts are:

evidence-based practice,
recovery,
participation,
social inclusion / social exclusion,
stigma, shame and discrimination,
spirituality.

Evidence-based practice

Defining evidence-based practice

Within the field of mental health, concepts of evidence-based practice have emerged as dominant influences in the way all disciplines provide clinical services (Tanenbaum, 2003). Originating in the evidence-based medicine (EBM) movement (Evidence-Based Medicine Working Group, 1992), evidence-based practice (EBP) involves the conscientious, explicit and judicious application of best research evidence to a range of clinical domains: diagnostic tests and interventions of therapeutic, rehabilitative and preventive nature (Gilgun, 2005). EBP focuses on

DOI: 10.4324/9781003148913-4

locating and evaluating research evidence according to research methods in which randomised clinical trials are seen to constitute the strongest evidence for efficacy. Qualitative studies, case studies, and anecdotal and 'expert consensus' evidence are less highly valued. There is an emphasis on quantitative indicators of outcome and an insistence that interventions that have consistently failed to be proven effective should be replaced by evidence-based interventions. Systematic review of the evidence using EBP principles provides the basis for the development of clinical guidelines for practitioners to govern the treatment and management of a range of mental health disorders. While most evident in psychiatry and psychology, all the mental health disciplines have adopted the language of EBP in describing their practice, and it remains the dominant theoretical approach to practice in contemporary mental health practice.

A very useful working summary of the EBP principles is provided by Drake (2005). He argues that EBP encompasses five basic principles:

It builds on basic health care values.
It asserts that scientific evidence should be considered as one important factor in making health care decisions.
It assumes that scientific evidence is complicated, hierarchical and often ambiguous.
It recognises that factors other than scientific evidence – for example, consumer preferences – are critical contributors to medical conditions.
It recognises that clinical experience is critically important to decision-making.

Within the social work literature there is a range of positions on EBP, with some writers asserting the importance of positivist scientific approaches and others absolutely rejecting EBP as managerialist and technocratic. Drake's (2005) model provides a practical middle position between these extreme views. Our professional values are important, as are the preferences of the consumer. Nevo and Slonim-Nevo (2011)[1] argue for use of the broader term *evidence-informed practice* as a way of denoting a more inclusive understanding of 'evidence' incorporating workers' values, experience and creativity. Plath's (2006) analysis of EBP in the Australian mental health context is similarly useful here. She endorses the importance of social work's engagement with the principles of EBP, pointing out the many positive benefits of drawing on available evidence to inform practice and the ethics of such an approach. She challenges a simplistic adoption of EBP, arguing that problems surround the definition of interventions, the nature of evidence and the choice of outcomes.

EBP demands an active engagement with the research literature as the foundation for practice. It is clearly most applicable in those clinical settings where interventions can be explicitly defined around tightly controlled variables and where outcomes are clearly defined. Drake (2005) reminds us that practice needs to be shaped by more than scientific evidence. We need to be mindful of professional values, the preferences of consumers and families, and our clinical judgement.

Implications for social work practice

EBP will continue to provide a central organising principle for the delivery of mental health services, and social workers will be increasingly drawn to evidence to inform their work. We have to engage fully in the EBP debates at the team and systems level to ensure that the particular focus of social work is best represented in the mix of services that teams will provide. Individual practitioners need to be informed about the evidence for any interventions they apply in practice. We need to understand the strengths and limitations of the EBP approach and be able to articulate the knowledge base for our practice. A starting point might be a preparedness to access the research literature to establish the existing evidence to inform a response to a problem from practice. At a broader level, as a profession, we need to apply research approaches to evaluating our practice so that we can be more active contributors to the knowledge base for practice.

At the same time, we recognise that EBP needs to placed alongside the other determinants of our work – our ethics, our commitment to client choice and self-determination, and the critical frameworks around disadvantage and empowerment. Valorising the lived experience of mental illness and the importance of relationship offers an alternative perspective to EBP. We don't just do things to people (that is, apply defined interventions); sometimes our work is much more subtle, based on engaging with people to facilitate a process of recovery or problem-solving. We need to be mindful of the need for evidence in our practice and actively seek knowledge that is well tested by research. We must also be mindful of the other principles that might shape our practice in different ways. Being prepared to apply a critical reflective process to the review of practice offers a potential framework which includes EBP and other approaches to developing practice.

Recovery

Defining recovery

The concept of recovery has emerged as a consistent unifying principle in contemporary mental health policies and services in Australia. Despite unanimous endorsement of the principle and the enthusiasm of service providers and policymakers to describe their services as recovery based, considerable difficulties remain in defining and applying it. The principle is essentially radical, challenging a preoccupation with illness and symptoms, diagnosis and standardised treatments, in favour of a concern for the individually based lived experience of illness. Recovery as a philosophy emerged partly from the rehabilitation movement based in Boston (Anthony, 1993), but mainly from the published first-person accounts of the consumer empowerment movement (Deegan, 1988).

Writers in the area of recovery theory have summarised the recovery principles in similar ways. In the following analysis of recovery principles, we will be drawing on the work of Bland and Wyder (2017) and Bland and Drake (2019).

Anthony (1993, p. 15) defines recovery as

> a deeply personal, unique process of changing one's attitudes, values, feelings and goals, skills and/or roles. It is a way of living a satisfying, hopeful and contributing life even with the limitations caused by illness. Recovery involves the development of new meaning and purpose in one's life as one grows beyond the catastrophic effects of mental illness.

The definition of recovery given by the Mental Health Commission (NZ) (1998, p. 113) is straightforward: 'Living well in the presence or absence of mental illness and the losses that can be associated with it'. In recent years, a number of studies have tried to synthesise the various dimensions of recovery (Davidson et al., 2005; Leamy et al., 2011). Slade (2009) draws a distinction between clinical recovery and personal recovery. Use of the term *recovery* can be confusing, particularly given the dominance of the medical discourse in mental health. One way to frame the model which can be helpful is to bear in mind an alternative sense of 'recovery': to 'take back' rather than 'get over'. The recovery model is a model of mental health which emphasises the act of taking back those things which both the illness itself and society (in its response to the illness) have taken away from the person with a diagnosis. These can range from stable accommodation, education, meaningful employment and a living income to physical wellbeing, dignity, respect and a life beyond diagnosis. A number of important principles can be identified:

1 The centrality of the lived experience of mental illness

In the mental health field, the dominant research narrative is that of the scientific delineation of diagnostic categories and the search for evidence to inform practice. These positivist approaches underpin broad areas of policy and practice, including psychiatric assessment, epidemiology, the development of targeted medications, the assessment and management of risk, and the articulation and evaluation of psychosocial interventions. Alongside these principles, and central to the definition of the domain of social work described in Chapter 1, is a recognition of the broader social context in which both disorder and treatment are experienced. This is an important dimension of mental health consumer advocacy over the last 20 years: an insistence that people are not defined by their diagnostic label and that the labels themselves do not effectively describe the experience of mental illness (Bland & Tullgren, 2016). This principle encourages us to focus not on a set of symptoms, but on the realities of life with a mental illness. When we do this we discover that people describe problems of isolation and loneliness, poverty, disrupted family relationships, housing and income security – social problems that are at the heart of social work practice. Lived experience becomes a starting point for understanding the impact of mental illness, not just for individuals but for their families as well (Bland & Renouf, 2017).

2 *The importance of journey and process*

Recovery is not the same as cure. It is a journey towards wholeness that may take a long time: for some, it is more linear and straightforward, while for others, it is a maze of constantly changing directions. It is not about controlling symptoms but about enabling the individual to live the life they want to live, with or without the symptoms of illness. Various writers such as Deegan (1988) have used their own first-person accounts of illness and recovery to describe this journey. Others, such as Hatfield and Lefley (1993), have used analyses of the first-person accounts of consumers and family members to construct descriptions of the stages of the journey.

3 *The importance of agency and empowerment*

As part of their recovery journey consumers learn to assume primary responsibility for their transformation from a disabled person to a person in recovery (Bland & Drake, 2019). The important concept here is a sense of agency. This process involves gaining control over one's life and treatment. Consumers often talk about having the opportunities to make choices and being given the dignity of risk, where they are allowed to make decisions that allow them to succeed and fail (Davidson et al., 2005; Leamy et al., 2011). Assuming control over their lives is complex and involves the ability to resume control of a life that has been controlled not only by an illness but also by a treatment system and possibly by family. As part of this process consumers learn to manage their own levels of distress, stress or depression. While complete symptom remission is not necessary, being able to manage symptoms in some way is essential for recovery (Davidson et al., 2005). Recovery always involves periods of good and difficult times, setbacks and accomplishments, and times when symptoms may be more or less controlled. A shift happens when consumers move away from simply receiving services to actively participating in and using treatments of their choice to bring symptoms under some degree of control, using their own coping strategies rather than being merely a recipient of other people's interventions (Davidson et al., 2005; Deegan, 1988).

A sense of empowerment and control over one's life also emerges when people in recovery begin to demand the same rights and take on the same responsibilities as other citizens (Davidson et al., 2005; Leamy et al., 2011). These citizen rights include the right to decide where to live, whom to love and how to spend one's time. Responsibilities include paying taxes, voting and volunteering. Becoming empowered is also linked to the concept of social inclusion, which has both a component of active citizenship and a sense of connection. Empowerment happens through accessing resources such as housing and employment and confronting stigma and discrimination (Tew et al., 2012).

Recovery is about choice, power and personal control over the many aspects that make up one's life. It is also about confronting the power of stigma and low expectations. Taking personal responsibility for one's life and moving towards citizenship are major themes of the recovery literature.

4 The importance of relationship and connectedness

A recognition that relationships with others provide the opportunity to be fully human, to grow through our problems and to find happiness is central to recovery. Recovery does not happen in isolation but through relationships with others. This principle is evident in the emphasis on family relationships, friendships and community relationships. Recovery work is about helping the individual to sustain and develop these relationships and provides social workers with an alternative locus of activity – not just working with individuals, but working with families, friends and the community. It's a reminder of the importance of the relationships that people make with mental health workers. These helping relationships – between workers and consumers and between workers and families – are seen as fundamental to the healing process. The relationships are based on a profound respect from workers for the lived experience of mental illness of consumers and families. This is an enormously challenging concept for mental health workers who have been strongly immersed in the scientific discourse of knowledge and skills of mental health.

5 The importance of hope

A central positive feature of the recovery journey is the importance of hope. A belief that things will get better is necessary to confront the painful realities of the present. Deegan's (1988) analysis of her own journey of recovery identifies hope as that which sustained her through the anguish that was central to her experience. The hope offered by family and mental health workers is also central to the journey of recovery. These significant others become 'hope carriers', supporting the individual at times when hope is needed to continue the journey. Hope is a complex concept, a part of the worker's *being* rather than necessarily anything that they do. Valuing hope in mental health practice is an acknowledgement of the humanity of working with others.

6 The importance of identity

Recovery involves the rejection of the power of mental illness as a central and defining identity. As part of their journey, consumers redefine themselves and start viewing their mental illness as only one aspect of a multidimensional identity rather than the mental illness being their primary identity. Many consumers, over time, have been able to rebuild and redefine a more positive sense of self. Family members need to move from an identity dominated by their role as caregivers. This task of rebuilding identity is invariably done through relationships with others (Bland & Drake, 2019). People recovering from a mental illness need to recover not only from the effects of the illness itself but also from social consequences and societal stigma associated with this (Davidson et al., 2005; Leamy et al., 2011). Many with lived experience of mental illness felt that they had struggled to overcome the stigma associated with mental illness and the impact this had on their sense of self. As we will show later in this chapter, peer-based programs offer both consumers and families opportunities to challenge stigmatising and limiting illness identities. A second strategy for identity change is the careful use of language, preferring strengths-based words and concepts over the pathology-saturated labels and language of psychiatry (Sartorius, 2002).

7 Meaning in life

Throughout their illness consumers start to make meaning of the experiences of mental illness and incorporate these into their lives. As part of this, many with the lived experience learn to accept the limitation imposed by their illness and discover talents, gifts and possibilities that allow them to pursue and achieve new life goals despite the presence of the disability. This can involve pursuing and achieving new life goals and/or increasing their quality of life (Bland & Drake, 2019). Those with lived experience will start to resume ordinary community roles such as spouse, worker, student, taxpayer and friend. This represents a turning away from isolated and restricted life opportunities to making meaningful contributions to a community of their choice (Davidson et al., 2005; Leamy et al., 2011). This journey of re-engagement with friends, family and community is often shared with the family, who have often been isolated by caring responsibilities and the shame and stigma that they feel in response to the mental illness. Families moved from 'fixing' and 'doing for' to 'being with' and 'journeying alongside' (Tew et al., 2012).

8 A focus on strengths, positive outcomes and the language of recovery

Long-term outcome studies from across a range of industrialised countries over many years have demonstrated that there have been significant levels of recovery from mental illness. The best known of these was conducted by Harding and colleagues (1987) in Vermont. This well-reported study built on the findings of earlier European research that found that while many patients diagnosed with schizophrenia were unwell at ten-year follow-up, a majority of patients did very much better after 25 or 30 years. Recovery was not just possible but likely for most people originally thought to be chronically ill and disabled. The recovery movement has challenged the power of the 'problem-saturated' language of mental illness which has stressed deficits at the expense of positive outcomes. The language of recovery has emphasised both the humanity of the experience of mental illness and the positive achievements of the person in recovery by deliberately using non-clinical language. There is a focus on the goals and the 'hopes and dreams' of the person, rather than the symptoms of a patient.

9 The role of the mental health services

Recovery is the work of the person; the role of the mental health service is to facilitate recovery. Writing of the 'work of recovery', Glover (2005) identifies five elements of individual recovery that are shared between individuals and their helpers:

the work of upholding hope
the work of engaging an active sense of self
the work of supporting personal responsibility
the work of unpacking discovery (moving from a sense of alienation and not knowing to discovery and meaning)
the work of remaining connected with self, relationships and community

10 Cultural differences in recovery concepts – individual or community

In an insightful exchange of opinions about the nature of recovery in Australia and New Zealand, O'Hagan (2004) and Rickwood (2004) reveal some interesting cultural differences between the two countries in the application of recovery principles. Rickwood asserts that Australia has adopted recovery principles in both the National Mental Health Strategy and the various state mental health services. O'Hagan insists that the New Zealand experience has been to take the highly individual definitions of recovery derived from the US experience and reinterpret these to emphasise the importance of community and cultural perspective unique to New Zealand. For example, the New Zealand models see recovery as the work of families and communities as much as that of individuals. There is greater emphasis on human rights and advocacy as a challenge to the power of stigma and discrimination.

From Ann: the concept of recovery

The concept of recovery has popular currency in mental health services. To live well in the presence or absence of one's mental illness has come to mean valuing hope and possibilities for change, taking responsibility for one's life by developing a sense of agency, and active engagement in society. The recovery concept grew from an analysis of books and articles written by people with a mental illness about their journeys towards healing. However, the writing and thoughts of authors have been used for purposes for which they were never intended, and they have been colonised by researchers, professionals and policymakers to develop new service paradigms. Again, the person with the mental illness has become the subject who is acted on, and little attention has been paid to the transactions of power involved in the misappropriation of others' ideas.

Any history of mental health services notes that ideas, concepts, paradigms all have a short shelf life. There is a constant professional restlessness, a search for innovative practice, the magic bullet which will achieve outcomes at least cost. This is known as 'keeping up to date'. Girded by new theories and interventions, the researcher or practitioner climbs the ladder of professional preferment. It is a consumerist approach to professional practice, and over the years many robust theories have been sent to the policy and practice rubbish tip, as the old is replaced by the new, regardless of value and efficacy.

Recovery, like any theory or practice, must be critically deconstructed. Definitions of the term vary. In Australia and the US the concept is underpinned by individualist and aspirational philosophies where hard work and application are always rewarded – the so-called prosperity gospel of the productive and prosperous developed nation. Such a definition lacks an understanding that society (government, organisations, people) also need to recover. By this I mean to learn to embrace and practise positive regard and honest belief in the worth and dignity of all people. When this is truly believed and deeply embraced, there is a consequent willingness to reach into the hip-pocket to fund services that support, enable and respect. Belief and practice become seamless.

Because of the centrality of outcome measures in service delivery, people with mental illness who fail to recover, who backslide or who don't recover in the permitted time can be blamed for poor results of programs. Poor compliance, lack of commitment to the process or a myriad of other explanations that focus on the malign 'other' are substituted for the failure of policy and practice. Recovery, then, becomes a get-out-of-jail-free card, which agencies, policymakers and politicians can use to explain poor outcomes.

Implications for social work practice

The recovery paradigm offers a coherent set of principles to guide social work practice in mental health. The emphasis on relationship; valuing the lived experience of illness; and the importance of hope, empowerment and strength are principles familiar to social workers. Topor and colleagues (2006) suggest that recovery-based work requires that the worker be able to 'stand alongside' the person in the early stage of recovery, moving to greater equality and reciprocity with an emphasis on encouraging personal decision-making and sense of agency later in the work.

Several writers have identified recovery theory as a natural fit for social work practice (Carpenter, 2002). In recent years, there have been attempts to test the usefulness of recovery theory in various areas of mental health practice. For example, are recovery principles relevant to understanding work with children and adolescents, or for people detained under mental health laws, or even for understanding the family response to mental illness? Social work research in these areas has the potential to inform not just our own practice, but broader mental health practice as well.

Participation

Defining participation

A central principle of policy and service reform in mental health over the past 15 years has been that of 'consumer participation' – the recognition that consumers of services should be vitally involved in all aspects of mental health services (Bland, 2002). Consumer participation is defined as 'any activity done by consumers where they have power or influence on the system and services that affect their lives' (O'Hagan et al., 2002). Typically, participation refers to the whole range of service activities, from services to individual clients through to service management and to education, training and research activities. Consumer rights to participation were first articulated as the Australian government's policy in the paper *Mental Health Statement of Rights and Responsibilities* (Australian Health Ministers, 1991). Among the rights and responsibilities listed in the document is an emerging acknowledgement that mental health workers need to talk with consumers about the way services are provided – that consumers should contribute to decisions made about their care. The principle of consumer participation is central to contemporary mental health policy in North America, Europe, Australia and New Zealand.

Similarly, there has been a recognition that family carers should also participate in all levels of policy and service development. The argument for carer participation is based on the recognition that families contribute enormously to the care and welfare of the person with the illness. They are so involved in the treatment system and treatment outcomes that they constitute both secondary consumers and secondary service providers (Bland, 2002). The principle of participation applies both to consumers and to families, though its application is different for the two groups. The specific policy of consumer and carer participation is discussed in the next chapter.

The rationale for consumer participation is summarised in two basic propositions:

Participation is a right. By this argument, the recipients of services have a right to be fully involved in planning, delivering and evaluating those services.

Participation ensures better services. By this argument, consumer participation in services is a way of improving services. Participation will strengthen accountability mechanisms and ensure increased responsiveness of mental health services to the needs of consumers.

A review of the literature suggests that arguments supporting the principles of consumer participation are based largely on rights and values, rather than on better services (Nelson et al., 2001). With few exceptions, consumer participation in mental health services is promoted as an expression of consumer empowerment principles rather than as a strategy for achieving better service outcomes (Honey, 1999). Within the broader health and disability areas, however, there is emerging evidence that consumer participation is associated with better service outcomes (Commonwealth Department of Health and Aged Care, 2000). Sometimes, rights and benefits arguments are jointly argued. Consumer advocate Cath Roper, for example, argues that consumers have a vested interest in their own health services that can be capitalised on and worked with for the benefit of the service, provider, consumer and wider community. She cautions that consumers are not offered the same choices in mental health services as they are in acute services. The very fact that consumers are often using the service in an involuntary capacity denies them certain choices that are commonplace in other health services (Roper, 2006).

Consumer participation in practice

By definition, participation is a radical principle – empowering consumers and family carers to share the decision-making with service providers and to enjoy a number of new roles in the mental health system beyond that of the sick role. Consumers and family carers are encouraged to be active participants in designing, managing and evaluating the mental health services and to take a more active part in the education of the mental health workforce. Participation is evident in a number of areas.

Consumer and carer participation in policymaking bodies

Consumers and family carers have been appointed to peak policy and administrative bodies. Local examples include Mental Health Australia and the various state and Commonwealth mental health commissions. The principle of consumer and family carer participation, developed in the National Mental Health Strategy, is also reflected in the mental health plans for each of the states. This is significant given that the provision of mental health treatment services is largely the responsibility of state governments. While most administrations will maintain a positive policy of consumer participation and make some minimalist attempt to apply the principle, to this point in time there is real difficulty in moving from the rhetoric of participation to the positive implementation of the policy in practice.

Linhorst (2005) provides a detailed argument for the promotion of consumer participation as central to empowerment. He argues that sites for participation include both individual treatment planning and service planning as well as policymaking and that participation is empowering and a desirable outcome in its own right. His analysis provides many examples for service providers seeking to encourage consumer participation. These include:

recognising the incentives for participation (for example, increasing confidence, gaining skills) and

promoting knowledge of, and access to, a wide range of participation structures (for example, advocacy groups).

Consumer and family carer participation in education and training of the mental health workforce

Education and training of the mental health workforce has been an important site for the implementation of the principle of consumer participation. There are two distinct areas concerning consumer perspective training for mental health practitioners. The first is the inclusion of a consumer perspective in professional training programs, the undergraduate and postgraduate courses preparing practitioners who will work in the mental health field. The second is the delivery of consumer perspective content in professional development activities for the professionals already in the mental health workforce. While there is not yet a systematic audit of the extent to which consumers are contributing to the education and training of mental health professionals in either area, there is some evidence that implementation of the policy is limited and inconsistent. The Implementation Plan for the National Practice Standards for the Mental Health Workforce (Bland, 2006) showed a wide range of models of consumer involvement in education and training. Some university programs employed consumers as guest lecturers in professional training programs, but very few had engaged consumers in developing or evaluating courses. Only one mental health region had employed a consumer educator as part of a workforce education and training unit.

More positive, perhaps, has been the success of the Mental Health Services Conference (TheMHS) and the Building Bridges Conference in Australia and New Zealand. These conferences have provided a focus for shared learning among mental health workers, consumers and family carers. In other positive moves, consumers and family carers are included in the editorial process for some mental health journals.

Participation in direct service delivery: clinical and non-clinical services

In recent years there has been an expansion of opportunities for consumer and carer participation through the employment of peer workers as part of the mental health workforce. In summarising the benefits of the peer workforce strategy, the National Mental Health Consumer and Carer Forum (NMHCCF, 2010) argued that when consumer- and carer-identified positions are well designed and are integrated into flexible and supportive workplace environments, consumer- and carer-identified workers can use their knowledge and skills to deliver:

- targeted peer support and mentoring to consumers and carers;
- extensive knowledge of what life is like for consumers and carers and the capacity to link traditional mental health care with the community,[5] providing an essential holistic and recovery-focused element to traditional mental health service delivery;
- role models for recovery for consumers, carers and the mental health workforce, as well as colleagues based outside mental health services (e.g., police, criminal justice), thereby challenging discriminatory consumer and carer stereotypes and helping to break down stigma;
- advocacy at both individual and systemic levels;

- valuable policy input, for example:
  - lived experience and the unique understanding of what mental health consumers and carers are experiencing and what they need from services;
  - intimate knowledge of the service delivery environment, to inform innovations or improvements which might be necessary and/or possible; and
  - ability to actively contribute to mental health teams as peers, thus placing them in a position to use their influence to contribute creatively to service improvement activities;
- enhanced visibility of the consumer and carer voice at both the individual treatment and service delivery level to inform cultural and structural change in service delivery, workplace culture and workforce development.

The peer workforce represents one tangible and exciting strategy to operationalise consumer and carer participation in mental health services. Significant difficulties remain, including questions of scope of practice, appropriate resourcing, training and supervision. There is some concern that service managers could see the advantage of employing peer workers as a relatively cheap solution to workforce building. At a very basic level, the introduction of a new player in the multidisciplinary team demands the inevitable negotiation of work roles in what is already a contest space. Social workers have a clear role in supporting the work of peer workers, and forging alliances and partnerships is fundamental to this.

Consumer participation in research

The obligation to engage more meaningfully with consumers in research has led to greater consumer participation in research studies. The subjective experience of the consumer perspective is now generally regarded as important information (or 'data'), so we are seeing more qualitative methods being incorporated into mental health research. Consumers are also being consulted more frequently to advise on key issues such as the design of questionnaires and survey forms, the best forums and techniques for more effective interviews and conversations with consumers, and the verification and evaluation of the outcomes of the research. In some places, consumers are actively participating in research even to the extent of occasionally being designated as 'co-researchers', and there are examples of innovative research projects which have been shaped by consumers' interests rather than those of other researchers (Rose, 2008). Despite these encouraging developments, we are still a long way from what could be called 'consumer research', that is, consumer-led or consumer-driven research.

Consumers' participation in their own treatment

The issue of a consumer's participation in their own 'treatment' is perhaps the area in mental health where there has been the least progress made, not only in consumer participation practice but even in its articulation as rhetoric and policy (Bland & Epstein, 2008). While services might work at applying the participation principle at planning levels, they are less successful in making it work at the level of individual treatment. Janet Meagher (2002) notes that although individuals are jointly responsible with their treatment professional for the development and implementation of their care plans at every level of their care, there are many behavioural, cultural, professional, legal and pseudo-ethical reasons why real consumer participation is difficult at this individual level.

Meeting the challenge of involving consumers fully in their own treatment is at the core of effective social work practice in mental health. This is one of the 'sticking points' where EBP has to work alongside the need to maximise choice and control for consumers in what they do with social workers to meet recovery goals. In later chapters, we provide some direction for social work practice in areas such as assessment, case management and working with families.

From Ann: participation in the mental health sector

All words have meanings specific to the environment in which they are used. *Participation*, when used in the mental health sector, has come to mean the involvement of consumers and carers in all aspects of service delivery, from policy formation, to service delivery, education, research and evaluation. It describes any activity where consumers have power or influence over the system and services that affect their lives. Participation has also been framed as a right: 'Nothing about me without me'. An alternative argument for participation is a functional one: that it is a tool to improve services and professional care, if only service providers ask the right questions, take the time to listen and reflect and were committed to service improvement. It comes as no surprise that while the rhetoric of participation is evident in policy documents, at the coalface it is more often observed in the breach.

While much attention has been given to fostering participation in specialist mental health services, far less (or no) attention is given to 'participation' in other programs or agencies which provide mental health care or welfare services to those with mental illnesses. For example, most medical mental health interventions are provided by general practitioners who usually work in private practices on a fee-for-service basis, yet the principle of consumer 'participation' in this sector is given little attention. Similarly, how do consumers participate in service delivery by psychologists and other practitioners whose services are paid for by Medicare?

However, people with mental illness spend very little time being diagnosed and treated. Our fullest vocation is not the 'career' of the patient, but as participants in the economic and social life of the community – whether we like it or not! Non-governmental welfare agencies and other governmental departments that provide services have very different definitions or expectations of consumer 'participation'.

It can be argued that the principle of 'participation' is stuck in an historical time warp, reflecting an era when people with mental illnesses were cared for in total institutions. The reality of life in the community is that health and welfare services are compartmentalised, and consumers must deal with multiple agencies in order to meet needs for treatment, accommodation, income support, rehabilitation, training and employment. It is the lived experience of all our lives that the rhetoric and practice of participation does not extend this far.

Participation and empowerment

Empowerment is a popular concept in social work, emphasising as it does the importance of the social justice focus for mental health practice. Linhorst's (2005) analysis of the meaning of empowerment in mental health is useful in identifying the practical dimensions of the concept. He argues that genuine participation in decision-making is central to empowerment. Another dimension is that of access to the resources – personal, organisational and community – that enable people to gain greater control over their environment and attain their aspirations (Hasenfeld, 1987). Linhorst argues that empowerment is both a process and an outcome, dependent on the establishment of deeply respectful relationships between consumers and service providers. He reminds us that empowerment is contextually specific and changes over time, so that good outcomes in one context may not transfer to other contexts and may be lost in time.

From Ann: participation as the new recovery

In the income support (social security) sector, *participation* has come to mean the active involvement of those who are poor, disabled or unemployed in the social and economic fabric of the nation. Participatory welfare is a far more contentious and oppressive concept than the rhetoric or practice of participation in mental health services. Yet the reality of our lives is that many spend far more time interacting with income support agencies and job placement firms than with mental health services. 'Participation' has become a blunt tool to enhance the social capital of communities as well as a way of empowering those who are marginalised by mental illness. Additionally, the policy push to 'participation' is informed by the changing demographics of developed societies because as ageing baby boomers retire there are insufficient workers ready to step into employment to replace them. Thus, people who are of working age but are not looking for work through disability or misfortune are now being 'urged' into employment, where years ago it suited governments to allow them to linger on disability pensions, so that they could not be counted among the unemployed during a time of economic downturn.

More recently, we have been told that the age of entitlement must end; the nation can no longer afford generous welfare and health systems. Everyone – even the mentally ill and the disabled – must become self-sufficient and participate in building national wealth.

Participation now becomes a stick, not a philosophical carrot underpinning recovery programs. 'Participation' (the involvement of consumers in all aspects of service delivery) is largely absent from this sector. The policies that inform income support and related services (participatory welfare) result from the exercise of political will, which is informed by policy think tanks, bureaucrats and ministerial advisers, not service users. Beyond electing governments every few years, we have few opportunities to participate in this process. Participation has become the new recovery. It is a process over which we have little real influence but with which we must engage.

Implications for social work practice

Consumer and family carer participation remain important principles in contemporary mental health services, research and education. Although official policy documents strongly endorse the principle, there remain difficulties in implementing it in practice. There is a need for more resources to support initiatives such as the employment of peer workers beyond unrealistic token levels. There needs to be a change in the culture of mental health services so that workers see consumer participation as core business, as central to their activities and as highly valued for what it contributes to those activities. This change of culture needs to be expressed in the language of the service; the way budgets are framed; the way staff are selected, trained and managed; and the way services are delivered. We need to develop the 'technology of participation' – the knowledge and skills to implement the philosophy of participation – since this remains largely undeveloped.

Central to effective participation is the establishment of respectful relationships among workers, consumers and family carers. This simple truth relies on a genuine commitment to the spirit of participation as a radical empowering philosophy that allows a shared responsibility for treatment and care. This is the challenge for all mental health workers.

Social inclusion / social exclusion

Defining social exclusion

In describing the nature of participation in this chapter, we have focused on the way the concept is applied in mental health policy, but the concept has relevance beyond mental health and includes a wide range of contexts related to broader ideas of citizenship, particularly that of economic participation. British mental health policy has addressed the nature of social exclusion as a primary issue, recognising the intimate connection between being mentally ill and being poor. If we conceptualise poverty as exclusion from participation in a wide range of domains (such as housing, income security, access to education, health services, transport and personal safety), we can understand the framework for social endeavour as multidimensional. This is significant because the focus on social exclusion redirects an understanding of mental illness away from a preoccupation with illness and symptoms and towards a more holistic focus on the social context and social consequences of illness. This expanded understanding is central to the domain of social work, and social exclusion is an area of primary concern. We will also look briefly at the issues of stigma and discrimination in this section. The concepts are closely related to social exclusion, and the impact of discrimination is to reinforce exclusion.

The report *Mental Health and Social Exclusion* (Social Exclusion Unit, 2004) summarises the research literature to argue that social exclusion should be a major focus of mental health policy and to locate mental health policy within broader social policy. It points to the very high numbers of citizens with major mental health problems who are unable to participate in the paid workforce, who rely on disability support pensions and whose social isolation as a result imposes further risk factors such as poor health, education and housing. The report asserts that mental illness constitutes a greater risk for social exclusion than does unemployment. It contends that stigma and discrimination, low expectations of people with mental illness, difficulties in accessing services and the absence of support in areas of housing and work constitute barriers for people with mental illness to participate effectively in the community.

In the Australian context, there is solid and convincing evidence of the social exclusion of people with psychosis living in the community. Large-scale national studies (Jablensky et al., 1999; Morgan et al., 2011) present a grim summary of the lived experience of mental illness for the most seriously mentally ill and disabled people in the community. The following are conclusions of the most recent study (Morgan et al., 2011):

People with severe mental illness have very high levels of poor physical health in areas such as heart disease, diabetes, oral health and obesity. Smoking, alcohol and other drug usage are much higher than the general population.

While a minority of people in the study were working, 85 per cent of the sample relied almost entirely on Centrelink benefits for their income.

Only 10 per cent of men and 25 per cent of women were in stable, marriage-like partnerships. Many people had very few friends. Loneliness was a predictable outcome of psychosis.

Education and literacy rates were lower for this group than the general population.

Suicidal thoughts and attempted suicide rates were high.

Very few people owned or were buying their home. Many described their current housing as unsatisfactory.

Other Australian studies (Butterworth et al., 2011) have shown high levels of mental health problems among the recipients of such Centrelink benefits as unemployment, supporting parents and student allowances. There is a clear connection between being poor and being mentally ill, and poverty is a clear and predictable consequence of major mental illness. The emergence of psychosis in young adulthood, and long-term consequent disability, provides the basis for a lifetime of poverty. This research helps us to understand the limits of applying an individual therapeutic approach to social work practice. Such structural disadvantage demands significant social change in areas such as housing and income security.

Rather than focus on poverty as an absence of resources, a social inclusion focus seeks to identify the dimensions of the positive and multidimensional concept of 'inclusion/exclusion' and has been applied to a growing body of British research into the social context of mental illness, suggesting both the nature of deprivation and possible ways of addressing the social impact of mental illness. Huxley and Vick (2005) and Huxley et al. (2005) have developed a set of dimensions of inclusion/exclusion to provide a base for both research and service development. They identify eight dimensions of inclusion, together with objective indicators for measurement:

Work and education – educational attainment, training opportunities, adult learning, type of employment, hours worked, reason for not working
Housing – accommodation type, tenure, facilities, neighbourhood
Finances – income, benefit level, financial difficulties
Family relationships – level of contact
Social relationships – social contact, activities
Leisure activities – community participation
Safety – victimisation, personal and neighbourhood safety
Physical and mental health – self-reported health status, contact with primary and secondary care services

In the next chapter, we examine the way in which social inclusion has been adopted as a policy principle in Australia and elsewhere. What is most important to understand about the social inclusion agenda is the inevitable interface between mental health issues and the wide range of other social policy matters. Governments have recognised the importance of inter-sectoral linkage in mental health policy and identify how a range of government sectors can promote mental health and recovery. These include education, housing, justice, work and income, child protection, and employment. The social inclusion / social exclusion agenda removes mental illness from an exclusive focus on matters of health and illness and relocates it to the mainstream of social policy.

Implications for practice

Concepts of social inclusion provide a solid and accessible entry for critical social work practice. Social work practice needs to be not just about working therapeutically with individuals but extends to family, friends and community (Tew et al., 2012). Working to make communities more inclusive is as important as supporting individuals to make helpful connections with their community. Practice cannot simply be about helping people to manage distressing symptoms. It has to be about working with individuals, families and communities towards social change. The social justice values of our profession demand that we work towards structural changes in the community so that a good quality of life is available to all citizens.

Stigma and discrimination

Goffman's (1961) early definition of stigma as 'spoiled identity' is still a useful starting point for our understanding of the nature of stigma. Bakshi et al. (1999) suggest that stigma in mental illness denotes an unjust and involuntary labelling process that misconstrues the character and personalities of individuals affected by mental disorder. The effect of stigma is to 'other' and dehumanise. The identity of the individual is 'spoiled', lost in the power of the label. In their analysis of the concept of stigma, Epstein et al. (2012) provide a consumer perspective on the lived experience of stigma. They argue that the label conveys expectations that people with mental illness are peculiar, dangerous and incompetent, but that the concept of stigma does not place sufficient responsibility with those who discriminate on the basis of such thinking. Table 3.1 illustrates the importance of language. The expectations and actions of others, and the internalised stigma of individuals, compound the very real difficulties already imposed by the illness. The impact of stigma and discrimination can be profound.

Consumers have written extensively about the power of stigma (Epstein, 1995) and the powerful and destructive impact of stigma for consumers. Epstein has argued that the stigma of some disorders is greater than others, that there is in fact, a hierarchy of stigmas in which depression and anxiety are widely accepted in the community, but personality disorder remains highly stigmatised. Other consumers have written about the experience of shame. Remi, for example, wrote:

> I think that the price of shame surrounding having or even knowing someone with mental health problems is too high a price to pay. Shame is why symptoms escalate, shame is why people don't go to therapy, it's the reason why people don't tell their family and friends, shame costs lives, it leads to suicide and strange behaviours that others don't or won't understand, shame is what causes isolation and keeps a person harbouring a secret that should not be their sole burden to bear when professional help is available.
>
> It has taken me so long to realise that the shame isn't worth it.
>
> (Remi's blog, www.time-to-change.org.uk/blog/stigma-and-shame-around-mental-illness-stopped-me-getting-support)

Table 3.1 Person-centred alternatives to commonly used words and phrases

Term	*Person-centred alternative*
Schizophrenic	Person with schizophrenia / a mental illness/ disability; Jane/John
Consumer	Recovery practitioner; person in recovery; survivor; service user; self-advocate
Decompensating / going downhill	Not him/herself today; he/she is experiencing symptoms
Manipulative	Resourceful
Crazy	Unique
Compliant	Might not be confident about personal choices or decisions; afraid; needing more information
Non-compliant	Beginning to think for him/herself; taking personal responsibility; needs more information
Sense of entitlement; aggressive; demanding	Aware of rights, making a choice
Resistant	Not open to; chooses not to; has own ideas; doesn't agree
Frequent flyer	Gives us many opportunities to intervene and support
Baseline functioning	What a person looks like when doing well
Unmotivated	Has other interests; bored; doesn't know how to begin
Helpless	Unaware of capabilities
Hopeless	Unaware of opportunities/possibilities
Grandiose	Has high hopes and expectations of self
Chronic	Unremitting; ongoing; persistent
Druggie; crackhead; junkie; comorbid	Person with an addiction or diagnosis of substance abuse
High-functioning; low-functioning; dangerous; danger to others / danger to self (DTO/ DTS)	Person who is showing these issues and characteristics
Case study	Individual example
Subject	Research participant
Lacks insight	Lacks access to information and resources

Research by Wyder et al. (2018) found high levels of shame among the families of inpatients detained under mental health laws. Confronting that sense of shame was identified as part of the family's recovery journey and involved developing a new identity, sense of self and sense of control over their situation. This study identified the treatment service as a source of stigma for the families and argued for a more 'family-centred' approach to inpatient care.

An analysis of the connection between social inclusion and mental illness (Leff & Warner, 2006) develops the ideas of stigma and discrimination as fundamental to social exclusion. Leff and Warner remind us that stigma can be imposed by a hostile or ignorant community, but it can be most effective in the form of 'self-stigma', the process of individuals and families absorbing negative stereotypes of mental illness and acting on these stereotypes. This results in low self-esteem, a sense of shame and low expectations – both of self and of service response.

Stigma is maintained through popular media. Although the 'coming out' of high-profile sporting personalities has significantly challenged negative stereotypes, there are very few positive images of mental illness in the community. The stigma of mental illness extends to the families of people with mental illness and even to those who work in the field of mental illness. Advocacy groups in Australia, such as ARAFMI, SANE and Beyond Blue, have worked hard to confront stigma and community ignorance about mental illness through community education and 'media watch' activities. These programs appear to rely on the assumption that bad attitudes are based on ignorance and that change will happen when people better understand the nature of mental illness.

It is significant, however, that Australian research (Mental Health Council of Australia, 2005, 2011) has found that a major site of stigma and oppression was the mental health system itself. Consumers reported that mental health workers often treated them with a lack of respect and were patronising, dismissive, blaming and judgemental. Some have argued that there is 'diagnostic prejudice': a hierarchy of disorders in which some are more acceptable than others. People diagnosed with severe depression, for example, might inspire some compassion, while a diagnosis of borderline personality disorder might inspire only contempt. These findings challenge the basis for an educational strategy to reduce stigma. Consumers reported that those who knew most about mental illness – the health professionals themselves – were capable of the most disrespectful and dehumanising response to people with mental illness. In recognition of this, the National Mental Health Strategy includes a major priority of engaging consumers and family carers in the education and training of the mental health workforce. *National Practice Standards* (Victorian Government Department of Health, 2013) set out in detail the attitudes and values of workers that reflect a respectful relationship with consumers that must be the start of non-stigmatising mental health practice.

The focus of anti-stigma campaigns remains difficult. Programs such as Beyond Blue have been successful in promoting the simple idea that depression is common and that treatment is available and effective. Others, such as the report *Living with Mental Illness* (Wesley Mission, 2007), take a broader approach, seeking to build awareness of mental illness and challenge misinformation in the community based on a concept of 'mental health literacy'. This task of community education and attitude change continues to pose a long-term challenge. Many campaigns seem to have the problem of explaining two competing truths: first, that people with mental health problems are not 'others' but 'us', and second, that mental illness is serious and profoundly life-changing. All of this is made more difficult by the wide range of disorders grouped uncomfortably under the common tag of 'mental illness'. In summarising the UK approach to confronting stigma, the Sainsbury

Centre's policy paper *The Future of Mental Health: A Vision for 2015* concludes that it is debatable how far stigma can be challenged: 'To achieve genuine change, increased investment in mental health promotion will be vital, but so will attitudinal change within services, among employers and in society as a whole' (Sainsbury Centre for Mental Health, 2006, p. 15).

From Ann: once I became my diagnosis there was no one left to recover

George Orwell said, 'If thought corrupts language, language can corrupt thought'. Thus, how practitioners think about, write about and talk about those with lived experience can affect how they might interact with us.

Skilful use of language:

is based on deep and respectful listening;
interrogates language that limits how consumers are thought about and talked about;
develops awareness about how language can sustain 'power over' and 'top-down' relationships;
acknowledges that practitioners have much to learn from consumers;
recognises the insidious practices of stigma;
is aware that those with lived experience can 'self-stigmatise' by interiorising others' limiting discourses;
helps us reframe how we think about and talk about our lived experience;
talks 'with' us, not 'to' us, so that together we might co-construct a better future;
takes time to explore our concerns, interests and aspirations;
notices and sustains change.

While stigma and discrimination are related concepts, it may be helpful to recognise that strategies to confront these issues may be different. Public education and marketing campaigns may be needed to present mental illness in a more positive light, but discrimination might be confronted more directly and with the weight of the law rather than the vagaries of public opinion. Clearly the efforts of governments and mental health advocacy groups in confronting stigma are important if the broader community is ever to develop more informed and inclusive attitudes to people with mental illness. Discrimination and human rights, however, are more accessible and immediate targets, and a focus on discrimination has the advantage of putting the emphasis on the unfair treatment which causes and compounds stigma (Sayce, 1998). In Australia, one of the earliest policy documents from the

National Mental Health Strategy was the *Mental Health Statement of Rights and Responsibilities* (Australian Health Ministers, 1991), an attempt to set out a non-legal set of rights for consumers, families and service providers. The most significant advance in the legal context of discrimination and human rights came with the Burdekin Report (HREOC, 1993). The commissioner took submissions from service providers, consumers and families in every state and territory and found evidence of systematic denial of human rights of people with mental illness. A separate section of the report deals with the denial of rights to families. The power of the report was based, perhaps, in its shifting the focus of concern away from mental illness as a medical issue to one of a human rights issue. It asserted that discrimination was a central feature of the experience of mental illness in Australia.

Perhaps the most valuable challenge to stigma has come from advocacy groups within the consumer movement. Agencies such as Our Consumer Place provide a strong consumer voice to support advocacy and public education. For example, they have prepared practical manuals for consumers engaged in public speaking or education work. They have challenged anti-stigma projects that promote positive views of some disorders, such as depression, while allowing stigma on other disorders to continue. Another challenge to stigma has come from the burgeoning information available to the public on the internet, where consumer voices can be easily accessed, along with good, practical information about disorders and treatments by advocacy groups such as SANE Australia.

The New Zealand experience has been based more strongly on principles of the protection of human rights through specific legislation. The New Zealand Bill of Rights (New Zealand Parliament, 1990) sets down basic rights in such areas as security, including the right to refuse medical treatment; democratic and civil rights; and protection from discrimination. The Human Rights Commission has a framework for human rights that includes:

> participation – people should be able to participate in society and decisions that affect them; accountability – those in authority should act justly and be answerable for their actions; no discrimination – people should be treated fairly; empowerment – allowing people to use rights as a leverage for action, linking decision-making to agreed human rights norms, identification of all relevant human rights and balancing various rights.
>
> (Mental Health Commission New Zealand, 2007, p. 180)

This emphasis on human rights overtakes a concern for confronting stigma. If the law can deal effectively with the impact of stigma there is less need to address the difficult challenge of changing community attitudes and values. A concern with social exclusion provides a natural focus for social work activity in multidisciplinary team settings, offering as it does an additional conceptual and practical paradigm for social work practice. It leads social work back to core business. It represents an additional focus for work to complement more therapeutic definitions of practice.

From Ann: thinking about mentalism/sanism

Mentalism is a concept that describes society's prejudices towards people diagnosed with mental illness. Mentalism circumscribes the humanity of consumers, carers and society. The idea has emerged from a critical/constructivist perspective, locating oppression and prejudice at the heart of social structures and social systems, including health and welfare services, mental health professions, the family, the media and the organisations that lobby and speak out on behalf of consumers. It is a limiting discourse. It informs tokenistic practices. Mentalism is enabled by normalism and ablism. All are pervasive and insidious, and like some alien creature they insinuate themselves into peoples' minds and set patterns for thinking and speaking about madness and the mad. They tell us what we can't do and what we ought to do.

For social workers to avoid mentalism there are a number of pitfalls. The first is the baby-and-the-bathwater pitfall, in which the practitioner denies the existence of mental illness, seeing other professionals and consumers and families as having been co-opted by the medical model. The second is about taking on the mantle of being the champion and advocate of people with mental illness, which can easily transform into benevolent othering and paternalistic practices. The third is about being aware of 'walking the walk, talking the talk'. This occurs when workers use the language of recovery and human rights, while subtly (and not so subtly) subverting the meanings attached to these critical concepts.

Mentalism highlights other-expert advice and other-expert goals. It has also become attached to ideological and philosophical ideas about individual responsibility, and broader social, organisational and political components of recovery are not addressed. Mentalism gave consumers a new name: persons-in-recovery. More recently, we've become persons-with-the-possibility-of-having-a-contributing-life. The labelling and defining is still being done by others.

To avoid mentalism, consumers ask that professionals acknowledge the expertise that emerges from the lived experience, that they develop a sensitive awareness of the transactions of power and that they always operate from a position of compassion, kindness and shared humanity.

I acknowledge my colleague Merinda Epstein from Our Consumer Place for her thinking about mentalism.

Example: Our Consumer Place – Empowerment through Collective Action
This original description of Our Consumer Place is taken from their website:

> Our Consumer Place is a resource centre run entirely by people diagnosed with 'mental illness' (we choose to call ourselves 'consumers'). We provide information,

> training, support and advice to consumer-run groups and projects (or more specifically, 'Consumer Developed Initiatives' [CDIs]). We also support what we call 'consumer perspective', recognising that the lived experience of 'mental illness' provides a crucial source of insight that is of value and must be respected. We believe that we are part of an important cultural shift, towards valuing and respecting the lived experience of 'mental illness'. Our Consumer Place has been developed by consumers for consumers.
>
> www.ourconsumerplace.com.au/consumer/aboutus

The organisation asserts that it is not a therapeutic resource or an advocacy group. Rather, the focus is on building the intellectual and skill base of the consumer movement and building a consumer community with the skills and resources to effect change for mental health consumers. The community building supported by Our Consumer Place is localised and contextualised. They run workshops and presentations for both professional workers and for consumers which focus on developing a distinct consumer perspective in mental health. One major activity has been the establishment of a clearinghouse of lectures, publications and websites to resource consumers as they engage in training each other and contribute to the knowledge base for the mental health workforce. Leading intellectuals at Our Consumer Place such as Merinda Epstein and Flick Grey have given consumers a powerful voice in the mental health community (www.ourconsumerplace.com.au/consumer/manifesto).

One of the distinctive contributions of the organisation has been that of challenging and reclaiming the language of mental illness. Merinda's cartoon drawings and deeply insightful and irreverent text offer an engaging and accessible set of ideas relevant to both consumers and professionals. The word *mad* has been embraced and promoted, featuring in such publications as *Mad Workplaces* and *The Mad-Quarry Dictionary*. Ann Tullgren, consumer and social worker and a regular contributor to the Our Consumer Place newsletters, has produced a helpful list of stigmatising words and alternative ways of expressing these. Judgmental phrases such as 'non-compliant' are reworked to become 'choosing my own treatment'. A constant message of Our Consumer Place is that the language we use constructs the reality of that experience, and challenging the negative, disrespectful and pessimistic language of psychiatry is an ongoing part of the struggle to defeat stigma.

How is this an example of empowerment?

- Providing resources. Our Consumer Place develops the intellectual property that forms the basis of education and training and makes it available to the consumer community. Individual consumers are connected with very skilled and committed activists. The quality training provided supports the good efforts of mental health workers as well as consumer activists.
- Reclaiming identity – a positive view of madness. In line with the recovery task of building a positive identity, Our Consumer Place can give isolated consumers and their families a language, role models, encouragement and hope

to be able to abandon the highly stigmatised and life-limiting role of mental health patient. There is another way to be mad, and there can be some pride, and indeed some joy, in that identity.
- Asserting authority and sense of agency. This is achieved through training and publication, promoting the consumer voice as a valid and important alternative to the dominant voice of mental health clinicians and academics. Our Consumer Place has been able to challenge the power of stigma and the hidden oppression of the anti-stigma campaigns. There is specific training in consumers using their experience to train others, moving beyond telling their story, to using their experience to challenge beliefs and values. Consumers recognise that they are the experts in their own experience, and that that expertise is powerful when shared with others.
- Establishing a sense of community. Our Consumer Place is a community of like-minded individuals, drawn together for mutual support and education. The newsletters and website provide a point of connection, pride and identity.

Spirituality

One of the key themes of this book is the importance of respecting the lived experience of mental illness of consumers and family as a starting point for helping. In recent years, an awareness has emerged of the importance of spirituality in understanding both the experience of illness and of recovery. This spirituality is not necessarily about religion, though many people do express their spirituality within the framework of a religious tradition. Neither is it about the ways in which the delusions and hallucinations of serious mental illness might be organised for an individual around religious beliefs. Rather, it is a preparedness to see spirituality in its wide variety of forms as fundamental to the human experience.

Towards a definition of spirituality

There are many definitions of spirituality, but most will include reference to the deepest human longings for wholeness, connection and transformation (Dudley, 2007). Three dimensions of spirituality are as follows:

Spirituality as meaning-making. In its simplest form, spirituality is about the way we make meaning of our experience of life. It allows us to struggle with the great questions of life – *What is the purpose of my life? Why did I become ill? Why do people suffer? Is there any justice in this life?* Consumers, family members and mental health workers may all struggle with these questions. Sometimes the questions are asked within a religious framework. For example, *Why did a loving God allow my son or daughter to get this illness?* These are the questions that Kushner (1981) deals with in his classic text *When Bad Things Happen to Good People.* Central to meaning-making is the nature and experience of hope.

Spirituality as offering transcendence. A second view of spirituality is that it is that which allows us to transcend the mundane and ordinary and connects us with the divine. We might call this transcendent power a *God*, the *sacred, nature*, or simply the *higher power*. Included under this meaning are beliefs about what is sacred.

Spirituality as that which enlivens. Rolheiser (1998) suggests that spirituality is also about the energy that inspires, enlivens and motivates us on our life journey.

Why is spirituality an important concept in mental health?

If we take this broad view of spirituality, then we can appreciate that it is much more than a set of religious beliefs or practices. First-person accounts of the experience of mental illness emphasise the profound impact of illness on the individual's sense of self (Deegan, 1988), and spirituality is that part of the individual's humanity that is involved in trying to make sense of that uniquely traumatic experience. As we have argued in reviewing the literature on recovery, hope is central to that process. Consumers and families will often struggle with issues of meaning-making and hope, and it is important that mental health professionals are respectful of that struggle. One of the most powerful aspects of the consumer and family self-help movements has been their capacity to provide a network of relationships within which meaning-making and hope can be shared and nurtured. In those relationships, individuals have often found the compassion and hope that have been too often absent from their relationships with health professionals. These relationships are often described as life-changing (Whitehead, 2002). It is our consistent argument through this book that helping happens through relationships, and we believe that where professional relationships are marked by respect and compassion, these too can be transformative.

We are not arguing that workers should necessarily look for opportunities to engage consumers and families in discussions about spirituality. It is sufficient, we believe, that workers should be mindful of the way individuals will seek to make sense of their experience and to be prepared to consider such questions as *How does this person find meaning in their life?* and *What makes this life worth living?*

Implications for practice

Beyond a general concern for spirituality, there is a growing interest in the potential for incorporating spiritual practices and beliefs in mental health interventions. Many so-called third wave cognitive-behavioural therapies are based in mindfulness and draw on meditation and other spiritual concepts and practices as an intervention for a widening range of mental health problems (Farhall et al., 2012). Mindfulness meditation is employed in therapeutic groups in mental health (Coholic, 2007). Kabat-Zinn (2003) warns, however, that we need to recognise the unique qualities of mindfulness mediation so that it is not 'seized upon as the next promising behavioural technique or exercise, decontextualised, and plugged into a behaviourist paradigm with the aim of driving desirable change, or fixing what is broken' (p. 145).

Spirituality and Indigenous cultures

The Social and Emotional Well Being Framework (Social Health Reference Group, 2004) reviews the literature on Indigenous mental health and the current range of mental health interventions. The report makes a powerful argument for understanding the historical and social context for Indigenous health and wellbeing, a necessary prerequisite for mental health. Wellbeing is seen to rely on a broad range of services including housing, education, employment, recreation, family services, crime prevention and justice.

Social and emotional wellbeing problems can result from a range of experiences all too familiar to many Indigenous communities – grief, loss, trauma, abuse, violence, child removals, family breakdown, racism and poverty. Care is effective when multidimensional solutions are provided which build on existing community strengths and capacity and include counselling and social support and, when necessary, support during family reunification. The report concludes that mental health clinicians must recognise the impact of cultural and spiritual factors on the way mental health problems develop and present, in order to provide accurate diagnosis and effective treatment.

The report adopts a number of guiding principles to shape service response (Swan & Raphael, 1995; Social Health Reference Group, 2004):

Aboriginal and Torres Strait Islander health is viewed in a holistic context that encompasses mental health as well as physical, cultural and spiritual health. Land is central to wellbeing. Crucially, it must be understood that when the harmony of these interrelations is disrupted, Aboriginal and Torres Strait Islander ill-health will persist.

Self-determination is central to the provision of Aboriginal and Torres Strait Islander health services.

Culturally valid understandings must shape the provision of services and must guide assessment, care and management of Aboriginal and Torres Strait Islander health problems generally and mental health problems in particular.

It must be recognised that the experiences of trauma and loss, present since European invasion, are a direct outcome of the disruption to cultural wellbeing. Trauma and loss of this magnitude continues to have inter-generational effects.

The human rights of Aboriginal and Torres Strait Islander peoples must be recognised and respected. Failure to recognise these human rights constitutes continuous disruption to mental health (versus mental ill-health). Human rights relevant to mental illness must be specifically addressed.

Racism, stigma, environmental adversity and social disadvantage constitute ongoing stressors and have negative impacts on Aboriginal and Torres Strait Islander peoples' mental health and wellbeing.

The centrality of Aboriginal and Torres Strait Islander family and kinship must be recognised as well as the broader concepts of family and the bonds of reciprocal affection, responsibility and sharing.

There is no single Aboriginal and Torres Strait Islander culture or group, but numerous groupings, languages, kinships and tribes, as well as ways of living. Furthermore, Aboriginal and Torres Strait Islander peoples may currently live in urban, rural or remote settings, in urbanised, traditional or other lifestyles, and frequently move between these ways of living.

It must be recognised that Aboriginal and Torres Strait Islander peoples have great strengths, creativity and endurance and a deep understanding of the relationship between human beings and their environment.

These principles are consistent with the social justice imperatives of the social work domain. The insistence on the broader principles of wellbeing, as distinct from mental illness, as the basis for Indigenous services offers a wide range of options for service development. These are consistent with principles of partnership, empowerment, spirituality and social inclusion discussed elsewhere in this chapter.

The spirituality of the worker

Questions of hope, meaning-making and transcendence are as relevant to the social worker as they are to the consumers and families with whom they work. Consumers and families have consistently reported that they really value the hopefulness and compassion of the worker, valuing these personal qualities as much as any technical skills of the worker (Deakin Human Services Australia, 1999). The journey of life and the search for meaning are challenges that we all face. Workers might struggle with their sense of personal inadequacy in the face of overwhelming distress among the people with whom they work. They might seek to connect with the wisdom and energy of their own spirituality in their practice, or they might seek the comfort of their religious beliefs and find meaning in ideas such as their own brokenness, giftedness and sense of calling. They might ask, *What is my place in the journey of this client or family?* In the positivist and scientific zeitgeist of EBP, there is, perhaps, less permission for them to own and explore their spirituality than there is for consumers or families.

Case example 3.1: spirituality – the annual ARAFMI workshop in Launceston

The ARAFMI group in Launceston, together with the Emmanuel Centre and the School of Sociology and Social Work at the University of Tasmania, held a workshop every year between 2003 and 2008 to explore spirituality and mental illness. These workshops brought together mental health consumers, families and mental health workers, in almost equal numbers and on neutral ground, to share their understandings of spirituality. Using stories, music and poetry as a stimulus, workshop participants explored one theme in depth at each workshop, covering themes such as hope, anger, grief, risk and forgiveness. The Emmanuel Centre provided a homely and welcoming environment, and the ARAFMI group provided generous hospitality in meals and refreshments. The workshop provided a safe space for sharing and nurturing spirituality, one of the very few places where the labels – consumer, worker or family – didn't really define or separate the participants.

Families represent a group at risk for compassion fatigue and depression. The effectiveness of the workshop relied on the ability of the organising group and the workshop leaders to provide a welcoming, nurturing space in which participants could enjoy reflection, support and encouragement. It built hope and was life-affirming. The ARAFMI group developed a strong sense of ownership of the workshop program over the years, and they are proud of its success. Evaluation of the project to this point has been based on feedback from participants – not only from the families, but also from the consumers and mental health workers – who have evaluated the workshops very highly.

Conclusion

In this chapter, we have seen that the context for social work practice in mental health is complex and dynamic. We have looked at a number of important concepts that shape the way mental health services are delivered. We have emphasised the critical nature of relationships and a respect for the lived experience of mental illness as fundamental to how we engage with these concepts in practice.

QUESTIONS FOR PRACTICE

1. Why is it important that we strive to establish opportunities for consumers and their families to participate in decision-making around treatment?
2. What is more important in working out how we do our work – the research evidence or social work values?
3. Is recovery an important goal of our work with all clients?
4. What are the human qualities that make me the person that I am that I bring to my work, and how do they make my work different from others'?
5. In what ways do I unintentionally label or stereotype people, and how does such labelling blame people, frame them as the problem and assume bad intentions?

6 Which 'hot-button' phrases do I use, and how do they ignore people's unique experiences and circumstances?
7 How does the language I use prevent or hinder change?
8 How can I use language in ways that are respectful and hopeful?

Websites

Australian Council of Social Service

The peak body for community services and welfare sector and the national voice for the needs of people affected by poverty and inequality.
www.acoss.org.au

Centre for Mental Health

Promotes a society in which people with mental health problems enjoy equal chances in life as those without.
www.centreformentalhealth.org.uk

Cochrane Collaboration

A global independent network of health practitioners, researchers, patient advocates and others promoting evidence-informed health decision-making by producing systematic reviews of research evidence.
www.cochrane.org

Hearing Voices Network Australia

Consumer led, promotes recovery and community. Provides information and links.
http://hvna.net.au

Intentional Peer Support

Promotes transformative relationships among peers. Practitioners learn to use relationships to see things differently, develop greater awareness of personal and relational patterns, and support and challenge each other in trying new things. Promotes social change in mental health.
www.intentionalpeersupport.org

INTERVOICE

International network for training, education and research into hearing voices.
www.intervoiceonline.org

Mental Health in Multicultural Australia

Provides a national focus for advice and support to providers and governments on mental health and suicide prevention for people from culturally and linguistically diverse (CALD) backgrounds.
www.mhima.org.au

Mental Health Services Conference

A learning network for improving services in Australia and New Zealand.
www.themhs.org

Our Consumer Place

Resources from a consumer perspective, e.g., *The MadQuarry Dictionary* and *Psychobabble: The Little Red Book of Psychiatric Jargon.*
www.ourconsumerplace.com.au

Royal Australian and New Zealand College of Psychiatrists

Statements and clinical guidelines about mental health.
www.ranzcp.org/Publications/Statements-Guidelines.aspx

Voices Vic.

Voices Vic. is a network of voice hearers, professionals and carers working together to reduce the distress associated with hearing voices.
www.prahranmission.org.au/hearing_voices.htm

4 The policy and legal context for practice

How do we get good mental health services in Australia? At the heart of any discussion of the purpose and implementation of policy and planning is a commitment to improving outcomes for mental health consumers, their families and carers. Understanding the policy and legal contexts for service provision is central to social work practice in mental health. In this chapter, we describe developments in mental health policy and law in Australia and suggest ways in which social workers can work to get good outcomes for the people and communities they support. Advocates for mental health reform, including the Australian Association of Social Workers, work to ensure the best policy, the right resources, accessible services, evidence-informed treatments and the best-trained workforce so that people with mental illness can get the support they need to lead better lives. Despite significant policy development and improvements in the resources available to treat and support people with mental illness, many consumers, families and carers do not believe they have good outcomes.

Fifty years ago, mental health policy and law were considered matters for the individual Australian states and mental health services and legislation varied accordingly; the Commonwealth government had no obvious leadership role. Pressure for major change built through the 1980s highlighting the failings of the mental health system. The National Inquiry into the Human Rights of People with Mental Illness (HREOC, 1993; also known as the 'Burdekin Inquiry') was a scathing critique of the mental health system in Australia, noting the lack of policy and program coordination and the high number of people experiencing homelessness following the closure of large institutions. From 1989, for the first time, Commonwealth and state governments worked closely together to produce a national approach known as the National Mental Health Strategy. The strategy has been articulated across a number of five-year plans (Australian Health Ministers, 1992a, 1998, 2003, 2009) (Commonwealth of Australia, 2017) with an overall aim to develop consistent policy, significant reform of services, common mental health legislation, and education and training of the mental health workforce. The Fifth National Mental Health and Suicide Prevention Plan sets out eight priority areas:

1 achieving integrated regional planning and service delivery
2 effective suicide prevention
3 coordinating treatment and supports for people with severe and complex mental illness

DOI: 10.4324/9781003148913-5

4 improving Aboriginal and Torres Strait Islander mental health and suicide prevention
5 improving the physical health of people living with mental illness and reducing early mortality
6 reducing stigma and discrimination
7 making safety and quality central to mental health service delivery
8 ensuring that the enablers of effective system performance and system improvement are in place

The Australian mental health system includes services funded and/or delivered by both federal and state and territory governments and the private and non-government sectors. The Australian government funds a range of mental health–related services through the Medicare Benefits Schedule (MBS) and the Pharmaceutical Benefits Scheme (PBS) / Repatriation Pharmaceutical Benefits Scheme (RPBS). The state and territory governments provide public sector mental health services that provide specialist care for people with 'severe' mental illness. Examples include specialist acute and psychiatric hospitals and community-based mental health care services. The private sector provides inpatient psychiatric care in hospital and private services provided by psychiatrists, psychologists and other allied health professionals. Mental health non-government organisations are private organisations (both not-for-profit and for-profit) that receive government and/or private funding.

In this chapter, we will outline the principles of contemporary Australian mental health policy and identify those aspects of policy which are most relevant to social work practice. Where possible, we will point to international perspectives relevant to the Australian context.

International perspectives on law and policy development

Analyses of mental health policy development in individual countries such as the United States (Mechanic et al., 2014) or the United Kingdom (Fawcett & Karban, 2005) reflect the influence of both local and international factors. For example, the decline of institutional care for people with long-term mental illness in favour of community-based care over recent decades has been an international trend, but the impact of the policy has varied from country to country, depending on the level of community support available for people and the broader health and welfare systems operating in those countries (Drake, 2014). Outcomes for community care depend not just on the availability of specific treatment services, but on access to such services as housing, work, health, income security, advocacy, education and public transport.

Two specific international developments are relevant: the development of UN Conventions on the rights of people with mental illness and the WHO's *World Health Report* on mental health (2001). The former set out the rights which have shaped the development of mental health law and procedures, and the latter established a set of principles for mental health service development, with a focus on prevention and addressing stigma and discrimination.

UN conventions on the rights of people with mental illness

The UN's Principles for the Protection of Persons with Mental Illness (Office of the High Commissioner for Human Rights, 1991; the Principles) sets out 21 principles to shape mental health law and policy. It starts with an elaboration of fundamental freedoms and basic rights, including:

> All persons with a mental illness . . . shall be treated with humanity and respect for the inherent dignity of the human person . . . here shall be no discrimination on the grounds of mental illness.
>
> (Principle 1)

The Principles specify other rights, such as the right to live and work, as far as possible, in the community. There are detailed provisions for the involuntary treatment of consumers, for the rights of children, for access to information, for confidentiality and for quality of care.

These rights are reflected in the policy documents of individual countries. Australia's *Mental Health Statement of Rights and Responsibilities* (Australian Government Department of Health, 2012), asserts the centrality of:

- respect for individual human dignity and worth;
- equity of access to health and mental health care, housing, education and training, work and employment, legal services, income maintenance and insurance;
- appropriate and comprehensive communication with service users about their diagnosis, options for care and treatment and the availability of services;
- information about ongoing assessment, support, care, treatment, rehabilitation and services that support recovery;
- informed consent processes, including the right to refuse medical treatment and other services, unless the individual is governed by mental health or guardianship legislation;
- the incorporation of age, social, economic, cultural/geographical background, sexual orientation, gender and gender identity and spiritual preferences into treatment, support and care;
- treatment environments which are safe and free of abuse; violence; and physical, sexual and emotional harassment and which facilitate recovery and minimise restrictive or intrusive interventions;
- involvement of families, carers and support persons in assessment, support, care, treatment, recovery and rehabilitation to the extent requested by the person;
- community participation to the fullest extent possible without discrimination, stigma or exclusion;

- the development and evaluation of social justice, health and mental health policy and services.

The 1991 Principles were superseded in 2007 by a more comprehensive Convention on the Rights of Persons with Disabilities (UN, 2006). While the convention does not establish new human rights, it does set out with much greater clarity the obligations on states to promote, protect and ensure the rights of persons with disabilities. Thus the convention not only clarifies that states should not discriminate against persons with disabilities, it also sets out the many steps that states must take to create an enabling environment so that persons with disabilities can enjoy real equality in society. It includes such provisions as:

- non-discrimination,
- full and effective participation and inclusion in society,
- equality of opportunity.

A consistent approach to international policy development has emerged from the WHO *World Health Report* on mental health (WHO, 2001). This report has set out ten principles that should underpin mental health policy and suggests targets for service development for low-, moderate- and high-resource countries. These policy principles, listed next, find expression in the policies of all contemporary mental health systems:

- Provide treatment in primary care.
- Make psychotropic drugs available.
- Give care in the community.
- Educate the public.
- Involve communities, families and consumers.
- Establish national policies, programs and legislation.
- Develop human resources.
- Link with other sectors.
- Monitor community mental health.
- Support more research.

From Ann: the history of mental health policy and practice

The history of mental health policy and practice is littered with the graves of ideas which have reached their 'use-by date'. History is often seen as evolutionary, with progress from the darkness of past ignorance to the light of science and the future. The embarrassing practices of yesteryear become redundant. In the rush towards best practice, history is often left unexamined, and its insidious impact on the practices of today is unacknowledged.

One unmarked grave of the past contains the bones of the eugenics movement of the late 19th and 20th centuries. From its roots in social Darwinism and theories about the survival of the fittest, eugenics became a popular discipline in England, Australia, the United States and continental Europe. It was concerned with encouraging the procreation of healthy babies, of a healthy population. The First World War concentrated examination of eugenics because many potential recruits were turned away due to ill-health. Additionally, with the wealth of nations being directed towards war, some thought that society could not afford to carry or support 'the disabled and mentally ill'. In fact, conditions in some asylums deteriorated markedly during the conflict.

European psychiatry has always emphasised its philosophical underpinnings, and it was natural that there should be discussion of the essential qualities of human beings – what life is worthy of life?

In Germany, many academic psychiatric researchers supported National Socialism, as they sought to distance themselves from psychoanalysis which they viewed as a 'Jewish' endeavour. Many worked at the Kaiser Wilhelm Institute for Psychiatry, Munich, which became a centre for expert opinion on eugenics. During the 1930s, staff at the institute identified people with manic depressive disorder and schizophrenia as being suitable for sterilisation. In 1939, 'mercy killing' was extended to the mentally ill. Psychiatrists assessed patients suitable for gassing, and brains were collected for the institute's collection. Reportedly, between October 1939 and May 1940, some 10 000 mentally ill persons were killed.

What is the relevance of this for a consumer perspective? Not to understand history is to be condemned to repeat it – though perhaps not in the same format. As a consumer, I firmly believe that this is our history. It is my duty, and the responsibility of all who work in this sector, to examine implicitly and explicitly held values that detract from the highest ethic of care. New situations require consideration of old ideas: consider the debate around the provision (or lack of provision) of mental health care to refugees and people in detention centres. It is vital to live in relationship to others, to value the worth and dignity of each person, to take a stand in history.

Identifying common principles

We will now identify a number of important common themes in policy development and suggest why these are important in shaping social work practice. Each section raises a number of key questions.

The importance of primary care as a site for mental health services

In line with the WHO Principles, there is a strong move towards locating mental health services in primary care settings. The emphasis here is to provide first-line treatment not in specialist mental health hospitals or clinics, but in familiar settings such as GP practices and community health centres. This is a key mental health policy principle and is set out in all the various Australian National Mental Health Plans (Australian Health Ministers, 1992a, 1998, 2003, 2009). The principle is echoed in the New Zealand policy, *Te Tāhuhu: Improving Mental Health: The Second National Mental Health and Addiction Plan* (Minister of Health, 2005). It is estimated that about 12 per cent of all visits to GPs are related to mental health, with depression as the most frequent presentation (AIHW, 2019). In recent years, the Australian government has further promoted the primary care approach to mental health through schemes such as the *Better Access Initiative* which fund general practitioners and allied health workers, including social workers, to provide mental health services to consumers in primary care settings.

This emphasis on primary care is designed to ensure easy access to first-line treatments in settings that are non-stigmatising. The inclusion of social workers and other allied health personnel in these services represents a significant expansion of fee-for-service work, greatly assisted by the extension of Medicare arrangements to suitably qualified social workers to provide such services, including telehealth services to people in rural and remote areas. In 2019, more than 2200 social workers had been accredited by the AASW to participate in the new Commonwealth schemes (AASW website, www.asn.au, 2019).

Mental health services are provided by a multidisciplinary workforce

This is a central principle of the Australian National Mental Health Strategy and is evident in all four national plans, the *National Standards for Mental Health Services* (Australian Government Department of Health and Ageing, 2010) and the National Practice Standards for the Mental Health Workforce (Victorian Government Department of Health, 2013).

Case example 4.1: The policy of providing service through a multidisciplinary workforce

An Australian Commonwealth/state initiative, the National Practice Standards for the Mental Health Workforce (Victorian Government Department of Health, 2013) address core elements of common practice across the five mental health professions; social work, occupational therapy, nursing, psychology and psychiatry. They are generic in the sense that all of the disciplines are expected to meet all the standards, and they are intended to complement each of the professional groups' discipline-specific practice standards or competencies. The standards are organised around 13 key areas, and many of them cover practice that is strongly familiar to social work. They include, for example, 'Rights, responsibilities, safety and privacy' (Standard 1), 'Working with people, families and carers in recovery-focused ways' (Standard 2), 'Meeting diverse needs' (Standard 3) and 'Treatment and support' (Standard 7). Each of the standards is written to identify the appropriate skills, knowledge and attitudes that the mental health worker would be able to demonstrate to practise at a satisfactory standard.

An emphasis on a multidisciplinary workforce has carried an expectation that social workers will share a knowledge, skills and values base with other health disciplines. To meet this expectation, the AASW developed *Practice Standards for Social Workers in Mental Health* (AASW, 2008b, 2014) and made amendments to the Australian Social Work Education and Accreditation Standards (ASWEAS) to ensure social workers can participate in programs such as *Better Access*, or in other fee-for-service work undertaken by social workers in private practice settings.

The policy of a multidisciplinary mental health workforce, then, represents not only a significant opportunity for social work to flourish and contribute strongly to the reform agenda, but also an ongoing threat to maintaining relevance and position in the 'unrelenting contestation' of the mental health workforce. It is increasingly common for positions to be advertised generically with descriptors such as 'crisis worker', 'case manager' or 'team leader', and many social workers compete successfully with other disciplines for these positions. The two challenges remain at the core of the practice of social work in mental health: maintaining the skills and knowledge of the general mental health worker, and developing, defining and defending a distinct identity as a social worker.

Quality mental health services depend on building partnerships among stakeholders

Mental health policies in Australia, New Zealand and elsewhere are based on a recognition that quality outcomes rely not on specialist mental health services alone, but on the maintenance of partnerships among key stakeholders. Partnership operates at a number of levels, and it concerns:

- the way primary health care and specialist services work together to provide continuity of care for consumers;
- the therapeutic alliances formed among service providers, consumers and families to achieve best outcomes;

- the partnership between governments that fund services and non-government organisations that use those funds to provide a range of support and recovery services;
- the way the various government departments concerned with health, income security, housing and transport need to work together to enhance opportunities for individuals to recover from the impact of mental illness;
- the way we partner with communities and cultural groups to work to ensure that services are safe, accessible and culturally responsive.

Social work's concern for the social context of mental illness and its recognition of the value of applying a systems perspective to assessment and intervention makes it particularly sensitive to the importance of ideas of partnership. Because social work in mental health has always worked beyond the framework of individual clinical treatment to include family, group and community work, as well as advocacy, research and policy, it has a tradition of engaging with any part of the system that is likely to be a locus of change. Because many social workers are employed in the broad range of health and welfare agencies and so encounter people with mental health problems in non-clinical settings, we are well placed to work at building partnerships with the consumer, their family and carers, and with other professionals to address a broad range of difficulties associated with the consequences of illness.

We have argued that relationships are at the heart of effective social work practice. This is as true in the area of building partnerships as it is in working individually with consumers and families. The relationships we develop with colleagues beyond the treatment team – and how we use those relationships to forge partnerships and promote positive social change – are fundamental to effective social work practice.

From Ann: public, private or something in between?

I've always felt embarrassed about revealing that I see clinicians in the private sector and have private health insurance. To admit that I use private mental health services seems to detract from my consumer credentials, as if I'm not a 'real' consumer unless I've been treated involuntarily, or had to consider whether or not to provide afternoon tea to the visiting community mental health team, or been forcibly injected, or placed in seclusion. Part of that discomfort reflects the debate about who is a 'real' consumer. Where is madness found? What is the difference between public and private mental health care?

In recent times there have been a number of changes in how mental health care is provided, characterised by:

- the domestication of care where individuals with mental illness, families and friends provide more care and support due to the shrinking of the welfare state;
- cost-shifting of the funding for mental health services between traditional state-funded mental health services (hospitals and community mental health teams) to agencies and services primarily funded by the Commonwealth;
- the blurring of the distinction between public and private mental health care. The private sector is, to various degrees, publicly funded under Medicare, various government grants, the Pharmaceutical Benefits Scheme and the private health insurance rebate;
- the expectation that citizens pay larger and larger gap fees, or co-contributions, as governments are prepared to fund less of the costs of care.

There is an argument that when consumers pay for care they become more than passive users of mental health services. In a sense they are employers on a fee-for-service basis of individual practitioners, some stand-alone, some in agencies and hospitals. Are service users in a commercial relationship with service providers or recipients of care? Implicit in any contractual arrangement is the idea that people can choose to purchase, or not, someone's skills and knowledge. Does this accurately describe the recent changes in service provision? Or, in reality, is the degree of choice more circumscribed and the amount of power held by consumers still illusory?

There are some other unintended consequences of this re-alignment of service provision; for example:

1. How does this affect traditional ideas about consumer participation and ways of influencing the manner and type of service delivered?
2. How do consumers and families influence how GPs and private practitioners provide services?
3. Is the notion of participation only available to the consumers and families of mental health agencies that have the time or money to support it?

Mental health policy is based on increasing access to, and provision of, quality services

The need for greater access to quality mental health services is implicit in Australian policies. The Better Access initiative of the Australian government, for example, seeks to make available a range of 'focused psychological interventions' in primary care settings. An emerging theme of all policies is the adoption of 'evidence-informed' interventions as the standard for services provided. This is reflected in all contemporary mental health jurisdictions, and there is a growing literature on the evidence base for the range of psychosocial interventions available to social workers and other mental health professionals (Stout & Hayes, 2005; Thyer & Wodarski, 2007).

Mental health policy should be based on principles of consumer, family and carer participation

A central principle of policy and service reform in mental health over the past 30 years has been 'consumer participation' – the recognition that consumers of services should be vitally involved in all aspects of mental health services, including design, delivery and evaluation. We defined consumer participation in the previous chapter as 'any activity done by consumers where they have power or influence on the system and services that affect their lives' (O'Hagan et al., 2002). Typically, participation refers to the whole range of activities, from work with individual clients through to service management, and to education, training and research activities. All policies stress the importance of engaging with families and recognising their need for support and inclusion in care planning.

In applying the policy of consumer and family participation in Australia, we need to find ways to make the principle work at every level – at the local level through the participation of families and consumers on policymaking boards, at board level for non-government organisations, in education and training, in service management and in service delivery. As we have argued, the most difficult area in which to make the principle work may be the work done between individual consumers and their mental health service providers. It is at this level that the principles of allowing service delivery to be directed as fully as possible by the needs and wishes of the individual consumer are both most needed and also most vulnerable. We acknowledge the fact that consumers don't share a common single view of how services should be provided. Nor do families and carers. Consumers and families may hold conflicting opinions about services, and within individual treatment situations they may hold conflicting beliefs about treatment or care plans. It is a mistake to think that adopting a principle of consumer and family participation will make the task of decision-making a simple one.

There are many practice implications for adopting a principle of consumer and family participation. While there are some very good examples of policy in practice emerging, there is a need for ongoing research into best practice in this area. It is clear that a central practice task of the mental health worker is to encourage consumer and family participation and then to work to engage positively with those competing perspectives.

Mental health policy should address the social and economic context for mental illness

The emphasis in Australia has been on the need for inter-sectoral links and integration of services (Australian Government Department of Health and Ageing, 2010) to ensure individual access to services across a wide range of health and welfare services. Implicit in the theoretical work to connect mental illness with social inclusion is the recognition that mental health policy is not just about the treatment of specific diseases and disorders. Rather, it is about acknowledging the capacity of mental illness to impact on all aspects of an individual's life. These impacts become the legitimate and core business of mental health policy. The social inclusion concepts provide a useful theoretical framework for considering those many areas of crossover between mental health and other social policies – areas where social work has traditionally been vitally involved in service delivery. Difficult areas exist in the intersections between mental illness policy and, for example, policies on child protection, homelessness, family violence and family welfare.

The social inclusion concepts are central to social work's domain as defined as the social context and consequences of mental illness. They are perhaps more relevant to the experience of severe and disabling mental illness than they are to the more high-prevalence disorders such as anxiety and depression. This suggests the importance of social work continuing to insist on a broad understanding of the impact of illness and to look for ways to address these impacts in all those agencies where social workers are employed. It also provides a conceptual framework within which social workers can define their domain and activities within mental health services, as well as an area in which social work might provide leadership in the process of policy and service development.

Mental health policy should promote recovery as a basis for mental health services

Recovery principles have been adopted as a central organising principle for mental health policy in Australia (see Chapter 3). As we have seen, the key principles of recovery are:

- empowerment through choice and self-management;
- an emphasis on strengths;
- services to meet individual need;
- the role of family and community;
- the importance of respect, hope and meaning-making.

The principle that recovery happens within relationships is enormously challenging. The idea is closely connected to the principles identified by the Australian consumers and families in the Deakin Human Services Project (Deakin Human Services Australia, 1999), which we described in Chapter 1. The Deakin project emphasised the importance of the lived experience of mental illness and the healing power of relationships – radical principles that challenge the dominant discourses of the technology of helping evident in the positivist and modern mental health interventions derived from evidence-based research. They emphasise the humanity of the worker as much as their competence and knowledge.

If we can accept that recovery comprises a range of different theoretical positions, it is still possible to identify a number of key practice issues that emerge from these various ideas about recovery. Workers need to keep in mind the big questions, such as 'What would a good life look like for you?' and 'How can I work with you to achieve that?' We would be concerned about the relationships that individuals have with friends, family and community. We would emphasise the development of trust and respect with individuals and families as a starting point for helping.

Mental health policy for specific communities

There is a growing recognition that broad mental health policy needs to be responsive to the specific needs of marginalised communities and population groups, including Aboriginal and Torres Strait Islander peoples, young people, people from culturally diverse backgrounds and older people. The Working Together project (Purdie et al., 2010), for example, seeks to inform mental health work with Australian Indigenous people through a detailed exploration of the connections among ideas of emotional health and wellbeing, a history of colonisation and dispossession, trauma, loss and grief, social disadvantage, and Aboriginal spirituality.

Mental illness, poverty and human rights

Social work's concern with social justice provides a useful framework for considering the development and application of mental health policy in Australia. There is strong evidence through the *National Survey of People Living with Psychotic Illness* (Morgan et al., 2011) and other research that poverty and social exclusion are closely connected with long-term mental illness. Butterworth et al. (2011) have shown significantly higher rates of mental illness among all groups of Australian citizens on Centrelink benefits, including full-time university students. They conclude that mental disorder represents a substantial barrier to work, community engagement and social participation. Unless this nexus between illness and poverty is addressed through broader social welfare programs, such as housing and income security, people with serious mental illness will be excluded from participation in Australian society.

The Human Rights Law Centre argues that despite the developments in policy and resources in mental health, services are significantly under-resourced in Australia, and there are widespread problems with access to care, quality of care and adequate accommodation for people requiring mental health services. They cite an international review of Australia's compliance with the Internal Covenant on Economic, Social and Cultural Rights that expressed concern about 'the insufficient support for persons with mental health problems, as well as the difficult access to mental health services, in particular for Aboriginal and Torres Strait Islander peoples, prisoners and asylum seekers in detention' (Human Rights Law Centre, 2011).

New social policy initiatives

The National Disability Insurance Scheme (NDIS)

The National Disability Insurance Scheme was introduced in Australia in 2013 to support people with disability, including people with psychosocial disability, to have greater choice, control and access to services that enable independence and participation. The NDIS provides individualised funding to eligible participants to purchase support services. A person is eligible if they are under 65 and an Australian citizen or permanent resident and:

- they have a disability that is likely to be permanent (including psychosocial disability);
- without support, they have a substantially reduced capacity to take part in the activities of daily living and effectively participate in society;
- they are likely to require support from the NDIS over their lifetime.

A recent review of the legislation that provides for the NDIS identified a number of barriers for people with psychosocial disability, specifically access for people with episodic illness. The review recommended that the legislation provide clarification for 'when an impairment is considered permanent for people with psychosocial disability, appreciating that their needs may be episodic and fluctuate over time; and that the determination of reasonable and necessary supports for people with psychosocial disability should be aligned with best practice recovery approaches' (Tune, 2019, p. 9).

Mental Health Commissions

Governments both at state and Commonwealth levels have established the office of Mental Health Commissions. The functions of these commissions vary from state to state. While some are directly involved in distributing resources, all are charged with setting standards for services and holding services accountable to these standards through independent monitoring and reporting. Rosenberg and Rosen (2012) suggest that the commissions offer hope that the complex network of government and non-government services across state and Commonwealth jurisdictions might be better 'joined up' to meet the needs of individual consumers.

Policy, resources or practice standards?

What will ensure good services for consumers and their families? Clearly good policy, adequate resources, and a highly trained workforce are necessary but possibly insufficient to ensure good outcomes. The individual worker is challenged to ensure that their 'knowledge from practice' is organised and fed back to policy-makers so that the impact of policy decisions is clearly communicated. A focus on lived experience reminds us that the quality of any service is determined not just by policy, resources and training, but by the actions of individual workers. Service quality is experienced at the level of the transactions between individual consumers, families and workers. This endows individual workers with a lot more power and responsibility than they might feel they have. It is an assertion of the importance of good practice and the value of the diligent, persistent, compassionate and imaginative worker.

Mental health law

An understanding of the legislation that shapes the way treatment can be provided for people is essential for all social workers, not just specialists in mental health services. Central to such legislation are the provisions for allowing the involuntary treatment of individuals who have mental illness. This is a complex and contested area, one in which the principles of right to treatment and protection compete with self-determination and individual civil liberties. Forensic mental health practice is a specialised area requiring a detailed knowledge of the specific legislation dealing with the connection between crime and mental illness. We will not try to cover this practice area in this chapter, nor will we deal with the specific mental health legislation of each state or national jurisdiction. Rather, we will provide a general overview of the legal principles that shape legislation in the broad areas of providing involuntary treatment in hospital and the community.

It is important to recognise that social work practice in mental health is also concerned with other legislation that impacts on the welfare of people with mental health problems. For example, it is important for social workers to have knowledge and understanding of social security legislation, as well as laws covering child welfare, family violence and housing. Effective case management and advocacy with consumers depends on the social worker's knowledge of these areas of law. We acknowledge the importance of these areas of law, although a more detailed discussion is outside the scope of this chapter.

International conventions

As we outlined earlier in this chapter, all recent mental health legislative reforms have been developed within the context of the UN Principles and Conventions. The emphasis on rights in these documents provides a positive context for mental health law, in which the focus is not simply on treatment arrangements, but also access to, and quality of, services.

Involuntary treatment

Most people who receive mental health services do so as voluntary patients, and a central principle of mental health legislation over the past 50 years has been to support voluntary care as the preferred basis for treatment. Mental health law provides the framework for the provision of treatment to those people who may be ill and are at risk of hurting themselves and others but who do not recognise and/or choose to access treatment. In summary, the law aims to provide treatment when needed and to protect both the community and the individual from harm and danger.

There is an enduring tension between the concepts of beneficence and social control. On the one hand, the concept of *parens patriae* insists on the obligation of the state to 'protect' citizens with mental illness from harm. In summary, if you are so ill that you cannot make a reasonable decision to seek treatment, then the state should protect you from harm by providing that treatment, even if that is against your will. There is, however, a principle of social control implicit in compulsory treatment provisions. Involuntary treatment is also about the protection of families and communities through a deprivation of the civil liberties of individual citizens. There is an inherent tension between beneficence and social control and the principles of individual freedoms and self-determination. The framing of mental health legislation and its implementation in practice need to address the tension between these competing principles.

Healy and Brophy (2002), in their review of Australian and international trends in mental health law, argue that involuntary treatment for individuals appears to rely on five common themes in legislation:

A requirement that the person be diagnosed with a mental illness. This raises issues of the definitions of mental illness and mental disorder that are applied in legislation and the capacity of the complex process and contested nature of diagnostic assessment to be contained in the law.

Refusal or inability to consent to voluntary treatment. The person refuses treatment or is unable to give consent to treatment.

The likely efficacy of treatment. There is an assumption here that the treatment services are accessible and effective. Healy and Brophy argue that implicit in the law is a recognition that involuntary treatment can only be justified on the basis of both the need for, and the availability of, that treatment. This extends the debate about the rights of people with mental illness to include a right to treatment. We consider this issue of right to treatment later in this chapter.

The likelihood of being dangerous or causing harm to self or others. Again, there is an expectation that an assessment of risk of harm can be made accurately.

Provision for judicial review of treatment orders. All jurisdictions provide for periodic review of involuntary treatment orders, typically at one-month and six-month intervals (Healy & Brophy, 2002).

The circumstances under which involuntary treatment are provided remain a highly contested area of practice for all mental health workers. The competing arguments are developed in some detail in a debate on whether it should be easier to commit people involuntarily to treatment (Schwartz et al., 1994). On the affirmative side of this debate, emphasis is given to the importance of laws that facilitate easy access to treatment.

Persons with severe and persistent mental illness have serious illnesses that impact on their capacity to make informed decisions, follow through with decisions about treatment or voluntarily participate in treatment. It is the responsibility of mental health professionals, aided by workable mental health laws, to help meet the care needs of these individuals, even if against their expressed wishes (Schwartz et al., 1994, p. 255).

In opposition to this position, Mosher (Schwartz et al., 1994) argues for the importance of civil liberties, outlining that it is wrong to define mental illness, to predict dangerousness or to ensure effective treatments. It is wrong, he argues, to deprive people of their freedoms under these circumstances. At the heart of this debate is the question of the nature of mental illness. If we accept an illness model, then it is easier to accept an argument for involuntary treatment. If we believe, as Mosher does, that mental illness is essentially socially constructed, then an argument for involuntary treatment is harder to sustain. The challenge for social workers in practice is how to work within the complex ethical dilemmas that accompany involuntary treatment, ensuring both the right of access to treatment when needed and the right to maintain maximum autonomy and dignity for individuals at all times.

Community treatment orders

Community treatment orders (CTOs) provide for involuntary treatment outside hospital. Their use is designed to offer less intrusive or less restrictive forms of involuntary treatment. While CTOs are provided outside hospital, the extent to which they are less restrictive is contested (see for example, Slade et al. [2014], O'Hagan [2012]) with many asserting that CTOs are inconsistent with recovery-oriented principles (Edan et al., 2019). To be effective and fair in practice, CTOs need to be backed up with sufficient, high-quality resources for community treatment, as well as strong review mechanisms. Where these elements are lacking, they are open to criticism as an unwarranted infringement on the human rights of the person for little or no benefit. Healy and Brophy (2002) contend that, while there is evidence of benefit for many clients, it is possible that the same benefit might be attained through the provision of well-resourced assertive community treatment (ACT) programs. Indeed, one of the big problems with CTOs is that, paradoxically, they may lead to less care and treatment being provided to individuals in the community because the element of compulsion may reduce the need for the kind of careful engagement that requires a lot of staff time and effort. CTOs provide a lot of control but not necessarily a lot of care. Consumer-based research conducted by the Mental Health Legal Centre in Victoria, where approximately 25 per cent of consumers of community mental health services are on CTOs (Edan et al., 2019), suggests that many consumers find the application of CTOs intrusive and stigmatising, challenging the assumption of some mental health workers that CTOs offer a more 'consumer-friendly' method of involuntary treatment

(Healy & Brophy, 2002). The social control dimensions of enforced treatment remain strong.

Practice issues in working with mental health law

Social workers are vitally involved in many aspects of the application of mental health law. In many health and welfare agencies, social workers may become aware of mental health problems for their clients and are frequently part of the assessment and referral process that leads to decision-making about involuntary treatment. In mental health services, all aspects of working with clients – in assessment and crisis work, in case management or in family work – may be shaped by issues of managing involuntary status. For example, a case manager working closely with a client experiencing a relapse of illness may need to consider the circumstances under which involuntary detention and treatment may be necessary. Using the law and working within the legal context are complex areas of practice. There are a number of practice issues for social workers that can be identified.

Competing perspectives: rights vs risk

As we have argued, there is an enduring tension between autonomy and self-determination on the one hand and protection and social control on the other. What do we do when a client for whom we might provide case management decides to stop taking medication, or refuses to keep appointments with other treating staff? How do we balance the client's right to choose or refuse treatment with the need to protect the client from a damaging relapse?

Case examples 5.1 and 5.2 illustrate the tension between self-determination and protection as competing practice priorities. Assessing the level of risk involved is part of the process of resolving the ethical dilemma.

Case example 5.1: driving a car

Richard takes medication to manage symptoms of psychosis. He has developed a good working relationship with Kate, his case manager, and has made some steady progress towards his recovery goals. Richard decides that he is ready to drive his car, despite the advice of his psychiatrist who is concerned that Richard cannot safely drive a car while taking his current medication. Richard tells Kate that he will stop his medication and drive his car. He will not tell his psychiatrist of his decision, and insists that Kate not disclose this information either.

What are the ethical issues for the case manager, and how might these be resolved?

Case example 5.2: moving on

A social worker, John, was the case manager for Alice, a woman with mental health problems associated with alcohol-related brain damage, who had been living in a boarding house. She had done very well in hospital on a memory support program, but since moving into the boarding house she had been misusing alcohol, and her behaviour was disruptive and difficult for the other residents. John tried a number of strategies with Alice, but a crisis was reached after there was unresolved conflict with the other residents. John wanted Alice to return to hospital and was hopeful that this would happen quickly given her positive response to previous treatment. Alice refused to seek admission to hospital as a voluntary patient and so, after extensive consultation with his colleagues, Alice was admitted as an involuntary patient under the Mental Health Act. When he tried to explain this decision to Alice and showed her the necessary paperwork, she told John she had decided to leave the boarding house and would travel interstate that day. John had to decide whether to call the police to enforce the order or allow her to move on.

What should John do?

In case example 5.1, there are risks both to Richard and to the general public in driving a car while taking medication, noting the specific side effects. If he doesn't drive, he may be a risk only to his own welfare and independence. There is a risk for the social worker in withholding important information from Richard's psychiatrist. What are the principles that should govern such disclosure? In case example 5.2, the worker has to balance the need to protect Alice from risk of harm against a violation of her right to choose her own solution to conflict in the boarding house. These are complex and difficult ethical issues for the social worker.

Competing perspectives: consumers and family and carers

One of the consistent arguments put forward by families is that treatment services are too slow to intervene by using the provisions of mental health law to arrange involuntary treatment for mentally ill family members. The law generally requires that involuntary treatment can be provided when the person appears to be mentally ill and there is some risk of harm to self and/or others. Families are understandably anxious to arrange treatment quickly when it is clear that a family member is ill. The person's behaviour at home may be disruptive and distressing to family members, but at what point does that behaviour become a threat to anyone? Treatment staff may suggest to families that they should insist that the consumer move out of the home if their behaviour is disruptive, but families are understandably concerned to add the stress of eviction and abandonment to the distress of an emerging illness. Clearly, families have a right to express their own needs and suggestions to treatment staff, but at what point do their needs for safety and security override the consumer's right to refuse treatment?

Family advocate Harriet Lefley makes a strong case for the rights of families:

> Families . . . suffer greatly when a relative's concept of self-determination means rejection of treatment, noncompliance with medications, substance abuse, or even homelessness. . . . The argument of self-determination, that leads mentally ill persons to reject involuntary treatment as an abuse of their rights, can also be used to support the self-destructive behaviours that make such interventions necessary.
>
> (Lefley, 1993, p. 8)

While Lefley is unable to offer a solution to the dilemma of competing rights, she suggests the need for ongoing dialogue among consumer groups, families, service providers and lawyers so that the needs of all groups continue to be addressed.

A right to treatment

Within this discussion of the rights of consumers and families, generally framed around the need to protect civil liberties, we also need to acknowledge that rights also extend to the 'right to timely and high quality treatment' (Australian Health Ministers, 1991, p. 1), whether consumers are voluntary or involuntary. Certainly, the uneven quality of services across and within Australian jurisdictions challenges this right for many citizens (Mental Health Council of Australia, 2005). As we argued in the introduction to this chapter, this problem of poor services persists despite the promotion of excellent mental health policies. Mechanic, McAlpine and Rochefort (2014) and Brophy (2012) argue a connection between the aims of mental health law and the availability and quality of services. Without access to good services, less restrictive legal options, such as CTOs, cannot be effective.

Working towards empowerment

The dimension of social control inherent in mental health service provision reinforces the need for social work practice with involuntary clients to be based on principles of empowerment. A commitment to empowerment principles provides some direction for the way in which we might want to influence the working of that system for consumers, their families and carers. A number of practical steps can be taken to promote empowerment, as shown in the following section.

Promoting empowerment

Be mindful and aware of the power exercised by the treatment system. By this, we simply mean that it is necessary to recognise the social control dimension of treatment systems. Providing treatment is not a politically neutral activity, and social workers should be mindful of the exercise of power in the delivery of services.

Maintain a detailed working knowledge of mental health laws and procedures. Maintaining this knowledge allows us to keep clients and families fully informed about the legal context in which treatment is provided.

Access good consultation and supervision in order to support decisions about involuntary treatment and to work through the consequences of those decisions.

Give consumers, families and carers the information they need to negotiate the treatment and legal systems. Most mental health systems provide written statements of consumer rights and responsibilities. These set out the details of such processes as appealing against treatment decisions.

Arrange for independent advocacy. Social workers may need to encourage and arrange for independent advocacy for consumers, families and carers. Social workers, when part of the treatment system, cannot claim to be able to be independent advocates for consumers. There may be times, too, when consumers and families and carers each need separate advocates.

Maximise opportunities for choice. Within the context of involuntary treatment, there remain opportunities for consumers to exercise choice and control of their circumstances. A good example of ensuring choice for people who may require involuntary treatment from time to time is the use of advance directives (also known as care directives or advance health directives), as discussed by Bland and Epstein (2008). They argue that advance directives offer the opportunity for consumers to participate more fully in making treatment and other decisions during times of distress. The idea of advance directives is based on the assumption that people who have been diagnosed with mental illness know about their own lives and have the right to participate maximally in the decisions that are being made about them, even when they are deemed to be 'very unwell'. Advance directives enable people with mental illness, particularly people with episodic mental illness, to document what they need if or when they become distressed or 'ill' again in the future. They are an exceptionally important mechanism for people who believe that it is likely that at some time in the future they will be deemed to have lost decision-making competence with the consequence of them being once again forcibly hospitalised and treated against their will.

Using advance directives, people can document treatment options that assist their recovery, as well as things that they don't want. They can, for example, document drugs that have, in the past, caused nasty side effects; whom they do and do not want to come and visit them in hospital; and opinions about electroconvulsive therapy (ECT). However, advance directives need not be restricted just to treatment decisions. They can also apply to essential mental health decisions like child care arrangements and the care of household pets.

While there is limited legal backing yet in Australian jurisdictions for advance directives, the Queensland government has implemented 'advanced health care directives for mental health' under the Powers of Attorney Act, 1998 (Qld) (Department of Health Queensland, 2020). Victoria, New South Wales and the ACT are exploring ways in which the concept of advance directives might be implemented for people with mental illness. Consumers are promoting the process of developing advance health directives as a way of encouraging family and treatment services to be sensitive to consumer rights and as a way of maximising the opportunities for consumers to participate directly in their treatment decisions (Bland & Epstein, 2008, p. 250).

Involuntary treatment and recovery

The use of coercion to detain someone against their will in a hospital and to require that person to submit to treatments that are experienced as intrusive and unpleasant would appear to violate all the principles of recovery. Involuntary treatment denies individual fundamental recovery principles of agency and citizenship. A large study in a Brisbane hospital (Wyder et al., 2013) has explored the tensions between recovery and involuntary treatment by exploring the experience of consumers, families and workers. It found that almost half of the consumers interviewed reported that, even while in hospital, they could see the need for involuntary treatment 'to protect them from the psychotic illness that had overtaken their lives'. A number of factors seemed to reduce the distress of coercion and treatment.

Consumers felt empowered when they were given appropriate information about their legal and treatment options and when staff took the time to explain the legal processes and genuinely engaged consumers as much as possible in choosing from treatment options. Similarly, consumers stressed the importance of being shown respect and compassion by staff. Some consumers did not accept the need for treatment and experienced all aspects of their care as intrusive and unwelcome. Others described how the attitudes of staff helped to make the experience less traumatic, and these consumers could see their involuntary treatment as a setback, but not a failure, in their recovery journey. It is possible to conclude that recovery principles remain fundamental to managing the experience of involuntary care. Where an individual's self-determination and sense of agency is overwhelmed by the psychotic illness, the relational dimensions of recovery become more important. The worker has to ensure that whatever choice is available is within the constraints of the compulsory treatment, work hard to ensure access to legal rights and independent advocacy for the individual, and work at developing a relationship with the person that is deeply respectful, supportive and hope-giving. The shared experience of arranging involuntary treatment among consumers, families and workers can become a starting point for the very challenging work of the recovery process into the future.

From Ann: risk and danger – you have been warned!

It is currently fashionable to place posters around agencies and mental health services stating that abusive and aggressive behaviour will not be tolerated and that perpetrators will be expelled from the facility. These confrontational notices appear to be directed at the client, not the worker or the client's relatives or friends. The image of the person with mental illness that is being constructed is that of a dangerous and unpredictable person. The posters appear to be informed by a belief that risk of aggression is ubiquitous, and that it can be reduced by warning would-be perpetrators about the consequences. They also appear to be a management tool, providing a legal basis for expulsion of violent clients without any challenges by client or family to duty-of-care failures.

Is there any evidence base that says signs work? The causes of aggression are complex. On the other hand, there is a plethora of research and reports of best practice that indicate that aggression can be reduced by altering the physical environment of the unit or agency and through the development of healing, trusting and supportive relationships between worker and client, where any build-up of frustration is noted early and defused.

What are the unintended consequences of the signs? They are deeply stigmatising, warning clients not to trust other clients (the dangerous 'other'), and they create a climate of fear, informing families and friends of those with newly diagnosed mental illness that the reports in the media about 'mad axe-murderers' or 'crazed gunmen' are true and that they should be wary of the mentally ill.

Whenever I read warning signs, I feel angry. I want to challenge the staff about their views, saying, 'We're not all like this', and then I realise that as a person with a mental illness I am 'othering' my fellow consumers, creating binaries (violent / not violent) which disempower and fracture our communal voice. So I walk into the agency feeling defensive and distrustful about the staff, wondering whether they see the 'real me' or whether I am covered in a patina of untested assumptions and biases by the very people who say that they care and want to help.

Conclusion

In this chapter, we have looked at the development of mental health law and policy as a context for social work practice. We began by raising the issue of the connection between policy and service delivery, arguing that the adoption of excellent policy in the Australian context over the past decade has not been translated into better services for many people. It is possible to see good policy as a necessary but insufficient basis for service reform. We identified important common themes in policy and suggested that these are important determinants of social work practice. We have reviewed the legal principles that underpin and shape mental health law and its application in the area of involuntary treatment. We have identified a range of practice issues for social work in relation to mental health law, and seen how relationships have emerged as a significant principle underpinning a recovery focus for service delivery.

QUESTIONS FOR PRACTICE

1 Why are families likely to be more prepared to seek early application of involuntary treatment provisions than either consumers or workers?
2 What are the principles that should guide treatment staff in deciding whether to recommend a community treatment order?
3 Is there a valid argument to detain someone in hospital under an interim treatment order but allow that person to refuse to take any treatment?
4 How are government mental health policies created? Who influences their development and review? How can social workers play a role in these processes?

Websites

Australian Government Department of Health

Information about mental health policy, programs, management of disorders, suicide prevention, publications, data, consumer and carer participation and useful links.
www.health.gov.au

Mental Health Legal Centre, Inc.

A Victorian site covering mental health law. Links to other states and overseas.
www.communitylaw.org.au

UN Convention on the Rights of Persons with Disabilities

Details of the UN Convention.
www.un.org/disabilities/convention/conventionfull.shtml

World Health Organization

www.who.int/

National Disability Insurance Scheme

www.ndis.gov.au/

National Mental Health Commission

www.mentalhealthcommission.gov.au/

5 Overview of mental health disorders

In this chapter, we provide an overview of some of the mental health disorders and describe common mental health treatments. We will start with the common disorders (anxiety and depression) followed by lower-prevalence disorders – psychoses, bipolar disorders and personality disorders. We are aware of how superficial such a review must be, given the huge and diverse literatures on the various disorders and the very wide range of mental health disorders across the lifespan. We focus on adult mental health – and even within this area there are many disorders that we are not able to cover.

A working knowledge of the system of classification of disorders is useful to all social workers and essential to those working in mental health services. Social workers share the tasks of assessment, treatment and support, so it is important for all social workers to understand the approach to classification of mental health disorders and to recognise the signs and symptoms of the most common disorders. In this chapter, we will sometimes use medical or classifying language to describe and define mental health disorders. It is important to note this is not the language of social work; however, it is a language that social workers need to understand, apply and critically engage with.

Defining and classifying mental health disorder

Simply put, the medical model is a way of understanding and organising symptoms and signs into categories (diseases, disorders and syndromes). The principal purpose is to determine and prescribe the appropriate treatment, but there may be other important purposes as well, such as to determine aetiology and suggest prognosis. *Symptoms* are patterns of reported experience recognised by the medical practitioner, and *signs* are patterns of characteristics that are observed. In medicine (although these definitions are not always used precisely), *diseases* are usually well-established entities, often with a clear biochemical or physiological cause; *disorders* are also well established, but their cause may be much less clear; and *syndromes* are collections of signs and symptoms that suggest treatment and prognosis but are not as clearly established as diseases or even disorders (Bland et al., 2012).

DOI: 10.4324/9781003148913-6

The Diagnostic and Statistical Manual of Mental Disorders 5th edition (DSM-5) offers the following definition of *mental disorder*:

> A mental disorder is a syndrome characterized by clinically significant disturbance in an individual's cognition, emotion regulation, or behavior that reflects a dysfunction in the psychological, biological, or developmental processes underlying mental functioning. Mental disorders are usually associated with significant distress or disability in social, occupational, or other important activities. An expectable or culturally approved response to a common stressor or loss, such as the death of a loved one, is not a mental disorder. Socially deviant behavior (e.g., political, religious, or sexual) and conflicts that are primarily between the individual and society are not mental disorders unless the deviance or conflict results from a dysfunction in the individual, as described above.
>
> (APA, 2013, p. 20)

This is an intensely pragmatic definition. There is no necessary assumption of disease and no assumption about specific aetiology, and the definition is careful to require that the presenting 'problem behaviour' be considered within a social and cultural context. The term *clinically significant* suggests a dimensional element, allowing for disorders to be diagnosed towards the extremes of what might be 'normal' thinking, emotion and behaviour. For example, the disorders of depression and anxiety represent forms of thoughts and feelings found in most people in the community, just as certain features of psychotic illness (such as hearing voices) are also common in the population of people without a diagnosis of mental illness and may have religious and/or cultural significance.

In this context, it is important to understand that most psychiatric categories remain essentially provisional. There are fierce debates within the field of psychiatry about the whole enterprise of psychiatric classification, exemplified by debates surrounding revisions for the DSM-5. The classification of major diagnostic categories such as depression and schizophrenia remain contested and, we can confidently predict, will continue to change over time.

In this chapter, we will try to align our descriptions of disorders with those in the DSM-5. The primary purpose of the DSM is to provide clinicians and researchers with a common language for research and for the treatment of people with mental health disorders, and social workers need to be familiar with its content and structure. The DSM provides a description of each of the clinical syndromes with a list of signs and symptoms to be considered and the criteria in terms of severity and duration under which a diagnosis might be made.

Issues of reliability and validity are relevant here. *Reliability* refers to the extent to which clinicians will identify the signs and symptoms in a consistent way to reach a similar diagnostic conclusion. *Validity* refers to the extent to which the specific list of symptoms and the necessary criteria for inclusion actually capture a distinct clinical syndrome. Psychiatric research continues to be challenged by fundamental issues of reliability and validity, but it is still fair to say that the DSM tends to give precedence to reliability.

From Ann: dimensions of diagnosis 1

Many of us report the relief of being diagnosed with a particular mental illness: 'Finally I know what is wrong with me'; 'Now that I know what is wrong I can be treated/cured'; 'Now that I know my diagnosis I can go to the library and do some research'.

Diagnosis is often seen as a scientific discipline, describing observation, collecting information and applying robust diagnostic criteria. But diagnosis also has a political dimension. Often, subsidised psychiatric medicine is only available to people who have a particular diagnosis. For example, some of the newer-generation antipsychotic medications can only be dispensed under the subsidised Pharmaceutical Benefits Scheme.[1] This is a way of the government containing the costs of medicine. Because some medicines are useful in treating other psychiatric conditions, the prescribing doctor is faced with an unenviable dilemma when the consumer cannot afford the full cost of medication: to lie or to prescribe medication which is less effective or has more side effects. Additionally, different diagnoses attract different services, or sometimes no service at all (witness how some mental health services refuse to treat people with personality disorders).

The DSM does not seek to address issues of causation. For example, it defines a disorder such as depression through its symptoms and not on information about whether it is biologically based or connected with psychological or social causes (Parker, 2005). We will not be focused on questions of aetiology in this chapter. While the medical model tends to direct attention to biological causes and, more to the point, biological treatment, it is quite capable of accommodating psychological and environmental causative factors and 'prescribing' psychological or social interventions.

In any case, psychiatric treatments are often not directed at the presumed cause of the problem. Antipsychotic medication, for example, acts on symptoms and behaviour, not on some specific process of psychosis. While it might legitimately be said that the identification of a bacterium 'justifies, decides and guides' the use of antibiotics to treat a bacterial infection, the underlying process of psychosis has not been identified (although of course there are many theories, some with more support than others) and hence there can be no corresponding treatment in this sense (Rosenman, 2013, pp. 191–2). So, within the medical model, psychiatric treatment is often prescribed not for disorders as such, but rather for symptoms. Furthermore, just as it is common for people to take medication for serious anxiety that they understand to stem from social situations, so, conversely, there are many effective psychosocial approaches to disorders that have a substantial biological component.

In the real world, mental health problems are often not discrete entities. For example, depression and anxiety often occur together, and there are a number of similarities, such as disrupted sleep, irritability and difficulty concentrating (Goldberg et al., 2010). In fact, as with a lot of mental health classification, the boundaries of these disorders are hotly debated in the psychiatric and scientific literature.

Dziegielewski's (2010) analysis of the relevance of the DSM for social workers in the United States is helpful in understanding the relevance of the classification system in Australia and elsewhere. While Dziegielewski acknowledges the significance of diagnosis generally for treatment and research in psychiatry, she argues for the importance of social workers to develop their assessment skills to extend the DSM model into areas of the social work domain. As we will argue in this book, for social workers, *assessment is not the same as diagnosis*, and we are mindful of the politics of assigning a label. The DSM assumes major importance for social work in the United States, as it provides the basis for third-party reimbursement of private practice fees and for establishing eligibility for agency services. Social workers in the United States need to be able to assign a DSM diagnosis in order to provide a service.

So, although *social workers need to understand the 'illness and diagnosis framework', we do not have to embrace it.* Its dominance, as Rogers and Pilgrim have pointed out, 'should not be confused with its conceptual superiority' (2010, p. 2). Mental distress has complex determinants, many of which are social. We do not understand the complexity of mental distress by simply making an accurate psychiatric classification.

Finally, it is important to remember that, as Ann points out, a diagnosis is often used as much to ration services as to inform treatment.

From Ann: dimensions of diagnosis 2

A study of the first 100 000 Iraq and Afghanistan conflict veterans seen at US Department of Veterans' Affairs facilities has shown that 25 per cent have received mental health diagnoses. Of these, 56 per cent had two or more diagnoses, the most common being post-traumatic stress disorder (PTSD), substance abuse and depression. The true number of veterans with mental health problems only becomes apparent some time after their return home. This is because veterans perceive that if they admit to problems before they are discharged from service, this will delay their return home. In addition to the suffering of veterans and their families, there is an added political dimension to the way in which the Department of Veterans' Affairs applies the diagnosis of a personality disorder (PD). In the first six months of 2007, the US military discharged more than 22 500 service members due to personality disorders. Service members diagnosed with PD rather than PTSD or some other mental health condition are generally not provided with military disability benefits because the military regards PDs as long-standing conditions which were evidenced prior to military service. This is despite all recruits needing to pass rigorous physical and mental assessment before being accepted into the armed service and passing another assessment before their overseas deployment.

Common mental health disorders

Anxiety and depression are the most commonly diagnosed mental health disorders. While it is often noted that general practitioners are in the front line of diagnosis and treatment of these disorders, it is worth reflecting on the fact that many social workers in a variety of settings are likely to work with people experiencing these problems, whether or not they have been diagnosed or are being treated. The expansion of primary mental health care provision in Australia, including the public funding of 'focused psychological strategies' (such as those identified in the Better Access Scheme described in Chapter 4) by social workers and other allied health professionals, is an attempt to increase the availability and effectiveness of treatment for people with common mental health problems.

Anxiety and depression are usually conceptualised and diagnosed separately, but commonly occur together (Goldberg et al., 2010). Indeed, a mixed anxiety and depression disorder is often proposed (Malhi & Henderson, 2013). This serves as a reminder that, in the real world, mental health problems are often not discrete entities. Within this chapter we will consider each disorder independently and outline the symptoms and common treatment for each, while recognising that terms such as *anxiety* and *depression* go only some way towards describing the disorder for many people.

Anxiety disorders

Textbooks of psychiatry generally introduce the discussion of anxiety disorders by arguing that anxiety is essential to human existence (Barton, Joubert, Alvarenga et al., 2012). As a response to fear or stress, it motivates us – in the classical fight or flight response – to physical action. As such, it is adaptive and has survival value. However, anxiety disorders are not simply a matter of excessive worry or anxiety in response to stress. Anxiety disorders are diagnosed when the anxiety:

- is excessive;
- is prolonged;
- interferes with our social, occupational or other important areas of functioning.

Anxiety can impact peoples' thinking, mood and behaviour, as well as physical symptoms such as breathlessness, fatigue, chest pain, headaches, muscle tension, dizziness and nausea. People may experience excessive worry and recurring fears, as well as disturbed or disruptive thought patterns, such as catastrophic or obsessive thinking. Some people will avoid situations that make them feel anxious, which can be disabling, and will place limits on desired opportunities and experiences. Most people have good insight that something is wrong and are often embarrassed to tell others about it (Barton, Joubert, Alvarenga et al., 2012).

There is a continuum of severity of anxiety disorders. Some people with mild symptoms may improve without treatment, especially as the specific stressors are removed or become less influential. However, anxiety disorders are often chronic and cause great personal distress and impairment of social and occupational functioning, so recognition and treatment are important.

Prevalence of anxiety disorders

The lifetime prevalence of anxiety disorders is 26.3 per cent and the one-year prevalence sits at 14.4 per cent (Slade et al., 2009). The most prevalent specific disorders are social phobia (4.7 per cent), agoraphobia (2.8 per cent), generalised anxiety disorder (2.7 per cent) and panic disorder (2.6 per cent) (Australian Bureau of Statistics (ABS) 2008). Women experience higher rates of anxiety disorder than men (18 per cent and 11 per cent respectively), and there is an overall tendency for anxiety disorders to become less common as people grow older. Anxiety is the most common mental health disorder reported by Aboriginal and Torres Strait Islander peoples (17 per cent) (Australian Bureau of Statistics [ABS] 2019). Mixed anxiety and depression is more common than any specific disorder alone (Davies, 2003), and anxiety is present as a feature of many other disorders, including schizophrenia and personality disorders.

Specific anxiety disorders

Table 5.1 Specific anxiety disorders

Disorder	*Symptoms and specific concerns*
Panic disorder	People experience recurrent and unexpected and/or expected panic attacks which are followed by persistent concern about having another panic attack or concern about the implications of the panic attacks. Following a panic attack people tend to avoid similar situations or locations.
Agoraphobia	People are anxious about being in a situation from which escape may be difficult or embarrassing, or in which help may not be easily available should a panic attack occur. The anxiety usually leads to avoidance of certain situations or requires a support person to be present (e.g., elevators, crowded places, travelling alone, motorways).
Social anxiety disorder (social phobia)	People are anxious about being in social situations, including being scrutinised or evaluated by others in case they do something humiliating or show obvious symptoms of anxiety. The anxiety usually leads to avoidance of certain situations (e.g., eating, speaking or writing in front of others, social gatherings).
Specific phobia	People have a persistent fear or anxiety of a specific object or situation (e.g., injections, heights, animals, flying). The fear leads to avoidance of those objects or situations.
Generalised anxiety disorder	People worry excessively and persistently about a number of areas of their lives, including their relationships, health, job or finances.

Source: Treatment Protocol Project (2004, pp. 211–2).

Treatment for anxiety disorders

Specific anxiety disorders each require specific treatment, but there is also considerable overlap (Brandish & Baldwin, 2012) enabling some general observations to be made. Psychosocial and pharmacological treatments can both be effective and may be used in combination, although most people prefer the former, especially in the medium to longer term.

Psychological therapies (talking therapies)

Cognitive-behavioural therapy (CBT) is an evidence-informed psychological treatment for anxiety disorders (and other mental health disorders, such as depression). CBT is a structured psychological therapy which recognises that the way we think and behave affects how we feel. Relaxation techniques are often used, including progressive muscle relaxation, guided imagery and mindfulness-based meditation (Kyrios et al., 2011). Behavioural strategies such as graded exposure – an effective but misunderstood therapy (Taylor & Abramowitz, 2013) – and response prevention are used in situations in which there is a specific stimulus. These may be combined with cognitive strategies which challenge and restructure beliefs leading to the anxiety. Problem-solving training is used to help people develop coping capacities and interpersonal skills and to prevent symptoms from reoccurring (Kyrios et al., 2011).

There are also numerous online resources available, such as videos facilitating guided mediations, breathing techniques and progressive muscle relaxation; online forums; and apps that provide education and information about anxiety disorders and strategies for being well.

Medication

It is regarded as best practice to use medication in the treatment of anxiety disorders if CBT is proving to be ineffective or if the person is also experiencing depression (Kyrios et al., 2011). Indeed, antidepressant medication is itself used as an effective treatment for anxiety disorders, especially the classes of medication known as SSRIs (selective serotonin reuptake inhibitors) and SRNIs (selective noradrenaline reuptake inhibitors). Benzodiazepines, which are anxiolitics with sedative properties, can be very useful in the short-term reduction of anxiety but are not recommended for long-term use because they can be addictive (Kyrios et al., 2011; Barton, Joubert, Alvarenga et al., 2012).

Depression and other mood disorders

As with anxiety, low mood is something we all experience. However, ordinary sadness, feeling blue or typical reactions to loss or stress are not the same thing as the disorder of mood known as depression, which is a serious, disabling and potentially life-threatening condition (Parker, 2004) characterised by the presence of sad, empty or irritable mood, with associated somatic or cognitive changes that significantly affect functioning (APA, 2013, p. 155). Depressive disorder is usually distinguished from normal unhappiness or sadness when the mood state:

- is severe and persistent;
- lasts for two weeks or more;
- interferes with our ability to function at home or at work.

It may be obvious that someone is depressed, but this is not always the case because people experiencing depression may withdraw or hide their thoughts and feelings. Somebody with depression may experience:

- lowered self-esteem – that is, a loss of normal self-confidence, and feelings of worthlessness and inadequacy. Pessimistic and self-critical thoughts are common;
- changes in sleep pattern – insomnia, broken or fitful sleep;
- changes in mood control – as well as feeling miserable, the person may have difficulty in controlling anger, guilt and anxiety;
- changes of mood through the day (*diurnal variation*) – some people with depression may feel most depressed in the morning and improve as the day goes on, while others experience the reverse pattern;
- changes in appetite and weight – people may lose or gain appetite and weight, crave food, alcohol or cigarettes, or experience constipation;
- changes in the capacity to experience and anticipate pleasure (*anhedonia*);
- changes in the ability to tolerate pain. This is because some types of depression actually lower the pain threshold, while others cause physical symptoms such as headaches and stomach churning;
- changes in sex drive – typically, libido is reduced or absent;
- suicidal thoughts – thoughts of death and either vague or specific plans for suicide;
- impaired concentration and memory;
- loss of motivation and drive – everyday activities seem meaningless. It can be difficult to get out of bed in the morning and to do even basic activities like showering and dressing;
- an increase in fatigue – feeling tired and lacking in energy;
- changes in movement – slowing down or agitation;
- psychotic features – sometimes people can develop delusions such as believing they are bad or evil or that they are being watched or followed. They can also experience paranoia, feeling as though everyone is against them or that they are the cause of illness or bad events occurring around them. They may develop specific beliefs and even hallucinations about their own body (for example, *My teeth are rotting and destroying my body*; *My guts are rotting inside me*).

Family conflict, financial stress, work stress or job loss, and problems with interpersonal relationships often accompany depression, and there is evidence to suggest that depression is associated with the experience of negative social interactions and low levels of social integration (Casey et al., 2012). Depression impacts people's ability to work, maintain relationships and care for themselves and others. People experiencing depression may be inclined to walk away from things like a job or a difficult relationship.

Depression can also impact decision-making capacity and the ability to weigh up advantages and disadvantages, consequences and outcomes. It is recommended that people avoid making life-changing decisions when they are experiencing depression, such as moving or changing jobs.

Prevalence of depressive disorders

The World Health Organization (2020) estimates that more than 264 million people experience depression worldwide, and it is now the leading cause of disability throughout the world. In the Australian context, the lifetime prevalence of mood disorders (most of which involve depression) is 15 per cent, while the 12-month prevalence sits at 6.2 per cent (Slade et al., 2009). Specific disorders include depressive episode (4.1 per cent 12-month prevalence), persistent depressive disorder or dysthymia (1.3 per cent) and bipolar disorder (1.8 per cent) (ABS, 2008). There is an overall tendency for mood disorders to become less common as people grow older. Women experience higher rates of mood disorders than men (7.1 per cent and 5.3 per cent respectively), and there is an association with the experience of domestic violence and other abusive relationships (Barton, Joubert, Alvarenga et al., 2012).

Perhaps 10 per cent of women experience depression during pregnancy (antenatal), and this increases to about 15 per cent post-partum (NHMRC, 2000). This is different from the more common 'baby blues' that are very common in the days immediately following birth. Depression is longer lasting and can affect not only the mother, but her relationship with her baby, the child's development, the mother's relationship with her partner and with other members of the family.

Because depression is so common, it is often encountered in primary care settings, such as general practice, although under-recognition by general practitioners has been widely reported (Mitchell et al., 2009). There is a high rate of undertreatment of depression and recurrence after treatment (RANZCP, 2004).

Symptoms of depression are associated with most other mental disorders and frequently with chronic physical illness as well, tending to worsen the prognosis for both types of conditions (Davies, 2003). We have noted already that anxiety and depression often coexist (and can be difficult to unravel), and there are other mental health disorders (such as schizophrenia and personality disorder) that may also accompany depression (Casey et al., 2012). Many people present with physical rather than psychological symptoms. Some physical illnesses (such as thyroid conditions, neurological conditions and infections) share symptoms with depression. There is a high level of co-occurrence with alcohol and drug use.

Specific categories of depression

There are a number of ways of classifying depressive disorders, based on the nature and severity of symptoms, and their cause. There is debate about whether it is more useful to see depression on a continuum from mild to severe, or whether a form of classification based on different distinct disorders is better. Although the old terms *reactive* and *endogenous* are no longer widely used, the problem remains of how to distinguish between a mental state that can be accounted for and understood as resulting from life events and a depressed mental state that seems to come more from within, without an identifiable cause (Durà-Vilà et al., 2013). It is important to acknowledge and respond to the seriousness of depression as a disorder, but so too is it important to retain an understanding of the experience of depression as a reaction to significant loss or trauma in our lives (Horwitz & Wakefield, 2007).

The DSM-5 identifies a range of specific diagnoses within this category; here we will focus on major depressive disorder (including major depressive episode) and persistent depressive disorder (or dysthymia).

Major depressive disorder

Major depressive disorder is characterised by persistent low mood and/or lack of enjoyment, together with other emotional, cognitive and physical symptoms and significant functional impairment. Major depressive disorder may be diagnosed when *five or more* of the following symptoms have been present for the same two-week period and represent a change from previous functioning. At least one of the first two symptoms (depressed mood or loss of interest or pleasure) must be included among the five (APA, 2013, pp. 160–1). The symptoms include:

- depressed mood most of the day, nearly every day;
- markedly diminished interest or pleasure in all, or almost all, activities most of the day, nearly every day;
- significant weight loss or decrease or increase in appetite nearly every day;
- insomnia or hypersomnia nearly every day;
- psychomotor agitation or retardation nearly every day;
- fatigue or loss of energy nearly every day;
- feelings of worthlessness or excessive or inappropriate guilt;
- diminished ability to think or concentrate, or indecisiveness nearly every day;
- recurrent thoughts of death, recurrent suicidal ideas, a suicide attempt or a specific plan for suicide.

Persistent depressive disorder

Persistent depressive disorder, or dysthymia, refers to chronic depressive symptoms that don't meet the aforementioned criteria. The mood disturbance is less severe, but persists for longer, with less chance of easing spontaneously. The DSM-5 (APA, 2013, p. 168) specifies the following diagnostic criteria:

- Depressed mood for most of the day, for more days than not, for at least two years, together with two or more of the following features:
    - poor appetite or overeating,
    - insomnia or hypersomnia,
    - low energy or fatigue,
    - low self-esteem,
    - poor concentration or difficulty making decisions,
    - feelings of hopelessness.

Treatment for depression

Specific treatment for depression should take account of the nature of the disorder, its severity and its impact. One good framework, advocated by the National Institute for Health and Care Excellence (NICE) in the United Kingdom, uses a 'depression continuum' to inform a 'stepped care' model for evidence-based treatment (see Table 5.2).

Medication

There are a number of classes of antidepressant medication, including serotonin and norepinephrine reuptake inhibitors (SSRIs and SRNIs), tricyclic antidepressants (TCAs) and monoamine oxidase inhibitors (MAOIs), each of which can be

Table 5.2 'Stepped care' model for evidence-based treatment

Focus of the intervention	*Nature of the intervention*
STEP 1: All known and suspected presentations of depression	Assessment, support, psychoeducation, active monitoring and referral for further assessment and interventions
STEP 2: Persistent subthreshold depressive symptoms; mild to moderate depression	Low-intensity psychosocial interventions, psychological interventions, medication and referral for further assessment and interventions
STEP 3: Persistent subthreshold depressive symptoms or mild to moderate depression with inadequate response to initial interventions; moderate and severe depression	Medication, high-intensity psychological interventions, electroconvulsive therapy, crisis service, combined treatments, collaborative care and referral for further assessment and interventions
STEP 4: Severe and complex depression; risk to life; severe self-neglect	Medication, high-intensity psychological interventions, electroconvulsive therapy, crisis service, combined treatments, multiprofessional and inpatient care

Source: Adapted from NICE (2009, p. 7).

effective but has its own profile of side effects. Doctors need to assess carefully the right medication for each individual, but it is fair to say that SSRIs are generally now the first line of treatment, largely because they are better tolerated than some of the other drugs, such as TCAs which had been the mainstay of treatment for many years (Barton, Joubert, Norrie et al., 2012).

Physical treatments

Electroconvulsive therapy (ECT) involves the delivery of an electrical current to induce a seizure for therapeutic purposes, under anaesthetic and using medication to relax the muscles to minimise the physical aspects of the seizure. ECT is often considered a controversial treatment because of its past use as a form of punishment and control and because of its poorly managed physical side effects. However, ECT has demonstrated effectiveness for quickly and significantly alleviating the symptoms of depression in certain situations and is regarded as a 'highly effective treatment with a strong evidence base, particularly for the treatment of severe depressive disorders' (RANZCP, 2013). While patterns of ECT use vary considerably, it is usually used when other treatments have not been effective, where there is a high risk of serious harm to the person and where depressive symptoms are severely disabling. Most mental health legislation provides for limitations on its use and special provision for consent. There is a range of promising newer brain stimulation treatments now starting to be used as well (Fitzgerald, 2011).

Psychological and psychosocial approaches

Among psychological and psychosocial approaches, the evidence for CBT and interpersonal therapy (IPT) is the strongest in achieving symptom reduction, and supportive psychotherapy is also commonly employed.

Cognitive-behavioural therapy. The goal of therapy is to use behavioural and cognitive strategies to effect change. CBT is generally provided by a clinical psychologist but is also increasingly within the skill set of other mental health workers such as social workers, doctors, nurses and occupational therapists.

Interpersonal therapy. This is a specialised form of psychotherapy that focuses on social roles and interpersonal relationships. Problems are identified in one or more of the following four specific areas: grief, role transitions, interpersonal disputes and interpersonal sensitivity. It relies on empathy, the therapeutic alliance and emotional expression, aiming to improve mood and functioning.

Supportive psychotherapy. This form of therapy provides support, education and counselling for the person. This includes a focus on enabling the person and their family to manage the impact of depression on their day-to-day lives. Because of the impact of depression on close personal relationships, it can be important to apply a family perspective to the experience of and response to recovery.

Preventative measures such as parenting interventions, school-based programs and interventions targeting job stress are among the many psychosocial approaches that can be effective in preventing common mental health problems such as depression and anxiety (Jacka et al., 2013).

Low-prevalence mental health disorders

The term *low-prevalence disorder* is sometimes used as a point of differentiation from common mental health problems, such as anxiety and depression, to refer to disorders that form much of the focus of specialist mental health services, such as psychotic disorders, eating disorders and severe personality disorder.

Psychosis

Psychosis cannot be simply defined, but the term is generally used to describe a mental health problem in which a person has lost some contact with reality (Kitchener & Jorm, 2009). Historically, the term *psychosis* came to be differentiated from neurosis to refer to mental health conditions without psychosocial biographical origins (Burgy, 2008), representing a break from the continuum of health. People with psychosis may experience severe disturbances in thinking, emotions and behaviour, and their lives are often disrupted severely. Relationships, work and self-care may be difficult to initiate and/or maintain (Kitchener & Jorm, 2009).

There are five key features of psychotic disorders: delusions, hallucinations, disorganised thinking (thought disorder), behavioural problems and negative symptoms. Drawing on the DSM-5, we next describe each briefly.

Delusions

Delusions are fixed but false beliefs that are not amenable to change in the light of conflicting evidence and are not shared by others of the same culture. Such beliefs are often held unquestioningly but may soften and be given up as a person becomes well. Sometimes a person's delusional belief during a psychotic episode may be held to be real for the past, even though the person no longer holds the delusion in the present. For example, the person might believe that the Roman Catholic Church was intercepting their thoughts but that they have stopped doing this now.

People commonly 'act on' their delusions. For example, if a person believes that their neighbours are trying to hurt them, they may be hostile and angry towards the neighbours. Examples include:

- persecutory delusions, in which the person believes that they will be harmed or harassed;
- referential delusions, in which the person believes that certain gestures, comments and environmental cues (such as a story in a newspaper or a song on the radio) are directed at him or herself;

- grandiose delusions, in which the person believes that they have exceptional abilities, wealth or fame;
- erotomanic delusions, in with the person believes falsely that another person is in love with him or her;
- nihilistic delusions, which involve the conviction that a major catastrophe will occur;
- somatic delusions, which focus on preoccupations with health and organ function.

Hallucinations

While delusions concern beliefs, hallucinations concern perception. Hallucinations are perceptual experiences in the absence of the corresponding appropriate stimuli. They are vivid and clear, with a compelling sense of reality and the full force and impact of normal perceptions, though they not under voluntary control. Hallucinations may be experienced in each of the five senses (sound, sight, taste, smell, touch), but auditory hallucinations are the most common, usually voices that are perceived as distinct from the person's own thoughts. The most common hallucinations involve hearing voices (auditory hallucinations), typically experienced as a voice or voices inside the head talking to or about the person. The voices vary in terms of frequency and content. Hearing the voices frequently or constantly can be very distressing. Depending on the content of the hallucination, the voice can be threatening, derogatory, intrusive or sometimes comforting.

Disorganised thinking (thought disorder)

Disorganised thinking (or thought disorder) is usually inferred from speech. Common examples include:

- switching from one topic to another (derailment or loose associations);
- providing answers to questions that are not well related (tangentiality).

Sometimes the term used is *formal thought disorder* to emphasise the essential point that what is abnormal is the *form* or structure of thought, as opposed to the content.

Behavioural problems

Certain behavioural problems including gross disorganisation and impacts on motor behaviour are associated with psychosis. Behavioural features of psychosis range from what the DSM-5 calls 'childlike "silliness"' to unpredictable agitation. Some people with psychosis exhibit and experience catatonic behaviour, which is a marked decrease in reactivity to the environment, such as resistance to instructions (negativism); maintaining a rigid, inappropriate or bizarre posture; or a complete lack of verbal and motor responses (mutism and stupor).

Negative symptoms

Generally, all of the features just listed (delusions, hallucinations, disorganised thinking and behavioural problems) are known as 'positive symptoms' in the sense that they are additional to normal experiences. Negative symptoms, on the other hand, suggest the loss of a capacity or a reduction or loss of function. The two most prominent are:

- diminished emotional expression;
- decrease in motivated self-initiated purposeful activities (called avolition) – the person finds it difficult to maintain activities of daily living, including housework and personal hygiene; family members and others may interpret this symptom as laziness.

Other negative symptoms include diminished speech output (alogia), a decrease in the ability to experience pleasure from good things (anhedonia) and a lack of interest in social interaction (asociality).

Schizophrenia

Schizophrenia tends to be used as an all-encompassing term for psychotic disorders that persist (Bennett et al., 2012). For a DSM diagnosis of schizophrenia to be made, symptoms must occur in at least two of the five areas outlined previously (including at least one of the first three) for a significant portion of time during a period of at least a month. It involves a marked reduction in level of functioning in areas such as work, interpersonal relations and self-care, and there must have been persistent continuous signs of the disturbance for at least six months. Despite extensive research into the disorder, there is a lack of agreement about whether schizophrenia is one illness or a number of different illnesses (Bennett et al., 2012), and despite recognition that there is a genetic component to the disorder, no unifying theory of causation has been accepted.

A diagnosis of schizophrenia suggests a disturbance of some of the most basic functions that give a person the feeling of being an individual, unique and self-directed (Treatment Protocol Project, 2004). There can be enormous disruption, tearing apart support systems and alienating the person from their daily contacts with family and friends (Dziegielewski, 2010). Historically, schizophrenia has been seen as a deteriorating disorder. When we communicate an assessment, it can have a profound effect for good or for ill. In the case of diagnosis, for example:

> it is commonplace in psychiatry to meet people who have lived much of their lives under a schizophrenia diagnosis and who were informed at an early stage of their difficulties that they should anticipate ongoing disability requiring lifelong antipsychotic medication. The insertion of an authoritative illness narrative into a person's life at a time of crisis may, in the short term, offer a thirsted-for sense of certainty, but also beckons towards a lifetime of restricted living.
>
> (Reed, 2013, p. 428)

It is, therefore, crucial that we remember that the majority of people with schizophrenia have the potential to improve and achieve long-term remission from symptoms and functional recovery, provided that good treatment is available (Zipursky et al., 2013).

A range of other psychotic disorders share symptoms with schizophrenia. It is the presence and combination of symptoms within specified time periods that allows the diagnosis to be made. The early phases of assessment and treatment may be difficult for the individual and their family while the diagnosis remains unclear. The initial presenting symptoms may be compounded or confused by the effect of drugs.

Related psychotic disorders include:

- schizoaffective disorder,
- schizophreniform disorder,
- delusional disorder,
- brief psychotic disorder,
- substance-induced psychotic disorder.

It is not uncommon for these diagnoses to be applied in early stages of the emergence of a psychotic disorder.

Prevalence of schizophrenia

The lifetime prevalence of schizophrenia appears to be well under 1 per cent, rather less than what is often presented by media. McGrath and his colleagues conclude that it would be fair to say that about seven individuals per 1000 will develop schizophrenia during their lifetime (McGrath et al., 2008). Their analyses challenge the view that schizophrenia is evenly distributed across all cultures and populations, identifying reported variation by race/ethnicity, country and urbanicity. According to the DSM-5, the sex ratio differs across samples and populations: for example, an emphasis on negative symptoms and longer duration of disorder (associated with poorer outcome) shows higher incidence rates for males, whereas definitions allowing for the inclusion of more mood symptoms and brief presentations (associated with better outcome) show equivalent risks for both sexes.

The Australian 2010 Survey of High Impact Psychosis (SHIP), which focused on people aged 18 to 64 receiving treatment for disorders such as schizophrenia, schizoaffective disorder, bipolar disorder and delusional disorder, estimated a 12-month prevalence of 0.45 per cent, about half of which was accounted for by people with a diagnosis of schizophrenia (Morgan et al., 2011).

Age of onset is typically in the late teens and early twenties (75 per cent of people with these disorders develop their illness between 16 and 25 years), though it can emerge earlier, with males developing the illness on average between three and a half and five years earlier than women (Kitchener & Jorm, 2009). The earlier onset for young men generally means that social and psychological development in the late teens is more disrupted, leading to higher levels of functional disability.

The risk of suicide for people with a diagnosis of schizophrenia is very high. About 20 per cent of people attempt suicide at least once, and 5–6 per cent die by suicide (DSM-5). Sometimes this is a response to hallucinations commanding harm; sometimes it is associated with depressed or hopeless thoughts which may be associated with the losses and dysfunction caused by the illness. The periods immediately following a psychotic episode and immediately following time in hospital may be associated with increased risk.

It is worth drawing attention here to some of the headline findings of the Study of High Impact Psychosis that we described in the previous chapter because they give an indication of the social context and social consequences of schizophrenia and other psychotic disorders (see box, 'Social context and social consequences of schizophrenia and other psychotic disorders').

Social context and social consequences of schizophrenia and other psychotic disorders

Many people living with psychotic illness are in relationships, study and care for children and others just like the rest of the population. They also experience particular disadvantages that, largely due to onset of illness in late adolescence and early adulthood, impact on their educational outcomes.

Psychotic illnesses can severely impact on people's ability to function in their daily lives in occupational, self-care and social domains.

People with psychotic illness receiving public mental health services also have poorer physical health than the general population, more often experiencing chronic conditions and being more at risk due to their high levels of obesity, smoking, and alcohol and drug use (as well as side effects of medications, including the masking of physical health symptoms). They are far more likely to harm themselves. They also think about and attempt suicide at rates far higher than the general population.

People with psychotic illness experience very high rates of unemployment and low rates of labour force participation. They are also at greater risk of homelessness. Factors contributing to these high rates include social isolation, family breakdown, stigma, discrimination and the need for acute care, including hospital admissions.

People with psychotic illness are often isolated by the symptoms of their illness and this isolation can be exacerbated by multiple episodes of illness, periods of hospitalisation and stigma and discrimination that make maintenance of family and social contacts more difficult (p. 10).

Source: Morgan et al. (2011)

A number of signs may be evident in the period before the onset of psychotic symptoms, including problems with disorganised thinking, suspicion, anxiety, depressed mood, fearfulness and withdrawal, as well as work and relationship problems. This period, called the *prodromal period*, and the months leading up to the crisis that will bring the person to the attention of the treatment system is a difficult and confusing time for the person and their family. It may take many months for a diagnosis to be made and for treatment to begin. A number of preliminary diagnoses may be applied before a diagnosis of schizophrenia is finally made. There is increasing evidence that active and aggressive intervention in the early stages of the illness may be effective in reducing the impact of the illness.

During the acute phase of the illness, the person will typically have the positive symptoms (delusions, hallucinations and thought disorder) accompanied by feelings of distress. In the residual phase of the illness, the person may experience fewer positive symptoms but will often have the negative symptoms such as withdrawal, apathy and affective flattening. A wide range of outcomes is possible, with some people making good recoveries and having no further episodes of psychosis. Others will make poorer recoveries and continue to live with the effects of the illness over several years. Davies (2003) argues that there is a critical period of between two and five years after the first episode of the illness when most of the impairment and disability arise. Therefore, active intervention is desirable during the early phases of the illness.

Simon Champ (1998) has written about his experience of treatment and hospitalisation during the acute phase of a psychotic illness:

> When I was psychotic, I often perceived hospitalisation and medication as a threat . . . as in one delusion when I believed that the hospital I was being held in was a concentration camp where I was going to be gassed. . . .
>
> The experience of hospitalisation gave me lasting negative messages that took me years to work through. Those messages were that I was unacceptable to society, that I was bad and that I had little power of my own. For me, these feelings are forever symbolised by the euphemistically called 'time out' room. Just at those times when I was least able to cope with the terrible fears I was experiencing because of paranoia, I was in solitary confinement away from other human beings who might have reassured me or genuinely cared for me. Such experiences taught me that society wanted to lock away and isolate what I was most afraid of, extreme states of mental anguish. I firmly believe that the act of putting me in solitary confinement in itself confirmed my sense of being an outsider. The experience of being locked away left me bitter and deeply alienated as did the rest of my first hospitalisation. Solitary confinement enhanced my feelings of guilt and the shame I felt at having a mental illness.
>
> (Champ, 1998, p. 56)

Treatment for schizophrenia

Contemporary treatment for schizophrenia should normally involve both medication and psychological and/or psychosocial intervention. Although some consumers still receive medication alone, clinical guidelines recommend that both forms of treatment should be offered (Galletly et al., 2016; Dixon et al., 2010).

Medication

Different forms of 'antipsychotic' medication have been used since the 1950s, to reduce or control psychotic symptoms. These are powerful tranquillising drugs that act to block dopamine receptors in the brain, and usually lead to at least some reduction in positive psychotic symptoms. Many different antipsychotic medications are in use, including, in more recent years, so-called second-generation or atypical antipsychotics. When first introduced about 20 years ago, it was widely believed that these newer drugs were generally superior in effect, tolerability and side effects, but the evidence suggests that this is an overgeneralisation. The selection of the 'right' antipsychotic medication for each individual is thus an important matter, and it can be a very difficult one. Part of the problem is that side effects are common and can be extremely troubling and disabling, including parkinsonism (muscle stiffness, decreased spontaneous movement and a shuffling gait), akathisia (agitation and restlessness) and tardive dyskinesia (usually a chronic, persistent, coarse, involuntary movement of the mouth, tongue and upper limbs). Some of these side effects may be treated, in turn, with other drugs. Second-generation antipsychotic drugs are often associated with substantial weight gain and other factors leading to diabetes and cardiovascular disease. While most antipsychotic medication is available only in oral form (as tablets or syrup) some are administered as slow-release ('depot') injections. A very useful detailed summary of the various drugs used in the treatment of schizophrenia can be found in *Mental Health in Australia* (Bennett et al., 2012).

Psychosocial approaches

Psychosocial interventions are relevant to both the positive and the negative symptoms of schizophrenia and offer considerable opportunity for preventing reoccurrence and relapse. However, their use in practice can be inconsistent, partly because services may be oriented more strongly to 'acute' treatment – crisis management and treating positive symptoms and disturbing behaviour – rather than addressing the negative and cognitive symptoms of psychosis and its disabling social consequences. Another part of the answer has to do with organisational factors and staff capacity (Haddock et al., 2014). The strong and developing evidence for psychosocial interventions (Drake et al., 2009) is not yet sufficiently influential to modify practices established over many decades of pharmacological dominance.

There is now a fairly standard list of clearly identified evidence-based psychosocial interventions that are effective for people with 'serious mental illness':

- family psychoeducation for reducing relapse and rehospitalisation
- cognitive remediation to improve cognitive functioning

- supported employment helping people return to the competitive workplace
- social skills training to improve social and community functioning
- CBT to reduce psychotic symptoms
- illness self-management training to reduce symptom distress and relapses
- integrated treatment for co-occurring substance abuse or dependence (Mueser et al., 2013)

There are also a number of 'promising practices' (for which there is less but developing evidence), such as assertive community treatment, supported housing, training in social cognition and cognitive adaptation training, that serve to create environmental supports to facilitate self-care and independent living skills. One of the most rigorous and authoritative sources of evidence for working with people with mental health problems is the Schizophrenia Patient Outcomes Research Team (PORT) (Kreyenbuhl et al., 2010). The PORT group specifies and recommends a number of specific psychosocial interventions, including almost all of those listed here. A comprehensive list of potential psychosocial interventions for schizophrenia, together with medication and other treatment guidelines, can be found in the *Royal Australian and New Zealand College of Psychiatrist Clinical Practice Guidelines for the Management of Schizophrenia and Related Disorders* (Galletly et al., 2016).

Bipolar disorders

Bipolar disorder, previously known as manic depression, is the name used to describe 'exaggerated swings of mood, cognition and energy from one extreme to the other' (Black Dog Institute, 2012, p. 1). Mostly, this takes the form of recurrent and oscillating episodes of highs and lows, although some people experience only the highs. Between the swings, people experience normal moods.

Subgroups of bipolar disorder

There are three main subgroups of bipolar disorder as described in the DSM-5:

Bipolar I Disorder, in which people experience a full manic episode, described as 'a distinct period of abnormally and persistently elevated, expansive, or irritable mood and abnormally and persistently increased goal-directed activity or energy' (APA, 2013, p. 124), preceded or followed by depressive or hypomanic episodes (where *hypo-* means *under*, hence elevated but not to the extent of full mania). This is the more severe form of bipolar disorder, in which people are more likely to have psychotic experiences such as delusions and hallucinations.

Bipolar II Disorder, which requires the lifetime experience of at least one episode of major depression and at least one hypomanic episode, typically accompanied by serious disruption of work and social functioning. Episodes may last only a few hours or a few days and the psychotic experiences associated with full mania are not present.

Cyclothymic Disorder, in which people experience at least two years of both hypomanic and depressive episodes, without fulfilling the full criteria for major depression, mania or hypomania.

We have described the symptoms of depression earlier in this chapter. The Black Dog Institute (2012) identifies the following as features of mania:

- *high energy levels* – feeling 'wired' and 'hyper', 'high' or euphoric, extremely energetic, talking more and talking over people, making decisions in a flash, being constantly on the go, feeling less or no need for sleep, racing thoughts and speech, decreased appetite, and weight loss
- *positive mood* – feeling confident and capable, optimistic that one can succeed in everything, delusions of self-importance, more creative, happier and feeling 'high as a kite'
- *irritability* – irritable mood, impatient and aggressive
- *inappropriate behaviour* – becoming over-involved in other peoples' activities, engaging in increased risk-taking (e.g., by over-indulging in alcohol and drugs and gambling excessively), saying and doing outrageous things, spending more money, having increased libido, dressing more colourfully and with disinhibition
- *heightened creativity* – 'seeing things in a new light', seeing things vividly and with crystal clarity, having heightened senses and feeling quite capable of great things
- *mystical experiences* – believing that there are special connections between events or that there is a higher rate of coincidence between things happening, feeling at one with nature and appreciating the beauty and the world around, and believing that things have special significance

Some of the other features that suggest a diagnosis of a bipolar disorder are:

- racing thoughts (for example, feeling like you are watching a number of different TV channels at the same time, but not being able to focus on any);
- sleeping a lot more than usual;• feeling agitated, restless and/or incredibly frustrated.

The manic phase of the illness may involve decisions or behaviours that have significant and adverse outcomes. For example, a person may make very poor financial decisions and lose large amounts of money. Research into the family experience of bipolar disorder shows that the manic phase of the illness, with its irritability and impulsive and inappropriate behaviour, can leave family members angry and confused (Bland & Harrison, 2000), wondering how much of this behaviour is the 'illness' and how much the 'person'. These 'difficult behaviours' during manic episodes can impact on the health and welfare of the person and their family and represent a major area of social work activity in the comprehensive care of people with bipolar disorder.

Prevalence of bipolar disorder

There is some debate about the prevalence of bipolar disorder. Parker (2004) has suggested that the rate of Bipolar II disorder may be higher than once thought, and may affect as much as 10 per cent of the population over a lifetime. Other estimates are considerably lower; for example, there is about 1 per cent lifetime prevalence for each of Bipolar I and Bipolar II (Malhi et al., 2009; Goodwin, 2012). Recent Australian data suggests a twelve-month prevalence of bipolar disorder as high as 1.8 per cent of the population (Slade et al., 2009).

Women and men develop Bipolar I disorder at equal rates, while the rate of Bipolar II disorder is somewhat higher in women (Black Dog Institute, 2012). While the aetiology of bipolar disorder is unknown, there is a strong genetic link (Duffy et al., 2014), typically developing in the late teens and early adulthood. Compared even with people with major depressive disorder, those with bipolar disorder experience a greater likelihood of being widowed, separated or divorced; are more likely to experience drug abuse or dependence; have greater disability, as measured by days out of role; have increased rates of treatment with medicines; and are at considerably higher lifetime risk of attempting suicide – all factors that reflect a 'sheer persistence of personal suffering' (Bebbington, 2004). Bipolar disorder is often a persistent, recurring disorder with a high relapse rate.

Treatment for bipolar disorder

Medication

The medical treatment for bipolar disorder is challenging because of the complexity of a disorder characterised by cycling phases (Malhi et al., 2009) and is the subject of much debate (Goodwin, 2012). A range of medications may be used. Lithium has been the first-line mood stabiliser treatment for many years, but it is less effective in treating rapid cycling and psychotic manic episodes. Other mood stabilisers and antipsychotic medication may be prescribed, as well as anxiolitics to control symptoms.

Psychosocial approaches

The psychological and psychosocial approaches we described for depression are relevant to bipolar disorder and are generally combined with drug treatments. Because bipolar disorder often persists over a long period of time, the emphasis tends to be on helping the person to manage the impact of the illness on their lives and supporting a process of recovery. The impact of bipolar disorder potentially across all life domains presents opportunities for social work activity in such areas as family, relationships, work and education. Cognitive-behavioural therapy and interpersonal therapy are both relevant approaches in areas such as developing with the individual a detailed knowledge of their illness, the unique stressors and coping responses, and the warning signs of relapse. Psychoeducation is a well-established therapeutic approach that seeks to restore the individual's sense of control over their life through gaining knowledge about the disorder and learning skills to manage and reduce its impact. Cognitive and functional remediation and mindfulness-based therapies may also be employed (Reinares et al., 2014).

Family work

Working with the person's family, either individually or in structured group approaches, has become standard best practice for both bipolar disorder and schizophrenia. The purpose of such family work is not just to enhance support for the person, but also to address the specific impact of the illness on the wellbeing of other family members. This is explored in greater detail in Chapter 9. We have noticed that building family understanding of the symptoms of the illness in bipolar disorder may be challenged by the specific behaviour of the individual in the manic phase of the illness. Disinhibition, hypersexuality and impulsive spending can create enduring problems for close family members well after the manic phase has passed.

From Ann: secrets of a magnificent medication manager

I take about ten different medications. Four of these are for my mental illness and the rest help me manage other health problems that accrue after a life lived with mental illness and treatment. Conventional wisdom suggests that if the doctor prescribes and the patient is compliant all will be well. I'd like to deconstruct this simplistic notion and let you into the secrets of managing the madness of medication. When asked to write about the experience of taking medication, I realised that consumers need an MBA in medication management! This is a fiendish tactic devised by the government to keep you mentally agile, able to multitask and 'job ready'!

In my tool-box are:

- a large ziplock plastic bag
- my diary
- the list
- my purse
- a large clear plastic container
- a dosette box

- a pill cutter
- a magnifying glass
- a computer

I keep all my prescriptions in a large ziplock bag, otherwise I lose them. Some prescriptions are issued by the psychiatrist, others by the GP and the rest by assorted specialists. Some scripts have two repeats, others with more; a few are single-use scripts with no repeats. At times I need the magnifying glass to read the tiny print on the labels on the boxes to see if it is indeed the final repeat.

You need to keep an eye on when you need a new prescription because, besides the risk of running out of medication, you generally have to go back to see the doctor for a new one. If I have to ring my GP for a script that I can pick up without an appointment it costs $15, not covered by Medicare, adding to the expense. Some doctors won't provide scripts after a phone call.

Of course you need to remember who prescribed what and their phone numbers so you can make an appointment. In my diary I write down contact details in the address section; it is best to include contact details for the chemist in case there's an emergency necessitating prescriptions to be sent from doctor to chemist. In the diary I note the date and time of appointments, along with what I need to talk about once I'm there, otherwise I always forget something important. It's most unfashionable of me to still use a diary in this digital world, but it works for me. My ultimate goal is to manage the whole process by developing a spreadsheet on my computer that interacts with the smart phone I can't afford, that sends messages to doctors and the chemist . . ..

When I go to the pharmacist I take the ziplock bag of prescriptions, which by now contains the empty packets. I hand them all over at the counter and head off for a coffee. A word about pharmacists – best to stick to the same one as they keep a record of how much you've spent in any financial year; I usually qualify for the Pharmaceutical Benefits Safety Net (reduced-cost prescriptions) about halfway through the year. When I get home I put the ziplock bag and the packets of pills into a large see-through container along with the rest of my stash and the magnifying glass. Then I need another coffee.

There is considerable debate about the best method to deal with multiple medications: to pop the pills onto the bench top just before taking them; to use a dosette box where once a week you place each day's tablets into their compartments; or to use a medication pack prepared by the pharmacist? I prefer a dosette box as this is the cheapest and helps me predict when I need a new prescription and when I'm about to run out of pills. I find medication packs are too expensive and not responsive enough to changes in dose or medication. Additionally, the pharmacist keeps the prescriptions. I also like to be in control of my medication and this includes knowing exactly what I'm on. However, I must confess that I sometimes make medication errors and that this is worse when I'm symptomatic.

Just when you thought you could breathe a sigh of relief at getting your head around all this, could I introduce you to the pill cutter and the concept of 'tweaking the dose'? As symptoms wax and wane, the dosage of your medication can change. Sometimes a new prescription for the changed dose takes care of this, but at others you need to chop the pill into two! While a pill cutter can achieve this, at times a pen-knife is better. For medication delivered by wafer, a pair of fine embroidery scissors works best.

Besides the need for a computer to design a spreadsheet, access to Dr Google is most helpful. Although it is 'best practice' for the doctor or chemist to warn you about side effects and to tell you how and when to take the medication, this often doesn't happen as they are busy, or concerned that consumers 'imagine' they've developed a side effect, or they don't want to worry you. So, you may need to get online to check these out with your alternative mental health practitioner, the internet.

A penultimate observation: I'm sure your mother told you never to leave home without wearing clean underwear in case you get run over by a car, and the same goes for The List, which I keep in my purse. This is a list of all the medication I take and the current doses. When I visit any of my doctors I show them The List, and if they're good, I let them keep it for their records. Then I return home to write out another one. I find that individual health practitioners are not terribly curious about what others are prescribing and so The List is a small aide de memoire, a little gift from me to them! Of course, if I do get run over by a car, The List informs the emergency department about what's what and who's who! The E Health Record achieves this too.

Personality disorders

A personality disorder is defined as 'an enduring pattern of inner experience and behaviour that deviates markedly from the expectations of the individual's culture, is pervasive and inflexible, has an onset in adolescence or early adulthood, is stable over time, and leads to distress or impairment' (APA, 2013, p. 645). Personality disorders have been clustered rather broadly as follows:

- Cluster A includes paranoid, schizoid (detached with a restricted emotional range) and schizotypal (involving cognitive or perceptual distortions and eccentricities of behaviour and discomfort in close interpersonal relationships).
- Cluster B includes antisocial, borderline, histrionic and narcissistic personality disorders. Individuals with these disorders often appear dramatic, emotional or erratic.

- Cluster C includes avoidant, dependent and obsessive-compulsive personality disorders. Individuals with these disorders often appear anxious or fearful. It should be noted that this clustering system, although useful in some research and educational situations, has serious limitations and has not been consistently validated.

There are unresolved debates about the appropriateness of categorical and dimensional models of classification – so much so that the DSM-5 details both a categorical and an alternative dimensional model for classifying personality disorders. Nevertheless, it is generally true to say that the emphasis in the personality disorders is the presence of personality traits in a relatively extreme form (for example, suspicion, isolation, histrionics, narcissism, dependence). Diagnosis is based on traits and behaviour that are not so much abnormal in themselves, but are judged to be maladaptive when considered in the context in which they occur (Davies, 2003). There is considerable overlap in the classification of personality disorders and other mental health problems (Rao et al., 2012, p. 534).

Borderline personality disorder

We have chosen to focus on borderline personality disorder (BPD) because of its relative frequency in treatment settings and across the human services and because of the extent of disability and distress experienced. The DSM-5 describes BPD as 'a pervasive pattern of instability in interpersonal relationships, self-image, and affects, and marked impulsivity that begins by early adulthood and is present in a variety of contexts' (APA, 2013, p. 663) and states that instability of personal goals and risk-taking and/or hostility are also features of the disorder.

People diagnosed with BPD often experience intense, even unbearable, emotional pain and distress. Linehan (1993a, 1993b) has argued that the central feature of BPD is emotional dysregulation, deriving from a combination of genetic, environmental and developmental factors. There is debate about the nature and causes of the disorder. Among other factors, connections between childhood emotional neglect, abuse and sexual trauma and the subsequent emergence of the disorder have been established through research (Pietrek et al., 2013), but not all people with BPD have had these experiences.

Features of BPD

The DSM-5 includes the following features of BPD:

- frantic efforts to avoid real or imagined abandonment
- a pattern of unstable and intense interpersonal relationships characterised by alternating between extremes of idealisation and devaluation
- identity disturbance: markedly and persistently unstable self-image or sense of self

- impulsivity in areas such as spending, sex, substance abuse, reckless driving and binge eating
- recurrent suicidal behaviour, gestures or threats, or self-mutilating behaviour
- affective instability due to a marked reactivity of mood
- chronic feelings of emptiness
- inappropriate, intense anger or difficulty controlling anger
- transient, stress-related paranoid ideas or severe dissociative symptoms

The pattern of oscillation between idealisation and devaluation in order to manage emotional responses in relationships is sometimes called *splitting*, a way of dealing with the ambiguities and subtleties of perception of self and others by rigidly assigning unrealistic positive or negative evaluations. This process often creates challenges for the worker in the helping relationship (Davies, 2003). Diagnosis requires special care, not least because it may be argued that the 'borderline' diagnosis often reflects an emotional (rather than rational or intellectual) response on the part of the person making the diagnosis and that the term tends to be used for ridicule (Vaillant, 1992).

There has been a lot of criticism of the treatment system's response to people with the disorder. The diagnosis can be highly stigmatising, and people so diagnosed are seen as a 'problem for the system', rather than requiring treatment and support. Some of the language used to describe behaviour sometimes associated with the disorder (words like *self-destructive*, *self-mutilating*, *manipulative* and *promiscuous*) reflects the judgemental attitudes of many health and human services professionals. Epstein (2004) has summed up this position as follows: 'I have been *diagnosed* with a number of illnesses, but I have been *accused* of having BPD!'

Prevalence of BPD

The prevalence of BPD in the general community is estimated to be 1–2 per cent. In psychiatric treatment settings, it is about 15–20 per cent, but these numbers are confounded because of particularly high comorbidity rates (Rao et al., 2012). While it is often observed that the diagnosis is much more common in women, there is an argument that this reflects a bias towards clinical (that is, in-treatment) rather than population samples (Hooley et al., 2012). The most common pattern is that the disorder emerges in adolescence, followed by instability in early adulthood, extending – but improving – into middle age, with a high risk of suicide and self-harm (Rao et al., 2012). The rates of reported childhood adversity are even higher than for other mental health problems (Pietrek et al., 2013).

Treatment for BPD

While some medications may be used to treat depression and anxiety associated with BPD, the most common form of treatment is long-term supportive counselling in combination with short-term crisis management and limited use of hospitalisation.

It is necessary to assert at the outset that people with BPD have a right to equitable access to treatment and support (Rao et al., 2012). Despite some misplaced pessimism about the efficacy of treatment for people with BPD (Grenyer, 2013), effective psychological and psychosocial therapy is available and recommended (NHMRC, 2013). Dialectical behaviour therapy or DBT (Linehan, 1993a, 1993b) is probably the most commonly applied specialist therapy. It combines the principles of CBT with mindfulness and acceptance. DBT targets mood instability and impulsivity, with a focus on the learning and practice of new skills. The 'dialectic' refers to the way in which extreme opposites of experience and 'either/or' thinking are reconciled, and DBT is based on a synthesis of total acceptance of the person while at the same time identifying areas that require change (Brodsky & Stanley, 2013). Other specialist treatments include mentalisation-based therapy, which is concerned with how the internal world affects the sense of self and relationships (Beatson et al., 2010), and cognitive-analytic therapy, which is a specialised collaborative 'doing-with' approach based on a highly relational view of the self, which aims to support the person to reflect on and ultimately revise dysfunctional 'reciprocal role procedures' and 'dissociated self states' (Ryle & Kerr, 2002).

The Australian Clinical Practice Guidelines (NHMRC, 2013) outline some of the general principles for effective work with people with BPD:

- gaining trust (for example, by showing a non-judgemental attitude and being consistent and reliable), taking care to manage any of the worker's own emotions that may lead to relational difficulty and poor clinical decisions
- setting boundaries that provide for agreed feasible and sustainable access to services
- managing transitions and endings in a manner that accounts for possible sensitivity to feelings of rejection and abandonment
- developing a single, tailored management plan, including a crisis plan
- paying particular attention to assessment and management of suicide and risk, for example:
    - recognising that many people with BPD live with persistent thoughts of suicide
    - trying to distinguish between self-harm and suicidality
    - assessing the risk to others, including dependent children
    - paying particular attention to any changes in patterns of self-harm and other risky behaviour
    - preparing for the consequences of adverse experiences

Childhood abuse is a common feature of the disorder, and so it may be necessary to address the enduring impact of this abuse within the support of a therapeutic relationship, with a focus on the here-and-now, taking care not to exacerbate the effects of past traumas. In the long-term counselling relationship, the worker should be able to provide consistent boundaries, support and encouragement. This is challenging work that requires personal maturity and commitment.

Engagement with families may be constrained by a perception of the family environment as a cause of BPD and by the diagnosed person's negative perceptions of the family, but treatment that adopts a systemic approach will take account of the significant family relationships of people with BPD, as well as the relationships between families and treatment providers (Giffin, 2008). Support for families, partners and carers is an essential part of comprehensive care, including support in times of crisis. People with BPD who are parents will often benefit from intervention that supports parenting skills and parenting relationships, and their children themselves may require additional support.

From Ann: aetiology of mental disorders

John Cawte, a former professor of psychiatry, describes one of the core technical skills he needed to do his job in a psychiatric facility in the 1950s as being an ability to perform lumbar punctures (Cawte, 1998). The diagnosis and treatment of mental illnesses is historically situated. Any effort of researchers to calculate incidences and prevalences must recognise this. Lumbar punctures were used to extract spinal fluid so that it could be tested for the presence of the spirochaete, which caused cerebral syphilis. Cerebral syphilis, also called general paralysis of the insane (GPI), accounted for a significant proportion of the asylum population before antibiotics became widely available. The clinical features of cerebral syphilis were largely unknown prior to the Napoleonic Wars in the late 18th and early 19th centuries, when large numbers of young and sexually active armed servicemen ranged across Europe and the naval ports of the various empires. In 1847 and 1879 respectively, Dr John Connolly and Dr Henry Maudsley – both eminent psychiatrists (then referred to as 'alienists') – noted the large number of asylum inmates with GPI. It was an epidemic that lasted more than 100 years, but today it is rare.

Conclusion

In this chapter, we have introduced the concept of mental health disorder and given a brief overview of some of the most common disorders. The research base for mental health and the simultaneous explosion of knowledge for consumers, as well as consumer-based knowledge about the disorders, is extensive and growing. Keeping up to date with this knowledge remains a challenge for social work practitioners.

Social workers in a range of settings need to have a good working knowledge of the signs and symptoms of a range of mental health disorders and evidence-informed treatment approaches, including the various medications and their side effects. Case managers, for example, need to recognise problematic responses to medication and work with their client and with other team members in resolving such problems.

At a basic level, symptoms, treatments, medications and side effects represent a substantial part of the lived experience of mental illness for consumers. This requires social workers to engage and respond with respect and curiosity. Our primary focus always remains on the personhood of the consumer – we are working with and supporting people, not illnesses.

QUESTIONS FOR PRACTICE

1. What is the relationship between psychiatric classification and the other assessment systems used by social workers?
2. What is the difference between assessment and diagnosis?
3. How well do descriptions of psychiatric symptoms capture the experience of mental illness?
4. Is a diagnosis ever a useful label? In what circumstances?

Websites

Anxiety Recovery Centre Victoria

Produces resources and an e-newsletter, together with training.
www.arcvic.org.au

BehaveNet

Provides comprehensive information about psychiatric drugs, diagnoses (including diagnostic criteria), practice standards, treatment guidelines, terminology.
www.behavenet.com

Beyond Blue

Provides information about mood and anxiety disorders for consumers, carers and professionals, including fact sheets and client handouts. Information on mood disorders in LGBTQIA+, CALD, Indigenous communities. Symptoms checklists, rating scales, outcomes measures.
www.beyondblue.org.au

Black Dog Institute

Covers all mood disorders. Fact sheets, rating scales, mood charts. Information for professionals that anyone can access. Online audio and audio-visual presentations. Research. Health professionals site.
www.blackdoginstitute.org.au

Diagnostic and Statistical Manual-5 (American Psychiatric Association)

Provides the text and other resources relevant to the DSM-5.
www.dsm5.org

Headspace – National Youth Mental Health Foundation

Links to Headspace centres in each state; fact sheets; online support. Information on personality disorders. Resources for professionals and families.
www.headspace.org.au

International Classification of Diseases (World Health Organization)

A disease-classification system used in most health services.
www.who.int/classifications/icd/en

Mind Health Connect

Information, links to services and other organisations. Section for health professionals. Provides a portal to online treatment programs, such as moodgym.
www.mindhealthconnect.org.au

Orygen Youth Health (OYH)

A youth mental health organisation based in Melbourne, Australia, with a specialised youth mental health clinical service, a research centre and an integrated training and communications program. Follow the links through to EPPIC (Early Psychosis Prevention and Intervention Centre), a service focused on young people with a first episode of psychosis. Offers training, education and resources for clinicians and researchers.
www.oyh.org.au

Our Consumer Place

Check old newsletters and the clearinghouse for conference addresses and articles written by consumers with personality disorders.
www.ourconsumerplace.com.au

Perinatal Anxiety and Depression Association (PANDA)

PANDA provides support and resources focused on the experience of perinatal anxiety and depression.
www.panda.org.au/

Royal Australian College of Psychiatrists

The college publishes and updates clinical practice guidelines for all of the mental disorders. For up-to-date information on treatment developments, you can access www.ranzcp.org/practice-education/guidelines-and-resources-for-practice.

RxList

An internet drug index that provides non-technical information about drugs in common use. Includes a medical encyclopaedia.
www.rxlist.com

SANE Australia

Provides fact sheets and podcasts on mental illness; reports and research. Includes stigma watch.
www.sane.org.au

Schizophrenia.com

Provides information, support and education related to schizophrenia.
http://schizophrenia.com/

Spectrum, the Personality Disorder Service for Victoria

Fact sheets, professional development, resources and links.
www.spectrumbpd.com.au

Note

1 www.pbs.gov.au/pbs/home.

Part II

Social work practice

6 Assessment for social work practice

Assessment is an ongoing process in which we come to an understanding of problems and strengths – those of both the client and their environment – for the purpose of deciding on action or intervention (AASW, 2008b). A comprehensive assessment seeks to consider all the factors that are relevant to the purpose of the work, and the approach we take to assessment will reflect (and, in turn, influence) the kind of work we aim to do. Depending on their area of work, mental health social workers will make a variety of formal and informal assessments. Social workers in other areas of practice will come into contact with many clients experiencing mental health problems and will therefore be in a position to carry out initial screening assessments.

'Doing an assessment' involves more than a one-off appraisal or making a diagnosis or formulation. Assessments often commence before the first contact between worker and client and should continue right through after the end, when the results of the work are being evaluated.

Assessment is one of the most challenging areas of social work practice in mental health. The legitimate reluctance to assign a label, combined with unease around some of the language and methods of psychiatric assessment, has led some social workers to neglect or reject assessment altogether – a response which denies clients the benefits of the social work perspective. A comprehensive, good-quality assessment relies on detailed knowledge about mental health, human development, family welfare and a range of other fields. Social workers will need to understand and draw on the language of psychiatry as well as their own core areas of expertise. One part of the challenge is to integrate the diverse elements of the assessment. Another is to make the assessment collaboratively so that the process occurs as part of a relationship with the client and the product is a shared thing that is negotiated over time with the client.

Our approach to assessment is reflective of our two major themes:

- the focus of mental health social work on the social context and social consequences of mental illness
- a focus on relationships in the lives of clients and on relationships as a central element of the work

There are implications for *what* we assess and also *how* we go about it.

DOI: 10.4324/9781003148913-8

What we assess: a focus on social factors, problems and strengths

In social work, the focus of our attention is usually defined as the person-in-situation or person-in-context. In psychiatry, the focus of attention is usually much more individual. A social work perspective on assessment in mental health includes this individual focus but has a broader field of vision. It also takes into account the families, groups and communities in which individuals live and the social issues and power relationships that impinge on or determine aspects of the lives of all involved. Simply put, it is a perspective that tends to view individuals as intrinsically social beings. Hence the focus of social work assessment in mental health is a broad one.

The broader unit of attention for mental health assessment is consistent with contemporary approaches to psychiatry, in which the mainstream approach is usually described as 'biopsychosocial'. This term, coined by Engel (1977), draws on 'systems theory' to draw attention to the interrelatedness of all aspects of an individual's experience – from the cell to the biosphere. We can contrast this with a 'biomedically reductionist' approach. Rather than focusing solely on symptoms, the biopsychosocial perspective provides a framework for assessing at all levels – biological certainly, but also behavioural, spiritual, individual, group, community and so on. More than this, it is based on the premise that each of these levels affects the others.

While in practice it is often easier to focus on each set of factors separately rather than attending to their interrelationship, a biopsychosocial assessment really aims to hold them together to give as complete a picture as possible. Mental health social workers work within the constantly shifting, complex space in which people and their environments intersect and interact. We seek to work with and understand people in the context of their family, material circumstances, culture and social networks. In practical terms, this means focusing on the factors that cause stress and difficulty and the factors that sustain and support people. In this regard, our assessments tend to differ from some others in the field of mental health, which, naturally enough, have a more specific focus on mental illness itself. People almost always come to the attention of a social worker because of a problem, and in a mental health setting accurate diagnosis or assessment of a problem is usually very important. However, if we treat the problem as the 'linchpin' of assessment and action, we risk an overly narrow understanding of the situation and the possibilities for recovery (Weick et al., 1989).

One of the fundamental elements of a social work assessment in mental health, then, is a consideration of both problems and strengths. Strengths may be understood as 'the capacity to cope with difficulties, to maintain functioning in the face of distress, to bounce back in the face of significant trauma, to use external challenges as a stimulus for growth, and to use social supports as a source of resilience' (McQuaide & Ehrenreich, 1997, p. 203). Strengths include personal qualities – attributes, talents and skills, interests and aspirations, and interpersonal skills – as well as strong intimate relationships, extended family, good neighbours, the qualities of family members and other supportive people, and attributes of the available environment (Saleebey, 2001). An assessment of strengths focuses on capabilities and aspirations in all areas of life to discover the individual and communal resources that are available and from which the client can draw. This requires careful and persistent listening and inquiry because the dominant story will often be one of difficulty, problems and pathology.

This does not suggest that problems be ignored, but neither does it mean just adding to existing pathology-based assessment formats. A strengths focus, in other words, recognises problems facing the client as an aspect of the client's experience rather than its defining characteristic. Other aspects – ones which can be understated by both clients and workers – include such basic (fundamental) things as the fact of the client's survival, their engagement – however it is framed – with the social worker and the moments of competence, coping and connection they have certainly experienced but have possibly forgotten in the face of crisis. There are simple strategies that can facilitate this: emphasising the client's own language while gathering information about symptoms and other difficulties, inquiring specifically about coping strategies and 'exceptions' to the problem (times when the problem is not present or is less influential). When taking a developmental history, it is important to ask specifically about physical, psychological, social and spiritual assets. When asking about relationships, work, education and community involvement, identify contributions and achievements as well as sources of support, skills, interests and plans. Corcoran and Walsh (2009) advocate the use of these and other questions as part of a simple approach to gathering information in a way that strikes a balance between problems and strengths.

How we assess: a focus on relationships

The social work mental health assessment is the work of understanding and as such it relies on the combination of expertise and empathy which characterises the profession. Assessments that include personal and social factors, as well as problems and strengths, require careful and detailed listening in a two-way flow of information and an ongoing conversation. Social workers aim to establish a 'shared understanding' within the assessment process. This involves applying the expertise of all parties – including the expertise of the client – collaboratively and not imposing from above one party's perspective or schema. The object of assessment is not a 'hidden truth' about the client, but rather we are trying to gain a greater understanding. Considered this way, assessment becomes a joint enterprise.

Much depends on how the mental health worker sets about the process of conducting the assessment. Three broad models of the assessment process have been identified: procedural, questioning and exchange (Smale et al., 1993; Walker & Beckett, 2011).

Procedural model – The worker completes a form or operates as if a form is being completed. The procedure or the form determines the agenda of assessment in this model. It is a simple, practical and relatively easy approach – but it may not necessarily go far towards meeting the actual or expressed wishes and needs of clients. It tends to be formulaic and uncritical.

Questioning model – The worker follows a format of questions, listening to and processing the answers. Implicitly, the worker behaves as if they hold the expertise, and the interaction follows and reflects the worker's agenda. The questioning model is often used when it is necessary to establish something clearly. Examples include situations in which eligibility for service needs to be established or situations in which risk is a big issue.

Exchange model – In the most sophisticated of the three models, the worker's assumed expertise is not so much an expertise in people and their problems and needs as it is an expertise in the process of problem-solving with others (Smale et al., 1993). The real skill here lies in involving the client actively, deliberately structuring assessment processes in order to achieve as much involvement as possible. It is more conversational and can be much more challenging to use – especially when there may be pressure to establish certain facts. The exchange model typically includes more people and takes longer (Smale et al., 1993). It gives implicit value to the contribution of the client and privileges clients' 'expertise by experience'.

The assessment process, then, can be the basis of an ongoing relationship. As we have emphasised elsewhere, this means that social workers must be willing to invest something of themselves in the interaction in a thoughtful and considered manner. The process of coming to understand the other necessarily 'also involves a process of coming to understand yourself in relation to the other' (O'Connor et al., 2006, p. 81).

Writing from a strengths and recovery orientation, Rapp and Goscha (2012) suggest an approach to assessment that is consistent with the exchange model: an assessment of strengths should evolve at the client's pace, should occur in the person's natural environment wherever possible and should be part of an ongoing process in which information is updated regularly. Simple-sounding strategies like this can be challenging to put into practice in some mental health agencies, but they are effective ways of really giving effect to the ideas behind the strengths-based approach.

The procedural, questioning and exchange models are not necessarily mutually exclusive, but the extent to which they feature in the interactions between the client and worker will have an impact on the process and on the quality of the relationship established during the assessment. At the same time, it is important to recognise that each model can be appropriate depending on the specifics of the client's situation. It will be clear that we consider the exchange model to be typically the most efficacious and aligned with social work values of respect and relational practice, but in situations of crisis, for example, a worker- or formula-led agenda can be crucial.

Many mental health clients will not view assessment as a benign process, with good reason. Yet, as far as possible, we advocate starting with the perspectives of the people most involved – the person themself and those close to them – recognising that people will be trying to make sense of their situation. The appropriate attitude is one of respectful curiosity, not making assumptions or jumping to conclusions. In the person's social network, there will often be conflict and power differences. In response, the worker needs to be both sensitive and clear about rights, responsibilities and confidentiality. As the assessment process unfolds, it will almost certainly reveal not one but a number of understandings of a given situation. Throughout, we seek to establish and maintain a respectful and empathic working relationship with the client and, in most cases, with other people who are important in the client's life.

Aspects of assessment

Discussing assessment in the abstract, as we are doing here, is potentially misleading because it is in many ways a fundamentally concrete undertaking which occurs between individuals in the moment. Statements of principle and outlines can only take us so far. It may be useful, then, to look at a particularly impressive contemporary model, synthesised by Kim Sutherland (2020) for use in Queensland public hospitals and health services.

Sutherland (2020, p. 12) identifies six 'core principles' as being 'fundamental to quality social work and psychosocial assessments'. These function as values-based focal points, informing and to an extent shaping the social worker's deliberations over each aspect or 'domain' of the assessment. The core principles include:

- the preferences, needs and values of the service user (person-centred care);
- the potential for a multiplicity of losses within the life circumstances of the person (changes in independence, status and role; the loss of dreams, ambitions and relationships);
- the possibility of trauma influencing the person's beliefs and psychosocial functioning (trauma-informed care);
- the existence of barriers to the person's engagement and recovery;
- the availability of collateral information – alternative perspectives from the person's family, social network and carers – and its incorporation into an assessment while maintaining a central focus on the person's own voice and perspective;
- the potential for intersections of social and structural forces (class, ethnicity, sexuality, ableness) to oppress and marginalise the person.

In Table 6.1 we summarise the psychosocial domains (condensing nine into eight) and Sutherland's operationalisation of each. These domains represent aspects of the person's life and experience which should be considered (through the lens of the six core principles) in any comprehensive assessment. Their operationalisation

Table 6.1 Psychosocial assessment domains

Domain	*Subdomains*	*Operationalisation*
The person	Person; culture; family (include concerns for safety of person or others in this domain)	Personality, relationships, significant networks; Strengths, challenges; Identity, sexuality, gender, language, religious beliefs, values, decision-making style; Parenting/partnering, intimacy, conflict, supports, coping strategies
Environment	Accommodation; participation; social media; education	Type and condition of accommodation (owner-occupier, rental; stability, size, safety, appropriateness); Location, access to services and amenities, transport options; Access to reliable online services; Isolation and connection to community, land or country; Changes in need
Finances	Employment; income; resources	Work history; Income source and reliability; Degree of financial dependence (on self, family, employer, welfare system, friends, charitable organisations); Financial confidence and literacy
Health (physical and mental)	Status; functioning; adjustment; cognition	Diagnosis, symptoms, co-morbidities, engagement with treatment/medication; Health literacy, insight, coping, capacity, resilience; Strategies, sleep, wellness, nutrition, hygiene; Substance use; Mood/affect, risk of self-harm
Legal	Advance care planning; guardianship and capacity; orders and applications; residency and visas	History; Assisted Decision Maker, advance health directives; domestic violence orders, child protection orders, forensic mental health orders, involuntary treatment orders
Developmental history	Significant life events; premigration history (if any); milestones; relevant educational history	Trauma (single-incident, complex, inter-generational); Relationships and attachment; Coping styles and patterns
Care needs and choice	Goals; support; future planning; involvement of caregivers; leisure interests	Personal wishes and plans; Care requirements; Significant people and agencies
Risk and protection	Risk factors; protective factors; safety plan	Child safety, domestic and family violence, elder abuse, suicidal ideation, carer stress, accommodation and income security, contributing factors (e.g., disability, literacy, numeracy)

Source: Adapted and abridged from Sutherland (2020, pp. 12–16).

is a particularly useful aspect of the approach, ensuring that at times ill-defined categories can be linked to observable aspects of the person's direct experience.

Part of such a critical attitude is sensitivity to the 'politics' of the referral. We want to know how the referral came about – who initiated it, what expectations they may have and so on. Does it concern someone who may not agree with these expectations, and may not even know about them? How does the person at the centre of the referral understand what is going on? Are there any other agencies involved and, if so, how? What legal or practical implications might the assessment have for the person at its centre and those around them? A critical part of this is being clear ourselves about our own statutory and other mandates to assess and intervene. Especially in situations of risk to the client or to others (see next), such obligations will inform both the manner and the purpose of the assessment.

It is helpful to consider these as steps because they describe the logical 'stepwise' relationship of the elements of the process, which helps to guard against forgetting and leapfrogging elements of the assessment – something that can happen easily in pressured situations. But in reality, it rarely works out just like this. All assessments should be an *ongoing process* of inquiry, and information should be updated regularly. It is important and useful for the worker to have a clear mental map of the assessment process, but of course we have to be flexibly responsive to the situation. Crises, when they occur, require an immediate containing response, and it is not necessary to know *everything* before we address pressing needs, such as needs for safety, containment, or housing or income support. And we will always be open to taking opportunities that may come up. The assessment is not simply an unproblematic information-gathering exercise at the start of the contact with a client.

Sutherland (2020, pp. 17–21) emphasises the importance of the clinical formulation at the assessment report's conclusion. This is a brief but challenging aspect of assessment in which the social worker presents an 'analysis and synthesis' of the client's history and situation. The formulation functions as the explicit rationale for future interventions and engagements. It is, by its nature, an encapsulation of a jointly produced 'moment in time' and thus more a hypothesis than a diagnosis. The challenge confronting social workers here is the ethical and practical one of prioritising their own professional 'voice' while at the same time ensuring that voice is placed at the service of the client (Sutherland, 2020, p. 17).

Sutherland suggests structuring the formulation along the lines of a 'clinical formulation matrix', which is itself a series of prompts particularly useful for new practitioners (see Table 6.2). The formulation itself comprises:

- an orientating statement in which key information is presented alongside a clear articulation of the desired outcomes and wishes of the person themselves;
- a statement of relevant background information;
- a statement of factors or issues which have triggered the current contact;
- a summary of aspects of the person's environment which contribute to the maintenance of the situation or problem;
- a final statement indicating the way forward.

Table 6.2 The social work clinical formulation matrix

	Biological	*Psychological*	*Social*
Presenting situation			
Background factors	**Prompts**: Genetic background Birth trauma Brain injury Physical illness/injury Medication Substance use Pain Developmental milestones	Personality Defences Coping strategies Self-esteem Body image perception Cognition Developmental experiences Early life experiences Attribution	Socio-economic status Social determinants of health Trauma Work Finances Social network connections Relationships Culture Education
Triggers	**Prompts:** Medications Trauma Drugs/Alcohol Pain Physical injury/illness Change in mental state Hormonal changes Developmental changes	Stage of life Loss/grief Treatment Stressors Trauma Life event	Work Finances Connections Relationships Migration Unemployment Family conflict Disasters Carer illness
Maintaining the concerns	**Prompts**: Medication Trauma Drugs/Alcohol Pain Physical impairment Chronic condition Physical environment	Stage of life Loss/grief Treatment Stressors Maintenance of social role Dysfunctional relationship Mental illness	Work Finances Connections Relationships Support mechanisms Unemployment Marginalisation Stigma
Strengths	**Prompts**: Physical health Medications Physical environment Genetic background	Engagement Insight Maintains medication regime Coping strategies Treatment Resilience	Good social network Employment Role in community Good service links Community networks Family

Source: Sutherland (2020, p. 20).

The following is an example formulation taken directly from Sutherland's work:

Madeline is a 22-year-old female with a new diagnosis of borderline personality disorder. Suicidal ideation following an alleged sexual assault and subsequent loss of employment. Madeline would like to report her attacker to the police and feel better psychologically but is not yet ready to look for alternative employment. **(orientating statement with person's wishes clearly articulated)**

Madeline has a history of childhood abuse, substance misuse and self-harm including one suicide attempt. (**background**)

Madeline enjoyed her job but recent risk-taking behaviour exacerbated existing feelings of poor self-esteem and worthlessness and is likely indicative of panic attacks at work. (**trigger**)

Madeline is using gin to self-medicate instead of taking prescribed medications. (**maintaining**)

From the information assessed it is critical we follow a sexual assault pathway and offer a forensic medical examination (FME) immediately ensuring a trauma-informed approach is utilised and mental health prioritised. (**final statement**).

From Ann: surfing paradigms

There are lots of different perspectives shaping the experience of living with madness. Those who assess/treat/manage/control/support us come from a variety of professional perspectives, each with a distinct epistemological tradition, each with its own unique viewing point, and each with its own power trajectory. There's the medical model using a positivist perspective that claims the evidence-based space for its own; they want to diagnose and treat us. The social control paradigm can sneakily inform treatment systems and the experience of involuntary care. There are those who want to help, care for and support us, who are well intentioned and determined to make changes. It's still them and us but is more benevolent in its othering. The managerialists want to manage madness according to their KPIs, protocols and policies. There are those that want to rescue us from biomedical dominance: the critical, constructivist mob. They believe that all these dilemmas and conflicts are redundant because there is no such thing as mental illness, as they campaign against human rights violations. Under the econometric tradition, bureaucrats, policymakers and politicians construct us as burdens, budget items to be managed, people with an overdeveloped sense of entitlement. Many of them believe that all will be well if only the government retreats from mental health care so that the private sector, underpinned by commercial principles, is allowed to efficiently manage all treatment and care.

Surfing these paradigms are consumers and families. Stormy waters indeed!

Psychiatric diagnosis and its place in assessment

'Diagnosis' has a particular meaning in a mental health context. A psychiatric diagnosis is 'the application of a medical label to a psychological abnormality' (Pilgrim, 2009, p. 6), using an accepted system of psychiatric classification such as the *International Classification of Diseases* (ICD) or the *Diagnostic and Statistical Manual of Mental Disorders* (DSM). Such systems of psychiatric classification seek to describe and define all those diseases, disorders and syndromes that fall within the ambit of the medical specialty of psychiatry – the major clinical clusters, which are:

neurodevelopmental disorders (for example, schizophrenia and autism spectrum disorder);
internalising disorders (for example, major depressive disorder and anxiety disorders);
externalising disorders (for example, substance use disorder and conduct disorder);
neurocognitive disorders (for example, delirium traumatic brain disorder);
other disorders.

The medical profession dominates the way mental health problems are understood and treated, and so this model of diagnosis is a central component of mental health assessment (Poole, 2004). Depending on the setting, the formal diagnostic process will almost always be undertaken by a doctor, preferably a psychiatrist. Traditional mental health assessment has been concerned primarily with psychiatric diagnosis because, within the dominant model of mental health care, it is diagnosis that fundamentally informs decisions about treatment.

Non-medical mental health workers need to understand the processes and categories of psychiatric diagnosis. As part of their own assessment processes, they will almost invariably gather information that will contribute to the diagnosis, just as their own assessments will, in turn, draw on the psychiatric diagnosis and its implications. Psychiatric diagnosis is an important component of a comprehensive mental health assessment, but not the only part.

Of course, there are limits to the usefulness of psychiatric diagnosis. Diagnosis is notoriously imprecise and unstable over time. 'Diagnosis may be more usefully considered as a hunch held lightly . . . rather than a decision to be defended' (Little, 2013, p. 882). In any case, decisions about intervention often rely more on the specific symptoms than the diagnosis as such. Further, social and psychological perspectives are often at least as important as the diagnosis. Finally, the diagnosis itself sometimes has significant negative effects, both because it tends to cement a particular view of the mental health problem that privileges certain voices (Jutel & Nettleton, 2011) and because problems of stigma and social exclusion are associated with mental illness (Poole, 2004). A social work assessment 'surrounds the diagnosis and informs it . . . [providing] both continuous feedback about the accuracy, usefulness, and relevance of the diagnosis, as well as continuous data and feedback to guide the goal-directed work of the helping partnership' (Miller, 2002, p. 45). Assessment is a much broader process than diagnosis.

Some mental health social work texts (especially American texts) are organised in such a way as to help social workers to gain competence in using the DSM diagnostic framework (Gray & Zide, 2008; Corcoran & Walsh, 2009; Dziegielewski, 2010) in the context of an approach to clinical practice that relies fundamentally on social work traditions, especially a strengths-based approach. This is not always easy to do, especially in clinical settings in which rapid assessment and short-term treatment are required. However, 'the importance of accurately identifying client strengths and support networks in the diagnostic assessment is critical, as these will be incorporated into the suggested intervention plan providing a means for continued growth and wellness lasting beyond the formal treatment period' (Dziegielewski, 2010, p. 30). Australian social workers wanting a specific working knowledge of psychiatric diagnostic systems will find these texts very useful, although we should remember that the DSM framework is itself the subject of extensive, at times even heated, debate among practitioners and researchers. The reasons for the widespread use of the DSM in American social work practice often relate to funding and billing requirements. Many social workers are attracted to 'the ease and clout' of the DSM, and alternative systems (person-in-environment, strengths-based systems and others) are used much less widely (Frazer et al., 2009).

From Ann: the archaeology of assessment

For four years I was an Official Visitor at a large and very old psychiatric hospital – one of the first asylums purpose-built for 'lunatics and imbeciles', which in the early days of the colony meant people with mood disorders, psychoses, alcoholism, tertiary syphilis, epilepsy and various developmental delays. To honour those who died after a lifetime spent in the hospital, I would read over their files and the early daybooks that recorded life on the wards. The files were slim despite the decades the people had spent in care.

Periodically the files would note changes in diagnosis and treatment. One man died with bipolar disorder but had once been diagnosed with 'masturbational insanity'. The archaeology of his treatment and care revealed the layers formed by changing theory, science and treatments.

Had he lived long enough to be discharged into the community, no doubt the size of the file would be exponentially increased with assessments for housing, income support, living skills, recovery and rehabilitation. But what would the size of the file mean? Better and more coordinated care? A greater depth of relationship? Improved outcomes? A robust paper trail for the auditors and managers?

The identification of common mental health problems

Like general practitioners, social workers are often in the 'front line' of recognition and assessment of common mental health problems such as anxiety and depression. This is not an easy thing. In order to improve recognition and outcomes, those in the front line need to be well connected to organised systems of mental health care for consultation and referral (Carey et al., 2014). Yet there are many missed opportunities. Social workers can be reluctant to ask about mental health problems because of their own discomfort in asking sensitive questions and responding to a client's distress, and in many settings there may be real time pressures (Thomas & Staiger, 2012, p. 635). Because of the prevalence and importance of mental health problems we believe that social workers in all settings should be aware of the basic 'building blocks' of psychiatric assessment: *cognition, thinking, perception, mood* and *behaviour*.

Areas of *cognition* to be aware of include conscious state, memory, concentration and attention, ability to calculate, and executive functions. Key disorders are delirium and dementia. In considering *thinking*, we pay attention to the thought stream (essentially, getting from A to B) and whether it is logical or not, and we watch for major themes of thinking such as paranoid or suicidal ideas. Psychosis is one of the key disorders associated with disturbance of thinking. Areas of *perception* to focus on include disturbance of any of the five senses (but most typically hearing and vision), particularly hallucinations. Again, these disturbances are associated with psychosis. *Mood* is an obvious area of interest in considering mental health problems, and the main disorders are depression, bipolar disorder and anxiety disorders. There are many relevant disturbances of *behaviour*, including eating, sleeping, social interaction and risky behaviour (including suicidal and homicidal behaviour); and the key disorders include personality disorders, eating disorders and substance use disorder.

In this book, we focus almost exclusively on adults, but the issues are different, of course, at different points in the life cycle. We need to be aware of serious emotional distress in *infancy*, which is a crucial time to reduce later developmental difficulties. Common disorders in *childhood* include anxiety, depression, conduct disorder (CD) and attention deficit hyperactivity disorder (ADHD). Emotional disorders (such as anxiety and depression) can seriously impair learning and development; and behavioural problems may disrupt social development and can lead to long-term mental health problems.

For young people in their teenage years and early twenties, mental health and substance-use disorders are 'the key health issue' (McGorry et al., 2007). Further, most adult-type psychiatric disorders begin between the late teens and the early twenties. Yet, recognition of mental health problems in adolescence and early adulthood can be a very vexed issue. Debates about the effectiveness and ethics of early recognition and early intervention for psychosis, in particular, are among the fiercest in contemporary psychiatry. The practical problem is how to move from noticing that 'something is not quite right' to the identification of a mental health problem. Families, friends and professionals all need to be able to differentiate between behaviour that might be considered 'normal but difficult' and what is abnormal for the person and indicative of a possible mental health problem. There is a very useful 'fact sheet' with some specific suggestions on the SANE website (listed at the end of this chapter).

The identification and treatment of mental health problems for older people is relatively neglected in Australia, despite its growing importance (McKay & Draper, 2012). Common mental health problems for older people are delirium, dementia, depression and anxiety – as well as the full range of pre-existing mental health problems experienced by people as they grow older. There are a range of social and psychological problems precipitated by ageing-related physical disorders and disabilities, so it is important to ensure that a thorough physical assessment is made, even though the problem seems to be cognitive or psychological. While it is important to emphasise that depression is not a normal part of ageing (beyondblue, 2010), there is a range of risk factors for depression associated with older age, including:

an increase in physical health problems;
chronic pain;
side effects of medications;
losses – relationships, independence, work and income, self-worth, mobility and flexibility;
social isolation;
significant changes to living arrangements;
admission to hospital;
particular anniversaries and the memories they evoke.

The mental state examination

The mental state (or mental status) examination (MSE) provides a specific structured format for making an assessment of cognition, thinking, perception, mood and behaviour. It is 'an inquiry into the symptoms and signs at the time of the interview, combined with a structured record of pertinent observations' (Singh & Kirkby, 2007, p. 102). It is an important part of a mental health assessment. MSEs are commonly undertaken by psychiatrists as part of the diagnostic process and, while only some mental health social workers will undertake MSEs, all will need a familiarity with the content and application of this tool, as it is ubiquitous in mental health practice. The dimensions of the MSE are fairly standard (see, for example, Singh & Kirkby, 2007; Meadows et al., 2012). There is a good example of a written MSE in Sawyer's (2009) chapter on mental health assessment.

Mental state examination

General appearance and attitude

Appearance includes physical characteristics, mannerisms, facial expression, dress and grooming. Attitude refers to how the client comes across and relates to the worker.

Behaviour and motor activity

This category refers to both the quantity and quality of physical activity, body movements, gestures, posture and gait.

Speech characteristics

Speech can be described in terms of quantity, rate of production and quality. For example, note how talkative the person is; the rate, volume and tone of the person's speech; any unusual speech patterns; and whether the characteristics of the person's speech are culturally appropriate, taking careful account of the person's language and language skills. Speech content may also be noted here, such as any characteristic themes of the person's speech.

Mood

Emotions and mood can be described on the basis of what a person says and also on the basis of what the worker observes. Affect is the observable manifestation of feelings, in contrast to mood, which is a more long-term reported feeling state. It may be important to identify whether the person's affect is congruent with what they report and whether the client shifts quickly from one feeling state to another (which is known as lability). Again, care needs to be taken to ensure that these assessments take proper account of the person's culture, which may influence greatly the degree of affective expressivity.

Thought process and content

We seek to infer information about thought from a person's speech and observed behaviour.

Thought *process* refers to the quality of a person's thinking as expressed in speech. For example, the person may express an overabundance of ideas or very few, may be slow or hesitant in their thinking or may have thoughts that might seem vague. The ideas the person expresses may appear to be unrelated to one another or connected in idiosyncratic ways (which is known as loose associations), or thought might be interrupted (blocked), circumstantial or tangential.

Thought content refers to the themes and preoccupations evident in the person's speech, including unusual or unrealistic ideas, preoccupations, obsessions, compulsions, delusions or ideas of reference. (Delusions are fixed false beliefs not accounted for in the context of the person's culture. Ideas of reference are ideas about the special significance of events for the person, such as the belief that the television or radio is speaking directly to or about him or her.) The presence and nature of ideas about suicide and harm to self and others would usually be assessed here.

Perception and sensory experiences

This refers to a person's ability to accurately perceive and process environmental stimuli. It includes any sensory impairment or the presence of illusions (distorted perceptions of actual external stimuli), hallucinations (false perceptions of sound, sight, smell, touch or taste in the absence of a corresponding stimulus), depersonalisation (the experience of feeling unreal, detached or numb) or derealisation (the experience that the external world is unreal, distorted or disfigured).

Intelligence and cognition

This addresses the client's general level of intelligence and intellectual functioning. It includes orientation, memory, attention and concentration, and abstract thinking in the context of education and culture.

Impulsivity

This refers to the ability to control aggressive, sexual and other impulses and may be estimated on the basis of observations during the interview as well as what is known about the person's recent history and behaviour.

Judgement and insight

Judgement refers to the person's ability to distinguish among thoughts, feelings, and actions; to examine alternative solutions to a problem; and assume responsibility for and understand the consequences of their own behaviour. Insight refers to the extent to which the person acknowledges the presence of problems and their own role in their development.

Mental health social workers will usually learn to carry out mental state examinations 'on the job', and here it is important that they do not forget their listening, interviewing and assessment skills. It is always useful to try to think about the process of being assessed and diagnosed from the perspective of the client (Coppock & Dunn, 2010). Different clients and their families will have different understandings of mental health problems, and some will fit more easily into the dominant medical paradigm than others.

The same point can be made about mental health professionals. The conceptualisation of mental health problems as primarily located *within* the individual tends to be associated with an assessment process oriented more to the *form* of the distress – depressive thoughts, delusions, hallucinations and so on – than to its *content* and *context* – the meaning of the experiences in the life of the client. If the attention of the person doing the assessment is focused on the form rather than the content of what the client is saying, the client may experience the assessment as quite literally not being listened to.

This leads to an important consideration for social workers conducting mental state examinations. As we have noted, the purpose of the MSE is to obtain a record of the person's condition at a given point in time. Functionally, this record will aid workers within the same service who may encounter the client months after the initial examination in assessing changes to the person's condition. In order to do this the report needs to be written in objective, clear language which will be comprehensible over time. There is little room for vague generalisations in an MSE. For social workers, this can pose a challenge: how do we look objectively at clients without objectifying them? How do we ensure that our professional strength and ethical duty – the empathic relationship – is maintained in the context of a necessarily jargon-ridden document?

One way of meeting this challenge is to remember that the mental state examination is not a checklist. It requires the application of the same skills as other assessments in social work – establishing a relationship and rapport, framing questions respectfully and effectively, a thorough curiosity, listening and observing carefully, and so on. It can be a real challenge to 'listen' simultaneously to both the *form* of a client's speech (and other clues to their thoughts) and the *content* and *real meaning* of what the client is communicating. It is very important, of course, to distinguish between subjective and objective judgements, and to take good account of cultural differences. An open and curious attitude rather than one that seeks to categorise and judge is required. For example, the final MSE category, judgement and insight, is not a simple matter of 'compliance'. Insight is not the same thing as agreeing with a 'professional' definition of the situation and the need to go along with the treatment as prescribed. Insight is much too complex a category to be reduced with any reliability to a simple categorical judgement, such as whether the person 'lacks' insight to the extent needed to justify involuntary status (Galloghly et al., 2013).

Assessing needs for service

If we are to work with clients towards their goals and their recovery, we must focus our assessments specifically on relevant life domains, to determine strengths and problems in these areas and the person's wishes and needs. Specific assessments of this kind will be particularly relevant to outcomes, whether it be in case management and other community settings or to a period of hospitalisation. Here we are concerned with aspects of human functionality and wellbeing that are often practical and the social context and consequences of mental illness. Different clients will have different, diverse wishes and needs. One older but still useful model (Victorian Government Department of Human Services, 1996, pp. 11–18) identifies several life domains or 'need categories' (see box, 'Need categories').

Need categories

Emotional and mental wellbeing
Dealing with stress
Personal response to illness
Personal safety and the safety of others
Friendships and social relationships
Work, leisure and education
Daily living skills
Family's response to relative's illness
Income
Physical health
Housing
Rights and advocacy

Source: Victorian Government Department of Human Services (1996, pp. 11–18)

Of course, these categories reflect the broad life activity areas commonly included in assessment and individual planning in many fields of human service, but in mental health services we typically give greater emphasis to dealing with stress and the personal and family response to the mental illness because of the importance of these areas in avoiding relapse and achieving recovery. The outcome of assessments in these areas should be a simple statement of priority needs and proposals for action, taking into account the varying perspectives of the different people involved. Not every category will be relevant to every client, and the assessment in these areas is one that will evolve and change over time.

Any assessment of needs for service should take into account the *availability* of service. Working in organisations, social workers carry a measure of responsibility to ensure that agency resources are deployed appropriately, relative to the different respective needs of clients. Decision-making about the allocation of resources is often one of the main purposes of assessment, just as negotiation over scarce resources is a critical part of the social work role (Walker & Beckett, 2011).

From Ann: access to social work services

Over the years I have been admitted to both public and private mental health facilities. Access to allied health care, especially social work services, is very different across these campuses. Privately run facilities generate profits for shareholders and owners. The profit motive influences which professional services are provided, or not. Social workers are a rare, if non-existent, breed in privately run facilities. Yet, privately run mental health facilities are major players in the Australian scene.

During 2017–18 there were 161 public mental health inpatient facilities. These provided 6,920 beds and 2,240,766 patient bed days. During the same period 66 private facilities provided specialised mental health care for admitted patients. They had 3,146 beds, and 1,179,991 patient bed days (Australian Institute of Health and Welfare, www.aihw.gov.au).

Mental health care in private settings tends to focus on diagnosis and treatment. Whole-of-person assessments, such as those provided by social workers and other allied health practitioners, are largely absent. Yet, those with private health insurance experience homelessness, family conflict, debt, domestic violence and income insecurity, just as those in the public system do.

What this means is that the 'social' part in the 'bio-psycho-social' assessment necessarily occurs in a variety of community service settings where social workers have an active presence. But this means that assessment is fragmented. Problems are atomised. Social workers must go the extra mile to liaise with other services in the interests of clients. That once prized notion of 'seamless service' has faded and has been replaced by the realities of 'phone tag' and frustration. This is also true for those competing for the scarce resources on offer in the public mental health system. Mental health work is done by social workers across a variety of settings.

I vividly remember one admission. Picture the dining room, not at meal time, but the dining room as a place to hang out and drink appalling institutional coffee. Then picture a fellow patient calling out to me 'I know you! You really helped me sort out my income support problems'. My anonymity fades and my chin hits the floor! Then . . . other patients ask me to help them to fill out forms, or seek advice about how to negotiate various services, and how to frame up their needs (language used) so that the correct assistance is provided. If I wasn't there, what would happen to those requests for assistance?

Assessing risks

Risk assessment is identified as a major part of the responsibilities of contemporary mental health work. A *risk* is simply the probability of something happening to a client or others in the client's social network; or being done by a client or others in the network. In mental health settings, it is usually applied to harmful or undesirable events, as in the following definition:

> Risk assessment is the process of assessing the likelihood of a harmful event occurring and of estimating the likely impact on the patient, carers, staff and others (the general public, the care providing organisation, etc.) should that event occur.
>
> (Wellman, 2006, p. 145)

Risks of this kind relate to the 'personal safety and safety of others' category in the aforementioned needs-for-service framework and include:

danger to self through self-harm or suicide;
danger to self through self-neglect;
dangers arising from the lack of treatment, poor treatment or poor compliance with treatment;
dangers arising from offensive or provocative behaviour;
danger of exploitation (emotional, sexual, financial) by others;
danger to others through assault (verbal, physical, sexual), exploitation (again, emotional, sexual, financial), or the abuse or neglect of children or dependent adults (Wellman, 2006).

A thorough risk assessment requires a consideration of both risk and protective factors. Where good clinical assessment instruments are available, they should be used, combined with 'actuarial' knowledge about the factors associated with particular risks. However, the majority of risks are difficult to predict accurately, and such approaches will always need to be combined with a professional judgement based on the unique circumstances of each situation. Most mental health services have a format for clinical risk assessment or employ formal risk assessment tools. It is a good principle to share the responsibility for risk assessment with colleagues wherever possible, rather than relying on an individual worker's judgement. Risk changes constantly and thus needs to be assessed continuously over time. Of course, the quality of the risk assessment is dependent on the quality of the information at hand.

We tend to assume that our role is to 'manage' risk by seeking to minimise or even eliminate it – often a difficult or impossible task. Yet, as Ramon (2005) has emphasised, this approach tends to draw attention away from the positive benefits of risk for clients and their families. Risk avoidance in the absence of risk-taking is not an effective strategy for human growth. Indeed, the willingness and ability to take risks in pursuit of improvement is a marker of social inclusion and an essential element of recovery. Risk is not simply something to be avoided; rather, what is required is a calculated approach to risk-taking, with the right balance of risks with protective factors – a goal that will look different for different people in different situations.

A 'positive' risk assessment will focus on the benefits, advantages and opportunities of a particular course of action as well as address the areas of risk, concern and potential harm. The aim is to do what is necessary to minimise harm while working towards the best likelihood of positive outcomes. This necessarily involves a monitoring role, and the active engagement of the client in the process – where it can be achieved – is an important factor in reducing risk and increasing the probability of a favourable outcome (Koubel & Yardley, 2012). It is worth emphasising here that the point of any risk assessment is to help to determine a plan: the whole point is to identify the risk factors so that they can be managed and the protective factors so that they can be built on. The goal of risk assessment should not be to categorise the person (Allnutt et al., 2013).

There are many specific elements of a comprehensive assessment of risk, including risks arising from dangerous behaviour (for example, arson, unprotected sex), disorganisation, memory problems, problems with making decisions about personal safety or legal or financial decisions, orientation deficit, provocative behaviour, wandering and a range of physical health risk factors. Here we will give special mention to only some.

Assessing risks arising from alcohol and drug use

The coexistence of mental health and alcohol and/or other drug problems is very common. Working with people with dual diagnosis poses special challenges because, overall, coexisting alcohol and drug use tends to lead to poorer outcomes in mental health care. People with dual diagnosis have been called 'a kind of mental health underclass' because dual diagnosis is associated with worse clinical and social outcomes, frequently poor general health and high levels of unmet need (Lawrence-Jones, 2010).

Moreover, it is more common for people with a dual diagnosis to experience a range of other problems: stigma; social, legal and criminal justice issues; housing; welfare; and other lifestyle issues. Further, there is strong, clear evidence of a higher risk of suicide and violence (Hughes & Phillips, 2012). There are some special principles for assessment and screening for drug and alcohol problems (see box, 'Principles for alcohol and drug assessment').

Principles for alcohol and drug assessment

Convey acceptance and be non-judgemental.
Normalise use.
Assume a higher level of use in your discussions with the client.
Ask about legal substances first.
Ask about past use before asking about current use.
Get specific information on amounts used and patterns of use.
Collect information from a variety of sources.
Have some awareness of diagnostic criteria for substance dependence and abuse.
Note, name and feed back concerns about substance-related risk factors.

Remember that coexisting substance use tends to be underreported in mental health settings. It can be useful to have a conversation about the client's pattern of substance use and identify factors that maintain substance use, interfere with sobriety or represent a risk of relapse (Drake, 2007).

Assessing the risk of violence and harm to others

Most people with a mental health problem do not engage in violence, but the likelihood of committing violence is slightly greater for people with a major mental health disorder who are not receiving effective treatment and have a co-occurring substance use disorder (Silver, 2006; Douglas et al., 2009; Short et al., 2013). Assessment of risk for violence involves making individual decisions. There are a number of readily observable risk factors for violence such as hostility and suspiciousness; expressions of anger, irritability and agitation; and specific psychiatric symptoms, such as severe thought disorder, delusions and hallucinations (Sands et al., 2012). Risks to others may result from factors such as command hallucinations or impulsivity, often related to the effects of substance use. As part of the risk assessment, it is useful to consider the role that mental illness may have played in past violence and could play in future violence (for example, as an organising or a disorganising factor). It is often pointed out that accurate prediction of violence is not possible, but we do not consider that to be an argument for avoiding an assessment.

Factors to take into account include the following, remembering that risk always has a dynamic (i.e., fluctuating) element and that it is sensitive to both contextual and individual factors (see box, 'Factors to consider in assessing risk of violence and harm to others').

Factors to consider in assessing risk of violence and harm to others

Aggression
Is there a history of aggression or a coercive personality style?
Is the person currently showing signs of aggressive or threatening behaviour?

Delusions
Does the content of delusions indicate risk of harm (to self and/or others)?
Do the delusions have a persecutory content?
Is the delusional content focused on particular people?

Hallucinations
Do the hallucinations create a sense of fear or persecution?
Is the person experiencing command hallucinations to harm (to self and/or others)?

Homicidality
Has the person expressed the idea of killing or harming others?
Is there an identified potential victim?

Neglect of dependants
Does the person have a reduced – or fluctuating – capacity to care for children or other dependants such as older family members?

Assessing risks associated with domestic and family violence

There is a strong link between mental illness and domestic and family violence. Many women and some men with mental health problems experience (and have experienced) domestic and family violence, and the link is strong across a range of mental illnesses including depression, anxiety, PTSD, eating disorders and psychosis (Oram et al., 2013). Some people (especially men) with mental health problems are violent towards family members. Yet some mental health workers are reluctant to ask about family violence, and in turn, survivors may be reluctant to reveal it, especially if they have no reason to believe that any disclosure will be taken seriously. The Queensland Department of Health (2020) has produced useful guidelines for identifying and responding to domestic and family violence, including potential indicators and suggested responses in discussing violence with survivors. Key principles identified are shown here.

Principles for discussing DFV with victims

Non-judgemental and careful listening

- Communicate belief
- Validate the experience of abuse
- Affirm that violence is unacceptable behaviour
- Show support toward the victim
- Make an initial assessment of safety
- Respond to any concern about safety

Source: Queensland Department of Health (2020)

Judging how and when to ask questions such as these requires social workers to prioritise safety, taking care with confidentiality, particularly with a view to ensuring that any violent situation is not made more dangerous. Working from a strengths framework, social workers will want to explore the ways in which the person has been able to cope with the situation, how they have been able to survive and what they believe needs to happen to make them safe.

From Ann: assessment and risk

During the past year, I have had a couple of brief psychiatric hospitalisations. As I had last been hospitalised more than 25 years ago, I noticed some changes in the experience. Looking back to the early years of my illness, inpatient assessment and treatments focused on symptomatology, suffering and response to treatments. Staff spent quite a bit of time with us patients, talking, playing games. They had a visible presence. There was no locked nurses' station.

My recent experiences were very different. Staff were largely invisible, spending much time within their locked office, with the blinds down. To speak with a nurse, I needed to ring the bell at their office and then wait for someone to come out and ask what I wanted. Often I needed to wait a long time. If I asked for some top-up medication, I was rarely asked why I wanted it, and there were no attempts to spend time with me to talk about the worsening of my symptoms that had led to me asking. Usually about once a shift 'my' nurse would come and talk to me, for about five minutes, almost always with a pen and piece of paper in hand. How did I feel? Was I feeling better or worse than yesterday? On a scale of 1 to 10 how did I feel? (It was not until the end of the hospitalisation that I discovered that 10, for them, was the best I had ever felt, but for me was the worst – so much for the accuracy of the assessment process.) I found this process degrading because it was obvious to me that they were asking me some questions with a view to writing their shift report in my file, not because they cared or wanted to help.

When I felt well enough to spend time with other patients, we usually sat in the dining room and drank tea or coffee, chatting, listening to each other's stories, offering advice and maybe playing games. Not once did a staff member sit with us to chat or take part in these conversations. They were largely oblivious to the tensions on the ward. We patients knew who was feeling low or edgy. We could predict who was going to 'blow', who was vulnerable.

There was a different culture of care in my recent experience of hospitalisation. It was more impersonal, less interactive, less wise, less healing. Staff appeared to have retreated behind their locked doors and the notices that said abusive or threatening behaviour would not be tolerated. I mourned the lack of opportunities for a relationship with staff, the possibilities of new insights or learning new strategies, for collaboration in my care. Hospital had become a place to wait until the change in medication took effect.

Does wisdom have a place when risk can be managed?

Assessing risks of suicide and self-harm

Assessing the risk of suicide and self-harm is one of the most important elements of a comprehensive mental health assessment, and all social workers, in whatever setting, need the skill and confidence to make this form of assessment and to respond effectively. But it is not always easy, and it is worthwhile for every social worker to undertake one of the good suicide intervention courses such as Applied Suicide Intervention Skills Training (ASIST). For those who have done so at some point, it is worthwhile considering refresher training.

A useful way of thinking about suicide risk and prevention is to consider the practical distinction between risk factors, warning signs and drivers

Risk factors and warning signs for suicide prevention

Risk factors

- An aspect of the person or their situation which statistically correlates with an elevated risk of suicide. These should be noted in the assessment, but they are not generally in themselves a cause for concern. They can include:
  - biological, e.g., male, age > 65 years, Caucasian;
  - psychological, e.g., substance use, untreated mood disorder;
  - cognitive, e.g., impulsivity, rigid cognitive structures;
  - social, e.g., unemployment, relationship breakdown, poverty;
  - proximal – sudden, immediate event, e.g., crisis in relationship, loss of job;
  - distal – chronic stressor, e.g., illness.

Warning Signs

- An observable shift in the person's thinking towards suicidal intent. These are typically person and situation specific but can include newly emergent expressions of:
  - hopelessness,
  - rage and a desire for revenge,
  - reckless and risk-taking behaviour,
  - feeling trapped,
  - increased alcohol and drug use,
  - anxiety,
  - changes in sleep pattern,
  - dramatic mood change,
  - lack of purpose.

Source: Tucker et al. (2015)

There are two points which are important to stress, owing to their somewhat counter-intuitive nature:

1. Suicidal ideation (thinking about suicide, even wishing for one's own death) is not a reliable indicator of intent. Such thoughts are much more common than actual suicide attempts (Large & Ryan, 2014; Silverman & Berman, 2014).[1]
2. Asking directly about suicide does not increase its likelihood (by somehow 'suggesting' it to the client). In fact, there is evidence that talking about suicide with high-risk adolescents can actually reduce their level of distress (Granello, 2010).[2]

If you think someone may be at risk, it is important to ask directly. Each of us will do this in our own words, at a time and in a way that is sensitive to the requirements of the situation, but the question should be explicit, such as 'Are you having thoughts of suicide?' or 'Are you thinking about killing yourself?' and 'Do you have a plan?'

Where a risk has been identified, it is critical to make an assessment of the seriousness of the risk, reflecting factors such as whether the person has a plan and the means to carry it out, the risk of impulsiveness (for example, due to alcohol and drugs) and any history of past attempts.

A suicide risk assessment should take into account a wide range of contextual factors, including a psychiatric assessment and an evaluation of risk and protective factors, and it should attempt to reach an understanding of the person's experience, including the quality and extent of inner pain and distress, and the meaning of that experience from the person's point of view. In suicide assessment, there is an established tendency to focus on the actual intended acts and their consequences – understandably so, given their potential finality. The *Australian Clinical Practice Guideline* (Boyce et al., 2003) focuses on self-harm regardless of intent. Yet, in relationship-based practice, there will naturally be a focus on meaning and intention – and this has practical, ethical and philosophical consequences (Fairbairn, 1998). Hopelessness, despair, agitation, shame, anger, guilt and psychosis escalate the risk. A history of previous attempts – not excluding ambivalent attempts – is strongly predictive (O'Connor et al., 2004).

Think about the characteristics of the person that might create a 'vulnerability' to risk – factors such as aggression, impulsivity, pessimism, substance use, personal or family history of suicidal acts, physical illness and poor social supports. Now, in the specific situation that is being assessed, consider how any of these or other factors may interact with situational stressors such as financial distress, social disruption, acute intoxication, the onset of a depressive illness, or awareness of other instances of suicide or self-harm. This kind of assessment can help the social worker to understand the risk and sometimes provide opportunities for prevention (Zisook et al., 2013). Strengths-based questions (Corcoran & Walsh, 2009, p. 29) might include:

> 'If you've had thoughts of hurting yourself, what did you do to get past that point?'
> 'Things sounded really hard then. How did you manage?'
> 'How did you stop things from getting worse?'
> 'What needs to happen now so that you feel a bit better?'

As with any kind of assessment, the quality of the relationship between the worker and the client is an important factor in determining the quality of the risk assessment, and the confidence that the worker can have in that assessment. It is not enough to ask the questions that lead to reassuring answers – the worker has to feel sure that the assessment is an accurate one. So, really, there are at least two assessments to be made at the same time: the degree of risk and the degree of confidence in the assessment. A judgement also needs to be made about how changeable the situation might be and when a reassessment might need to be made, as well as whether there is any associated risk to others including children.

The assessment of suicide or other risk carries with it a potential responsibility to act. Sometimes this will result in the person being admitted to a hospital or other place of safety. Often, though, it will be a case of establishing a careful plan involving the person and their family and friends: marshalling supports to maintain safety, ensuring that the person has good psychiatric treatment, reducing psychosocial stressors and building protective factors, and, importantly, planning in advance for contingencies. Every plan of this kind carries its own element of risk. For the worker, this is a heavy responsibility to be taken deliberately and carefully, on the basis of the most thorough assessment possible. Assessments and plans of this kind can prevent many suicides. So-called no-harm contracts may be reassuring, but they are no substitute for a proper plan to manage the crisis safely, ideally in the context of a continuing relationship. Talking to a client about suicidal thoughts and being willing to help them with a plan for managing their situation makes it less likely that the person will kill themselves.

However, we should always be aware that it is really impossible to *predict* completed suicide. Ryan and Large have made the important point that it is not, therefore, a 'comprehensive suicide risk assessment' that is required for each client, but rather a comprehensive assessment of their situation and needs. Any suicidal ideas are only one part of that wider picture. As they argue, 'This is not to say that we should abandon patient safety. Bolstering family or social support, restricting access to lethal methods of suicide or making a crisis plan are steps that should be taken for all patients in psychological crisis – not just those whom we imagine might be more likely to suicide than others' (Ryan & Large, 2013, p. 463).

Family assessment

Some very different forms of family assessment are used, as appropriate to the different types of work to be done with families. It is important to bear in mind that families have often reported experiencing the assessment as contributing to a sense of being somehow at fault and blamed for the mental health problem of a family member – something we wish to avoid for both ethical and therapeutic reasons. As with individual clients, we start from the premise that we seek to build a partnership with families, and the assessment is carried out in this context.

The focus of the family assessment is on understanding the point of view of each family member and how the family is experiencing the issues it confronts while also looking at issues that will be relevant to the work that will follow, such as how family members communicate together, how they solve problems and the resources at their disposal to meet their needs in the context of a family member's mental illness.

The first thing is to listen to their knowledge, experience and perspective on the situation. It is generally useful to ascertain a range of details, for each family member (Falloon et al., 2004) (see box, 'Initial information for family assessment').

Initial information for family assessment

Basic information, such as details about physical and mental health problems, other significant stresses in their life, and whether they know whom to contact in the service.

The way the person understands the client's mental health problem and its treatment, including what factors lead to improvement and what things tend to make the problem worse.

The way the mental health problem affects the person and their coping strategies.

Each person's daily life pattern, and sources of sustenance and satisfaction. Each person's personal goals and their goals for the family as a whole.

Family psychoeducational approaches rely on an assessment of this kind, together with an assessment of strengths and problems for the family as a whole in communication, problem-solving and goal achievement. (See Chapter 9 for more discussion of family psychoeducational approaches.)

Genograms, which are adapted family trees, are often extremely useful tools for identifying and discussing important issues for families across generations, especially when they are constructed collaboratively, 'shoulder to shoulder'. They help with engagement, the expression of information about family experiences and clarifying family patterns, and they often enable family issues to be seen in a new light (Milewski-Hertlein, 2001). They should be used routinely as a part of the family assessment. Family therapy, which is not discussed here in detail, requires more specialised assessment.

Culture and assessment

The attitude of respectful curiosity which we seek to bring to all assessment is a necessary stance in working with people from different cultures. It is often impossible for mental health professionals to have a detailed knowledge of such diverse experiences and to apply these in a mental health setting, so social workers need to make contacts within their communities and seek out sources of cultural expertise. However, it is certainly possible for social workers to learn to be sensitive to the dangers of misunderstanding that can affect assessment across cultures.

Each of us has our own set of values, beliefs and practices, shaped in part by our social and cultural context. We take much of this for granted. It seems natural to us, so difference will always challenge us to some extent. Getting to know any other person requires some encounter with difference, and the same applies to families or groups, to each of which we may attribute a distinctive 'culture'. Culture usually refers to the values, beliefs and practices that pertain to a given ethnocultural group, including familial roles; communication patterns; affective styles; and values regarding personal control, individualism, collectivism, spirituality and religiosity (Betancourt & López, 1993), but there is a sense in which virtually any assessment we are involved in is 'transcultural'. We make this point here because we want to emphasise the importance of self-awareness and critical reflexivity in making an assessment. Social workers seek to understand the client's experience, so we need to be as conscious as possible of our own taken-for-granted assumptions.

Basic elements of a cultural assessment

What is the cultural identity of the client?

What is the cultural presentation and what are the cultural explanations of the illness?

What cultural factors are related to the psychosocial environment and to levels of functioning?

What are the cultural elements of the relationship between the client and the worker?
What is the overall cultural assessment and formulation for diagnosis and care?

Source: Andary et al. (2003, p. 20)

There are potential cultural barriers to establishing a therapeutic relationship, and we need to exercise special care and sometimes specific strategies to build partnerships and trust and to negotiate a shared understanding of each other's perspective. Whenever required, skilled interpreters should always be engaged. Assessment instruments should be available in community languages but, even so, we need to be aware that assessment instruments and diagnostic systems contain cultural biases. Specific instruments such as the *Cultural Awareness Tool* (Multicultural Mental Health Australia, 2002) may assist in correcting these biases and improve the level of understanding across cultures.

When considering the impact and influence of culture it is important to avoid making generalised assumptions. No human culture can be characterised in a few paragraphs, and no two 'members' of a cultural group will have the same experience and relationship with the traditions and beliefs of their background. What does the culture mean for the client? Does the client identify with a certain set of beliefs? Do particular practices hold significance for the client? How is that significance expressed? As always, a relationship-based exchange with the individual client is crucial.

Social and emotional health assessment with Aboriginal and Torres Strait Islander people

The concept of social and emotional wellbeing is based on an Indigenous definition of health, reflecting a holistic and whole-of-life view of health, including social, emotional and cultural wellbeing (Social Health Reference Group, 2004) and encompassing individual, family, wider tribal group and the land, all of which are connected in a 'complex set of relational bonds and reciprocal obligations' (Dingwall & Cairney, 2010, p. 21). Social and emotional wellbeing is a positive concept, but it incorporates a number of factors that can have a positive or negative impact. Loss or disintegration of positive connections will lead to mental ill-health, and for this reason it is not possible to understand social and emotional wellbeing in isolation from the history of colonisation, dispossession, dislocation, inter-generational trauma and disadvantage that Indigenous Australians live with.

Different meanings and experiences of social and emotional health require different approaches to assessment, and the process is just as important as the content. For an accurate, culturally responsive assessment in Indigenous mental health, Drew et al. (2010, p. 204) emphasise the point that 'assessment of Aboriginal people cannot be moulded into a Western framework and that it is not only the individual but also the family and community that play an integral role in assessment and treatment'.

Drew et al. (2010) highlight the need to:

- identify your own attitudes, values and beliefs;
- respect community protocol – that is, whether there are any ceremonies that may coincide with your visit to the community;
- find out who is the right person to speak with in the community;
- ask whether it is appropriate for you to see this client;
- consider engaging a cultural consultant (the consultant should be appropriate for the engagement, for example, in their relationship to the client and in their gender);
- reflect on the person's behaviour within the cultural context;
- consider whether assessment tools are appropriate;
- ask what factors you need to consider when interpreting the data;
- consider traditional and non-traditional healing practices when deciding on appropriate intervention – that is, practices of elders and community healers.

Social work often has a 'bad name' in Indigenous communities; it can be associated with fear, trauma, anger and mistrust. In large part this 'bad name' has been acquired through processes of colonisation and recolonisation, racism, and the role social workers have played, and continue to play, in the forced removal of Aboriginal children (Bennett et al., 2013). Building genuine, respectful relationships takes commitment and investment over time; social workers need to listen deeply, privileging the centrality of storytelling and yarning in Indigenous cultures. There may also be specific skills for non-Indigenous social workers to learn here: appropriate forms of address; verbal and non-verbal skills including eye-contact, posture and gesture; and so on (Drew et al., 2010).

There may be an opportunity to learn from expert Aboriginal mental health workers or cultural consultants. There are some useful resources for guiding assessment with specific groups, such as the Strong Souls assessment tool, developed for use with Indigenous young people in the Northern Territory (Thomas et al., 2010), and the AIMhi (Stay Strong) Health Plan (Menzies School of Health Research, 2013). Among the websites listed at the end of this chapter, the Royal Australian and New Zealand College of Psychiatrists and Beyond Blue (n.d.) have developed well-researched online guidance for working with Indigenous people, including the Dance of Life matrix, which describes in some detail the elements of interrelated physical, psychological, social, spiritual and cultural dimensions of social and emotional wellbeing. In addition, the Australian Psychological Society (n.d.) provides resources for learning about ways of meeting the social wellbeing and mental health needs of Indigenous people and communities, including some screening and assessment tools and examples of promising practice.

Writing assessments

Generally speaking, all written assessments should include succinct statements of the following, in a disciplined and specific manner:

a statement of how the situation is understood
a statement of needs
a statement of the desired outcomes of care and treatment

We must write with great care. What is written stays in place for a long time and is for different people to see, so it can be important and can have enormous influence. A good plan is to write as if the client will read what you have put down. Better still, in most situations, ask the client to read it.

Increasingly, mental health agencies encourage or require the use of specific data collection instruments and assessment frameworks. Tools such as genograms, ecomaps, social network maps and life charts can be used as part of a collaborative inquiry. These inform, but do not replace, the assessment.

Because assessment is an ongoing process, each entry in the file contributes to the written assessment. The best way of doing this is to work to a general template, such as the 'SOAP' model, which is simple and provides an excellent discipline. It was developed in relation to problem-oriented record keeping but lends itself to use in almost all mental health services. A template for recording is shown (see box, 'Template for recording').

Template for recording

Subjective: What the client tells you; what they say; how they say it; expressed feelings and perceptions.
Objective: What you observe.
Assessment: Your analysis of the problem; explanations, hypotheses, diagnoses; interpretation of the subjective and objective information.
Plan: Following from the assessment: interventions used/planned to achieve goals; treatment progress.

Source: Cameron (2013)

Where there are different points of view, these can be included in written assessments and reports. In mental health settings, assessments should be written in such a way as to maximise the client's understanding of, and contribution to, the situation (MacDonald-Wilson et al., 2001). Participative report writing seeks to include the client in the actual production of the report, or at least to ensure that the client's perspective is properly represented. Regular reviews of the assessment need to be undertaken to incorporate new information and perspectives and also to retain the focus on shared understanding of problems and strengths – the basis for development and review of a plan of action and joint work.

Outcome measures

We will return to consider outcome measures in the final chapter, after we have had the opportunity to discuss social work practice approaches, but we mention it here because we want to emphasise that ongoing but explicit evaluation is an essential part of assessment. In order to do this, we need to be setting goals of some kind, and we need a clear idea of what we regard as a desirable outcome. Some goals – for example, those relating to risk assessments – might be quite conservative: that the person remain safe and that harm is avoided. In the mental health field, the outcome is frequently measured in terms of the extent or influence of symptoms.

Conclusion

Mental health social workers will seek to use the assessment process to establish, as collaboratively as possible, what constitutes a good outcome for each client and each piece of work. The achievement by a client of particular personal or interpersonal goals (for example, in some of the domains of the needs-for-service assessment), improving quality of life and social inclusion (Huxley & Thornicroft, 2003; Coombs et al., 2013), or increasing choice and freedom from restraint – these are the areas in which the outcomes of effective mental health social work are likely to be most evident.

QUESTIONS FOR PRACTICE

1. Before seeing a consumer for the first time, do you talk to other staff about them, and do you read their case notes? Why or why not?
2. In what ways can clients take a collaborative role in assessment?
3. Should clients 'own' a record of care, much like a record of vaccination?
4. How can information be shared between workers and services in ways that are respectful to clients?
5. How can thorough and holistic assessments avoid intrusiveness and loss of dignity?
6. How might a focus on risk diminish a creative approach to assessment and intervention?
7. How can client confidentiality be respectfully managed when families are included in assessment and treatment?
8. Reflecting on your own culture, how is mental health and illness understood? How might this inform/shape your work with clients, families and communities?

Websites

Australian Indigenous Mental Health

A website from the Royal Australian and New Zealand College of Psychiatrists and Beyond Blue. A site to support the work of health professionals in improving knowledge and understanding of Aboriginal and Torres Strait Islander mental health issues.
http://indigenous.ranzcp.org/index.php

Centre for Rural and Remote Mental Health

Sections on Indigenous wellbeing and rural mental health. Newsletter and resources.
www.crrmh.com.au

Children of Parents with a Mental Illness (COPMI)

Includes many resources useful for the assessment of families where a parent has a mental illness.
www.copmi.net.au

Living Works Australia

Training courses for professionals and the community in suicide awareness, risk assessment and intervention.
www.livingworks.com.au

Mental Health in Multicultural Australia (MHiMA)

Resources and handouts translated into community languages.
www.mhima.org.au

SANE Australia

Includes the 'not quite right' fact sheet mentioned in this chapter.
www.sane.org

Social and Emotional Wellbeing and Mental Health Services in Aboriginal Australia

Promising practices, assessment and rating charts, personal accounts of illness and recovery for clients.
www.sewbmh.org.au

Transcultural Mental Health Centre NSW

www.dhi.health.nsw.gov.au/transcultural-mental-health-centre

Notes

1 Large, M. & Ryan, C. 2014, 'Suicide Risk Assessment: Myth and Reality', *International Journal of Clinical Practice*, vol. 68, no. 6, pp. 679–81.; Silverman, M. M. & Berman, A. L. 2014, 'Suicide Risk Assessment and Risk Formulation Part I: A Focus on Suicide Ideation in Assessing Suicide Risk', *Suicide and Life-Threatening Behavior*, vol. 44, no. 4, pp. 420–31.

2 Granello, D. H. 2010, 'The Process of Suicide Risk Assessment: Twelve Core Principles', *Journal of Counselling and Development*, vol. 88, Summer, pp. 363–370.

7 Social casework in mental health settings

Social casework in the mental health field entails work with individuals, their interpersonal social systems (family and others) and a very wide range of areas relevant to their personal and social functioning and recovery. Depending on their own needs and wishes, these areas might include, for example, family responsibilities, social and occupational role and functioning, alcohol and drug problems, legal issues, safety, physical health issues and the secondary effects of treatment. In this chapter we outline an approach to social casework and the organisational context in which it is often undertaken – the case management system.

Before going any further, however, we need to acknowledge the problematic nature of the terminology. The idea of a 'case' is a familiar one in social work, but the term does not sit comfortably with all consumers or families – certainly it fails to capture the centrality of relationship, partnership and therapeutic alliance to good mental health practice in the community. At the same time, an alternative such as 'working with individuals' (the nomenclature adopted in the Australian Association of Social Workers' Practice Standards, for example) is equally misleading. As we have emphasised, social work in mental health entails a focus on more than the service user – it encompasses communities, families and interpersonal networks, a breadth of scope traditionally associated with 'casework'. In the absence of a viable alternative we have chosen to retain the term, recognising always that effective and ethical casework is entirely inconsistent with practices, attitudes or language which reduce or dehumanise the service user to a file number or a 'case'.

Relationship and the application of partnership

Throughout this book we emphasise the crucial role positive relationships play in the recovery process. While we naturally emphasise the relationships between service users and those in their familial and social networks, we also need to recognise the significance of the service user's relationship with their social worker as a determinant of the success or otherwise of practice (Davidson & Chan, 2014). Research evidence and much of the subjective experience of case workers and clients suggests a clear, positive connection between a working relationship that is open, trusting and collaborative and successful therapeutic outcomes in mental

DOI: 10.4324/9781003148913-9

health, including quality of life, symptomatology, attitudes towards medication, satisfaction with treatment and especially the person's subjective experiences of community living (Solomon et al., 1995; Hamovitch et al., 2018. Person-Centered Care and the Therapeutic Alliance. Community Mental Health Journal, 54[7], pp. 951–8). One of the key early descriptions of case management in mental health emphasised the human relationship factor in the following terms:

> Simply stated, the human element cannot be taken out of the human service system. When connecting with clients, the case manager establishes a close bond with the client. The case manager treats the client as a 'person' rather than a client, attending to the client's need to be physically, emotionally, intellectually, and spiritually close to another person.
>
> (Anthony et al., 1988, pp. 222–3)

There is evidence that clients generally value the quality of their relationship with the case worker more than they value the structural aspects, such as frequency of contact. One aspect is the importance of someone 'really believing in me' or 'seeing something inside of me that I couldn't see' (Davidson et al., 2006b, p. 483); another is sustaining hope (Hobbs & Baker, 2012). Some clients may have few other relationships, so the connection with a case worker may be all the more important to them. Recovery is a personal experience that is shared through relationships in social situations – it exists as much between people as within them (Best, 2012).

This raises a great challenge inherent in social work practice: the ability to relate in a genuinely empathic fashion while retaining a purposeful disposition. In the absence of the former, social workers risk becoming simply one more 'expert' the service user is required to speak with (Slade, 2012); in the absence of the latter, accountability and appropriate professional boundaries are compromised, potentially to the confusion and distress of the client. If the relationship is to be authentic, case workers must be willing to invest in it personally; to act naturally, in a way that reflects their own personality; and to communicate aspects of their own personal experience. Doing so professionally means always having an eye to the primary purpose of the relationship, which is to encourage and support recovery for the client. How can this balance be achieved?

The first task, as we argued in Chapter 1, is to really listen; then it is necessary to learn from these communications and to respond meaningfully. This means paying close attention to the client's own perceptions and understandings of the situation, getting to know them as a person and responding to their actual needs. As Simon Champ has put it:

> the best professionals involved in my care have, like me, opened themselves to the mystery that is schizophrenia. They have gained my trust, sharing and supporting my inner search for meaning and for an understanding of the relationship between myself and my illness.
>
> (Champ, 1998, p. 59)

This does not always have to be complicated. Case workers may position themselves more as companions and helpers in a partnership with their clients, supporting everyday solutions to everyday problems, rather than adopting the position of expert. Elements of skill are involved here, but also human qualities and values.

The relationship must be safe enough for clients to feel able to communicate frankly. Workers should recognise that clients will make their own choices about what they communicate in the interests of solving problems and seeking to meet their needs. Although these relationships involve reciprocity, the case worker is not simply a friend or a peer, and there will be differences in, and inequalities of, power.

We have a tendency to think about a line that we should not cross in order to keep our relationships 'professional'. We tend to characterise 'professional' relationships as more distant and considered than ordinary human relationships. Davidson (2005) has usefully proposed that, rather than thinking in terms of a clear line, we should aim instead for balanced relationships that are neither too 'entangled' nor too 'rigid'. Too much entanglement or (at the other end of the continuum) too much rigidity can each lead to breaches of a professional relationship. 'Balanced' professional relationships are authentic and caring, while maintaining clear boundaries. There is no clear set of rules for this; it is a matter of responding to each client's unique needs. This requires professional judgement, self-reflection and decision-making that is accountable to other professionals. In a balanced professional relationship, such authority as comes with the professional role is used with care so as to neither exploit the clients' vulnerabilities nor infringe on their rights (Davidson, 2005).

Power imbalances between staff and consumers in a mental health system find their way into the language used by staff in small, seemingly benign interactions, for example, by presuming to 'know', by presuming to use terms of endearment, or by making 'suggestions' that are really directions. Such patterns of control within the service system may have a profound impact on the client's ability to regain control over the rest of their lives (Melville-Wiseman, 2012). During the consultations about the development of the Australian Mental Health Social Work Practice Standards, focus groups of consumers and families identified that it was often the common, basic courtesies that were most appreciated: phone calls being returned, a non-judgemental attitude, being treated with respect as an intelligent human being and being listened to (AASW, 2004). These are simple, everyday markers of a decent relationship that can form the basis of partnership with the potential to support recovery.

Many consumers in mental health settings will have previous experiences of coercion or unsatisfactory 'treatment' relationships, may feel that services have little to offer and may be rightly sceptical about a new relationship with a case worker. Sometimes this scepticism is described as 'difficult to engage' or, worse still, 'non-compliant'. Case workers need to be curious and engage *with* the consumer to explore their past experiences of social workers and the services system – this tells us about what's important to the consumer, what dignity and respect looks like to them and what should be avoided in the relationship. If services focus solely on immediate outcomes or on medical treatment, they might not seem relevant to what consumers actually want; and of course this can be compounded in involuntary treatment settings. Mental health services need staff with the appropriate skills and the time and resources to achieve engagement (Sainsbury Centre for Mental Health, 1998). Relationships of this kind are not possible without persistence and consistency (Davidson et al., 2006a). Case workers also need to develop the skill of respectful and assertive engagement. The principle of assertiveness, applied to this context, means being proactive, patient and gently persistent in initiating and maintaining contact.

The prominence of recovery ideas in mental health services has led to some serious rethinking about the role of social workers and other mental health professionals. Firstly, it involves a fundamental repositioning of the place of mental health treatment:

> Overall, proponents of a recovery approach seek to reverse some priorities. People with mental illness don't need treatment – they need a life. Treatment may contribute to the process of striving for a life worth living, but it is a means, not an end.
>
> (Slade, 2012, p. 704)

Naturally, positive changes in psychiatric symptoms are often critical to recovery, and this is facilitated by access to good-quality mental health care, but response to treatment is not at all the same thing as recovery, and different consumers will follow different trajectories. Recovery is something that only consumers can experience and achieve, but they do so in the context of social relationships, including relationships with mental health professionals. The point of professional activity is to support recovery (Diamond, 2009).

Individual service planning

Support for recovery is aligned with social participation and inclusion (Gardner et al., 2019) – what the Australian National Mental Health Commission (2014) calls a 'contributing life'. How social inclusion is defined can be a complex question. Leamy et al. (2011) discuss inclusion in generalities of empowerment and control, while Gardner et al. (2018) note the combination of objective factors, such as economic position, and subjective factors, such as one's perceptions of acceptance and engagement. As so often in mental health social work, it is the interaction of structural factors (potentially both constraining and liberating) and personal/interpersonal factors which defines our focus.

At the same time, it is important to avoid conceptualising social inclusion as unproblematically linked to social participation, which itself should not be considered a self-evident good. The extent to which a person chooses to socialise or take part in social activities (one metric of participation) need not be a function of mental wellness; indeed, assuming, for example, that a withdrawn or solitary disposition is linked to the mental illness with which a person may be diagnosed is in reality a form of stigma. What matters here is the extent to which a person is able to exercise their agency. Social inclusion can be understood as the right to choose whether or not to socially participate and the absence of structural barriers to the exercise of that choice.

What this means for any one service user is very much open to negotiation and depends on the assessment of what is wanted and needed. It is not a matter of 'maintaining' people with mental health problems in the community, managing all the attendant risks and reacting to crises and other difficulties as they arise; a much more active approach is required. Each person's situation and goals will be different, so the work will not take a standardised form; rather, it needs to be devised and negotiated with each person in consultation with the people who are important to them. An individual service plan (ISP) provides a structure that can be used to decide on priorities and actions. An ISP should be simple, straightforward statements of needs and goals and the steps that will be taken to achieve them within a timeframe. It may include a wide range of areas of activity, such as (those which are set out in detail in Appendix II (see also Chapter 6)) emotional and mental wellbeing; dealing with stress; personal response to illness; personal safety and the safety of others; friendships and social relationships; work, leisure and education; daily living skills; family's response to a relative's illness; income; physical health; housing; rights and advocacy.

Individual service planning needs to be done collaboratively with the client and needs to include the contributions of mental health professionals and others. Where an ISP is used, it should form the basis of the service that is provided by the agency, so the case worker must ensure that it *includes* and takes account of medical, psychiatric and other specialised forms of treatment. It should not merely sit alongside another parallel treatment plan; it is central to mental health treatment and care, not an adjunct. Some of the work identified in the ISP is to be done directly by the case worker, some by others in the agency and some indirectly through liaison, negotiation and coordination with other service providers. Whatever the mix in each particular case, the basis of good social casework is the relationship with the client.

Effective social casework of this kind is complex but often also very practical work because it aims to focus on the everyday situations clients are experiencing. It is important for social workers not to lose sight of the value of practical work with clients. The more people see our services as useful and practical, the more likely they are to stay engaged (Rapp & Goscha, 2012).

From Ann: so, you're applying for the job as my case manager?

It's true – I am so much more than my diagnosis or presenting problem.

You may want to manage, I may want to consult. Could we start by saying 'hello' to each other?

I don't 'do' 9 a.m. appointments!

Do you see yourself as my case manager or an enabler, co-creator of possibilities or partner in recovery?

Please don't 'hot-label' me: non-compliant, difficult, demanding, challenging, ungrateful. . . . These labels stick, and I always get to hear about them.

Just because I have a mental illness doesn't mean that I am more or less intelligent than you, more or less educated, have more or fewer friends, am more or less loved.

Don't assume, ask.

I really hate the term *consumer*. Would 'Ann' do?

If I have difficulties speaking English, would you mind using an interpreter each time I see you?

How I experience my symptoms may be different from how they are described in your textbooks. Would you like me to tell you about this?

Get to know me before you read my notes or are influenced by other clinicians' stories or opinions of me.

I'm a very good source of information about what medication suits me, what has worked for me in the past and what treatments/interventions I would prefer in the future.

Could we plan ahead for the unexpected?

I may not want to see you and might prefer to see someone else.

There really is no point in leaving glossy brochures about forming partnerships and consulting us if you don't really mean it.

When I'm episodic, I can become disorganised and lose track of appointments and things I have to do. Please be flexible.

Please, deeply listen. Show respect and curiosity.

There will be things I choose not to share with you.

At the front door to your service, there is a sign that says that abusive language and behaviour will not be tolerated. I presume it refers to the workers in this service. I'd heard that you are all stressed and that your workloads are huge. I didn't realise it was that bad. Should I be alarmed or go somewhere else?

Keep the relationship fresh. I change. You change. Isn't life wonderful?

It's OK to say, 'I don't know, but I can find out'.

It is possible for people with a mental illness to have rich and fulfilling lives.

I really hate being handed around from worker to worker when you go on leave or change jobs.

If you leave, don't forget to say goodbye. I may want to thank you.

I have a whole other life outside this service.

Because I have a mental illness, my physical health may not be as good as yours; my teeth may be in a worse condition; I may be poor; I may experience housing insecurity; I may not have many friends. Alternatively, I may be a former politician, or a famous football player. . . . You never know!

Sometimes, you may have to carry my hopefulness for me, just until I get stronger . . .
Your timetable for my recovery may not dovetail with my timetable, or where I'm at just now.
Do you have any idea how humiliating grand rounds are for me?
If you're going to discuss me in your case conferences or committees, you might like to ask me what I think, or want, or hope for.
I may have things to offer you too!

Supporting strengths

The strengths-based approach is perhaps the dominant approach in contemporary social casework in mental health. There is evidence that a strengths-based approach makes a greater contribution to both personal recovery and symptom alleviation, compared with other common approaches (Barry et al., 2003; Fukui et al., 2012). It was first articulated in North America in the context of a challenge to the emphasis on individual pathology in mental health service delivery, related to psychodynamic and biomedical discourses. The model aimed to 'humanise' mental health services for people with severe and persistent mental illness (Taylor, 2006). This impulse receives renewed emphasis in the context of contemporary focus on recovery (Oades & Anderson, 2012; Rapp & Goscha, 2012). Strengths-based social casework provides a conceptual basis for transforming practice away from pathologising discourses towards a focus on 'resilience, rebound, possibility, and transformation' (Saleebey, 1996, p. 297). All people have strengths and abilities, including the ability to build their competence, so service systems need to be designed to give people the opportunity to display use and build such strengths. The strengths-based approach has been applied specifically to a form of case management (Rapp & Goscha, 2012) which emphasises client self-determination and strengths rather than pathology, with the case worker working optimistically and assertively with the client.

It might be argued that there is little or no difference between the strengths-based approach and 'good basic social work practice', and the principles are very straightforward. The work is concerned with what the person has achieved so far, the available resources and the person's knowledge, talents and aspirations. The community is viewed as an oasis of resources; the focus is not just on the strengths of the individual but the strengths of the environment. The following principles apply (Rapp & Goscha, 2012):

The client is the director of the helping process, so case managers should only act with the client's approval, involving them every step of the way.
The case manager–client relationship is primary and essential.
The primary setting for our work is in the community.

Strengths include personal and environmental resources and attributes. In a sense, they are ordinary. They are the things that are not necessarily mentioned in formal case discussions, and they can get submerged and forgotten when considerations of illness and risk are to the fore. But they can be the most important particular things. Strengths include:

skills like gardening or caregiving for children;
talents like playing the bagpipes or cooking;
personal virtues and traits like patience or a sense of humour;
interpersonal skills like comforting the sick or mediating conflict;
interpersonal and environmental resources like an extended family or good neighbours;
cultural knowledge and lore like healing ceremonies and rituals or stories of cultural perseverance;
family stories such as narratives of overcoming obstacles or migration and settlement;
knowledge gained from struggling against adversity, such as how one came to survive and overcome barriers or how one developed and maintained faith and hope;
knowledge from occupational or parental roles like caregiving for others or planning events and celebrations;
spirituality and faith such as a transcendent system of meaning to rely on or a declaration of purpose beyond the self;
hopes and dreams such as personal, familial, social and occupational goals and vision, or positive expectations about a better future (Saleebey, 2001, p. 185).

The case worker needs the skill to listen for, ask about and value 'ordinary' strengths of this kind. The Australian consumer consultant Allan Pinches has conceded that it might sound sentimental to relate to 'hopes and dreams' or that this may be a bit of a luxury for which service providers have neither the time nor the resources. However, he says, 'if we don't factor in the person's "hopes and dreams" which are important innermost and holistic parts of that person's world, a large proportion of the person is not being addressed' (Pinches, 2014, p. 11).

It is most important to ensure that a strengths-based approach does not elide the challenges faced by the client. In working to identify strengths (a collaborative process, of course) the worker needs to ensure that they are not adopting a tone of 'looking for the silver lining' or in some fashion minimising difficulties. In other words, an emphasis on goals and strengths should by no means preclude careful attention to the person's mental illness and their life problems. But the case worker seeks also to avoid rumination and a simple rehearsal of past struggles. Issues are viewed from the perspective of a practical optimism, a foundational belief that any circumstance can change. In this sense, a strengths perspective involves identifying and providing resources for the person to address adversities, for example, by learning information about mental illness and its treatment and by developing skills for reducing relapses, dealing with stress and coping with symptoms (Substance Abuse and Mental Health Services Administration [SAMHSA], 2003).

This approach emphasises the importance of 'natural' supports – family, friends, neighbours, sports and other clubs, faith communities, arts centres and so on – rather than professionally delivered services. Case workers thus require detailed knowledge of the actual communities in which they work, not just knowledge of formal and specialist organisations. Hence, they must themselves be active participants in the community. The focus is on real-life goals in real-life settings, and here too a lot of the work is very practical.

Working with involuntary clients

As we have acknowledged, much mental health social work involves the exercise of some degree of coercive power. Many mental health consumers are not voluntary. For some (perhaps many) social workers participation in such a system represents an ethical dilemma which may be insurmountable. We hold that an uncritical collusion with medical and legal mechanisms of control is unethical, and as a consequence we affirm the importance of mental health social workers actively engaging with issues of systemic governance as a core responsibility. At the same time, we consider ideologically pure refusals to engage with the field to be an abnegation of responsibility to service users.

Partnership and strengths-based approaches are no less applicable in these situations, but there are particular challenges in their application. While it might be argued that having a role in a system with statutory power can help to protect and even empower consumers by ensuring that their rights are safeguarded and the least restrictive treatment options are used (Wilson & Daly, 2007), the plain fact is that a lot of mental health settings are much less respectful and empowering than they might be.

There are different ways to think about 'involuntariness'. In mental health settings, involuntariness is a common legal status, with particular meanings that vary according to the jurisdiction. Involuntary mental health status commonly restricts the person's right to refuse treatment, and as a consequence, case workers will often be in the position of monitoring and even enforcing treatment compliance. Voluntary clients, on the other hand, have the legal freedom to make their own decision about whether or not they accept any specific treatment. Clients may be subject to other legislation in areas such as guardianship, social security, child and family welfare, and criminal law. As a result, they may have restricted freedom in a range of areas – even about where they live. Case workers need to be absolutely clear about what legal role, if any, they have to play in monitoring and reporting on any legal restrictions – and about the limits of that role. Case workers should ensure that their clients also understand these issues and how they apply to the individual. For example, while a client's involuntary mental health status may mean they have no choice about whether to take a certain medication, this does not of itself restrict them in making all kinds of life decisions, such as how to spend time and money and so on. Clarity about such matters – the limits of confidentiality, any divided obligations and the potential outcomes for the client – forms one of the fundamental bases of an honest, direct, trusting and collaborative relationship (Regehr & Antle, 1997). Further, as we will see, there will always be room for choice and negotiation within the parameters of specific legal restrictions.

In reality, the distinction between voluntary and involuntary status is not so clear, and it might be useful to think of this as a continuum or a complex dynamic that changes in response to the situation. Like clients in other fields of health and welfare, people experiencing mental illness do not necessarily seek out available services, which are often experienced as being stigmatising or irrelevant. Clients who are legally 'voluntary' will almost always have some degree of reluctance – just as, conversely, clients who are legally 'involuntary' may well be willing to participate in all or at least some of the work that occurs in a case management relationship. The task for the case worker is to expand opportunities for more collaborative service agreements that explore clients' concerns while addressing mandates, agreeing on clear contracts that include collaborative tasks and avoiding unnecessary or unethical coercion (Rooney, 2002).

Fundamental principles of strengths-based social work in statutory settings will be of use in these situations. Differences in power between the worker and the client are inevitable, and there will be matters over which the client has no choice, but this does not prevent a social worker from working energetically to establish a partnership and offer as much genuine choice as possible in the circumstances. For example, there may be no choice about whether the client goes to a hospital because of a legal order, but there may be many possible options about when, how and with whom they attend. Having offered the choice, workers should respect and honour the client's decision and do their best to implement it; otherwise the option should not be offered (Jack, 2005).

An effective approach to empowerment requires the realisation that power is not a finite commodity to be divided up between worker and client. On the contrary, empowering practices affect both worker and client positively. Mental health workers are more likely to use intrusive, coercive approaches if they work in a demoralising organisational climate and hold negative and unhopeful attitudes towards people experiencing mental illness (Manuel et al., 2013). In contrast, the development of the attitudes and skills that underpin collaborative work with clients is empowering for the professionals concerned (Sousa & Rodrigues, 2012). To the extent that this can be achieved in involuntary contexts, it is all the more true.

Balancing risks

Mental health services are established for a range of purposes and simultaneously provide support and treatment while also providing a framework for managing risks, such as the risks of harm to self or others that we identified in the previous chapter (Rose, 1998). Indeed, from a public policy perspective, risk assessment and risk management are 'at the heart of effective mental health practice' (Department of Health, 1999, p. 22). Case workers operate within mental health systems that are set up to provide both care and control, and both functions should be recognised (Furlong, 1997). What is required is an approach to practice based on the principles of partnership that identifies and takes seriously issues of risk and acknowledges the worker's statutory and ethical responsibilities. However, this is a sophisticated undertaking that requires great skill as well as a well-managed and well-resourced service system. In practice, there is a tendency to emphasise either risk or relationship at the expense of the other. Some workers, committed to the principles of the therapeutic potential of a partnership with consumers, seek to minimise their role in assessing and managing risk. Others, influenced by a requirement to minimise risk, put less energy into the development of such a partnership, resulting in a demoralising and defensive form of practice. The best practice relies on the capacity to hold both dimensions in an appropriate balance on the basis of a negotiated partnership with the client and family carers. Workers should always avoid adopting a controlling or authoritarian position but should explain as directly as possible their concerns when they arise and the reason for their actions. They should support positive risk-taking. For example, anxious periods such as starting a new job might be a good time to temporarily increase medication.

There is a strong ethical and moral dimension to this work when it is done well, and it draws on personal qualities such as belief, optimism and caring (Ryan et al., 2004) as well as wisdom, courage and fortitude. The importance of hope is frequently emphasised (Hobbs & Baker, 2012), and rightly so. In mental health work, as in other contested fields where there is a lot of concern about the management of risk (Stanford, 2011), hope is a necessary risk, and hopeful practice is part of a moral response to risk.

From Ann: singing the bipolar blues, a melody in two parts

Part 1: a chorus singing of fractured lives and lost possibilities

It has been called the most important issue facing psychiatry today. I'm not talking about compliance with treatment regimes or the pin-the-tail-on-the-donkey exercise that identifies where we are in our recovery journeys. The real 'issue' is the extraordinarily high rates of morbidity (illness) and mortality (death) experienced by people with enduring mental illness.

It has been known for many decades that we suffer far worse physical health than the general population. We continue to die around 20 years sooner. While this has been acknowledged by the psychiatric great and good, few inroads have been made into these shameful outcomes.

In a nutshell, compared to 'normals', we have higher rates of:

- diabetes and cardiovascular illness;
- HIV, hepatitis C and tuberculosis;
- kidney disease;
- poor oral health;
- respiratory diseases;
- cancer;
- asthma;
- skin cancer;
- osteoporosis;
- middle ear infections;
- obstructive sleep apnoea;
- fibromyalgia;
- arthritis;
- chronic back and neck conditions.

Additionally, women:

- are less likely than the general population to have regular pap smears and breast checks;
- have limited access to contraception;
- face increased risk of complications in pregnancy and birth.

And men:

- are less likely to have prostate checks.

Why is this happening?

Health practitioners, the government and Big Pharma are quick to blame the individual for illness and early death. They point to smoking, lack of exercise and obesity underpinning 'lifestyle' diseases. This sleight of hand in attributing responsibility to the individual reduces complex health, economic and social problems to a kind of personal moral failure. This strategy takes the spotlight off some critical facts. Health and illness are determined by a complex interplay of factors having to do with the individual, the practitioner, the sticky and perverse nature of much mental illness that makes it imperfectly understood, and the systems within which we live and health care is delivered. Disease and disability are found on the very margins of society. We live in enclaves marked by social exclusion, poverty, housing insecurity, low rates of literacy, high rates of incarceration and a myriad of problems that mark our 'otherness'.

Relationship between mental and physical illness

How mental illness is linked with physical illness in a genetic or biochemical sense is little understood. It would appear some mental illnesses are intrinsically linked with particular diseases. Whatever this nexus, while acknowledged statistically, it is yet to be fully understood.

What is known clearly is that some medications used to treat the symptoms of mental illness, especially the atypical antipsychotics, are associated with the metabolic syndrome that leads to diabetes and cardiovascular illness. Part of the explanation here is that psych medications can cause the weight gain and sedation that make it harder to keep slim and active. But, it is also now acknowledged that they also cause elevated blood glucose and fats quite independently of weight gain or 'lifestyle'.

Fat really is a pharmacological issue and a LapBand is not the answer!

Applying the evidence

There is now a fairly well-agreed set of evidence-informed psychosocial interventions that are effective for people with 'serious mental illness' (Kreyenbuhl et al., 2010; Mueser et al., 2013):

- family psychoeducation for reducing relapses and rehospitalisations
- cognitive remediation to improve cognitive functioning
- supported employment assisting people return to the competitive workplace
- social skills training to improve social and community functioning
- CBT to reduce psychotic symptoms
- illness self-management training to reduce symptom distress and relapses
- integrated treatment for co-occurring substance abuse or dependence

Assertive community treatment (ACT) is also usually mentioned in this connection, as are a number of 'promising practices' for which there is emerging evidence, including supported housing and cognitive remediation (Ventura et al., 2019; Goering & Streiner, 2015; Australian Housing and Urban Research Institute AHURI, 2017). However, the mainstay of mental health treatment remains medication, evidenced by the high rates of GPs prescribing antidepressant and anti-anxiety medications and the use of antipsychotic medication for people experiencing psychosis, especially people with schizophrenia (AIHW, 2019). There are many reasons for this. One of the most fundamental is an entrenched practice culture, dominated by the medical model, that focuses on the containment of risk over active support of recovery (Harvey & O'Hanlon, 2013). Another problem is the difficulty in translating the recommended interventions to 'real-world' consumers and situations. In any case, social workers have been much less active in research than psychiatrists (where studies are often funded by large pharmaceutical companies) and psychologists, so there are significant gaps in the 'research base' for the interventions fundamental to our approach.

In general terms, a feature of some evidence-informed approaches is a rather narrow focus on alleviation of symptoms, rather than psychosocial 'functioning' or quality of life. Indeed, if we define recovery as 'a way of living a satisfying, hopeful and contributing life even with the limitations caused by illness' (Anthony, 1993, p. 527), we might conclude that much broader measures are necessary if we are to focus on the most meaningful outcomes. The relevant question for research and evaluation – so far largely unaddressed – is 'What is the evidence that this approach leads to satisfying lives or other recovery goals such as social inclusion?' (McPherson et al., 2009). Nevertheless, there really can be no excuse for working in ignorance of available knowledge, and social workers should ensure that they are familiar with the available evidence in a changing field.

Social workers as case managers

Case management, such an essential part of modern mental health systems, has its origins in social casework. The model of case management most prevalent in Australia has been called 'clinical and rehabilitation-based case management' (Fossey et al., 2012), a model that seeks to integrate and coordinate psychosocial aspects of care with psychiatric treatment and direct therapeutic (or clinical) work. In this model, the case worker simultaneously applies specific mental health clinical skills, establishes and maintains a sustained relationship, and works with the client in natural and formal environmental systems, and interventions are focused on three domains (Kanter, 1989):

- the environment (through linkage with community resources, consultation with families and other carers, maintaining and expanding social networks, collaborating with treatment services and advocacy)
- the client (through individual psychotherapy, developing living skills and psychoeducation)
- the relationship between the client and the environment (through crisis intervention and monitoring)

There is an explicit acknowledgement of the importance of continuity of care, flexibly altering the level of support and structure in response to the client's changing circumstances.

The *processes* of case management are familiar to social workers trained in social casework. There is a systematic and collaborative approach to:

- assessment of the client's needs,
- planning and coordination of the treatment or intervention,
- monitoring and review of the symptoms of mental illness and other aspects of the client's situation and progress,
- planning for case closure or discharge.

Case management in mental health does not deserve its image as a routine, 'common-denominator' activity. The case management role is crucially important for many clients because when it is done well it combines a number of critical factors:

It provides a therapeutic relationship.
It provides access to services.
It coordinates and interweaves medical and other treatment for mental illness with psychosocial intervention aimed to support clients to fulfil major life roles.

In practice, case management systems can become stretched and strained and can stray from these principles and degenerate into routine monitoring with an emphasis on risk control. Under such conditions, they may lose their effectiveness, but there is better empirical evidence for the efficacy of more intensive 'full service' models of case management such as assertive community treatment (ACT), which has strong social work origins (Mowbray & Holter, 2002), is based in outreach and seeks to engage with clients in natural community settings (Mueser et al., 2013).

We observed earlier some of the problems with the term *case*, and the term *case management* is even more problematic as it seems to suggest control and direction, rather than support for the recovery of people experiencing mental illness. Further, it may conjure up ideas of control and direction that are not appropriate to the role. Case managers themselves need to think through and be very clear about exactly what, if anything, they really seek to 'manage' as they carry out this complex role.

To do it well, case managers need skill and experience in engagement, assessment, planning, therapy and working with complex social networks. Case workers are there for the long haul and are in crisis situations with individuals and families. Their work requires that judgements always need to be made about priorities. The potential of the work is such that no one could possibly do it all, and the case worker needs commitment and resilience. At its core, case management is a form of work that calls for a willingness to engage with clients and their families in their daily lives, exactly where social workers have traditionally aimed to work.

From Noel: case managers in hospitals

Case managers are based in the community, but in most services their role is to work with the client wherever they may be, including during any periods of hospital stay. Indeed, at times of crisis such as hospitalisation, the case manager role can really come into its own. Psychiatric hospital staff necessarily have a very partial view of the life situation of consumers, coming to know them at a point when they are most unwell and perhaps most vulnerable. It is also often a time when the person's social support system is under great stress. Hospital staff meet clients outside their normal social milieu, and it can be difficult or even impossible for them to establish and maintain an image of their patients in their normal social roles – parent, partner, son or daughter, friend, worker and so on. At times like this, it can be crucial to have the longitudinal view of someone who knows the client over time and knows something of the client's world and their place in it. The decision about the right time to leave hospital, for example, will depend on whether it is the right time in the person's process of recovery. This is an area that community-based workers are likely to understand much better than the hospital staff.

Mental health social workers outside the public sector

The private practice sector in mental health social work in Australia has always been relatively small, but it is growing very rapidly. In recent years, the Australian government has provided Medicare rebates for mental health social work within a range of schemes, the largest of which are currently the Better Access to Mental Health Care and Access to Allied Psychological Services (ATAPS) programs (Department of Health and Ageing, 2010). There is an accreditation scheme to ensure that mental health social workers in Australia have and maintain the clinical skills for this work. Under these programs, benefits are available for a specific range of interventions, based on a brief model, including:

psychoeducation (including motivational interviewing),
CBT (including behavioural interventions and cognitive interventions),
relaxation strategies (including progressive muscle relaxation and controlled breathing),
skills training (including problem-solving skills and training, anger management, social skills training, communications training, stress management and parenting programs),
interpersonal therapy (especially for depression).

There is flexibility to include narrative therapy for Aboriginal and Torres Strait Islander people (Australian Government Department of Health and Ageing, 2006).

These forms of intervention have been called *focused psychological strategies* and are said to be 'evidence based', although their effectiveness in real-world primary settings is more difficult to establish (Moulding et al., 2007). We know that the clients of accredited mental health social workers often experience complex problems, including poor or unstable housing, low incomes and unemployment, social isolation, domestic violence, discrimination, relationship difficulties, and grief and loss. When funding is available to address only specific aspects of a mental health problem, it is more difficult to broaden the focus to include the social context and social consequences of those problems, despite their importance. So far, it seems most social workers have been able to negotiate these difficulties in a way that has brought benefit to their clients (Pirkis et al., 2010).

In 2010, mental health social workers waged a successful campaign against government attempts to reduce the participation of social workers in these arrangements. The campaign relied on an argument that social work participation in the programs was important for addressing social disadvantage (Mendes et al., 2012).

Gaining mental health accreditation

The Australian Association of Social Workers oversees accredited mental health social workers (AMHSW) in Australia. There are six criteria to the accreditation process for social workers:

Criteria 1: Hold current membership of the AASW
Criteria 2: Have at least two years full-time equivalent (FTE) post-qualifying social work experience in a mental health setting. An applicant must be able to articulate how their experience meets the AASW Practice Standards for Mental Health Social Workers, 2008b, 2014
Criteria 3: Have received at least two years full-time equivalent (FTE) post-qualifying supervision in a mental health field
Criteria 4: Have met the Continuing Professional Development (CPD) requirements
Criteria 5: Demonstrate ability and knowledge of clinical social work practice
Criteria 6: Arrange an employer or supervisor to provide a referee statement

Maintaining mental health accreditation

To remain eligible to provide mental health services as a Medicare provider, social workers must maintain their AMHSW status, including maintaining CPD and supervision requirements.

AMHSWs are required to complete 50 hours of CPD activities each year, including 20 hours relevant to mental health practice and ten hours relevant to the current list of Focused Psychological Strategies. These strategies are a requirement set by Medicare for all allied health professionals to ensure ongoing eligibility for providing services under the Better Access Initiative (AASW, 2020).

From Ann: funding models and models of practice

Although social workers welcome government acknowledgement of their knowledge and skills by providing funding for private practice, there is a risk in restricting interventions to those prescribed in the funding model. When someone is hungry, or homeless, or fearful, focused psychological strategies may not work well. Social workers need to work tirelessly towards developing models of practice, assessing their effectiveness and promoting this to policy 'wonks' and government.

Conclusion

In this chapter, we have shown how different work settings within the mental health system require us to work in quite different ways – such as operating within a particular model of case coordination or case management, with a particular therapeutic approach or with a particular focus on advocacy. Some of these sit more easily with the principles of social casework, such as those based in systems thinking or narrative approaches, those oriented to recovery and those that value advocacy and activism. Models that emphasise individual pathology present much greater challenges, but the principles outlined in this chapter will provide a solid basis for social casework in mental health, whatever the service setting.

QUESTIONS FOR PRACTICE

1. What would you need to learn and what skills would you need to develop in order to fit Ann's requirements for a case manager? What personal qualities would you bring to the role?
2. Ann asks, 'Is it possible for people with mental illness to have a rich and fulfilling life?' What stops people from achieving this simple goal?
3. How would you manage the issues of power and control in a case management role?
4. Is it possible to acquire an objective truth about what works in mental health work?
5. How can social workers respond creatively and safely to risky situations in mental health?

Websites

Centre for Clinical Interventions

Resources for mental health practitioners.
www.cci.health.wa.gov.au

Centre for Mental Health (UK)

Criminal justice; policy; training; physical health; employment and recovery.
www.centreformentalhealth.org.uk

Commonwealth Department of Health

Practice guidelines and standards for services and professionals. Literature reviews. National Practice Standards for the Mental Health Workforce.
www.health.gov.au

Dulwich Centre

Narrative therapy training, research, publishing.
www.dulwichcentre.com.au

Mind Australia

Resources on recovery include links to literature, research, government policies.
www.mindaustralia.org.au

National Institute for Health and Care Excellence (NICE) (UK)

Provides national guidance and advice to improve health and social care; sets standards for social care; treatment guidelines.
www.nice.org.uk

Research into Recovery

Site of the Recovery Research Team at the Institute of Psychiatry, London, with resources for clinical practice.
www.researchintorecovery.com

St Luke's Innovative Resources

Strengths-based resources: cards, books, training and other conversation-building tools for practitioners.
www.innovativeresources.org

8 Working with people with mental illness across service systems

In this chapter, we will focus on social work at the points where mental health and social life intersect and in situations where other kinds of health and welfare services are delivered. Fortunately, there is a much better understanding developing at the level of public policy that health and wellbeing are intimately connected with social and psychological factors. On the ground, this simply means that we should expect to find that mental and physical health and psychosocial problems will probably be interconnected. In Chapter 1 we defined the domain of social work practice as that of the social context and social consequences of mental illness. Clearly, the interface between mental illness and a range of other social problems like homelessness, income security, family welfare and family violence is a key aspect of social work practice.

For example, one person may be dealing with ongoing physical ill-health, depressive symptoms, the experience of violence at home, a history of sexual abuse and financial problems. Another – perhaps the perpetrator of violence – might at the same time be contending with substance abuse issues and the associated effects on physical wellbeing, as well as social role problems and difficulty in managing anger. Depending on the service setting, 'the point of entry' may be the physical health issues, or the violence, or perhaps the financial difficulties, and the person may or may not want to deal with other aspects of their situation. It makes sense, however, to try to understand the interconnections between the difficulties and, if possible, to deal with them in an integrated way. Even if the first line of response is, say, a pharmacological response to one person's experience of depression, there will be value in a broader approach that addresses some of the psychosocial issues that might be relevant to the recovery process (Van Hook, 2003). Separating out and isolating one problem for intervention often leads to failure (Sessions & Lightburn, 2006).

As we identified in the first chapter, the ubiquity of mental illness means that no matter where social workers choose to practise they will invariably work with people who have mental health problems. It is commonly said that the rates of mental disorder in the population are of the order of 'one in five', but even this is a substantial underestimation if we are talking about lifetime risk, in which case 'one in two is much more like it' (McGorry, 2005, p. 6). The rates of mental illness in the caseload of most social workers – wherever they work – are likely to be

DOI: 10.4324/9781003148913-10

considerably higher, of the order of 50 per cent at any given point according to an authoritative source (Huxley, 2008). What has been said about the primary health care system (Regier et al., 1993) is true also of social welfare services: these are the de facto mental health systems because of the critical role that they can and do play in identifying and caring for people with mental health problems who are not receiving care or treatment from mental health services. Almost two-thirds of people with a mental health problem do not use or have access to any form of mental health service (McGorry, 2005; Slade et al., 2009), and for people aged 16–24 (the age range with the highest prevalence of mental illness) the situation is even worse (Reavley et al., 2010). Social workers in all settings should be able to identify and respond to mental health problems and their effects. The experience of mental illness will often colour and complicate other human problems, including poverty, housing, physical health, and family and relationship difficulties.

Similarly, mental health social workers will often need to work in partnership with social workers in other practice settings. On the basis of a collaborative partnership with the client, the social worker will often need to engage with a range of other service providers and community members as required by the specific needs and circumstances of each client. The need for social network interventions is increasing in the current environment (Whiteford & McKeon, 2012) because many clients have complex needs that require joint work across the boundaries of multiple service systems (for example, income security, child protection and family welfare, justice, health, alcohol and drug services, and so on) and engagement with important systems in the client's life (for example, employment, education, extended family systems and so on). Mental health services are frequently criticised for being unresponsive and poorly integrated with the community and other health and welfare services. They should not be a 'one-stop shop'. Social workers need to adopt an informed, planned and skilled approach to working at the interface between the mental health service system and the community to ensure that mental health care is provided in an integrated way, to advocate alongside their clients for their needs to be adequately met and to build new service networks to address service gaps, such as inadequacies in affordable and accessible housing and vocational opportunities.

Recognition and early intervention

Social workers working in many different settings are in a good position to recognise and respond to mental health problems, and this opens up the possibility of early intervention and also health promotion. Better recognition is the first step. In the case of psychotic disorders, for example, there is evidence that being in contact with a health care professional may actually delay recognition and treatment of the mental illness, perhaps because professionals may not be acquainted with the phenomenon and may tend to attribute the difficulties to other conditions or normal adolescent behaviour (Reed, 2008). Certainly, the early signs of psychosis that normally occur in adolescence, such as sleep disturbance, depression or withdrawal, do not always amount to a clear-cut picture of mental illness. It is not a good idea to be quick to label such early warning signs as mental illness, but social workers *should* be quick to identify the *possibility* of mental illness and be willing and ready to discuss this with the individual concerned and – wherever it is reasonable in the circumstances – with family and friends. All will potentially benefit from support, including support in gaining access to good assessment and treatment via a general practitioner or a specialised mental health service such as a community mental health centre. General principles of early intervention are set out in Chapter 10.

In Chapter 6, we set out some steps to assist in the recognition of common mental health problems. Like general practitioners, social workers will often encounter people who are feeling anxious, depressed or distressed by a relationship or life crisis, suicidal thoughts or other mental health concerns. Social workers have particular expertise in working with people whose mental health problems coexist with other problems, such as family distress, drug and alcohol abuse, unemployment, disability, poverty and trauma. Social work expertise in working collaboratively with other professionals is a distinguishing feature of their approach to primary mental health care.

Consultation and partnership principles

Service responses that bring good mental health care to people in everyday health and welfare settings will almost always be based on partnerships between social workers and other health and welfare professionals with specialist expertise. The skill of providing consultation within a service network is an essential part of the work of a mental health social worker. The person providing the consultation brings expertise: specialist knowledge about mental health problems, skill in responding, knowledge and influence within their agency and service network, and the willingness and ability to impart their expertise to others. More than this, effective consultation is a partnership:

> Consultation is joint exploration partly of the question at hand, partly exploring the alternatives for managing it, and partly exploring what there is in oneself, in the consultative relationship and in the work setting that helps the work advance.
>
> (Luntz, 1999, p. 28)

Mental health consultation may centre around concerns about an individual client or a group of clients and may focus on the knowledge and skill of the worker(s) or organisational systems and policies. It is useful to distinguish three levels of consultation, based on the work of Jennifer Luntz (1999, 2000), who articulated the 'Victorian model' of consultation:

In primary consultation, the consultant is first briefed and then meets the client, and then a joint decision is taken about what might happen next.

In secondary consultation, the consultant does not actually meet the client, but rather discusses the situation and offers suggestions based on information that is put together by the consultee.

In tertiary consultation, the discussions focus more on agency structure and functioning, rather than the interactions between workers and their clients.

Social workers need to develop skill in both seeking and providing consultation. Some mental health services identify consultation as a specialist function and establish specialist teams to support and enhance the capacity of primary care providers, especially general practitioners and community health services, to recognise and respond to mental disorders more effectively. They provide consultation, liaison, education and training services to primary care providers working with people with a mental illness.

From Ann: some guiding principles

Each contact with a person who may have a mental health problem presents the social worker with a 'window of opportunity' or 'point of entry' to establish a relationship. The 'presenting problem' is often the tip of the iceberg.

All things are interconnected.

Early intervention can either occur early in the development of a disorder, or when a person first reaches out for help. Early intervention is the opposite of the revolving door.

To avoid departmentalisation of problems, inter-sectoral networking is critical.

Remember:

Respectful listening – It is critical to listen respectfully to the client's account of their lived experience.

Recovery – A focus on recovery puts due emphasis on promoting resilience, emphasises strengths and allows a hopeful attitude to guide the healing relationship.

Resources – Social workers are privileged to be aware of knowledge, resources and skills which could be of value to clients, families and friends. Social workers can provide effective 'jumper leads' to kick-start a client's recovery.

Referral – It is never enough to 'refer on' a client for assistance with one of their presenting problems, such as homelessness or need for urgent dental care. The next step is: Was the referral successful? If not, what alternatives might exist?

Respectful collaboration – Working closely in collaboration with other professionals is key.

Co-occurring substance use problems

The coexistence of mental health and alcohol and/or other drug problems is very common. Its incidence varies among different groups, but it is fair to assume that it is the norm rather than the exception. Substance use is a major factor driving the higher prevalence of mental health problems among younger people (aged 16 to 24) (Reavley et al., 2010). Treatment options in the highly specialised area of co-occurring substance use and mental illness have been summarised in the major report *Guidelines on the Management of Co-occurring Alcohol and Other Drug and Mental Health Conditions in Alcohol and Other Drug Treatment Settings* (Marel et al., 2016).

The Queensland Health Policy on treatment of co-occurring mental health and alcohol and other drug problems (Queensland Health, 2008) provides a good overview of the principles for intervention and service design, which have been summarised as follows (Lee et al., 2013):

Effective *collaborative partnerships* of mental health and alcohol and other drug services with professionals in primary care, social services, housing, criminal justice, education and related fields are required.

Individuals with dual diagnosis are the *expectation, not the exception.*

An *integrated care approach* that ensures continuity and quality between mental health and alcohol and other drug services, as well as across other service sectors, is needed.

A *'no wrong door' approach* is used that provides people with, or links them to, appropriate services regardless of where they enter the system of care.

The development and maintenance of a *therapeutic alliance* based on mutual respect are required.

Integrated service provision involves a *biopsychosocial approach* comprising an array of physical, psychological and social service interventions in the provision of engagement, assessment, treatment and care.

A *harm-minimisation approach* is used and promoted.

A holistic, *recovery-based approach* is used in the provision of assessment, treatment and care, involving direct service provision for mental health and alcohol and other drug problems and effective linkage with the broader social service network.

Within the treatment context, both mental health and alcohol and other drug problems are *considered of primary importance to the clinical presentation.*

Needs change over time.

The active participation of the *person, primary carers, family or significant others* in the treatment and care occurs wherever possible.

Working across systems requires flexibility, patience and an endless capacity for doodling as you play 'phone tag'.

Intervention is often challenging. People with psychosis and co-occurring substance use problems may see less good reason to change and be harder to engage and keep involved. There is no single correct dual diagnosis intervention and no single correct program; intervention should be individualised. Clients will proceed at their own pace, and it can be very hard to end an addiction, so it is important to give credit for this. Mental health services should be 'welcoming' to people with dual diagnosis (Minkoff, 2001), and access to either mental health or substance misuse treatment should not be restricted on the basis of one or the other problem; rather, the aim is to provide continuity of care in an integrated way. Even in programs where abstinence is a *goal*, it should not be a pre-condition of intervention. Assistance with fundamental needs such as housing will often be required. The 'stages of change' model is well known and can be useful for structuring and targeting psychosocial interventions through pre-contemplation, contemplation, preparation, action and maintenance stages (Prochaska et al., 1992).

Cognitive-behavioural approaches are employed successfully with people with dual diagnosis, and the foundation for most psychosocial intervention is motivational interviewing (Hughes & Phillips, 2012). Motivational interviewing emphasises personal choice, responsibility and awareness of the risks and benefits of substance use (Horsfall et al., 2009). It seeks to make links between the person's life goals and problems related to substance use. There is active engagement around the actual concerns of the client, and the worker also supportively fleshes out and challenges any ambivalence towards substance use and the client's interest in change. Typically, work of this kind would seek to develop strategies for avoiding specific situations at high risk of substance use and build on alternative constructive, non-substance-related activities. This approach is consistent with a harm-minimisation approach, which recognises that users have an active role in making choices and taking action around their drug use, and focuses on the harmful consequences of use. Motivational interviewing is often complemented by cognitive-behavioural and group and family interventions. Some of the same principles of good psychosocial work with people with mental illness 'alone' apply in at least equal measure: aim to establish a therapeutic relationship, work contextually, work actively and assertively over the long haul and pay attention to warning signs of relapse.

Housing and homelessness

Safe, affordable, good-quality and secure housing is a critical factor in maintaining wellbeing. Housing is not simply a matter of providing a physical dwelling. Housing problems may result from poor-quality housing and housing conditions, insecurity and debt relating to housing, and the lack of a feeling of 'home' (Robinson & Adams, 2008). Homelessness itself is commonly associated with mental illness in the public imagination, and for good reason. A significant minority of homeless people have a mental illness: people with psychosis make up 18–29 per cent of the 'homeless population' and problems with substance use are also common. Recent research undertaken by the Australian Housing and Urban Research Institute (AHURI) (www.ahuri.edu.au/policy-analysis/mental-health-and-housing) estimates that 32 per cent of people accessing homelessness services in Australia experience mental health problems.

Mental illness often makes it more difficult for a person to break out of homelessness, but the relationship between mental illness and homelessness is a complex one. There is some evidence that it is often the homelessness that comes first (Chamberlain et al., 2007). People come into contact with homelessness services for a range of reasons, including:

interpersonal issues such as domestic violence, relationship breakdown and conflict, and the need for time out from family;
financial reasons;
accommodation difficulties such as overcrowding, eviction and emergency accommodation ending;
health issues such as mental health problems and problematic use of drugs (AIHW, 2007).

Social workers who are working with public housing tenants will encounter many people with mental illness – particularly psychosis and alcohol and drug problems, personality disorder and, in the case of older people, dementia. Many of these people are already using mental health services, but typically this is independent of their housing providers (AIHW, 2013). Social housing is the largest single component of non-health expenditure for people with a mental health problem in Australia (Medibank & Nous Group, 2013).

People with mental illness may move in and out of homelessness (Holmes et al., 2005). Poor housing conditions – such as those in many boarding houses – can serve to make mental health problems worse. For example, some people may seek to avoid the violence and intimidation associated with such settings by withdrawing and becoming more isolated. It is useful to identify individuals and groups at particular risk of becoming homeless and to put in the effort to help them maintain or re-establish housing. Young people coming out of care are one such group, and older people with psychotic disorders are another (Craig & Timms, 2000). Improvements in housing conditions will often have a positive effect on mental health and wellbeing, as is demonstrated by the results of programs to improve environmental and housing conditions so that people's living conditions are healthy and safe (Blackman & Harvey, 2001). Indeed there is good evidence to suggest that providing 'housing first', rather than focusing on treatment compliance, contributes as much to good outcomes for people as effective community services (Padgett et al. (2006).

From Ann: addressing homelessness among people with mental illness – a dilemma

In *The Soloist*, journalist Steve Lopez (2008) recalls his first meeting with Nathaniel Ayers, a 'beyond 50' African American living in Skid Row who played a two-string violin, next to his shopping cart, which was heaped over with all his belongings. Lopez subsequently learned that, 30 years earlier, Ayers had held a scholarship at the Juilliard School of Music. Then came his psychotic breakdown and homelessness. Lopez wants to change Ayers's life – to find him accommodation and help him reconnect with his family and musical career.

One of the central dilemmas Lopez explores is this: should they first assess and treat the disorder and then connect Nathaniel with financial support, housing and so on, or is it most important to gain his trust, build a sustaining relationship and establish a home, and might Nathaniel then choose to seek treatment?

Of course, real life is rarely about an 'either/or', but about the messy reality left when the binary is shattered: structured intervention versus supportive environment.

When people with a mental illness make contact with homelessness services, it is a 'critical moment and it is crucial to get the right sort of assistance quickly' (Chamberlain et al., 2007, p. 7). Many specialised services use an outreach or linkage model. The biggest issue is to get the services effectively to the people: accommodation services must be linked directly with mental health services, and the response has to be quick, non-bureaucratic and at once highly individualised and wide-ranging in order to meet different individuals' needs (Craig & Timms, 2000).

However, people's capacity to make meaningful choices about housing is constrained by poverty and the lack of low-cost and social housing. Supported housing programs for people with mental illness are an important part of the needed response. In the early stages of the deinstitutionalisation era, supported housing was conceived on a continuum, the aim being for people to move progressively to more independent accommodation. Congregate care settings in which people share close quarters under strict house rules are constraining, and this model of group living is no longer dominant. In recognition of the simple and unsurprising fact that most (but not all) people prefer to live in a dwelling of their own, and not necessarily with another person with a mental illness, most programs now attempt to bring the support to the person. Supported housing that offers people their own house or flat on the basis of their preferences can be 'a form of personal liberation' (Padgett, 2012, p. 720). One study of people with a mental illness who maintain successful housing tenure found that they regarded the most important element of their success as being able to manage regular rent payments (Healy et al., 2005), so effective recovery-oriented money management programs can make a critical difference (Elbogen et al., 2013).

People with physical ill-health

In Australia, people with mental illness may experience the kind of health outcomes normally associated with the developing world. Physical and mental health problems are often related. There is increasing recognition of the fact that people with mental health problems tend to have poorer physical health, and much of the gap has social determinants. For many people, poor physical health compounds the burden of shame and stigma associated with living with mental illness.

From Ann: where the mental and physical collide

Long-term use of psychotropic medication can have some unfortunate consequences. Weight gain and inactivity may lead to a diagnosis of type 2 diabetes. Additionally, there's now some evidence that some medications affect lipid and blood sugar levels independent of their effect on weight and activity.

Exacerbations of the mental illness may require increased dosage of psychiatric medications which may increase blood sugar levels, requiring changes to diabetes medication. Then, diabetes leads to increased vulnerability to infections, and being sick means that the experience of mental illness is harder to live with. And then, people with diabetes are at an increased risk of stroke and cardiovascular disease, both of which worsen depression. It's not a pretty picture.

Yet there is a real danger that this interest in physical health has unintended consequences, making people with mental illness subject to further professional and societal 'gaze', where they are observed, classified, judged and further regarded as 'the other'. Government policy, the complex systems of service delivery, the actions (or lack of) by health professionals and the responsibilities of Big Pharma also need to be held to account. This is about making the person political and about including the critical with the clinical.

The life expectancy for people with schizophrenia, bipolar disorder and other long-term mental health conditions is between ten and 25 years below that of the general population (Osborn, 2012). People with a mental illness become seriously ill and die at a much faster rate than the general population, and this 'mortality gap' is currently increasing in Australia (Lawrence et al., 2013), as in most developed countries. The overwhelming majority of excess deaths are due to physical illness such as cardiovascular disease and metabolic complications (Lawrence et al., 2013), and much of the mortality gap results from death at an early age, not late in life (Chwastiak & Tek, 2009). Suicide accounts for only about 14 per cent of the higher death rate of people with a mental illness. People with mental illness experience a higher occurrence of risk factors for many chronic diseases and some types of cancer and suffer from the adverse physical effects of some psychiatric medications and poorer access to health care than the population as a whole. Poor health monitoring may result from 'diagnostic overshadowing', with health care providers attributing physical symptoms to a person's mental health problem (Sinding et al.,

2013). Discrimination on the part of busy health care providers who 'see' only the mental illness may lead to a failure to provide equal access to health care in hospital emergency departments and other primary and specialist health care settings. This is one reason for lower levels of routine screening and proper treatment.

Many of these health problems and excess deaths are preventable. The National Mental Health Commission (2012) has recently identified physical health as an urgent area for action. Similarly, an international consensus statement to improve the health of young people with psychosis has been released (International Physical Health in Youth [iphYs] Working Group, 2013). A focus on youth and prevention needs to be complemented by strategies that target older consumers as well, including improving professional and consumer awareness and education, diagnosis and management, and enhanced inter-sectoral links between mental health services and physical health systems. Yet much of the gap is indicative of a lived experience of poverty, housing insecurity, marginalisation and discrimination. It is not simply a matter of individuals taking more responsibility for their own health, nor is it a matter only for doctors. Social work skills in assessment, referral and systemic advocacy can make a critical difference in the context of a respectful and hopeful helping relationship.

From Ann: a confession

It's time to fess up, put aside my shame and embarrassment, and confide in you, gentle reader, about my various, complicated and costly health problems. I've been taking an array of psych medications since I was 19. I currently take three different ones for my bipolar disorder – an antidepressant, a mood stabiliser and an antipsychotic. Then there're another five different tablets for diabetes, cholesterol and blood pressure. Finally, there're three other pills for other diseases that are chronic, unpleasant and incapacitating.

In a way I'm fortunate – I can advocate for myself with my GP and various specialists. I'm organised and informed, I remind them when blood tests are due, I turn up to appointments and fill the prescriptions. Being treated for my physical illnesses may mean I'm less likely to die prematurely, but I don't expect to make old or healthy bones. It isn't easy keeping all the mental and physical health balls in the air, but I have to say I'm not a bad case manager for myself – but that's because I'm a social worker who has worked in health! But how very confusing, alienating and confronting it must be for my consumer sisters and brothers.

I'm repeatedly struck by the lack of communication between my mental health team and GP but suspect this isn't unusual. If I didn't advise both systems about changes in medications or the results of blood tests or other investigations, neither would know! This ignorance or disinterest can be potentially life-threatening because of drug interactions and the effects of certain diseases on other diseases. GP systems of care are also really inefficient and haphazard. I'd like to see their computers generate reminders about tests due, or when repeat prescriptions should be written. Would it be asking too much for GPs to proactively follow up patients who miss appointments? All the policies and procedures and consensus statements in the world won't make a difference if no one heeds them!

A final word about money: paying for prescriptions and visits to doctors and various tests is really expensive. Most people who live with psychosis are reliant on Centrelink benefits and pensions. Even with a health care card to subsidise the cost of medical appointments, pathology and prescriptions, difficult decisions have to be made – 'Can I afford to get this prescription or do I really need to eat today?' The reality of the cost of health care these days is that everyone (doctors, chemists) wants a co-contribution. So, if I can't afford to see a doctor or pay for a prescription, does this mean that I am 'non-compliant'?

Working with people experiencing poverty

In developed countries, the association between low socio-economic status and mental health problems is 'strong and significant' (Das et al., 2007, p. 467). People in the lowest economic strata are about two and a half times more likely than those in the highest strata to have a mental illness (Bauer et al., 2005). There are a number of ways to account for this relationship, each of which may be relevant to an individual's situation. The so-called social causation hypothesis suggests that poverty leads to mental health problems because of stress, the circumstances of deprivation or poor access to amelioration and treatment. The 'drift' hypothesis suggests that poverty is a *consequence* of mental illness. Third, the relationship may be due to other factors associated with both poverty and mental illness, such as poor physical health or exposure to violence (Das et al., 2007). These issues are contested, although there is considerable evidence that class position generally precedes the disorder (Siegel, 2008). For our purposes, however, this is not really the point. Whatever the cause, the association is strong. People with mental health problems like schizophrenia and depression are much more likely to be unemployed and isolated from their family and to have poor educational outcomes. Mental health problems are much more prevalent among income support recipients than others (Kiely & Butterworth, 2013). Many have experienced hardship and trauma in their lives, including events such as unemployment and redundancy, separation and divorce, and disability. These are risk factors for the development of mental health problems and will tend to affect adversely the outcome of existing mental illness.

The important thing to remember in practice is that psychosocial factors are a significant part of the picture, a common trigger for mental illness. The 'stress-vulnerability' model of mental illness expresses this simply. In the context of a vulnerability to mental illness (due to one or more genetic, physical, environmental, psychological or social factors in combination), a significant stressor provides the trigger for the onset of mental illness. For example, significant loss, a difficult relationship and financial problems may all lead to the onset of depression (and, of course, exacerbate the ongoing experience of depression). The experience of victimisation, such as that resulting from physical or sexual abuse in families or physical or sexual harassment at work, is another clear factor associated with depression as well as traumatic stress. The stress-vulnerability model tends to emphasise the psychological experience of stress, so it is well to bear in mind that such psychological experience is often linked to external (social) stressors.

For people living in deprived circumstances, there is a link between common mental health problems and poor community resources and connections (sometimes referred to as *social capital*) (Stafford et al., 2008). Mental health problems are associated with social disadvantage, trauma and stressful life events, and the experience of poverty is itself potentially associated with many related stressors: isolation, uncertainty, frequent negative events and little access to help. So it is unsurprising that sadness and low morale are associated with poverty. For example, low-income women who are also mothers have a rate of depression (25 per cent) about double the rate for all women (National Alliance on Mental Illness, 2008), and in Australia, sole parents on income support have a rate of anxiety and depression between three and four times the national average, with 45 per cent of lone mothers experiencing a diagnosable mental illness (Butterworth, 2003). Exposure to traumatic events may result not only in PTSD but also in depression, anxiety disorders, substance misuse and adjustment disorders, and it may be associated with other problems that cause distress such as financial difficulty, housing problems, lack of information and relationship breakdown (Bisson et al., 2007).

From Ann: the community health social worker's role

Although my friend Kay's doctors would link her steady progress towards recovery to judicious use of medication, I would like to think that Kay herself would also emphasise the role the community health social worker played in helping her to:

secure accommodation with a spare bedroom for visits from her young son in foster care,

negotiate with Child Protection to have overnight access visits for her son,

establish Centrepay deductions from her disability pension so that her rent and money for electricity and the phone are deducted before her pension reaches her bank account,

make a referral to the Mates Program and link her with a buddy/friend to meet her weekly for coffee,
link her with a mentor she can meet for coffee and encouragement,
find a peer worker who is also a mother and who can support her in developing her parenting skills,
find a neighbourhood centre for cooking classes and ideas about stretching her limited budget further.

The toll taken by poverty on human development and emotional health is due to cumulative rather than single sources of stress (Sessions & Lightburn, 2006). Physical and psychosocial conditions in the homes of people living in poverty increase the risk of harm to the psychological wellbeing of children as they grow and develop; conversely, improving the economic wellbeing of poor families translates into improved psychological wellbeing for young people (Dearing, 2008). Generalist social work methods, such as strengths-based and problem-solving models, can make a real difference to mental wellbeing in the context of an ecological understanding and a commitment to empowerment and social justice (Bauer et al., 2005), disrupting the cycle of poverty and mental illness by helping to achieve tangible improvements in people's living conditions, social relationships and inner resources.

Income security and workforce participation

Contemporary social welfare policy tends to support measures to increase workforce participation for people with mental illness, partly as a way of breaking the cycle of poverty and ill-health (unstable housing, inadequate food and clothing, heavy reliance on emergency relief agencies and regular disconnections of electricity and telephone) and partly as a way of minimising the costs of social welfare. Participation in work is one of the most important markers of social inclusion and, for many people with mental illness, one of the most significant elements of recovery. It may bring not only greater financial security but also meaning, development of personal skills and qualities, and many more personal and social connections. Non-participation in work and education is often associated with the early experience of mental health problems in young people (Rickwood et al., 2014), with consequences for later life. Effective programs for establishing and maintaining employment for people with mental health problems are well established in some places, but there is a huge unmet need in this area (Harvey et al., 2013; Waghorn, 2013). It may be relatively easy for private and other providers to offer employment support to people with mental health problems who have good employment prospects while effectively discriminating against those who are most disabled and hardest to place – people who also have a great deal to gain from workforce participation.

Allan Summers's job

Allan Summers is a man in his late twenties. A psychotic illness was diagnosed six years ago, but Allan had been experiencing difficulties well before that – he had been homeless since he was 14 and had not completed secondary schooling. In recent years, he had never found it easy to get on with others, he was edgy in social situations, and there was something about his appearance and manner that made him stand out. About two years ago, after he had spent some time in a psychiatric hospital, he decided to accept the offer of a place in a shared flat with connections to a recovery program that offered home-based outreach support. He faced many challenges there, including the challenge of getting on with his new flatmate.

One of Allan's biggest goals was to get a paying job – something he had never really been able to maintain. His key worker helped him to look, and they were both pleased and a bit surprised when Allan got a job that was advertised in the local paper, restacking supermarket shelves. The job involved shifts that started late at night and went into the early morning, and Allan found that this work seemed to suit him perfectly. He had no trouble adjusting to the hours, he learned the requirements of the job, and the money was better than anything he had received before. He loved the job. Each night he cycled to and from the supermarket. One night, just a month after he had started, some adolescent boys yelled abuse at him on his way home, and Allan shouted back at them. The next night, they were waiting to attack him. His head needed many stitches, and his bike was broken. It would be weeks before he could go back to work, and of course he did not have any sick leave to fall back on.

This was a catastrophe with many ramifications for Allan, but the wonderful thing was what the supermarket manager did: he bought Allan a new bike and held the job until he was well enough to return. It was an act of kindness and decency by someone who recognised the importance of the work to Allan and the fact that Allan was a good worker.

From Noel: supporting people to work

Psychosocial rehabilitation programs have been well established in Australia for many years now – residential rehabilitation, clubhouses, support for living skills, home-based outreach support and other good creative programs – but it's striking how hesitant we have been to really tackle the need to support people in employment, compared with some other parts of the world.

I remember when a new rehabilitation program was being set up in a 'good' suburb in Melbourne in the early 1980s and meeting a lot of opposition from the local community. They were sophisticated and well organised in their campaign to have the program moved to someone else's backyard. The director of the service was a creative and visionary man, and he decided to set up a 'home maintenance' service in the area. It was a deliberate strategy to maximise the face-to-face contact between the participants in the program and the community, and at the same time it offered participants an opportunity to learn and develop good practical skills, earn some money and provide a service to the community. Given the amount of hostility and suspicion in the community, I don't think I would have been brave enough to go ahead with this plan (let alone think of it!), but it was exactly right – the program established its place in the neighbourhood, and the home maintenance service thrived, as did many of the participants.

Nowadays, the good creative programs operate as social firms or support people in open employment. A recent radio program describing a cafe and catering business employing a significant number of people with a mental illness attracted callers critical of the enterprise because it was encouraging 'wage slavery' rather than personal growth. I suppose that I shouldn't be surprised by this new form of community opposition, but it seems terribly wrong-headed to me. We would never want to force people into work, and I agree that a lot of work is very low paid with poor conditions, but for most of us work is absolutely fundamental to our financial security and social success. I think it's essential that we do whatever we can to ensure that people with mental illness are not excluded from the opportunity to work in a good job with a decent wage.

Child and family welfare

It is only relatively recently that there has been an emphasis on supporting people with mental health problems in their parenting role and meeting the needs of children of parents with a mental illness. Social workers in Australia have played a leading role in redressing this striking neglect. Naturally, people with a mental illness can, and do, make very good parents, but often they need considerable support to do so. Children themselves are likely to experience problems with a lack of information and openness, predictability and instability, fear, loneliness, loss and sorrow (Trondsen, 2012). They may experience problems with their own development and mental health, and there may be protective concerns (Darlington & Feeney, 2008).

Services for meeting the needs of families where parents have a mental illness have tended to focus on the clinical treatment of mental illness within families and, often, on individual-level issues such as the knowledge and skills of parents and measures to improve the mental health of children. Yet, social factors such as poverty, stigma and poor housing are known to prevent good outcome for many such families. It follows that a range of social care agencies need to be involved in meeting these needs, and that interventions should include community development and public health approaches as well as individual and family-level education, treatment and support (Fraser et al., 2006; Siegenthaler et al., 2012). Work with families where a parent has a mental illness aims to strengthen and support children to enhance protective factors that contribute to the children's mental health while also identifying and reducing the risk factors in parents with a mental illness, their family and the community.

Parents have the right to the support they need in order to do their best for their children (Sayce, 1999) and to keep families together. Social workers can take some simple steps to support this: ask consumers about their children; find out where there is low-cost child care in the area; make people aware of respite programs, family support services, and mainstream parenting resources and self-help groups; discuss parenting issues as part of their work with consumers; support parenting and parental rights; and encourage the development of support services specific to parents. Parents with a mental illness will want to do the best for their families, but they may be constrained from seeking help for themselves and their children because of the fear of interference and lack of understanding from child protection services, and the possible loss of custody of their children.

Most parents with a mental illness are very good parents, but much mental illness is episodic, so for some families this means periods of particular difficulty from time to time. They may rightly fear that any sign of not coping will lead to catastrophic outside intervention. Social workers need to respond by developing close, respectful relationships with these parents to help them to manage crises and ensure that they have access to the community support they need to carry out their parenting role. It is important that parents who are particularly vulnerable have access to high-quality preventive early intervention that works intensively with families facing actual or potential child protection issues, such as programs that combine peer support, quality early education and personal development in a safe and supportive environment (Mondy & Mondy, 2008).

Of course, children will usually have caring and loving feelings towards their parents, even though they may well be distressed and sad because of what is happening to their parent and in the family. Sometimes the family will be relatively isolated from contact with other family members and friends. Somers (2007) found that the children of parents with schizophrenia experienced more psychiatric disturbance, more problems with school and less contact with relatives, and they spent more time at home. Children of sole parents who are mentally ill may be especially vulnerable, and there is evidence that substance abuse is a particularly potent factor in separating parents with mental illness from their children (Jones et al., 2008).

In child and family welfare settings, many families are experiencing mental health problems, either because the children have psychological or developmental difficulties or because there is an adult with a mental health problem. Parents with a mental illness are much more likely to be involved in the child welfare system and to have lost custody of their children. Families in which a parent has a mental illness are more likely to experience poverty, housing problems, family disruption, marital conflict, reduction in social and leisure activities, disruption of children's schooling and isolation (AICAFMHA, 2004). Difficulties commonly encountered include behavioural problems among children and parental mental illness: psychotic illness, drug and alcohol problems, and depression and anxiety. Grief associated with a child's disability may be a significant issue.

In order to meet the needs of children of parents with a mental illness, there needs to be an overall framework that looks at the system as a whole. Relationships are the key to tying the system together and connecting people to the services that they need. Connecting with new services is difficult and stressful for people, and we need to acknowledge that. Social workers who are able to establish the right relationship with families can try to support people in getting the help they need. Specialist mental health services have a pivotal role not only in recognising and addressing the needs of children in families where a parent has a mental illness but also as active sharers of expertise, deliberately working together with other parts of the service system rather than being suspicious and critical of other service providers. Families are generally not helped by provision of services in disconnected 'silos', with specialist mental health services in one place and specialist child and family welfare services in another.

Conclusion

In this chapter, we have seen how some social workers choose to specialise in mental health work and do so through specialist settings or other counselling roles. Others need to develop expertise in understanding and responding to mental health problems simply because they encounter these issues in virtually all fields of practice. The complex interplay of problems and challenges is the bread and butter of social work in many settings, and mental health problems are often a very big part of this picture. Social workers in everyday settings are very well placed to identify and support people experiencing mental health problems. Of course, this does not mean that personal difficulties should all be construed as psychiatric illness or that social workers working outside a mental health setting should attempt to provide 'treatment' to people experiencing psychological distress. Nevertheless, at the end of the day it is often the work that is done to address the real-world problems of people with mental health problems that really makes the difference.

QUESTIONS FOR PRACTICE

1 How can housing programs be made more responsive to the needs of people with mental health problems?
2 How can mental health and child protection services work together to ensure good outcomes for families?
3 What can social workers do to promote good physical health for people with mental health problems?
4 Can you suggest some ways that social workers might balance the need to support parents through a mental health crisis and still protect the safety and welfare of children?

Websites

Australian Drug Foundation

Information and research relevant to alcohol and other drugs.
www.adf.org.au

Children of Parents with a Mental Illness (COPMI)

Site for families, young people and professionals. Offers professional tools and information such as eLearning courses and evidence-based information and research.
www.copmi.net.au

Rethink Mental Illness

Provides a comprehensive range of materials for professionals in primary and secondary care. Includes material on the physical health needs of people affected by mental illness.
www.rethink.org

Health.Vic

Practical guidelines for mental health workers supporting parents with a mental illness.
www2.health.vic.gov.au

9 Working with families

Introduction

Social work with the families of people who have a mental illness has emerged as a major area of practice, yet a focus on families has always been a feature of social work practice (AASW, 2008b, 2014). Social workers have been pioneers in the area of family therapy, and the vast majority of work in the child and adolescent mental health field has been family focused. These have been specialised areas of practice, each with its own theory base and often requiring additional specialist training and supervision. While we will draw on knowledge from both areas, in this chapter we will focus primarily on family work as a broad area of practice in generic mental health settings. We are most interested in the impact of mental illness on individuals within a family context, and as such we recognise the importance of families as providing the primary supportive relationships in which illness is experienced, treatment is provided and recovery is pursued.

We emphasise the network of relationships provided by family and friends in the chapter on social work assessment. This chapter will consider the impact of mental illness on the family, an area where social work has had some leadership. While the research literature has focused largely on the impact of psychotic illness, we accept that all forms of mental illness, including the more common disorders such as depression and anxiety, have the potential to impact greatly on the intimate relationships in the person's social network. Indeed, the defining basis of an impact on family is the severity and duration of the disorder, rather than the diagnostic category. This chapter will reflect this long-standing focus on families and psychotic illness. It is in this area that the concept of 'family caring' has been most relevant and where most of the therapeutic work has been with families has been focused.

We start with a review of the diverse theoretical perspectives informing family work. Recovery theory will be applied as an overarching set of principles for understanding the family experience and directing social work practice. As in other chapters in this book, we will emphasise some key themes, such as strengths, resilience and the importance of understanding the social context and consequences of illness. We see the work with families as happening through respectful relationships that social workers build with families. In this chapter, we also argue for the importance of two principles: the centrality of building a therapeutic alliance with

DOI: 10.4324/9781003148913-11

the person with an illness, their family and the treatment staff, and the importance of respecting the needs of families, not just insofar as that is relevant for our work with individuals, but also in their own right. We see families as directly and powerfully impacted by serious mental illness, and responding to family distress is core business for social work practice.

Towards a theory base for family work

While family work has always been a traditional area of social work practice in mental health, the theory base for practice has evolved over the last 40 years through a number of competing research directions, theoretical conflicts and ambiguity about how to work with families. Bland and Foster (2012) have identified a number of competing perspectives of families in the mental health literature and argued that confusion about these perspectives has both theoretical and practice approaches to families. Families have variously been seen as causing mental illness in a family member, as carrying the burden of care or as carers for the ill family member. We will outline these competing perspectives briefly before considering in greater detail the application of recovery theory to the family experience.

The early follow-up studies from the deinstitutionalisation movement from 1950 to 1990 were largely concerned with patient outcomes and the extent to which discharged patients created a burden for families (Drake, 2014; Hoenig & Hamilton, 1969; Bland, 1987). The key concept here of *family burden* encouraged mental health workers to consider the cost to families, as a balance to the benefits to the 'patient', of community care. These studies sought to measure both *subjective* and *objective* family burden.

These same outcome studies were the origins of a vigorous and highly influential body of research known as the *expressed emotion* (EE) studies (Vaughn & Leff, 1976, 1981; Hooley, 1985). The focus of these studies was the identification and measurement of certain specific family traits – criticality, hostility and emotional over-involvement – which could predict the likelihood of relapse of people with schizophrenia. It was believed that these traits created potentially toxic emotional environments, a form of chronic stress that contributed to relapse in vulnerable people. The original work with people with schizophrenia was extended to other diagnostic groups such as major depression and bipolar disorder (Goldstein & Miklowitz, 1994). Families who were hostile to, or critical of, ill family members, or who responded to the withdrawal and disability of illness by becoming overprotective, were assessed as having high EE and were seen by treatment staff as a threat to the person's recovery. Through the lens of this theory, families were seen not as a resource to be supported but as a risk to be managed. The theory encouraged a series of family interventions designed to reduce EE in high-risk families. No family intervention was needed for low-EE families.

An alternative theoretical understanding of the family response to mental illness came through the strong growth and assertion of the family self-help movement in North America, Europe and Australia (Hatfield, 1978; Hatfield & Lefley, 1987).

The movement focused on the lived experience of mental illness of families and asserted the importance of families as *caregivers*. Writers such as Hatfield (1978) emphasised the serious impact of severe mental illness not just on individuals but on whole families. Family carers were not just parents but could be partners, siblings, children and extended family (Wasow, 1995). The illness created enormous stress for families, not just at times of crisis, but in the long-term care of family members with serious mental illness. Families were not simply a burdened resource or a threat to be managed. They were an integral part of the experience and impact of mental illness, and they had needs for support and service in their own right and not just as an adjunct to the treatment of the person with mental illness. Families were highly critical of the neglect and abuse they had experienced in treatment systems that ignored their needs or, encouraged by the EE theories, treated them as a threat to the patient's recovery.

Some negative aspects of the EE theories are as follows:

The theories served to blame families – to interpret the responses of parents to the impact of illness on a loved one and on themselves as pathological. The theories interpreted the collateral damage of illness as contributing to the illness.

The theories served to misinterpret the grief, guilt and shame of family. The pain of many families was diagnosed as pathology, and those families were treated with suspicion, when the human response required from workers was compassion.

Hatfield and Lefley (1987) argued that family response to mental illness was best understood not in terms of underlying family pathology, in toxic emotions that clinicians needed to repair, but in more ordinary processes like coping, adaptation and response. Emerging illness, they argued, created a deep crisis for the family. The illness, and the subsequent caring and support, disrupted the ordinary maturational processes of building identity, gaining independence and interdependence, and maintaining traditional family roles. The caregiving role overwhelmed other roles such as parent, partner or sibling. Family members needed to learn new ways of coping with the crisis to find a balance between the demands of caregiving and meeting their own needs.

This view of families as caregivers has emerged as a dominant theme of the mental health policy in Australia and elsewhere, as argued in Chapter 4 of this book. This official policy reflects the assertions of the family self-help movement that mental illness impacts profoundly on whole families and not just individuals; that mental health services should address the needs of families; and that treatment responses should be based on therapeutic alliances among consumers, families and treatment staff. These principles are set out in the range of state and national mental health policy documents over the last 25 years, for example, the revised National Mental Health Policy 2009 and the Fourth National Mental Health Plan, An Agenda for Collaborative Government Action in Mental Health 2009–2014. The *National Practice Standards for the Mental Health Workforce* (Australian Government Department of Health 2012), for example, specifies the knowledge, skills and values that workers need to be able to work effectively with family carers. Carers are seen as having a right to participation in all aspects of service development, delivery, management and evaluation, and in the training of the mental health workforce.

Families and recovery theory

There has been little systematic interest in the changing role and experiences of families throughout the emergence of illness, crisis, seeking of treatment and subsequent recovery. Most of the research literature describing family experience, particularly descriptions of the caregiving role, has been rather static, ignoring the way the family response changes over time. Early work on the stages of family responses to mental illness by Terkelsen (1987) emphasised the importance of the crisis of an emerging psychosis as a 'tipping point' for families. Using his experience as a clinician, Terkelsen described the different emotions and changes for the family while they search for help during the crisis of acute illness and subsequent treatment, including the painful adjustments to the ongoing illness that are needed. Hospitalisation and involuntary treatment were identified as a critical time, not only for the consumer but also for their family. These stages, however, are not stops on some linear timeline but are part of a longer journey (Wyder et al. 2018). Wyder and her colleagues have sought to apply principles of the recovery paradigm to the changing experiences of families over time, building on Terkelsen's work and offering a model for engaging and working with families. The challenges and tasks of recovery change over time, and are reactive to the development and treatment of the illness.

Table 9.1 Competing theoretical perspectives for family work

Paradigm	*Theoretical issues*	*Issues for intervention*
Families and pathology	How do families contribute to the emergence or course of the illness process?	Therapeutic interventions like EE theory–based interventions
Families and burden	Cost/benefit of family vs institutional care	Policy responses designed to limit burden
Families as carers	Instrumental, cognitive and affective dimensions of the family response	Policy to support carers, Family Support Program approaches, individual family work
Beyond caregiving – families and recovery	Carer or family Family as the only consistent support for many people who have been isolated by the illness process	Supporting the recovery journey for families over time. Asks us to consider what is most helpful for the family at each point in time. Crisis work. Balancing the needs and rights of all family members. Balancing the roles and responsibilities of individuals, families and communities.

In Chapter 2 we have reviewed the basic principles of recovery theory. In the following section we summarise the analysis of recovery theory in relation to family work, as developed by Wyder and Bland (2014). We believe that this approach best synthesises the diverse research literature on families and provides a solid theoretical basis for social work practice in the area.

Wyder and Bland (2014) draw a distinction between *recovery-oriented support* and *family's recovery journey*. They argue that, certainly, families have an important role in supporting their family member's recovery, but families face significant challenges in managing their response to the emerging mental illness of a family member. We can conceptualise the response to those challenges as making their own journey of recovery. Using the framework for recovery as developed by Davidson (2005) and discussed in Chapter 2, we can identify the central aspects of this recovery journey for families.

Understanding the family recovery journey

Principle 1: renewing hope and commitment

Davidson et al. states: 'Hope is at the centre of the recovery journey for consumers. People with lived experience need to have a sense of hope that recovery is possible' (Davidson et al., 2005, p. 484). While this is true for consumers, hope plays a central part in the recovery journey of families (Bland & Darlington, 2002).

For families, holding hope is complex. At times, they may need to hold the hope for their loved ones, in particular when the symptoms they are experiencing are severe and disabling (O'Grady & Skinner, 2012). This often involves balancing the uncertainties of the illness with the possibilities of marked improvement, recovery and even cure (Rose, 1998). This is difficult, particularly during the early stages of the illness. Families also need to be able to maintain hope for themselves, that they are able to continue their caring responsibilities while leading their own fulfilling lives (Bland & Darlington, 2002). There is now mounting evidence that when families experience hope for their loved ones, they often also experience hope for themselves (O'Grady & Skinner, 2012).

Principle 2: redefining self

Perhaps the most overarching aspect of recovery, redefining self, involves reconceptualising mental illness as simply one aspect of a multidimensional identity rather than assuming a primary social role as 'mental patient' (Davidson et al., 2005, p. 484). For many families, a defining role is that of 'family carer', so that other family roles such as parent or partner are overwhelmed. For many, particularly during the early stages of the illness, the caring role can become all-consuming (Magliano et al., 1998; Saunders, 2003). The recovery journey for families over time involves moving away from seeing themselves as having a primary role of a carer to a place where the caring role becomes only one aspect of their lives (O'Grady & Skinner, 2012). This transition, or redefining self, reflects the recovery journey of the consumer and can be understood as essential to the family's recovery journey.

Principle 3: incorporating illness

Acknowledging and accepting the limitation imposed by one's illness helps one discover talents, gifts and possibilities that allow a person to pursue and achieve life goals with the presence of disability (Davidson et al., 2005, p. 484). Families need to find a balance between accepting the limitations imposed by their relatives' illness and encouraging their loved ones to reach their potential (Tew et al., 2012). This can be a difficult task for families as it often highlights tensions between consumers' and families' needs and wants. For example, while consumers may seek independence, families may worry about their wellbeing and want to protect them. In their own recovery journey families also need to adjust to the limitations imposed by their caring responsibilities and the secondary impact of their loved one's illness. The impact of long-term caring and the need to sustain a caring, comfortable and loving relationship can alter a carer's self-efficacy and coping capacity (Row, 2011; Wilkinson & McAndrew, 2008). Again similar to consumers, many families will need to discover new possibilities and pursue and achieve different life goals. O'Grady and Skinner (2012) described this process in which families move away from the preoccupation with their family member's journey to finding their own separate but parallel recovery pathway as 'journeying on'. Families moved from 'fixing' and 'doing for' to 'being with' and 'journeying alongside'. Tew et al. (2012) describe this difficult task as moving from 'standing with' the person to being able to encourage independence.

Principle 4: being involved in meaningful activities

As part of a recovery journey, families need to expand their own social role beyond that of being a carer. This process involves letting go of the all-absorbing preoccupation with their relative's illness and reconnecting with ordinary life tasks such as work and social activities.

Principle 5: overcoming stigma

'Recovery involves developing resilience to stigma and/or actively fighting against it' (Davidson et al., 2005, p. 484). In their supporting role, families need to find ways to encourage their loved ones to overcome the impact of mental illness and stigma (Rose et al., 2002). This can be very difficult as families will often experience stigma themselves, and many families are hesitant about seeking support from others as they anticipate negative reactions. As part of their recovery journey, families need to overcome their own sense of guilt and shame and the stigma of mental illness.

Principle 6: assuming control

People must assume primary responsibility for their transformation from a person with illness to a person in recovery. Assuming control over one's life and treatment contributes to the redefined sense of self as an active, effective agent. Opportunities must be available for people to make choices, and people must have options from which to choose. People must also be afforded opportunities to 'succeed and fail' (Davidson et al., 2005, p. 484). This issue of assuming control over their own lives is complex as consumers need to resume control of a life that has been controlled not only by an illness but also by a treatment system and possibly by family. Similarly, families also struggle with the issue of control and have to make a decision about who has ultimate responsibility for managing the illness. Wyder and Bland (2014) describe the difficulties faced by families as they struggle to balance the family members' needs to take control of their own lives against the need to encourage positive risk-taking for the person with an illness, which is central to the consumer's recovery journey. A reluctance to take risks based on a fear of relapse sometimes accounts for the sense of being 'stuck in the caregiving' that mental health professionals recognise in the family response.

Over time, most families reassume control of their own lives and develop a life that extends beyond their caring role (O'Grady & Skinner, 2012; Rose et al., 2002; Saunders, 2003). As part of their recovery journey many families engage in self-reflection, looking back and appreciating how far they have come from the initial days of the illness, reviewing personal philosophies and carefully considering their own future (Ayres, 2000; Rose et al., 2002). Many families find that when they let go of wanting to control their relative's behaviour, they also gain back control over their own lives (O'Grady & Skinner, 2012).

Principle 7: becoming empowered and exercising citizenship

As a sense of empowerment and control over one's life emerges, people in recovery begin to demand the same rights (e.g., the right to decide where to live, whom to love, how to spend one's time) and take on the same responsibilities (e.g., paying taxes, voting, volunteering) as other citizens (Davidson et al., 2005, p. 484). Empowerment happens through accessing resources such as housing and employment and confronting stigma and discrimination (Tew et al., 2012). Families can play an important part in encouraging and supporting consumers to engage in activity in any of these domains of social inclusion.

Carers and families, as well as consumers, can also feel isolated, unrecognised by health care professionals and powerless (Wilkinson & McAndrew, 2008). This sense of feeling powerless is increased when families feel discouraged from approaching services, are not given any information about their relative's illness or treatment plan and are seen as part of the problem (Gray et al., 2008; Row, 2011). For many families the ability to move from feeling disempowered to a position where they can advocate effectively not only for their loved ones but also for themselves is an important part of feeling empowered, which is essential to their recovery journey (Row, 2011; Slade et al., 2007).

Principle 8: managing symptoms

Although complete symptom remission is not necessary, being able to manage symptoms in some way is essential for recovery. Recovery involves periods of good and difficult times, setbacks and accomplishments, and times when symptoms may be more or less controlled. A shift occurs from simply receiving services to actively participating in and using treatments of one's choice to bring symptoms under some degree of control' (Davidson et al., 2005, p. 484). The family's role can be that of encouraging consumers to find ways of managing their symptoms. Associated with their role in supporting consumers, families themselves often experience psychological distress such as anxiety, depression and insomnia. Many caregivers are exhausted from coping with the day-to-day crises of severe mental illness (Row, 2011). This not only impacts on their caring abilities but also on their own lives. Many families at first are reluctant to deal with their own stress; however, research suggests that when families decided to do something about their own physical, emotional and spiritual health, many of their other problems would also become more manageable (O'Grady & Skinner, 2012). As part of their own recovery journey families need to find effective ways to manage their stress.

Principle 9: being supported by others

Recovery is not done alone. Becoming interdependent in one's community and having supportive others and role models, whether they are family members, friends, professionals, community members or peers, provides encouragement through the difficult times and helps celebrate the good (Davidson et al., 2005, p. 484). Families and friends can be central in offering this support (Australian Health Ministers Advisory Council, 2012; Slade, 2009). There is now mounting evidence that families themselves also need to be supported, and this support can be considered central to the family's journey of recovery. Social support has been identified as crucial to a family's ability to cope, and there is evidence to show that families who felt supported by mental health services were less stressed, were better able to cope and experienced less psychological distress (Rose et al., 2002; Row, 2011; Saunders, 2003). In summary, social support serves as a protective factor which facilitates coping and family functioning (Row, 2011).

The family response to mental illness

This section describes in some detail the research literature on the lived experience of family carers. It draws on the clinical work broadly described as family support and psychoeducation. The first-person accounts of families, the writings of key family advocates such as Agnes Hatfield and Harriet Lefley in the United

States (Hatfield & Lefley, 1987), family advocacy groups such as the Alliance for the Mentally Ill and the Association of Relatives and Friends of the Mentally Ill (ARAFMI) in Australia, and high-profile family advocates such as Anne Deveson (Deveson, 1991) have contributed a solid understanding of the family experience of mental illness. These non-clinical writings represent a form of alternative discourse about families and mental illness that has challenged the dominant medical and therapeutic discourse that has emphasised family pathology. Social work research (Bland, 1987; Cowling, 2004) has built on this knowledge to provide a solid empirical basis for social work practice with families. Certainly, families experience a range of specific problems associated with the illness, such as isolation, worry, discrimination, decreased participation in the workforce and restricted life chances. The caring responsibilities generally fall more heavily on women, with often severe impacts on their health and workforce participation.

Central to this knowledge base about families is an understanding of the instrumental, cognitive and affective dimensions of the caregiving role and the diversity of family response to a range of different illness behaviours.

From Robert: family reunions

Maria was the eldest daughter in a family of seven children. When her younger brother Duncan became ill with schizophrenia, all of the family members rallied round their parents to support them and to give Duncan whatever help they could. As Duncan's illness continued to be serious, the family's coping resources were stretched to the limit. Maria said that family get-togethers which had been important and fun for all were now dominated by discussions about how to best help Duncan. She said: 'We would promise each other each time we met that we would not talk about Duncan, and then when we met we would talk of nothing else'.

This is a great story about the way that illness impacts on the whole family. It's about the way that siblings may try to share the caregiving with parents and how family members will struggle – not always successfully – to restore a balance in their lives that has become dominated by the illness of one family member.

Caregiving as an instrumental role: the doing of caregiving

Hatfield (1991) and Bland (1987) have described the range of tasks that families undertake as caregivers for family members who develop mental illness. These include assisting with day-to-day tasks and activities such as providing meals, cleaning, supervising medications and treatments, solving problems and managing difficult behaviour. It is this view of caregiving that is at the heart of the national mental health policies. Providing home and shelter within the family has made community life possible for many people unable to cope on their own. Families claim that they have to learn a range of advocacy skills to ensure that they receive services their family member needs. As we have suggested, caregiving is not just about parents caring for adult children with long-term illness. Partners, siblings and children can also be caregivers. As recent research has shown, people with long-term illness are at risk of homelessness and poverty (Drake, 2014), and families are often the last defence against these outcomes (Hinton, 2007).

From Robert: Michelle's mother

Michelle was a competent, intelligent young social worker. Her mother, Jean, had long-standing bipolar disorder, and Michelle was a primary caregiver for Jean through Michelle's teenage years. At the times when Jean became unwell, Michelle would take over the household tasks, deal with Jean's erratic behaviour and try to negotiate with the hospital ward for Jean's admission. Sometimes she was able to persuade Jean to accept treatment as a voluntary patient, but on two occasions she needed to arrange an involuntary admission. Jean would settle well on medication and be discharged to Michelle's care. This pattern lasted over a 12-year period until Michelle was in her mid-twenties. At no time did any of the staff discuss with Michelle the impact of her mother's illness on Michelle or her younger brother. Despite the presence of a social worker in the treatment team, Michelle was never offered an appointment.

The story illustrates the way that children can become caregivers for their parents, assuming a range of tasks that include household management, caring for siblings and negotiating with, and advocating for, treatment services. It shows the way that ordinary family roles are distorted by mental illness. Michelle cared for both her mother and her brother through her teen years and early adulthood. This is a contemporary story, not one from the distant past. It illustrates the capacity of treatment systems to neglect families and the difficulty for even assertive caregivers to be heard in the system.

Caregiving as a cognitive role: the knowing of caregiving

The family self-help movement has identified the enormous challenge confronting families as they struggle to make meaning of the emergence of mental illness in a family member. Terkelsen (1987) describes the various stages of family response to emerging illness by suggesting that recognising unusual and disturbing behaviour as the symptoms of an illness is a difficult process for families. Families have to learn about the illness and develop an understanding of their family member as a 'person with an illness'. This recognition of symptoms, the presence of an illness and the need for treatment are learning hurdles both for the individual and for their family. Such emerging understanding or 'insight' takes time and is particularly difficult in the early stages of emerging psychotic illness.

It is easier to accept, perhaps, when the illness is more familiar and within the family or community experience – for example, depression or anxiety. In some psychotic disorders, such as schizophrenia, the symptoms may be so bizarre and disturbing that it is difficult for families to deny the presence of severe illness. More difficult perhaps are those disorders such as bipolar disorder and personality disorders where the symptoms constitute very challenging behaviour which the family can easily interpret as deliberate, harmful and offensive acts (Goldstein & Miklowitz, 1994; Bland & Harriso, 2000). Getting an illness perspective on these behaviours may be difficult.

From Robert: Josh's mania

Josh, a gay man of 34, had bipolar disorder. When he was well he was able to hold down a steady job and lived with his partner, Donald. In the manic phase of his illness, he would have enormous energy, was full of grand plans and was careless with his money. He would go to nightclubs and pick up men for casual unprotected sex. Donald was unable to cope with his difficult behaviour, and was angry and hurt by Josh's actions. During one of his episodes, Josh contracted HIV. When the mania cycled to depression, Josh was overwhelmed with guilt and anger. He was ashamed of his behaviour but angry that his partner and friends had not acted more forcefully to prevent the harm he had caused to himself and others.

This story illustrates the challenge of understanding the difficult behaviours of mania as the symptoms of an illness and responding to that understanding. What the treatment staff would call 'hypersexuality' appeared to Donald to be simple promiscuity. Josh's insight into the illness process emerges only in the depressive phase of the illness, and the consequences of his behaviour are catastrophic.

Being able to see such difficult behaviours as symptoms of an illness often remains problematic for families. Our experience in working with families of people with schizophrenia and bipolar disorder over many years suggests that families will often struggle with knowing what is the illness and what is the person. Attributing all unusual behaviour to the illness suggests that the person is not responsible for any of this behaviour. For example, a high level of anxiety might lead a person to make constant demands for reassurance, creating frustration for those close to the person. Does the person have no control over this demanding behaviour? Fear can lead to intimidation and threats of violence – are these parts of the illness or simply 'bad' behaviour? Hatfield and Lefley (1993) argue that part of the recovery process for individuals is taking responsibility for *all* behaviour and being able to see the choices open to each of us in response to the illness. There are no easy answers to any of these questions, and the solutions for individuals and their families can only be worked out patiently over time.

There are many other dimensions to the 'knowing of caregiving' for most families. They have to learn about treatments and medications, mental health laws and how the complex mental health system works. They need to learn about the roles of various mental health professions. They need to be aware of their rights. They have to learn to navigate the social security system, welfare services and recovery-based services.

Caregiving as an affective response: the feeling of caregiving

The emergence of mental illness in a family member brings a range of difficult and enduring emotional responses. The early writers from the self-help movement helped to transform thinking about family experience from judgmental concepts like 'dysfunctional', 'enmeshed' and 'over-controlling' to thinking about family distress, grief and guilt (Hatfield & Lefley, 1987; Terkelsen, 1987). Understanding grief and guilt in families remains central to appreciating the family experience of mental illness.

From Robert: the family photos

On a home visit, I noticed a series of family photos proudly displayed on a mantelpiece. Among them was a photo of Emma, a consumer where I worked and the daughter of the woman I was interviewing. I said to the mother that it was a lovely photo. She said, 'Yes. That was Emma before she became ill. You don't know her like this, you only know a patient'. She was right. The Emma I knew seemed very different from the shining, happy young woman in the photo.

This is a story about grief and loss. It's hard sometimes for treatment staff to understand the magnitude and nature of loss that families might experience. As the mother said, 'You only know a patient'. Hopefully we also know the person who for a time is a patient, but we may not know the person before they were ill. We may not know their youthful hopes and dreams or those of the parents before the onset of the illness. Of course, recovery is possible and some level of restoration is inevitable, but there are times of deep distress, particularly in the early stages of the illness, and grief may be present through many years. It is often hard for parents to put the experience of loss into words. For me that loss is defined by the difference between the shining young woman in the photo and the person I know 'only as a patient'.

The nature of this mother's grief is based on a sense of loss (Bland, 1998; McGregor, 1994; Highet et al., 2004), though this loss may be difficult to define. The impact of serious psychotic illness such as schizophrenia may involve a loss of employment or study, loss of friends, loss of income and diminished life opportunities. Families may also lose a sense of the future hopes and dreams for a life that might have been very different but for the illness. McGregor (1994) lists the losses as loss of the child's personality, loss of the child's role in the family, loss of joy and potential and loss of hope for the future. External losses include loss of privacy, financial security and social network. This sense of loss of confidence and hope for the future is often unexpressed and unacknowledged.

In non-parental family relationships, the sense of loss may also be profound. In writing about loss and major depression in families, Highet et al. (2004) suggest that depression causes a loss of intimacy and spontaneity in relationships. Depression is called 'the thief of joy'. Wasow (1995) describes the impact of illness on grandparents, who endure the 'double whammy' of the grief for a grandchild with severe illness and also for the impact on their own children, the child's parents. Siblings may also be affected (Bland, 1987), and children experience loss in response to a parent's illness (Cowling, 2004). This sense of loss of childhood may be a lifelong grief.

Case example: a grieving daughter

Elaine explained that her family had struggled with the illness of her mother over many years. There were frequent hospitalisations, and Elaine's father managed to care for his wife and children through these. However, Elaine's mother remained emotionally distant and troubled by withdrawal and lack of motivation. For Elaine, the sense of loss was most profound when, as a young adult, she had a miscarriage: 'I didn't realise how much I needed my mother until then, and she just couldn't be there for me. I was so sad'.

The grieving is complicated. Doka (1989) calls it 'disenfranchised grief' because there is little community permission for families to understand their response as grief or to express it. The object of loss is still alive, and that which is lost is not clearly defined. The grief is also 'recycled', complicated by the variable course of severe illness. Families re-experience the grief at times of relapse of the illness, as hopes for recovery are threatened by each setback. The grief is unexpectedly awakened at significant anniversaries and at times of the achievements of peers.

From Robert: a grieving father

Will was the father of a young man, Ben, who had been admitted to the unit with a diagnosis of schizophrenia. During Ben's admission, Will attended the Family Support Program over six Monday evenings, often with other family members. Will spoke of the pain he felt seeing Ben so ill and disabled by the illness: 'He was a wonderful son – a great athlete, so full of promise'. During the groups, Will was open about the profound impact that Ben's illness had on him and his family, but he saved the most painful disclosure for the very end of the program. As he left the group, he shook my hand and thanked me for the help we had given him. But as he did so, he drew me to one side and said that he could not leave before he told me the very worst. He told of how he came to visit Ben one evening on the ward. As the lift doors opened on the ward, he could see Ben at the end of the corridor, not in his ward but locked in the seclusion room off the nurses' station. He remembered Ben's face framed in the Perspex security window – confused and frightened. The nurse told Will that Ben had been fighting. Confronted with the image of Ben locked behind the Perspex, Will tearfully confided that he realised that no matter what he did, he was not able to protect Ben from the illness. He had never felt so helpless or defeated.

This story has remained for me one of the most powerful learning experiences in my working life. At one level, it is about the profound grief of this loving father and the terrible loss of confidence in his capacity to care for and protect his family. At another level, it is about his enduring capacity to struggle to be that loving father – something that filled me with hope even as I shared his present distress. Then it is about the sense of privilege of his confidence in me – in disclosing 'the worst' – and the power to engage with him and his family as they sought to find a way through this awful crisis. Finally, the image of the young man imprisoned behind the Perspex window is a powerful metaphor for schizophrenia. I cannot tell this story from my practice without being moved to tears.

Guilt is similarly common and difficult to deal with. Parents may feel responsible for the emerging illness of their children and guilty about their feelings of anger and frustration. Partners will also feel guilt at perceived failure to continue to be loving partners in the face of loss of the quality of past relationships. Siblings may feel a sense of 'survivor guilt' – how was it that they avoided an illness that a sibling developed? This guilt may not be based on any real failing, and family members may know that the guilt is unreasonable, but guilt is a slippery emotion – not necessarily open to defeat through reason. In a perverse way, it may be part of preserving a sense of agency. Parents, for example, may believe that if they caused the illness, they can also defeat it. Families may prefer to hold to this sense of agency rather than see the illness as some uncontrollable external force, random in its attack and unresponsive to their efforts.

Anne Deveson's powerful account of the loss of her son to schizophrenia describes her grief and anguish not just in response to the illness but also in response to the failure of the treatment system to care for him (Deveson, 1991). Indeed, this is a consistent theme of the literature of the family self-help movement. McGregor (1994) argues that mental health workers have not seen grief and guilt as a normal and necessary part of family response to the impact of illness but have either ignored families or treated their distress with suspicion. Certainly families have felt blamed by health professionals, adding to the sense of guilt they may already feel (Highet et al., 2004).

The limits of the concept of caregiving

The emphasis on caregiving in the policy documents is perhaps based on the intention of the policy writers to locate families in the mainstream of mental health services, to avoid any suggestion of blaming families for mental illness and to emphasise the contribution that families make to recovery. Certainly the recognition of the importance of families as caregivers over the last 20 years has helped to challenge the dominance of the family pathology discourse among mental health professionals. These advantages notwithstanding, the focus on caregiving and carers throughout the National Mental Health Policy may limit a recognition of other family issues beyond the confining though important role of caregiving. The cumulative research on family response to mental illness suggests the complexity and variability of family response. It involves, for example, issues of grief, impact across generations, cultural variability and changes over time based on family life stages. These important issues are not captured within the simple concept of the caregiving role.

Families do other things associated with protection, identity and resources. They provide a predictable and safe living situation for people who would otherwise be dependent on hospital, hostel or the streets. They keep order and routine, lend money when needed and offer encouragement. They persist, they remember, they open the door when you knock – unlike many mental health services that give up, close down and move on (or move the person on). Families are open all hours, and they're there on the weekend. Sometimes they absorb a lot of anger. They remember birthdays and maintain family rituals. They offer a space where people can be loved and love others. Family connectedness and interdependence provide a great protection from the two evils of mental illness: loneliness and hopelessness.

Another risk to families is based on the assumption that families of people with mental illness are inevitably carers, or should adopt caring roles, or should constantly be carers. To define families as carers and to honour the caregiving role is also to convey an expectation that family members will readily accept this role and the enormous personal costs it may bring. Certainly the struggle for family advocacy groups through the decades has been for better mental health services so that the wider community can relieve individual families of some of the burden of caring for ill family members. At some point, families need to be able to stop being carers and just be family.

It is also important to challenge the concept of consumers and carers locked in some eternal, unequal relationship. Caring is a family role based on need and opportunity. It is not all one way, and it changes over time. The real danger of a focus on caring and carers is that mental health professionals will ignore the broader family context in which caring is provided. Caring happens within a complex set of relationships, and the appropriate focus of understanding this complexity is probably the family context, rather than the caregiving role. It is the variation in family relationships, as much as the variation in illness and disability, that determines the particular way in which families will respond to the illness of a family member.

Children of Parents with a Mental Illness (COPMI)

In the last two decades there has been an increased recognition of the needs and experience of children whose parents have a mental illness. It is estimated that 21–24 per cent of Australian children live in a household where at least one parent has a mental illness (Maybery et al., 2005). The caring role that these children undertake may vary from helping out to more extensive care (Sanders, 2004).

The AFRC monograph 'Family Relationships and Mental Illness: Impacts and Service Responses' (Robinson et al., 2008) reviewed the literature in this area and concluded that the effects of having a parent with a mental illness may impact on children in different ways. Children may be affected in terms of their own direct care or indirectly through impacts on their social and emotional health and well-being. Core attachment needs such as love, physical and emotional nurturing, and security may be at risk. Children may have to deal with a range of emotions and reactions that come from having a parent with mental illness. These include confusion, fear, questions about normality, disruption of connections with the unwell family member and worry that they will also become sick. Children also felt awkward and embarrassed having friends over and grieved for the parent they once knew.

The COPMI movement has worked nationally at a number of levels to address the needs of families and specifically children. Taking a strong advocacy approach, the movement has sought to build greater understanding of the needs of both parents and children, challenging the stigma and suspicion of parents who have mental illness. Certainly COPMI is concerned with the welfare of vulnerable children, but the movement has sought to empower and resource parents to provide the best care for their children. They have worked to increase awareness and uptake of the COPMI guidelines and resources among relevant individuals and services, to promote education and training of health and other relevant workforces, and to increase the availability of resource materials for children, family members and other parties affected by parental mental illness.

In 2007 the COPMI program was included under the Council of Australian Governments' New Early Intervention Services (NEIS) for Parents, Children and Young People measure. The COPMI website describes the aims of the program under this scheme as supporting mental health promotion, prevention and early intervention for all children through universal evidence-based school and early childhood programs and through targeted programs aimed at children who are at highest risk of developing mental health problems (or who have early signs, symptoms or diagnosis of mental health problems). The measure provides a framework for mental health promotion, prevention and early intervention for children from birth to 12 years (www.copmi.net.au/).

A real benefit of the COPMI initiatives is the development of excellent resources not just for mental health workers but for young carers themselves. A particularly useful set of resources are the GEMS, providing mental health workers with concise evidence-based guidelines for practice across a wide range of topic areas. The focus of social work activity with families should be multilayered. It is not just about recognising and supporting vulnerable children but also about supporting parents with mental illness to be the best parents they can for their children. This work is sometimes at the interface of the statutory child protection system, so a further dimension of social work practice here is to work to ensure that the systems of care and protection, of treatment and support, work well together in the interests of children and families. It is skilled and challenging work but clearly an area of core business for social work in mental health.

Confidentiality and privacy

There is evidence that despite the good intentions of policymakers in Australia many families continue to experience difficulties in relationships with service providers and in accessing services. The failure of services to address the needs of families has been a consistent theme in the submissions from family advocacy groups to the various national inquiries into mental health over the last 30 years (for example, the Senate Select Committee's report *A national approach to mental health: From crisis to community* [Commonwealth of Australia, 2006] and the Mental Health Council of Australia's *Not For Service: Experiences of injustice and despair in mental health care in Australia* [Mental Health Council of Australia, 2005]).

These problems exist despite the spirit of the various state and Commonwealth mental health policies that proclaim partnership between family carers and service providers, and despite various reports in the research literature about the management of confidentiality matters with family (Furlong, 2001; Leggatt, 2002).

One of the points of tension in the relationships among consumers, families and carers is around the area of confidentiality and privacy. For example, many families who are closely involved in caregiving roles feel that the treatment staff don't give them sufficient information about the consumer's treatment. Treatment staff can be so worried about disclosing any information to families about their work with the consumer that they avoid engaging with families. The debates in the workplace generally focus on the extreme positions such as situations of risk of life and safety, for example, when treatment staff might consider the consumer a risk to themselves or to family members (Szmukler & Bloch, 1997; Leggatt, 2002).

Rather than frame this debate in terms of insoluble adversarial positions, we think it's more appropriate to consider the common needs of consumers, families and workers and the way information can be shared to meet those needs. The discussions between the consumer and treatment staff are protected by a legal and professional framework of privacy and confidentiality. So too are the discussions between workers and families. Where families provide direct care for the consumer, the family carers need the right information to provide that care. A partnership between treatment staff and families is possible only if the treatment staff respect the family's need for reasonable information and advice about treatment. A general discussion among consumer, family and workers around the treatment plan, medication, expectations, side effects and situations that are stressful for consumer and family will help to set a solid basis for shared commitment to the treatment plan. Treatment services need to find creative solutions to this dilemma that are based on forming treatment alliances among consumers, families and workers. For example, in treatment teams it may be possible to assign a staff member to work closely with families of consumers who insist on keeping treatment matters confidential and separate from families. In other teams, staff can insist on meeting with the consumer and their family to review treatment so that families have an opportunity to feel heard about decision-making, and consumers can determine what information is shared.

The importance of relationship

These principles of family work are echoed in an authoritative statement from the World Fellowship for Schizophrenia and Allied Disorders, which identifies 15 principles for family work. These begin with the fundamental requirement of ensuring 'that everyone is working towards the same goals in a collaborative, supportive relationship. Working together ensures that the goals for treatment and care are understood and agreed by the treatment team which includes the family. This will overcome the isolation that is experienced by both professionals and families' (Leggatt, 2002, p. 53). While this might seem so fundamental as to be obvious, such a principle actually suggests a radical reworking of strongly entrenched traditions of mental health work, which have tended to split the needs and perspectives of individuals and their families – when the latter have been considered at all. The construction of a 'team' that includes professionals, the consumer and the family is a complex and sophisticated undertaking. For example, particular skill is sometimes required in negotiating issues of confidentiality (Furlong & Leggatt, 1996) and situations in which family relationships have been badly damaged – perhaps even by family violence and abuse.

Building supportive relationships with family members is at the heart of family work, and developing and sustaining these relationships over time is core social work business. As we have argued here, families have to deal with a range of powerful feelings – including grief, guilt and shame. Families may be angry. They may have found accessing treatment services for their family member or themselves frustrating and may not feel that they have been treated with respect by the health professionals they have met in the course of their family member's treatment. It is not surprising, then, that many mental health workers find family work difficult. Dealing with powerful, painful feelings is always difficult.

It has been our experience that really effective family work is possible provided the worker is prepared to engage respectfully with family members. It takes courage to work compassionately with very distressed people. Sometimes the grief and anger will threaten to overwhelm us as well as those we are trying to support. When family members are angry and difficult, we need to be able to reach beyond their difficult behaviour to understand the painful feelings behind it. We need to be able to encourage hopefulness in family members. There is research evidence to show that working with families can make for good outcomes – not just for families, but for individual consumers as well. The technology of this work is underpinned by the quality of the relationship that will make that work possible.

Conclusion

Working with families is a core activity of social work practice in mental health. At the heart of this family work is a recognition of the broad impact of mental illness – not just on individuals but on their families too. Families provide the immediate social context for individuals and are intimately connected with the important issues of identity; safety; security; and social, emotional and economic wellbeing. In this chapter, we have emphasised the importance of the family's lived experience of mental illness and the need for supportive relationships with families as a starting point for family practice.

QUESTIONS FOR PRACTICE

1 Why do mental health workers often find it difficult to engage with family members?
2 How does recovery theory apply to the experience of family and carers?
3 How might the experiences of parents be different from those of siblings, partners and other family members and close friends?
4 What are the principles that apply to the sharing of information with family members, and what skills are required to do this well?
5 How might you, as a social worker, best respond to parents' feelings of guilt?

Personal accounts

Jo Buchanan, *Wings of Madness: A Mother's Journey* (New Holland Publishers, Sydney, 2004). Jo tells the story of her son, Logie winner Miles Buchanan, her own sister and her nephew as they battle with mental illness. Jo's quest to find the answers takes her into the archives of an asylum. A story of enormous grief, faith, resilience and recovery.

Catherine E. Camden-Pratt, *Out of the Shadows: Daughters Growing Up with a 'Mad' Mother* (Finch Publishing, Sydney, 2006). Brings together the stories of 11 women who tell their stories of living with a mentally ill mother, the impact that this had on their lives and the richness that comes from making sense of it all.

Anne Deveson, *Tell Me I'm Here* (Penguin, Ringwood, 1991). Writer, broadcaster and film maker Anne Deveson tells a deeply personal and moving account of her son's experience of schizophrenia. Told with intelligence, passion, humour and searing honesty.

Raymond Gaita, *Romulus, My Father* (Text, Melbourne, 1998). Raymond Gaita is a professor of philosophy. He writes about his father, a compassionate and honest man who taught his son the meaning of living a decent life. It is a story about passion, betrayal, madness, friendship, the joy and dignity of work, character and fate, and affliction and spirituality. Now also a film.

Nathaniel Lachenmeyer, *The Outsider: A Journey into My Father's Struggle with Madness* (Hill of Content, Melbourne, 2002). A profoundly moving examination of Nathaniel's father, a professor of sociology who developed schizophrenia, which cost him his family, his career and even a roof over his head. Nathaniel has also written a picture book titled *Broken Beaks* (Michelle Anderson Publishing, Melbourne, 2004) about the friendship between a small sparrow and a homeless man. It highlights the heroism and dignity of people with mental illness.

Websites

La Trobe Bouverie Initiative

A Victorian statewide clinical, academic and consultation agency specialising in family approaches in mental health service provision.
www.latrobe.edu.au/bouverie

SANE Australia

A national advocacy and information organization.
www.sane.org:

Mental Health Foundation of Australia (Victoria)

www.mentalhealthvic.org.au

Association of Relatives and Friends of the Mentally Ill

Site contains links to state associations.
www.arafmiaustralia.asn.au

National Alliance for the Mentally Ill (US)

US based advocacy organization for consumers and family carers.
www.nami.org

National Network of Carers Associations of Australia

www.carersaustralia.com.au

Australian Young Carers

www.youngcarers.net.au

Multicultural Mental Health and Suicide Prevention

Information and resources in community languages.
www.mmha.org.au

Mental Health Care

UK based mental health information for friends, family and carers.
www.mentalhealthcare.org.uk

Carers UK

UK website with information for carers.
www.carersuk.org

10 Working with communities

Introduction

One of the key themes of this book has been the need for mental health services to look beyond the treatment of symptoms to the social environments in which people live and the ways in which the experience of mental illness and those environments interact. In this chapter we consider a logical 'next step' from this position – the provision of health promotion and illness prevention services outside clinical settings. While some of these are provided in mental health services, most are located within the broad range of health and welfare services and address more general health and welfare goals. Many social workers in community-based agencies dealing with housing, income security and family welfare may not even conceptualise their work within a mental health promotion or prevention framework. They might instead describe their work as being aimed at giving people the skills and resources to exercise greater choice and control over their lives. They would argue for the principle of empowerment rather than mental health as underpinning their practice.

We will start with a broad theoretical description of the principles of health promotion and illness prevention, leading into the argument that group-based and community approaches to practice offer an alternative focus for social work activity beyond specific clinical work with individuals and families. These group-based and community activities include population health approaches, working with identified vulnerable groups and working with people with mental health problems to reduce the impact of illness and disability. Much of the social work practice in these areas is based on an empowerment model which is ill-suited to the empirical or quantitative evaluation which tends to dominate mental health policy and clinical practice. For many preventive approaches, however, qualitative evidence for effectiveness abounds. We argue that social workers need to be able to locate their work within clear conceptual models of practice and seek ways to evaluate and validate that work.

In this chapter, we will use lots of examples to illustrate social work practice in group-based and community approaches. We want to encourage social workers to see the opportunity for highly creative approaches to their work in this area and to value this work as being capable of making a significant contribution to individual and community wellbeing. The key themes of this book, valuing lived experience

DOI: 10.4324/9781003148913-12

and the importance of relationship, are as relevant to community work as they are to clinical work.

Important theory and concepts that underpin community work

A conceptual basis for much of the group and community work approaches that social workers use can be developed through an understanding of concepts such as risk and wellbeing.

I Risk, resilience, protective factors and vulnerability

In his analysis of the theory of prevention in mental health, Singh (2012) argues that effective prevention relies on the identification of both causal and protective factors in the development of mental illness. Queensland Mental Health Commission (2015) extends this analysis of risk and protective factors by considering structural, social and economic, and personal factors in understanding risk and protection (p. 16). Structural risk factors, for example, include poverty and discrimination, social isolation, and migration. Personal risk factors would include poor education and low self-esteem. Protective factors at a structural level would include equality, safe and secure housing, personal safety, and social support. Personal protective factors would include self-confidence, problem-solving skills and good physical health. Risk factors refer to biological, environmental and psychological factors that increase the probability of development of a mental health problem. Protective factors produce resilience to the development of psychological difficulties in the face of adverse risk factors (Singh, 2012). Risk and resilience operate in some dynamic interaction through the life cycle of the individual. The strengths perspective discussed in previous chapters of this book emphasises the personal resources and coping skills of the individual, and certainly evidence of resilience in resisting stress and risk is an example of individual strength that needs to be considered as part of individual assessment.

While the concepts are typically applied to individuals, they are just as relevant to families, groups and communities, and broader social factors can be considered as part of both risk and resilience. For example, long-term high levels of unemployment in a rural town might be considered a risk factor for the broader welfare of that community, threatening its ability to provide strong supportive networks for community members. Such a community might have a high rate of crime or youth suicide. Alternatively, a severe natural disaster such as bushfire might result in a positive community response, demonstrating a high level of community resilience in the face of adversity. The experience of confronting and sharing adversity might be seen as building strengths in the community.

The interconnections among risk, vulnerability and resilience in conceptualising preventive approaches and interpreting outcomes of interventions are complex.

Statements about causal relations are fraught with difficulty in mental health social work: as we noted earlier, our evidence base rarely includes the empirically derived data which would support such conclusions. In this context, however, we argue that defining the particulars of connections between, for example, levels of social support, the experience of past trauma, economic disadvantage and mental health outcomes is less important than identifying the connection itself.

From Robert: the junior basketball team, an example of a group project to build resilience

I had been a university teacher, social worker and coach of junior basketball teams for many years. I was aware of the opportunities created by junior sport to build confidence, social skills and self-esteem in children. I was aware of the way that sport provided a positive point of connection between children and their families and could also bring families and communities together to share the experience of competitive sport. With the help of a social work student (Rob), I approached a local primary school in his area and talked with the school administration about the possibility of working with some of the more marginalised children in the school. I suggested that we work with the children to select and train a couple of teams to take to an inter-school competition. I explained that I was interested in working with children who came from poorer families, some of the African refugee children and some of the children with behaviour problems. I was very keen that the teams would also include some of the more popular and skilled players. I didn't want the teams to be seen as just for 'problem kids', and I also wanted the teams to be competitive in the inter-school competition. The school administration agreed to the suggestions, and it was decided to form two teams – one for under-14 boys and one for under-14 girls.

Rob and I were careful to promote the positive opportunities that the project would offer the children. Sponsorship from local business meant that we could buy good playing uniforms. We were able to secure some court time in a local gymnasium to train the players. Rob worked hard to make contact with the families of the children and to include them in some of the team activities. The six weeks of training provided many opportunities to get to know the children and their families, to set challenges for the children and to build their skills and confidence. At the inter-school competition, both teams were competitive, and the children enjoyed the experience very much. The local newspaper covered the event and wrote a very positive story about the team, illustrated by photos. The project was evaluated by gathering informal feedback from the children, their families and the school.

This project can be conceptualised as one of resilience-building for a group of children who were identified as carrying some of the risk factors for mental health problems (low socio-economic status, early childhood trauma and deprivation through forced migration, behavioural problems). The use of competitive sport as a medium for social work activity ensured a positive, non-pathologising basis to engage the school, the children and their families. That the children really enjoyed their participation was central to the success of the project. The aims of the project were very broad, and it was considered inappropriate to insist on the children submitting to a series of psychometric tests to determine changes in levels of confidence and self-esteem. The work is considered to be highly creative and not a little risky. It was important, for example, that the newspaper didn't portray the children as needy children benefiting from a mental health project. Careful negotiation with the newspaper journalist ensured that the children would be portrayed positively.

If we were to do this again, we might try to make the aims more explicit and seek to measure outcomes more rigorously against these aims. This might be more professional, but it may not be as much fun!

(*Source*: Bland & Pearce, 2006)

2 *Wellbeing and prevention*

Contemporary understandings of mental wellbeing and recovery have emphasised the importance of recognising the dual continua – presence or absence of mental illness on one continuum and flourishing or languishing on a second continuum.

This conceptualisation encourages us to see the importance of supporting the goals of wellbeing, even for people who might continue to experience the symptoms of mental illness. As such it mirrors the definitions of recovery that focus on living well despite the presence or absence of illness. It reminds us that social work activities can be directed beyond specific treatments to include a range of individual and community activities designed to improve wellbeing. As we have seen in the discussion of social inclusion and recovery in other chapters, improving outcomes in areas such as employment, housing, friendship and family supports is highly valued by people living with mental health problems.

3 *International conventions*

A number of international conventions have emphasised the connections among social factors and health outcomes for communities. The Ottawa Charter (World Health Organisation, 1986) and the Jakarta Declaration (World Health Organisation, 1997) both recognised the importance of social equality, strong communities and building community capacity as fundamental to health promotion. The Melbourne Charter (Global Consortium for the Advancement of Promotion and Prevention Mental and Behavioural Disorders, 2009) identifies the principles and actions that governments, communities, organisations and individuals can take to

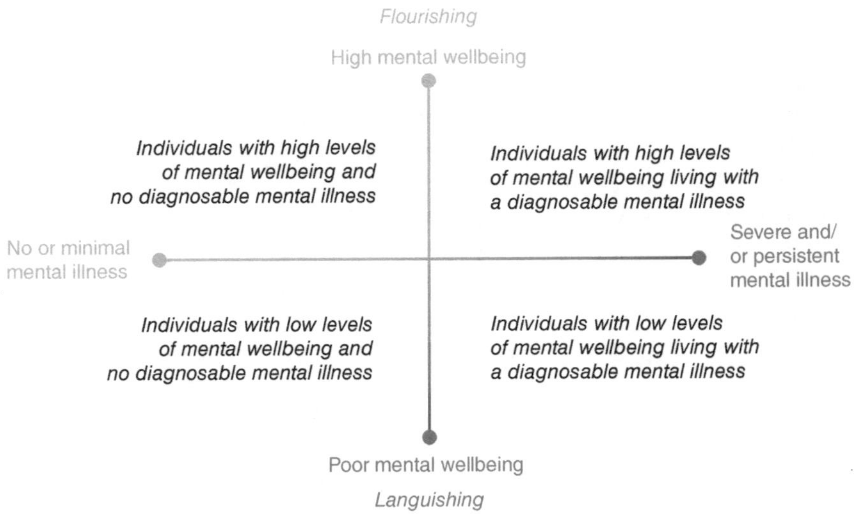

Figure 10.1 Dimensions of Wellbeing and Preventions

Source: Queensland Health Commission, 2015

influence the social and economic factors that influence mental health and wellbeing. The charter asserts that mental health is the fundamental right of every human being and is threatened by poverty and inequality, conflict and violence. Mental health is advanced through respectful and participatory means where cultural diversity and heritage is acknowledged and valued.

The Queensland Mental Health Commission (2015) argues that the things that support good mental health and prevent mental illness include:

- being socially connected;
- having control over one's life;
- having a sense of purpose and future;
- meaningful participation in learning, work and community;
- having access to housing, income and other measures;
- being safe and free from violence and discrimination.

These principles, articulated in the Queensland Mental Health Commission Plan (2018), resonate strongly both with the dimensions of social inclusion and of recovery discussed in Chapter 3 and throughout the book.

Creating supportive environments

The creation of supportive social, cultural and physical environments is a key strategy for encouraging positive mental health in communities (Commonwealth Department of Health and Aged Care, 2000). We have discussed in earlier chapters the importance of community safety, housing and transport as central to social inclusion and basic to good mental health. Projects that encourage safety, for example, might include an anti-bullying program in schools or a neighbourhood watch project in a community.

Social support, strong social networks and a sense of integration and inclusion are key predictors of mental health. Loneliness and isolation reduce people's ability to cope with stressful life events and increase the risk of mental illness and suicide (Commonwealth Department of Health and Aged Care, 2000). To encourage participation, social environments need to be inclusive, non-discriminatory, non-stigmatising and encouraging of access for all members of the community (Commonwealth of Australia, 2017). The Queensland *Shifting Minds* strategic plan (2018) identifies the importance of early intervention through enhanced family support, whole-school programs of education, strengthened human rights legislation and investment in diversionary programs to address the over-representation of people with mental illness within the criminal justice system as key priorities.

Mental health promotion was framed within the Queensland Mental Health Commission's 2015 report *Early Action* as enhanced social and emotional wellbeing. These outcomes are linked to strengthened individual capacity resulting from addressing 'social inequities such as economic disadvantage and social exclusion' (p. 15).

Case example: the Kalahari Driving School, an inclusive community-building program

Lloyd, a lecturer with a university Rural Health School in Launceston, had developed an interest in the welfare of the local African refugees. Over time, he came to know many of the families and realised that some of the older boys had difficulties finding work, making friends and developing a sense of connection with the local community. He realised that many of these boys were unable to achieve that most basic of qualifications for inclusion in a rural community – a driver's licence. Through assembling local resources and using his own community connections, Lloyd was able to establish the Kalahari Driving School – essentially a group of volunteers who were prepared to teach the young men to drive a motor vehicle and prepare them for the licence tests. The outcomes of the project extended well beyond the tangible acquisition of a driver's licence. They included the development of confidence and agency in the young men and the forging of supportive relationships between the young men and the volunteer helpers. The volunteers learned first hand about the challenges the young men faced in adjusting to the new lifestyle in Australia.

This is a great example of inclusive community work. Getting a driver's licence represented a significant transition for the young men, allowing them to participate more fully in the community, to seek employment and to enjoy a social life beyond their immediate families. It gave the young men a sense of achievement and independence, and in the process it allowed them to form friendships with local volunteers that further encouraged their participation in the community. At the same time, for the volunteers it helped to build a real understanding of the African refugees as individuals – as people with needs and aspirations. The outcomes were positive for all parties.

Mental health promotion and prevention

Prevention is defined as 'interventions that occur before the initial onset of a disorder to prevent the development of the disorder' (Mrazek & Haggerty, 1994, p. 23). Singh (2012) acknowledges the traditional classification of the levels of prevention (Caplan & Caplan, 2000) as useful in mental health. The Everymind *Prevention First* model (2017) conceptualises mental health intervention responses along a continuum from primary to tertiary prevention with promotion as a necessary adjunct. **Primary prevention** refers to interventions targeting the whole community with the expressed goal of preventing mental ill-health's onset. Examples of these interventions include education campaigns around bullying, the development of culturally appropriate information and the targeting of specific support programs for groups identified at higher risk, such as people from regions affected by drought or natural disaster, LGBTQIA+ people and Aboriginal and Torres Strait Islander people. **Secondary prevention** involves interventions for people who are showing early signs of mental ill-health. Interventions in this category attempt to reduce the duration and severity of symptoms. Examples range from education programs regarding symptoms to assist early detection and the promotion of culturally appropriate screening tools to response-capacity building among health professionals. Tertiary prevention includes interventions designed to reduce the impact of mental ill-health for people in recovery. These can include activities such as the creation of ways for people with a diagnosis to participate socially and the development of relapse prevention plans and programs to challenge stigma.

Mental health promotion is any action taken to maximise mental health and wellbeing among populations and individuals (Commonwealth Department of Health and Aged Care, 2000). It aims to protect, support and sustain the emotional and social wellbeing of the population by promoting the factors that enhance mental health. It is a relevant concept across the spectrum of interventions – before, during and after the onset of mental health problems and mental disorders. The evidence base for effectiveness of promotion activities is developing in key areas of social and economic activity: social connectedness; violence and discrimination; and increased economic participation such as access to work, income and housing (Keleher & Armstrong, 2005).

In her overview of the scope of mental health promotion, Barry (2007) argues that promotion relies on three key determinants of mental health: social inclusion, freedom from discrimination and violence, and economic participation. This assertion connects broader promotion and prevention activities with the social justice themes of social work practice. Health promotion is not just a marketing strategy or educational activity but the art of a political process of building more just communities. Barry suggests the importance of both 'top-down' and 'bottom-up' approaches working together to achieve social goals – good national policy and national programs interfacing with strong local initiatives driven by local communities to meet local needs. By implementing this model, many of the community work projects of social workers, including those not developed from mental health settings, can be conceptualised within a health promotion framework.

The terms *health promotion* and *prevention* are used almost interchangeably, but some significant differences need to be acknowledged. Health promotion activities can apply to people with well-established illnesses and as such are not essentially preventive. For example, stop-smoking programs for people with long-term schizophrenia seek to mitigate the negative health impacts of cigarette smoking.

Case example: Choir of Hard Knocks, a health promotion project for people with an established mental health problem

The Choir of Hard Knocks was formed in 2006 as an initiative of Reclink in Melbourne, Victoria. The choir director, Jonathon Welch, invited homeless men and women to come together to form a choir that would share a love of music. His project became the subject of a highly successful television series that followed the development of the choir through early difficulties to celebrated performances in the Melbourne Town Hall and later at the Sydney Opera House. Many of the people in the choir had long-term mental illness. Some had serious alcohol and substance abuse problems. All were poor and disadvantaged. The Reclink staff provided substantial organisational support and some resources. This provided Jonathon with the space and resources to establish the choir and to challenge the choristers to learn and interpret the music. While the experience of being a part of the choir was sometimes stressful, most of the choristers were able to develop confidence, self-esteem and new hope for the future. As well as a series of successful concerts, the choir has produced a best-selling DVD and CD and is in great demand to perform publicly.

The Choir of Hard Knocks is a story of real magic. Its music has inspired many of us in the mental health field to appreciate the capacity for healing that comes from vision and commitment. Through all the sadness and poverty of the choristers emerges the beauty of the human spirit that remains untouched by mental illness.

Sites and activities for action in building supportive environments

There are a range of key strategic sectors, including the home, child care, education, employment, corrections and the media, that can be seen as potential sites for partnership between mental health and other services to produce activities of health promotion or prevention. A number of key areas identified here which are likely to include social work involvement are set out in Table 10.1.

Put simply, the monograph (Commonwealth Department of Health and Aged Care, 2000) argues that there are many sites of opportunity for mental health services to form partnerships with community-based organisations to develop health-promotion and preventive projects. While there are examples of such partnerships, particularly in the area of community health generally, there is not a strong tradition of mental health services adopting a strong community-based outreach to local community health and welfare services. While social workers in general health and welfare settings are actively engaged in many projects that would meet the definitions of health promotion or prevention in mental health, these social workers do not traditionally define their projects in this way. The preferred language to describe their services is drawn from community work and community development, which emphasise the empowerment of citizens to make decisions over resources and life circumstances. The organising principles for these services stress choice, power, agency, resources and relationships.

Importantly, however, the Commonwealth Department of Health and Aged Care (2000) monograph encourages us to adopt the principle of seeing mental health and wellbeing not as an isolated and unique responsibility of mental health

Table 10.1 Key strategic sectors, settings and people for mental health partnerships

Sector	*Settings*	*People – individuals or groups*
Health	Includes prenatal and postnatal health care settings, general practice, hospitals, community health, Aboriginal health services	Includes clients, patients, carers, staff, GPs, social workers, allied health staff, policymakers, managers
Welfare	Includes child and family welfare services, counselling services, child protection services, employment services, disability services	Includes clients, carers, counsellors, clergy, youth workers, social workers, consumer organisations
Housing	Includes housing services, refuges and shelters, residential aged-care settings	Includes clients, staff, managers, policymakers
Community	Includes communities, recreational groups, clubs, associations, sporting groups, Aboriginal community groups, churches	Includes volunteers, consumer groups, club members and management, professional organisations, community group members and staff

Source: Commonwealth Department of Health and Aged Care (2000, pp. 38–9).

services but within the matrix of broader community services that need to work together to ensure the mental health and wellbeing of citizens. This truth is central to the key themes of this book – that the domain of social work in mental health is that of the social context and consequences of mental illness and that social inclusion principles are central to social work practice. Social work as a discipline is probably closer than any other to these health-promotion and prevention strategies.

Case example: the Vietnam Veterans Heart Health Group, a health-based prevention program

The Veterans and Veterans' Families Counselling Service (formerly called the Vietnam Veterans Counselling Service) has run a series of group-based interventions for its clients over many years. These include health-promotion and preventive programs such as:

- stress and anger management, assertiveness and self-esteem skills;
- PTSD post-program development groups;
- partners' support groups;
- health education groups for veterans or their partners;
- couples' communication skills groups;
- lifestyle management;
- groups for sons and daughters to help them deal with the impact of having a parent who has been to war;
- retirement planning.

The heart health program offers veterans a series of classes and structured exercise sessions that are designed to reduce the risk of heart disease. The course builds positive attitudes to health care, diet, weight management, alcohol use and general fitness. It also brings veterans together in a supportive group to build motivation and enhance wellbeing. The program reduces veteran isolation by encouraging positive friendships and support in an ordinary social context. Evaluations of the project have been positive, not just in its capacity to reduce the risk of heart disease in participating veterans but in the broader benefits of reducing isolation, building supportive friendships and enhancing a sense of wellbeing.

This program is a good example of the connection between physical and mental health and the many benefits that can flow from a group-based approach that is sensitive to the culture in which it is introduced. The gym environment is more welcoming and appropriate than trying to bring men together to discuss their health problems. Accessibility and sensitivity are central to the success of the project.

Community education as a method of health promotion and prevention

Many of the group and community work projects undertaken by social workers contain a strong element of education. This is based on the principle that change happens for people through developing knowledge and understanding and through the learning of new skills to cope with life. As Hatfield (1987) argues, an educational focus provides a much more positive paradigm for change than does treatment or therapy. Hatfield has been able to develop specific skills-focused training programs for families of people with mental health problems based on learning theory and principles of stress-coping and adaptation. Examples of learning-based models include programs to teach parents of adolescents good communication skills (parent effectiveness training) and psychoeducation programs to help people with schizophrenia to understand their illness and develop effective coping strategies to deal with some of the distressing symptoms. The family support programs described in Chapter 9 are good examples of learning-based work.

Case example: Beyond Blue community lectures, a learning-based project

As part of its broad range of activities, Beyond Blue works to build community understanding and awareness of depression. Though based in Melbourne, the organisation regularly runs information sessions in rural and regional centres. These sessions follow a format of lecture and discussions, typically with an 'expert' speaker who has a mental health background and another 'expert' speaker who has experienced depression. The lectures cover topics such as the nature, causes and course of depression, as well as the treatments and help available. Members of the public are welcome to attend, and the lectures are well covered by the local media.

The Beyond Blue lectures provide a non-stigmatising opportunity for people to learn about depression. They are a starting point for finding help for oneself or a family member and a way of building community support and understanding for people with depression. They provide a space for people who could not easily ask about depression to start a journey of help-seeking and recovery.

Other, more formal community education projects are designed to educate large groups of people. The 'Be You' initiative was launched in 2018. Funded by the Australian federal government and managed by Beyond Blue, the project provides early childhood services and primary and secondary schools with evidence-based mental health promotion, prevention and early intervention training and resources. Be You's objectives are to promote mental wellness through the development of teachers', parents' and carers' capacity to influence good mental health and to intervene early when challenges are identified (Be You, 2018). The Mental Health First Aid Course (Jorm & Kitchener, 2011) provides basic information about mental health problems and skills in responding to mental health crises. The program is designed to provide useful information for ordinary members of the public but is particularly useful for people in the human services such as teachers, police, and ambulance and welfare workers. Anti-stigma projects, such as those run by SANE in Australia or Mind in the United Kingdom, generally rely on educational strategies to build community awareness and understanding of mental health issues.

Mutual support groups

One of the traditional ways that social workers in community settings have sought to work with people with specific needs has been to assist people to form support groups. This strategy has been based on the power of collective identification to confront isolation. People who were alone can find a sense of common cause, mutual support and strength in the group. People can learn new ways of understanding their experiences and take collective action to address a sense of powerlessness that comes from isolation. The mutual support model is central to some of the most successful interventions in the mental health area, such as the Alliance for the Mentally Ill (AMI) in the United States; the Association of Relatives and Friends of the Mentally Ill (ARAFMI) in Australia; and the many consumer support networks that have been formed by consumers – or mental health survivors – throughout the world, such as Being in NSW.

Case example: Hearing Voices Network, a mutual support group

The Hearing Voices Network was established in the Netherlands in 1987. Its aim originally was to develop the further understanding of and research into hearing voices. Similar organisations have since been established around the world, and there is an international network known as INTERVOICE – the International Network for Training, Education and Research into Hearing Voices. Members of the network include people who hear voices, family members and friends, and professionals. The philosophical underpinnings of the network place an emphasis on the personal engagement of voice hearers and others. INTERVOICE asserts that all participants are experts in their own experience. Each voice hearer is a person first, secondly they are equal partners and thirdly they have different but mutually valuable expertise to offer. The movement regards itself as post-psychiatric and argues that the central issue is one of respect for human rights. It therefore challenges the way societies and professions perceive hearing voices. It seeks more holistic health solutions to problematic and overwhelming voices that cause distress. The network asserts that many people successfully live with their voices, and that the voices in themselves are not the problem.

The network is a good example of consumers challenging professional definitions of mental illness and pathology. While social workers in mainstream mental health services might feel uncomfortable talking about the network with their clients, we believe that it may offer an alternative and useful resource for some people. By definition, such consumer-directed programs are not developed or managed by social workers or other health professionals. Skills in working collaboratively with consumers are needed here.

It is important to note the increasingly important role played by 'peer support' or 'lived experience' workers in mental health. The Queensland Mental Health Commission (2019) based its framework for further developing this workforce on the recognition of the potentially powerful interventions people with direct experience of mental ill-health and services are able to make. There is a clear resonance with fundamental underpinnings of the recovery model as we have previously discussed it. The framework also recognises the difficulties which can arise for workers when their roles and boundaries are not adequately defined and when governance arrangements are lacking. There is considerable international evidence for both the importance of the role and its challenges (Kemp and Henderson 2012; Simpson et al. 2018; Walsh et al. 2018).

From Ann: the joys of being part of a 'permanent draft' community-building document

When Our Consumer Place announced a competition for entrants to *The MadQuarry Dictionary* I knew I had to be part of it! The word had gone out to the far cyber reaches of consumer land around Australia (and dare I say, without manic pretensions, The World) that an A-Z Dictionary was being put together featuring consumer re-definitions of words, phrases and acronyms commonly used in the mental illness world.

My little offering was 'FIFO, noun, Fly In Fly Out, aka acute psychiatric care'.

I've read it many times, sometimes roaring with laughter and at others discomforted and angered. *The MadQuarry Dictionary* comes from the genius and pathos of madness and holds a mirror to the sector/industry that shows what we see when the emperors are wearing insufficient clothes!

To this day it helps me feel part of a strong, diverse and energetic consumer community.

Collective action

Sometimes the focus of group and community action is on bringing about change. Many of the mutual support groups like NAMI and ARAFMI have adopted a strong advocacy role, challenging discrimination and stigma in the community. A commitment to social justice and social change is central to social work practice, and many social workers have established social action projects in the mental health area to bring about social change.

ALTERNATIVE
Example: Our Consumer Place – Empowerment through Collective Action
This original description of Our Consumer Place is taken from their website.

> Our Consumer Place is a resource centre run entirely by people diagnosed with 'mental illness' (we choose to call ourselves 'consumers'). We provide information, training, support and advice to consumer-run groups and projects (or more specifically, 'Consumer Developed Initiatives' [CDIs]). We also support what we call 'consumer perspective', recognising that the lived experience of 'mental illness' provides a crucial source of insight that is of value and must be respected. We believe that we are part of an important cultural shift, towards valuing and respecting the lived experience of 'mental illness'. Our Consumer Place has been developed by consumers for consumers.
>
> www.ourconsumerplace.com.au/consumer/aboutus

The organisation asserts that it is not a therapeutic resource or an advocacy group. Rather, the focus is on building the intellectual and skill base of the consumer movement and building a consumer community with the skills and resources to effect change for mental health consumers. The community building supported by Our Consumer Place is localised and contextualised. They run workshops and presentations for both professional workers and for consumers which focus on developing a distinct consumer perspective in mental health. One major activity has been the establishment of a clearinghouse of lectures, publications and websites to resource consumers as they engage in training each other and contribute to the knowledge base for the mental health workforce. Leading intellectuals at Our Consumer Place such as Merinda Epstein and Flick Grey have given consumers a powerful voice in the mental health community (www.ourconsumerplace.com.au/consumer/manifesto).

Our Consumer Place seeks to empower consumers in a number of fundamental ways:

- Providing resources. Our Consumer Place develops the intellectual property that forms the basis of education and training and makes it available to the consumer community. Individual consumers are connected with very skilled and committed activists. The quality training provided supports the good efforts of mental health workers as well as consumer activists.

- Reclaiming identity – a positive view of madness. In line with the recovery task of building a positive identity, Our Consumer Place can give isolated consumers and their families the language, role models, encouragement and hope to be able to abandon the highly stigmatised and life-limiting role of mental health patient. There is another way to be mad, and there can be some pride, and indeed some joy, in that identity.
- Asserting authority and sense of agency. This is achieved through training and publication, promoting the consumer voice as a valid and important alternative to the dominant voice of mental health clinicians and academics. Our Consumer Place has been able to challenge the power of stigma and the hidden oppression of the anti-stigma campaigns. There is specific training in consumers using their experience to train others, moving beyond telling their story to using their experience to challenge beliefs and values. Consumers recognise that they are the experts in their own experience and that that expertise is powerful when shared with others.
- Establishing a sense of community. Our Consumer Place is a community of like-minded individuals, drawn together for mutual support and education. The newsletters and website provide a point of connection, pride and identity.

Case example: Flying Solo

Annette was a social worker at a community health centre in a regional town. She noticed that a number of clients referred by GPs for help with depression were women who were struggling to rebuild their lives following the death of a partner. She established a group called Flying Solo to help women cope with this difficult transition. At first the group operated like a mutual support group as the women shared their experiences of grief, but over time it moved to a social action project. Among the many difficulties confronting these women were the policies of banks, utilities and other services that required some action to change account details from their partner's to the their name. The women found the paperwork required to manage such changes was excessively bureaucratic and patriarchal. Services frequently sent mail to the women but addressed to their deceased partners, and the women found that they had to work hard to get the necessary changes to arrangements and that services were often unresponsive, slow and unconcerned about the stress that such arrangements caused the women.

Annette helped the women to plan a campaign to change the procedures that banks and utilities used at such times. They wrote letters and organised deputations to meet key staff in the agencies. They developed a Guide for New Widows that provided a wealth of practical information following the death of their partner. As a result of their action, a number of small but significant changes were made to the procedures of target agencies. As well as a strong sense of solidarity and support among the women – an effective protective factor, perhaps, against the possible onset of depression – there were tangible social outcomes from the project.

This is a great example of creative social work intervention that addresses both the critical and the clinical dimensions of practice. These functions are not in opposition here but offer a complementary direction for practice that in the end is effective and relevant.

Responding to disasters

Social workers in Australia have a long history of working with communities during and after disasters, both internationally and locally. Centrelink social workers, for example, take an important role in Australia's international disaster response team. They were present in Bali, caring for survivors and their families following the bombings and providing ongoing support during the court case and anniversary commemorations, again in Lebanon and Cyprus during the evacuation of Australians during the civil war, in Cyclone Yatsi in North Queensland, and when the tsunami impacted Thailand.

On the home front, environmental disasters are part and parcel of Australian life, principally bushfires and floods, and occasionally earthquakes. Climate change sees their increasing frequency, and enquiry after enquiry says community recovery needs to be conducted in more effective ways through better preparation, targeting interventions in a more focused manner, spending disaster money more wisely, using and contributing to best practice, and working collegially and more strategically. Mental health work is a core component of community recovery endeavours and social workers play important roles in the immediate and subsequent responses to disaster.

Significant mental health, physical health and welfare stresses follow the experience of catastrophe. In the period following disaster, social workers are most often found assisting people to come to terms with their loss, easing the transition to new lives, navigating complex bureaucracies and dealing with the mental health sequelae of trauma. While there is general acknowledgement of the value of such social work involvement in disaster response, we face the challenge of conceptualising and theorising this work so that the lessons learned from disaster work can be shared, taught in social work programs and applied again when needed.

As well as counselling traumatised individuals in an individual casework approach, a community work approach would seek to engage groups of people in the community to build on established networks of support or build new supportive relationships that help communities to confront the problems they face. A focus on community strengths and resilience, rather than pathology, can lead to creative and effective interventions. For example, in a Victorian town badly affected by the 2010 bushfires, the local fire brigade held monthly community barbeques which became a focus for sharing, encouragement and recovery. This very 'ordinary' approach provided a non-stigmatising point of connection for citizens who could face together what might be difficult to face alone.

Community example – Central West Rural Wellness Network

Through the last eight years, much of Eastern Australia has been subject to drought, with serious economic and social problems in rural communities in Queensland, New South Wales and Victoria. The severe stresses for farmers and graziers, and for rural businesses, have threatened the mental health and wellbeing of many people. While the most obvious problems surround a lack of income from drought-affected properties, farmers also faced the struggle to feed animals and the distress of stock losses. There have been concerns about the risk of depression and suicide among vulnerable individuals.

There are few specialist mental health services in many communities. Sometimes the well-intentioned government responses, using programs drawn from urban experience, have proven problematic. Importing outside experts – either as financial advisors or as specialist drought counsellors or mental health experts – may create problems for the target group for whom help is intended. It's difficult to establish the kind of trusting helpful relationships when the outsiders lack local knowledge. Accessing help anonymously might be impossible in close knit communities where privacy is limited. Some local communities have been able to do highly creative and effective work, not by importing expertise but by building on local service networks that emphasise community strengths.

One such group has been the Central West Rural Wellness Network. This group began their work in 2014 as an informal network of service providers in the Longreach area. The rural family support officer organised a meeting of local workers from the GP network, alcohol and drug treatment services, financial counsellors, ambulance services, police and the Royal Flying Doctor Service. As a collective, they had a deep, intimate knowledge of their community and were able to work together to connect vulnerable people with the local supports available. They were people who were often well connected and well respected by local people. Help was offered in a respectful way by people who understood the needs of the community – local people helping local people. Among the network, the group was able to access whatever resources were available and to distribute resources. They were able to advocate for additional resources which saw opportunities for additional funding for community initiatives. Services like the police and faith-based institutions became front-line mental health providers.

Over time the community has shown considerable resilience and moderated the worst impact of the drought, not by importing expertise but by working with the strengths of the local community. One such strength has been the integrity of helpful individuals who can use the relationships of trust to connect people with helpful others. In these circumstances, referral involves facilitating connection to trusted people, not formal services.

The example is instructive on a number of levels. It is a clear reminder that communities have strengths and resilience that can be the basis for good outcomes. It's a lesson about the risks of well-intentioned outsiders failing to understand the nature of local communities. The network of relationships among community leaders is built up over time, and the local culture can be complex and subtle – it's hard for outsiders to work effectively with the community until a level of trust can be established. Concepts of supporting hope and sense of agency – central to recovery – are basic to this story of community response to drought. Finally, it is further evidence of an underlying principle of this book: that helping happens through relationships.

Practice principles for group and community work

This chapter has identified a number of theoretical principles to construct a model for social work practice in the area of community work in mental health. This remains a significant and major area of social work practice – with its own literature and theory base, and it is beyond the scope of this chapter to cover this area in any depth. We can, however, identify a number of practice principles that can be applied to this work.

A commitment to empowerment principles

Thyer and Wodarski's (2007) analysis of social work interventions being based on psychosocial frameworks emphasises the scientific and positivist dimension of practice. Many of the interventions we have discussed here, however, reflect the social work commitment to its value base, specifically that of social change, social justice and empowerment. These principles, central to community work practice, are basic and relevant to mental health social work generally and particularly useful in shaping group and community approaches in social work in mental health. They give a distinctive social work emphasis to the work of health promotion and prevention. The discussion of approaches to practice in this chapter revives the importance of avoiding the critical/clinical binary discussed in Chapter 1. Good social work practice is sensitive to both clinical effectiveness and issues of power and powerlessness.

Linhorst's (2005) analysis of empowerment principles in mental health practice offers a detailed and insightful theoretical framework to describe many of the community work projects described here. His chapters on housing and employment argue strongly that projects in these areas meet not just the needs for shelter and resources but provide opportunities for people to exercise personal agency in their lives. For example, when discussing housing, Linhorst identifies a number of practice guidelines for group and community work projects that encourage empowerment outcomes. These include:

- providing skills training in the setting in which people choose to live,
- supporting an array of housing options,

- educating landlords and neighbours about psychiatric symptoms,
- working with landlords to develop trust and respect.

The importance of relationships as a vehicle for change

A constant theme of this book has been the importance of relationships as the vehicle for change. This is as evident in the discussion of group and community work approaches as it is in the individual work described earlier. Social workers engaged in group and community work approaches need relationship skills in order to assess, engage, encourage and sustain others in planned activity. As the examples show, group and community work can have a transformative impact on all participants. The power for change emerges through the relationships formed by the worker with clients, with families, with other service providers and with ordinary citizens.

Engaging with evidence

As we have argued elsewhere in this book, the dominant cultural paradigm within the mental health services is that of evidence-based practice. Many of the interventions described here are broadly based programs, in which both the intervention itself and the desired outcomes might be difficult to specify. Certainly, there may not be the clear research base to provide a confident expectation that the program planned is protected by ready evidence. In the absence of such ready evidence, social workers may struggle to justify their activities to managers insisting on evidence-based practice. Under such requirements, health promotion and prevention activities run the risk of being seen as 'not core business', a luxury that hard-pressed services cannot afford to support. How, then, do they shape our work?

Many of the strategies already identified in Chapter 3 are relevant here. They include:

- attention to a detailed description of what the program will do. It is important that social workers can describe clearly what it is they do and why they will do it;
- locating the planned program within the available evidence and theory. Attention to the research literature will ensure that whatever research has been done in the area can be assembled to shape and defend the proposed project. The concepts of health promotion and prevention described here provide a useful theoretical framework for much of the group and community work undertaken by social workers;
- locating the project within current mental health policy. Since the Second National Mental Health Plan (Australian Health Ministers, 1998), health promotion and prevention have been identified as priority policy areas;
- evaluating programs as effectively as possible against identified aims. This is an internal response to the need for evidence – how effectively does the project meet the identified aims?

The need for creativity and the concept of multiple sites for intervention

One of the salient features of many of the examples used in this chapter is the creativity of the individual workers involved. Through engaging with people around their strengths and interests, they have been able to find multiple sites for intervention. So junior sport became a site for building self-esteem and resilience in the basketball project. Learning to drive became a site for building a sense of agency, confidence and community integration in the Kalahari Driving School. Teaching homeless people to sing in a choir became a site for personal recovery in the Choir of Hard Knocks. The creative spirit remains the greatest strength of the effective social worker.

Conclusion

All community work relies on building effective relationships, and the power of relationship shines through in the stories of mutual support, social action and community building. Social work practice with groups and communities remains a potentially important area of practice in mental health. It is important not just for social workers in specialist mental health agencies but is relevant to social workers in a diversity of health and welfare settings.

QUESTIONS FOR PRACTICE

1 What strategies might a mental health social worker use to ensure that community work activities are embraced as mainstream mental health practice?
2 In the example of the Longreach community drought response, could the outside experts have approached their work more effectively, or was it always going to be impossible?
3 What is the place of relationship in building resilience in individuals, groups and communities?
4 What is the connection between resilient communities and individual mental health?

Websites

Australian Emergency Management Institute

Comprehensive free publications about emergency management, including disaster health; Guidelines for Psychological Services Practice Manual 10 – Mental Health Practitioners Guide.

www.em.gov.au

Mental Health Promotion

Provides links to resources for planning, research, evidence and key policies to support the policymaking process.

www.health.vic.gov.au/mentalhealthpromotion

Mental Health Pro

An online interactive network for professionals to share research, resources and ideas relating to mental health promotion. It provides access to the latest research, policy, news and events posted by moderators and members.

http://mhpro.health.vic.gov.au

Melbourne Charter

The charter reflects the input and support of organisations from all over the world. It articulates some common principles and recommendations that should be part of our future action in mental health promotion and mental illness prevention.

www.vichealth.vic.gov.au/-/mmedia/ProgramsandProjects/Melbourne-Charter

The Ottawa Charter for Health Promotion (World Health Organization)

www.who.int/healthpromotion/conferences/previous/ottawa/en/

11 Sustaining social work in mental health agencies

Throughout this book, we have emphasised that what makes social work distinctive in the mental health field is its focus on the social context and social consequences of mental illness and the advancement of social justice, and we have drawn out the implications for a critical approach to the work that is fully engaged with consumers and their families. In this final chapter, we focus on what might sustain and nourish work of this kind. We want to acknowledge just how challenging social work mental health practice can be. We will discuss here the organisational environment of mental health social work and seek to emphasise some of the factors that might sustain us individually and collectively: clarity of purpose, applying the principles of relationship-based practices in organisations and service networks, an ethical commitment to social justice in the mental health field and a commitment to the active improvement of services. We conclude with a discussion of competence and expertise in this field, and we suggest the kinds of supervision and professional development that support the growth of competence.

The organisational context of social work in mental health

Most mental health work is done in organisations and teams, and the landscape is changing. Only ten years ago, when we talked of mental health social work in Australia, we referred almost exclusively to the work of social workers in the public mental health system, sometimes including non-government agencies with a focus on psychiatric rehabilitation. Since that time, many of these agencies have been transformed and the environment has diversified to include substantial numbers of accredited mental health social workers working in primary mental health settings including independent private practice and community health organisations. A number of social workers are operating within the NDIS framework as case coordinators or individual therapists. As new funding models seek to offer consumers greater choice about mental health services, the working environment will continue to become more complex. Where the work has traditionally been organised around multidisciplinary teams, existing roles are tending to become less clear, and new roles are emerging, due in large part to improvements in consumer and carer participation and influence over system design. Moreover, mental health

DOI: 10.4324/9781003148913-13

social work is carried out increasingly in organisations with a focus and mandate other than mental health and in teams in which colleagues may have limited understanding of, or commitment to, the mental health of their clients. The mental health field itself is characterised by:

the expectation of interprofessional working, even sometimes in the absence of agreed models and purposes;
a high level of organisational complexity and change within the mental health service system;
the necessity of effective cross-sector working if good outcomes are to be achieved.

The agency or organisational setting is 'the hidden reality of social work' (Weissman et al., 1983, p. 3) because it has a profound effect on what transpires between workers and consumers. When we think about our work and its difficulties, as often as not it is the organisation that causes us concern, sometimes more than our work with clients. We often find ourselves thinking and worrying, even losing sleep, about our relations with colleagues, or the paperwork, or the rules and requirements of the organisation, or how our performance is being judged by others. There is a tendency, often, to think about the work that goes on between a worker and a consumer as the real work and what goes on in the agency as an unwelcome distraction. However, there are skills involved in working effectively with the agency, just like other parts of the consumer's ecosystem, and effective mental health social workers will need to work at contributing to, and deriving support from, their agency.

The purpose of the work

Given the level of need relative to resources and the emotional and other demands and strains of the work, it can be easy to work busily in the moment without a clear and conscious sense of purpose. Mission statements sometimes seem abstract and dry, possibly imposed from outside or comprising empty statements not well connected to actual practice. Mental health services are under enormous pressure, seemingly expected to do too much, so they need an articulated primary task that is manageable and meaningful, with effective gatekeeping so the service is not overwhelmed.

Reflecting the principles we set out in Chapter 1, mental health services should be organised in such a way that they give primacy to the lived experience of consumers and families, and the therapeutic power of relationships. Different organisations and workplaces have different contributions to make, but whatever the specific function of the organisation or team – crisis assessment and community treatment, case management, treatment in hospital and community settings, residential rehabilitation, home-based outreach support, supported employment, specialised treatment or a combination of these – we will want to organise the work so that both its ends and its means support people with mental illness *as they themselves experience their lives*, along with their families and friends, in a manner that supports and strengthens healing relationships with professionals and others. Many contemporary mental health services fall somewhat short because their purpose is defined more by the imperatives of established professional modes of intervention or by administrative or even political requirements, or because they are overtaken by short-term concerns, such as a preoccupation with the management of risk.

Clarity about the purpose of the work can help guard against an 'adjustment of expectations' away from the true purpose of mental health work and towards crisis control and stability (Woolford, 2013). Wharne (2005), for example, describes a familiar situation: a community mental health team in which it seemed that frequent client 'crises' were making it difficult to plan and organise the work, causing a lot of stress for staff and threatening to call into question the efficacy of the team. What was required was a reorientation of the team's efforts to give primacy to a range of practical and demanding work tasks designed to address the sorts of things that were causing the crises, which were mostly triggered by relationship conflicts or lack of money – usually associated with problems with symptoms, social withdrawal and often increased alcohol or drug use. This particular team was an assertive outreach team, and the 'reorientation' described was actually a 'return' to the principles of Test and Stein's (2000) original model of assertive community treatment (ACT), as Wharne identifies. The team had to refocus on the life difficulties and 'ordinary' hassles of its clients. This is a good illustration of the need for constant reaffirmation of the real purpose of the work in teams and the easy drift back into ways of operating that have more to do with the comfort zone of the professional than the needs of consumers, or even the mission of the agency.

The need for a clear sense of purpose is particularly important for social workers because, as we have discussed, the identification of the specific social work domain has often appeared elusive in practice. Social workers should hold fast to the overall purpose of their mental health organisation through a specific focus on the social consequences and social context of mental illness and on promoting social justice for people with mental health problems and other affected people in the community. These broader principles have to be translated into clear workplace priorities that reflect the specific work setting. For example, social workers who work with significant numbers of young families may decide to pay particular attention to work at the interface between child welfare and mental health service systems.

An example of reframing services around core values (ARAFMI Queensland)

ARAFMI has been a strong family-based community organisation providing support and advocacy for families of people with mental illness for over 30 years. One service was to provide respite for family carers in ordinary houses in the community. These houses were also used to provide temporary housing for consumers, again with a focus on respite for carers.

With the introduction of the National Disability Insurance Scheme, ARAFMI decided to compete for contracts for individual consumers, providing care coordination and personal support. This work was very successful and the organisation budget expanded considerably, so much so that the family support work that had been the core business of ARAFMI became secondary to the NDIS work. At the same time the block funding for community organisations, which had supported ARAFMI activity over the years, was wound back and replaced by NDIS funding. This posed a significant challenge for the organisation – should they continue to grow in the NDIS space but let go of core family business?

After considerable deliberation, ARAFMI decided that effective NDIS-based consumer care had the potential to contribute greatly to family welfare. They decided to redefine their commitment to NDIS work with individuals to reflect a broad family focus in a unique ARAFMI model of NDIS care and in 2020 adopted the following statement of service:

1 Care planning is based on the right of individuals to choose those services that they want to live a satisfying and contributing life. The individual's right to choose the services that they want and need should drive service planning.
2 Services are individually tailored and each plan is unique.
3 Assessment of individual need and service planning should recognise the social and personal context of the individual. This includes the person's family and close friends.
4 Assessment should include an awareness of the impact of support plans on family carers. Comprehensive support plans for each individual should include the potential for families to be supported as well.
5 Changes to the person's life circumstances because of NDIS support will have an impact on family. While the family is likely to benefit greatly from additional support to the individual, some families might experience additional stress. Service planning should anticipate this and ensure families are supported through stressful changes.

Focus on the lived experience of consumers and families

The greatest challenge for mental health agencies, and the greatest potential for transformation, flows from consumer and family participation. Consumers and families have been influential in establishing and changing mental health policy. Sometimes they have done so through lobbying and activism from the 'outside', and sometimes consumers and families have formed alliances with professionals to defend services that may be under threat and to advocate for new ones. Some mental health organisations are controlled by consumers or families, but most are not. All need explicit systems for supporting the expression of consumer voices and for listening and responding. Consumers and families have specific expertise that is not shared by professionals or managers. They have both the experience of living with mental illness and the experience of receiving – consuming, if you like – treatment and care. Each organisation needs a way of knowing about and learning from both – in the establishment of its priorities, its culture, its knowledge base and its practices. At the agency level, there are three related realms in which to give effect to the principle of participation: organisational governance, organisation-wide systems of participation and 'feedback' mechanisms, and participation by consumers and families in their own treatment and care.

In the realm of governance, there will be opportunities for boards of management, advisory committees and the like to include people who can speak from the experience of consumers and family carers and bring that experience to the 'high-level' organisational decision-making.

Within the agency, there is now considerable experience in the engagement of consumer consultants and carer consultants. Their roles vary, but generally they work as part of a multidisciplinary team to provide a range of services, including support and individual and systemic advocacy, as well as management and advisory roles. Increasingly, they are involved in staff selection procedures. These are very challenging roles; commonly, there is a single consumer and/or carer in a service with a wide range of positions to 'represent' and limited resources. The positions sit in a difficult position organisationally, in some ways a part of and yet in other ways apart from the mental health service. They are not always treated as equals by their colleagues, and the experience of mental illness, and the very qualities of sensitivity and compassion that consumers and family members bring to their work, may make them even more vulnerable to the stresses of working in the mental health system. Such roles rely for their success on an open and receptive organisational culture, and they are yet to penetrate the whole of the service system.

Effective participation, as discussed previously in Chapter 3, requires that adequate resources be allocated. For example, it may be necessary to invite a small group of consumers, rather than a single consumer, to contribute to a committee. Consumers who are 'seldom-heard' because they do not participate in formal participation processes should not be neglected (Hernandez et al., 2010). Consultation must be timely, rather than after the real decisions have been made. 'Consult early and often' is a good principle. Partnership carries with it the potential for conflict, so we need to be prepared to work through potential conflicts in a respectful manner. Encouraging independent and empowered consumer or family carer voices will invite the opportunity for productive disagreements.

The support for consumer and carer participation requires careful work. The following practical suggestions, developed in the United Kingdom by Hanley and Staley (2005) and elucidated by Campbell and Davidson (2012), provide a good framework for social workers seeking to improve their agency's focus on the lived experience of consumers and families. Each point may seem obvious, but it is worth remembering that effective consumer and carer involvement is usually very challenging for an organisation, so it might be necessary to address each issue carefully and explicitly in order to be successful:

Be clear about why you want to involve service users and carers.
Develop a strategy for involvement in partnership with stakeholders.

Be clear about who you want to involve.
Ensure you have all the appropriate policies and procedures in place.
Identify the resources required to support user and carer involvement.
Be ready to constructively challenge people's attitudes and beliefs.

Here are their key points about the *process* of involvement:

Give service users and carers a choice about how, when, where and how often they get involved.
Think about the level of involvement you want – consultation, collaboration or user control.
Ensure you involve a wide range of people – make special efforts to involve people who may often be marginalised.
Provide training and support for service users, carers and staff – think about expenses and payment, training, access issues, information, involvement in meetings and emotional support.
Ensure user and carer involvement has an impact.
Keep all stakeholders informed of the success of user and carer involvement.
Involve service users and carers in measuring the impact of user and carer involvement.

The third realm of participation in the agency is probably the most complex: allowing the consumer 'into the system' at the point at which decisions about treatment are being made. This may mean a shift from a model in which the worker assumes all or almost all of the responsibility for protection, diagnosis and prescribing treatment, in which the voice of the consumer is subordinated or lost. It is precisely at this point that the principles of relationship-based practice are tested and come into their own. Such principles can be encouraged and supported by agency managers and professional supervisors, but they depend on the knowledge, skills and values of each worker for their realisation.

Teams that are both creative and effective need the autonomy and common values to be able to support the needs of consumers and can assist the agency to move beyond service-led and crisis-oriented forms of work to something more proactive and client-led. For this to occur, the worker has to hold in mind the situation of the consumer in its fine detail in such a way that needs can be anticipated, rather than waiting until people experience acute difficulties or cause problems in the home or in the community. Technical expertise is important, but it has to be applied in a way that properly engages with the actual experience of the consumer, striving for a relationship that will be a vehicle for change.

In work environments that are busy and under strain, where staff struggle to deal with mental illness, conflict and risk, attention can be diverted from this focus, to be replaced by a concern with the pressure of time, routine work processes and organisational tensions. We can forget, for a time, to organise our work and interactions around its primary purpose, and we can forget the language of compassion and care (Crawford et al., 2013). Because consumers and families often have negative experiences of the mental health service system, any failure or lapse in common decency can make the situation worse. So too can an over-reliance on the conventional methods of psychiatry in a way that foregrounds the illness rather than the person.

There is a growing movement towards formalised peer support work as an integral element of mental health services. This is the logical consequence of a focus on the lived experience of consumers, and some suggest that peer support workers should comprise about half of the mental health workforce (Sainsbury Centre for Mental Health, 2009). Peer support is

> a system of giving and receiving help founded on key principles of respect, shared responsibility, and mutual agreement of what is helpful. . . . It is about understanding another's situation emphatically through the shared experience of emotional and psychological pain which may lead to peers respectfully challenging one another to 'move beyond previously held self-concepts built on disability and diagnosis'.
>
> (Mead et al., 2001, p. 135)

Peer support workers may be employed within public mental health services to work alongside other members of the multidisciplinary team as a 'supplementary adjunct' (Holmes et al., 2013). A new consumer workforce has come into being. Some peer support programs have their own organisational base, and some form part of peer-controlled services. There is growing evidence for the effectiveness of peer support programs for both clinical and recovery-oriented outcomes (Repper & Carter, 2011; Walker & Bryant, 2013). For the 'old' workforce, including social workers, new ways of working are required to support and nurture this fundamental change to the way mental health services are delivered.

From Ann: the sum of all our journeys

Deep Dialogue is a radical process in mental health where presumptions; paradoxes; contradictions; practices; closed-loop, self-sealing ways of thinking and unmentionables can be surfaced, shared and re-examined. Without critical reflection, business as usual can result in the displacement of the highly prized values and goals that underpin contemporary agencies.

The concepts were developed during a three-year consumer evaluation of acute psychiatric hospital practice between 1993 and 1996, the Understanding and Involvement Project (Wadsworth, 2001). Using a participatory action research methodology, it developed a process of consumer-driven deep conversations between those who work in the sector and those who receive services from them, with the goal of making real changes to services.

This was a radical endeavour in 1998, yet the ideas and concepts remain fresh and provoking.

The Lemon Tree Learning Project (Epstein and Our Consumer Place, 1997) was an ancillary project funded under the First National Mental Health Strategy. It developed a more structured version of Deep Dialogue between consumers and professionals that sets aside logic and analysis and uses tools of intuition and creativity.

Since then Deep Dialogue has been modified by consumers so that groups of consumers can develop theory that is grounded in lived experience. It supports consumers to speak to and hear from each other to develop a new logic where people aren't always and only the most vulnerable/incapable. It seeks to claim and reclaim the consumer voice, nurture it and co-construct new, emergent discourses.

Outcome measures

One good way to keep the focus on the real purpose of our work is the use of the right outcome measures. There are many challenges here because of the dominance of outcome measures in the clinical and administrative domains. Health is properly defined not only as the absence of disease but also as the presence of mental, physical and social wellbeing. It might be argued that the most relevant overall outcomes concern quality of life (Prigent et al., 2014), or satisfaction with life (or happiness), which is normally included as a component of quality of life. Clinical measures, such as compliance and symptom reduction, are relevant to these outcomes, of course, as are administrative measures, such as levels of service use and length of stay in hospital, but not in a straightforward way. To illustrate, for people with schizophrenia, most of the negative impact on wellbeing may be related to the symptoms of depression and anxiety and problems in psychosocial functioning, rather than psychotic symptoms as such. Among psychotic symptoms, hallucinations and suspiciousness may be more of a problem for wellbeing than disorganisation or delusions (Fervaha et al., 2013), so simply measuring symptom reduction may have very limited relevance.

There are recovery-oriented outcome measures in development and in use (Burgess et al., 2011; Shanks et al., 2013; Sklar et al., 2013), and there have been attempts to develop good measures of other relevant outcomes such as social inclusion (Coombs et al., 2013). Their relevance will vary with the service setting. In recent years the framework offered by the *Recovery Star* (www.outcomesstar.org.uk/using-the-star/see-the-stars/recovery-star-4/) has been used consistently across a wide range of services. The most promising approach aims to measure the outcomes that consumers find most relevant. A good ISP (individual service plan) can do this for an individual consumer, and it is essential that the views of consumers are reflected in service-wide measures as well. Where this is attempted it is likely to lead to positive service change, with improvements in consumer involvement in the service, peer support, and more responsive care and treatment, and a greater focus on the person rather than the illness (Happell, 2008). We can expect that services that involve consumers in an empowering way achieve better recovery-focused results than those that do not (Segal et al., 2010). Even in situations where their agencies do not develop outcome measures according to these principles, social workers should try to do so. The ways in which we (and our agencies) measure the results of our work will have a determining impact on the type of work that we do.

The need to improve outcome measures reflects a broader issue: while the knowledge and evidence base continues to come to us top-down (in the form of clinical practice guidelines, for example) or from outside our profession (for example, from psychiatry and psychology), it will always tend to be inadequate for our purposes. Mental health social workers will continue to face a major problem in influencing policy and practice while our own 'evidence base' remains undeveloped. Research is not something better left to others, yet we observe that too few mental health social workers read the research literature or engage in routine evaluation of their own practice, let alone conduct and publish 'formal' studies. Martin Webber's book *Evidence-Based Policy and Practice in Mental Health Social Work* (Webber, 2011) is important because it provides some of the tools that social workers need to construct more evidence about mental health practice on our own terms, based on questions that are relevant to our practice and a respect for a wider range of research paradigms, including collaborative research with consumers and carers.

Using relationship in teams

If we are serious about creating and working in an organisation that really values the quality of the relationship between consumers and workers, a good way to start is to develop good-quality relationships with colleagues and to value such relationships as a source of growth in the work. Writing about work with clients in unpredictable situations, Ryan and Morgan (2004, pp. 58–59) say that 'our most valuable tool becomes a trusting working relationship. With this, we can have confidence in what is said and agreed between parties. Without it, we are working in the dark'. The same is just as true for our work with colleagues in teams.

Teams are everywhere in the mental health field, and there is a general belief that multidisciplinary teams provide the best possibility of providing good care because of the rich range of skills available for the work. However, not all teams of this type are structured in the same way, and the differences present significant challenges:

Multidisciplinary teams comprise members from a range of disciplines working in parallel, coordinating, cooperating and conferring.

Interdisciplinary teams have all the features of multidisciplinary teams, as well as a system of collaboration, joint activity and some degree of shared responsibility.

Transdisciplinary teams, while they comprise a range of professions, place little emphasis on the members' different disciplinary backgrounds but are organised on the principle that, as much as possible, everyone will do the same work in essentially the same way.

It depends on the circumstances, but we generally strive for *interdisciplinarity*. The normal model of interdisciplinary teamwork describes shared common tasks (like case management or key working) together with some specialist professional tasks (like therapy or specialised advocacy). This model aims for a balance between the expression of individual professional expertise, identity and responsibility on the one hand and shared interests and qualities on the other. The aim is to make the service comprehensive and maximise the opportunity for consumer choice.

Innovative practice will often occur when two or more professionals work together, for example, when a social worker and consumer peer support worker contribute together to a peer support program or when a social worker and psychiatrist jointly provide education and support for family members. It is not just a matter of different knowledge and skills; sometimes the differences in style and approach produce a beneficial creative tension. There has to be sufficient middle ground, but a collaborative approach will celebrate the differences, rather than tend to obliterate or homogenise them. The team needs to produce something different, not just the sum of its parts. Interdisciplinary work can be encouraged by putting the emphasis on the bigger picture, such as projects that achieve outcomes for the organisation and its consumers (rather than emphasising specific component tasks), and by ensuring that there are valued opportunities for interprofessional communication about the direct work and joint education and research.

There are various ways to promote specialist professional work in teams. It might consist of some extra and different activities (for example, only the social worker works with families) or shared activities done with greater expertise (for example, many team members work with families, but the social worker is the expert in this area and thus works with families facing more complex problems). Operating on a shared terrain, each profession will bring its own perspective to the activity, 'looking at the same thing, and not seeing the same thing' (Baxter & Brumfitt, 2008, p. 240). The richness resulting from a range of perspectives is indeed the main point of interdisciplinary teamwork, but it may cause some tensions and conflicts.

Each team member needs a professional role definition that is sufficiently clear that they can make an effective and valued contribution to the team and its work. It needs to be a secure base from which to work – a secure basis for negotiation, not an inviolable position or a defensive bulwark (Woodhouse & Pengelly, 1991). This is why it is so important that social workers hold onto a firm commitment to their professional domain in mental health: the social context and consequences of mental illness and social justice. The special contributions of individual team members, based on their profession and other attributes, should be respected and nurtured, as well as the interdependence of team members – 'to recognise the value of each member's skills and to magnify the skills many times through the skills of other professionals' (Engel & Gursky, 2003, p. 49). The specific contributions of individual professions can be supported through profession-specific supervision and the encouragement of profession-specific tasks within job roles.

There can be a lot of disagreement about how the team should be set up and function. Some differences result from 'outside' factors such as workforce availability, team size, and the requirements of different service models and regional differences. Some result from the way that the tensions play out, such as different professional and personal positions and interests. Indeed, different professions may be socialised to value and expect quite different things from teamwork itself. Team members may hold too tightly to their own ways of doing things; they may have difficulty in finding a 'common language' for working together; and they may even develop negative attitudes towards one another, which will be a problem for teamwork whether they lead to conflict or avoidance. This can be demoralising and exhausting.

There is a very real risk that the interests and voice of consumers and/or families will be caught up in differences within the team and thus will lose out. Different team members may see a situation differently or take up different aspects of a situation. It is when they find themselves in dispute that there can be trouble – even more so when the underlying reason for the tension goes unrecognised. For teamwork to succeed there needs to be something keeping everyone's eye on the primary task and engaged in the real work. The focus needs to be on clients' recovery, not on the team's politics. A key task for the leader is to ensure that the team has and works with an explicit binding philosophy, based on the needs and aspirations of consumers. The fundamental collaboration is that between the worker and the client. The driving forces for interprofessional working are the goals, problems and needs of clients, so this is the basis of collaborative work within teams and among agencies (Miller et al., 2001). Instead of thinking about consumers and family carers as if they are *outside* the team and the organisation, a modern model of collaboration places them at the *centre* (Whittington, 2003).

Using relationship in the service network

Consumers with a range of needs for support (income security, housing, employment, mental health treatment, family support and so on) will often depend on good-quality service networks because it is often necessary for the different services to work together. For example, income security agencies need to cooperate with supported employment services; supported employment services may need to cooperate with family support services; and these in turn may need to cooperate with treatment services, and so on. Service networks can be very complicated, and it can be difficult to make them work effectively – keeping the consumer at the centre of the work. Most service networks will be improved not by adding a new service so much as ensuring that someone is willing and able to help consumers to navigate the existing service system and make it work better together. The social worker is often a critical link between the agency (team) and the service network.

Collaborative care – working with multidisciplinary teams, families, consumers and other people and agencies relevant to their lives – is frequently espoused, though not always achieved.

Many of the principles and dynamics of teamwork also come into play in inter-agency working, with roles being determined by both professional and organisational affiliation; however, there are differences because there is usually much less face-to-face communication and usually no shared operational policy. The result can be very complex indeed:

> Interagency networking is the development and maintenance of a system of inter-organisational linkage characterised by collective decision making and a set of positive feedback relationships between the internal structure, systems and values of participating organisations and the interorganisational network of which they are all members.
>
> (Trevillion, 1999, pp. 88–89)

Collective decision-making across agencies would be difficult enough were it not for the complexities of each agency's own structures, rules and ways of doing things, let alone the dynamics of the network system that tries to hold all these things together. Different agencies will quite properly bring different perspectives to the joint enterprise. In joint work with a parent with a mental illness, for example, child protection services might put the emphasis on the 'best interests of the child', while other child and family services may focus more on the family as a whole, and the adult mental health service may tend to be concerned with the interests and 'rights' of the parent. Collective decision-making requires that each party steps outside its own 'silo' and takes account of the range of relevant considerations.

In practice, it can be easy to pass the buck, take offence and enact rivalries that have little or nothing to do with the needs of the consumer who depends on the efficient functioning of this network. In any collaborative activity, it is necessary to let go to some extent and to be willing to tolerate some uncertainty about the task and the outcome. It is like this working in partnership with a consumer; it is like this in teams; and it is like this in complex service networks. Further, the more players there are, the more complex it can be. There will need to be some degree of joint decision-making. It is relatively easy to make a referral from one agency to another, but inter-agency collaboration involves joint work at the boundary of each agency's core responsibility, with each agency retaining some, but not all, responsibility for an outcome that neither can fully control. The interdependence and lack of control can be very anxiety provoking for those involved – more so than if the parties were in competition (Krantz & Gilmore, 1990). So there needs to be good leadership and a deliberate, concerted focus on effective inter-agency work.

Good external referrals require skill as well as resources, including the capacity to maintain up-to-date databases about the services available, eligibility criteria and referral pathways. In addition they require organisational policy and guidelines and a technology to facilitate the process (Makregiorgos et al., 2013). An effective referral may be difficult to achieve and may involve a number of complex steps (for example, as with most referrals to supported housing services), but often they are relatively simple and quick (as with some referrals to private clinicians, where responsibility is completely handed over). In either case, a level of cooperation is required to ensure that referrals are made and accepted competently.

Sorting out protocols for sharing information and dealing with confidentiality is probably the most important thing that can be done to facilitate good inter-agency working. Each agency will have its own practices for dealing with information, and each consumer will have their own preferences. Each participant in the inter-agency network needs to be very clear about their own roles and responsibilities – but this is only the starting point because the real purpose of the joint work lies outside the responsibilities of any one agency, by definition. There is a wider, shared purpose that transcends each agency's responsibility, so, having put effort into being very clear about stating their own role, each participant needs to take care to focus on the real task, not to go on defending their own perspective or interests. Successful networks are capable of a flexible response based in strong engagement and holistic work with consumers and families – something that requires strong leadership across agencies.

An Australian study of inter-agency collaboration (Scott, 1993) has identified some straightforward considerations. Conflict is to be expected, but it should be recognised as structural, not personal. Goodwill needs to be built and cultivated at both the interpersonal level and the inter-agency level. Workers and agencies should avoid making alliances by turning others into a common enemy. They should work to form coalitions on a broader agenda of change, and they should use their own experience to build the knowledge base on effective collaboration. Further, it is worth working at the development of a 'common language', ensuring that words mean the same thing to each party (Salmon & Rapport, 2005).

Professional service networks need a clear task – one that does not conflict with the task or interests of any of the collaborating bodies – and there has to be a way of sorting out conflicts. It needs a substantial investment of time and commitment from the right people – those with a real contribution to make and sufficient authority to be able to deliver on behalf of their own agency. It has to be backed up by the managers in each of the participating agencies. It needs humility: no one always knows best, and certainly no one 'owns' the client. And, as with all the work, the real test is whether the actions of the professionals are working in tune with the needs and experiences of the clients and their real-world networks.

For individual consumers, the really important networks will usually extend beyond the formal service system to include perhaps the general practitioner, some members of the extended family, the local shopkeeper, the priest, the football coach and so on. The complexity is such that this cannot be left to chance. It requires a lot of ongoing work – with resources specifically devoted to maintaining the network.

Working for social justice

All agencies have a responsibility to apply the fundamental principles of law and rights we identified in Chapter 4, including freedoms, dignity, equality and entitlement, and respect for diversity. This means using the minimum coercion and involuntary treatment, supporting consumers to live in the best possible environments, being able to exercise as much choice and freedom as possible consistent with their responsibilities as citizens and advocating for their right to the best possible mental health care.

Within every agency setting, there is the opportunity to work for social justice by ensuring that access to the agency's services is fair and open to those who need them, including people from diverse cultural backgrounds. At a fundamental level, this means ensuring that the agency presents itself as what Weeks (2004) called an 'attractive service which citizens want to attend'. In Chapter 10, we outlined a range of community work activities that confront aspects of inequality and disadvantage. Chapter 3 described the dimensions of social exclusion that impact directly on people with mental illness. We argue that while addressing inequality and disadvantage is challenging and complex, the pursuit of social justice remains an important principle that underpins much of social work activity in mental health.

As the goal of social inclusion has become a more central element of mental health policy and practice (Thornicroft, 2011; Coombs et al., 2013), so too have social justice issues achieved greater recognition. Good policy is a necessary but insufficient condition for good mental health services. We need ongoing reform to improve the focus and quality of those services. The whole enterprise of community mental health has been described as 'an impossible task' (Willshire, 1999) in the sense that it attempts to resolve conflicting imperatives that will always, at best, be balanced in tension – the need to provide for the care and treatment of individuals and their families, the need to protect and advance the civil and legal rights and liberties of those individuals and their families, and the social function of 'managing' the effects of mental illness in the community and the community's response to mental illness. It is not an easy balance: it is maintained under pressure, always threatening to break down. To some degree at least, these imperatives will tend to produce tension at all levels of the work. It is as if all the issues of mental health public policy are played out in each mental health service and each team.

Core concerns of social work – human rights, self-determination, family relationships and welfare, employment, housing, community, life chances – are central to mental health. As every social worker knows from experience, each of these areas is affected by social inequality. Contemporary mental health policy statements accord a high importance to adhering to human rights; providing services to those who need them most; and ensuring that consumers have access to a wide range of good community services, including housing, health and welfare services, income security and child protection. In their day-to-day work, these are often the areas of focus for mental health social work. There is unrealised potential for advocacy and social change around these fundamental social conditions.

Supporting self, supporting colleagues

Establishing and maintaining working relationships with clients, families and colleagues is stressful work that provokes fundamental anxieties. In relationship-based practice, there is always a fundamental anxiety about the balance of rewards and costs involved in an authentic human relationship between workers and consumers. It is often the crises that produce the most obvious stress – having to respond quickly and creatively to serious, sometimes life-threatening situations in the context of little time and few resources – but stress also comes from the burden of work that can be demanding emotionally, intellectually and physically and that requires concentration, skill and persistence.

Adding to this stress is the fear of blame, both personal and institutional, if something goes really wrong, exacerbated by including the ever-present prospect of review, inquiry and being held to account. A key element is the way the service responds to risk. In almost every practice setting, there will be situations in which the risks of self-harm, harm to others (including children) and violence need to be given the highest priority. Frequently, these risks occur in crisis situations, requiring a crisis response, even one that overrides the expressed wishes of the client. Beyond this reality, the organisation has a choice about the extent to which it supports positive risk-taking or the extent to which it seeks to contain the unexpected. Workers need to be able to think quickly, to respond flexibly and to act with imagination because these issues cannot be dealt with properly simply by establishing and applying rules and procedures. If practice becomes too defensive in response – avoiding risk situations – consumers will tend to get frustrated, feeling held back. In the long run, it is frustrating for staff as well, as it undermines their primary objective in undertaking the work in the first place.

The personal issues of workers will inevitably have an effect on their relationship with consumers and other aspects of the work. Being part of a good team is a protective factor against work stress for mental health social workers. The team is a ready-made arena for sharing and dealing with such stresses and anxieties, but when things are not working so well, this might just mean that the problems get passed around – possibly getting absorbed, but not really getting resolved.

Supervision

There is a strong tradition of supportive professional supervision in social work, but some special challenges are inherent in the mental health social work context. The reporting requirements of organisations, the need for accountability, and the pressure of work can lead to a form of 'micro-management' that is a poor platform for offering support to staff. Although social workers have, by and large, always valued a supportive approach to supervision, this is not the case for all the mental health professions. Profession-specific supervision is not always available and, in many service settings, it is not sufficient.

The word *supervision* has a specific meaning in social work that goes beyond the concept of accountability in administrative and line management terms. The quality of social work supervision is central to the development and maintenance of high standards of practice. This applies to social workers at all levels and across the full range of practice roles. The primary purpose of supervision is to support and ensure competent independent practice. There is no one right way to structure supervision, although there are many developed models. There are individual and group supervision practices, each with its advantages. Small-group supervision gives the supervisee a unique opportunity to hear about other people's work, just as it can sometimes generate rivalry and competition. Supervision by peers can create a wonderfully collaborative environment for learning and exploration but can sometimes feel frustratingly like the blind leading the blind.

It is a real skill to work as a good supervisor. Kadushin's model (Kadushin & Harkness, 2002) remains influential for good reason. Kadushin describes the way in which the three principal functions of supervision – administrative, educational and supportive – are interrelated. The administrative function concerns planning, distributing, monitoring and evaluating the work and activities in the team and those of each supervisee. The educational function seeks to ensure that the team members' developing needs for knowledge are addressed so that they can do the work as well as possible, and the supportive function recognises that the work, which has its inevitable inherent stresses as well as rewards, is being done by a *person*. Here, too, we need to focus on the actual experience of the worker, as well as the quality of the supervisory relationship; a good supervisory relationship engages with both the vulnerabilities and competence of the supervisee. This emphasis on relationship has a long tradition in social work supervision: 'The effectiveness and success of supervision depends largely upon the ability of the supervisor to institute and sustain a helping alliance with the clinician, which in turn serves as a paradigm for the helping process' (Fox, 1989, p. 148). Supervisees typically want a supervisor who can listen, empathise and respond in a flexible way (Cousins, 2004). In fact, although the supervisor may have particular responsibility, this is a two-way process.

Kadushin's model has tended to emphasise the educational and supportive aspects of supervision. Every organisation needs a good system for supporting good work and holding its workers accountable for the quality of their work – and this can be complex in the case of team or shared care. In general, each person involved in work with a consumer is responsible for their own actions and decisions in dealing with the situation. In addition, the organisation (as well as the supervisor) has a responsibility for providing the necessary supervision and support and for ensuring that staff are not required to act outside their proper area of competence and responsibility. Good supervision is honest and seeks to deal with the realities of the work and the real situation of the consumer.

An approach based on critical reflection (White et al., 2006) is well suited to supervision in mental health settings. Central to this approach is engagement with practitioners to look closely at what they do in their work, taking into account the distribution and operations of power. This may be done in a structured way, as shown in the box 'Example: a model for using critical reflection in supervision'.

Example: a model for using critical reflection in supervision

First, workers are encouraged to choose a critical incident from their practice and, using a series of simple structured questions, are helped to develop a nuanced understanding of what happened in their work (What did you do? How do you make sense of that?). They are asked to identify the knowledge they are applying in developing this understanding. The process of patiently sorting through the understandings, beliefs and affect of the various participants serves to 'deconstruct' the practice. It helps to make explicit some implicitly held knowledge and values. It also helps the worker to see the complexity and ambiguity of each situation. The worker is asked to record and summarise their understandings.

Second, workers are invited to consider alternative understandings. This might involve asking the worker to suggest how other stakeholders in the incident might understand the work. Central to this second stage of the process is consideration of the alternative sources of knowledge and the operations of power (What does the literature say about this? What are the dominant understandings? What are the marginalised understandings?). Then the worker is encouraged to write about 'reconstructed understandings' that emerge from this activity of reflection.

Third, workers should choose knowledge from the literature to inform practice. Having made explicit the range of knowledge and positions on offer, the worker actively chooses to shape their practice accordingly.

Individuals and teams need regular feedback on performance, and there should be an expectation that each team member's performance will be assessed and supported. Consequently, supervision should be provided within the organisation and is the responsibility of the organisation's leadership since it is a necessary condition of effective professional practice. The supervisor needs to have the skills necessary to support work that is consistent with the organisation's task and values and with the professional approach of the worker (so, in the case of social work, focused on social context, social consequences and social justice) and grounded in the real needs and wishes of the consumers of the service. Of course, the content of what a supervisee wants and needs to discuss in supervision often has as much or more to do with the organisation and its processes and requirements as it does with the 'direct' work with the client. The supervisor has responsibilities to both the organisation and the supervisee and may be located at the 'nexus' of the relationship between worker and the agency (Shaw, 2004). Although it is an organisational responsibility to provide supervision of this type, in some cases these requirements are served most effectively by engaging someone outside the organisation with the necessary skills. If this is the case, there needs to be a clear, open line of communication into the organisation because supervision in this model is not a private arrangement. Many of us will make our own private arrangements for supervision and consultation as well, but this is a separate matter.

From Robert: being human at work

Mental health workers face many competing demands. On the one hand there is the power of contemporary mental health practice that insists on the adoption of evidence-based interventions and the application of practice standards and mental health and agency policy. Challenging this imperative is the consistent message from consumers and families that they really value the humanity of the worker. They value the worker's compassion, energy and preparedness to be vulnerable. How do we hold these two competing imperatives together? Throughout this book we have encouraged social workers to value the power of the relationships they make with consumers and with families and to see those relationships as the vehicle for change. At one level this reliance on relationship seems easy, but our experience has been that this kind of work is both enormously challenging and enormously rewarding. To this commitment to relationship is added a commitment to engage with the evidence base for practice. You can't be the best social worker without being both fully human and fully professional – and that is the greatest challenge to each of us.

Developing expertise

The nature of the work can challenge a worker's sense of effectiveness and expertise. Mental health social workers are often subject to unrelenting demands, which is made much more difficult if they do not have clarity about their mission and roles. We may come to believe that we are picking up the pieces of shortcomings in the system while simultaneously having to take the responsibility and even the blame. The community has legitimately high expectations, but this can lead to feelings of helplessness among workers. As job demands increase without good systems for managing workload, there is reduced time for training and personal and professional development. Mostly, there is reduced time to do the job well. Conversations with mental health social workers often revolve around common themes: high-pressure and high-intensity work, concern about risk, and concern about burnout.

Expertise is something to be developed over the course of time, not a status to be achieved, and it relies on an honest and conscientious commitment to ongoing learning and personal and professional development. We have mentioned the Australian research that identifies the fundamental human qualities of belief, optimism and caring (Ryan et al., 2004) as essential components of expert mental health social work practice. Eileen Gambrill, a strong proponent of evidence-based social work practice, suggests that caring, courage and critical thinking are a 'formidable threesome' (2013, p. 622). 'Caring' relates to a focus on the lived experience of the client, and critical thinking requires a curious and inquiring mind. As Gambrill says, it takes courage as well as empathy to truly see what is going on for clients – especially in the absence of readily available means to relieve the situation – and to ask the hard questions. To these lists of human qualities there is one more that we would particularly add: perseverance – because good outcomes are often such a long time coming, and recovery is such a hard-fought process for many consumers.

Technical knowledge and skill are essential and, for many mental health social workers in Australia, need development. So too is an openness to knowledge beyond the technical, such as knowledge derived from theory and the knowledge that consumers and family carers bring. The strategies of critical reflection are very useful in developing and integrating this expertise and consciously linking and applying technical skills to the human encounter. They provide a structure for examining practice (and the assumptions implicit in ways of practice) together with the knowledge, skills and values that are being used in that practice.

There is a wide recognition that we need to develop the mental health workforce by improving knowledge, skills and attitudes. We should not forget that some of the most serious and damaging experiences of stigma and discrimination occur within mental health services. Perhaps contrary to expectation, mental health professionals sometimes share the same prejudices and negative views about mental illness that are found in the general population. Consumers report that mental health workers often treat them with a lack of respect and are patronising, dismissive, blaming and judgemental (Mental Health Council of Australia, 2011).

A professional approach to training and professional development is a systematic approach: from the initial assessment of needs, definition of development objectives and devising of evaluation measures (so that everyone can know how well they are going in achieving the objectives), to the development of content, methods and training materials. Staff will need to be allocated, and staff time dedicated, to the staff development activity, and an ongoing evaluation will feed back into further refinement and development of the training content, methods and materials. The aim should be to make a difference to the actual work, so the means of evaluation should, if possible, go beyond reflection on the content and process of staff development itself to assess and measure change in work practice and the outcomes as they are experienced by consumers.

Conclusion

In this chapter, we have demonstrated that, although congenial workplaces exist in the mental health service system, they are very rare. Throughout this book, we have tried to convey our passion for mental health social work and our conviction that the mental health field needs social workers who are skilful and effective with a clear and strong sense of their particular contribution. To reach this potential personally and professionally, all of us need support in our work. We are sustained by the relationships and partnerships we are able to develop. In turn, such partnerships provide us with a vehicle for contributing to a better mental health service system – one that reflects the fundamental principles and outcomes that lie at the heart of our reason and motivation for working with people with mental health problems and their families.

QUESTIONS FOR PRACTICE

1 What changes to the workplace environment could make it more welcoming and comfortable for staff and clients?
2 Within your agency and work team, how does what you do and what you say reflect your own values and professional commitments?
3 What are the challenges for social workers moving from direct practice to management positions?
4 How do you demonstrate to other staff / your supervisor / the family / your client that you are competent? What do you understand as 'competence' in mental health work?
5 Looking at consumer and carer accounts of using mental health services, what themes can you identify? In what ways can such accounts be seen as 'evidence' to inform practice?

Bibliography

ABC Radio 2007, *All in the Mind: Deep Listening – Working with Indigenous Mental Distress (22 December)*, 9 November 2008, transcript, www.abc.net.au/rn/allinthemind/stories/2007/2096863.htm.

Allnutt, S. H., Ogloff, J. R. P., Adams, J., O'Driscoll, C., Daffern, M., Carroll, A., Nanayakkara, V. & Chaplow, D. 2013, 'Managing Aggression and Violence: The Clinician's Role in Contemporary Mental Health Care', *Australian and New Zealand Journal of Psychiatry*, vol. 47, no. 8, pp. 728–36.

American Psychiatric Association (APA) 2013, *Diagnostic and Statistical Manual of Mental Disorders: DSM-5*, 5th edn, American Psychiatric Association, Arlington, VA.

Andary, L., Stolk, Y. & Klimidis, S. 2003, *Assessing Mental Health across Cultures*, Australian Academic Press, Bowen Hills.

Anthony, W. A. 1993, 'Recovery from Mental Illness: The Guiding Vision of the Mental Health Service System in the 1990s', *Psychosocial Rehabilitation Journal*, vol. 16, no. 4, pp. 11–23.

Anthony, W. A., Cohen, M., Farkas, M. & Cohen, B. 1988, 'Clinical Care Update: The Chronically Mentally Ill', *Community Mental Health Journal*, vol. 24, no. 3, pp. 219–28.

Australian Association of Social Workers (AASW) 1999, *The Development of Competency Standards for Mental Health Social Workers: Final Report*, AASW, Canberra.

——— 2004, *The Development of Competency Standards for Mental Health Social Workers: Final Report*, 2nd edn, AASW, Canberra.

——— 2007, *Submission by the AASW to the Inquiry by the Senate Community Affairs Committee into Mental Health Services in Australia*, Community Affairs Committee, Department of the Senate, Canberra.

——— 2008a, *Indigenous Health Position Paper*, AASW, Canberra.

——— 2008b, 2014, *Practice Standards for Mental Health Social Workers*, AASW, Barton, ACT.

——— 2012, *Australian Social Work Education and Accreditation Standards* (ASWEAS) 2012 Guideline 1.1: Guidance on Essential Core Curriculum Content, AASW, Canberra.

——— 2020a, *Australian Social Work Education and Accreditation Standards (ASWEAS)*, AASW, Canberra.

——— 2020b, *Gaining Mental Health Accreditation,* aas.asn.au

Australian Association of Social Workers (AASW) Project Team 2003, *Review of Social Work Education and Training Re: The National Practice Standards for the Mental Health Workforce (Report to the Commonwealth Department of Health and Ageing)*, AASW, Canberra.

Australian Bureau of Statistics (ABS) 2008, *National Survey of Mental Health and Wellbeing 2007: Summary of Results*, 4326.0, Australian Bureau of Statistics, Canberra.

Australian Government Department of Health and Ageing 2006, *Better Access to Mental Health Care: Questions and Answers*, Commonwealth of Australia, viewed 8 March 2009, www.health.gov.au/internet/main/publishing.nsf/Content/coag-mental-q&a.htm.

——— 2007, *Living Is for Everyone: A Framework for Prevention of Suicide in Australia*, Australian Government Department of Health and Ageing, Canberra.

——— 2010, *National Standards for Mental Health Services 2010*, Australian Government Publishing Service, Canberra.

Australian Government Department of Health 2012, *Mental Health Statement of Rights and Responsibilities*, Australian Government Department of Health, Canberra.

Australian Health Ministers 1991, *Mental Health Statement of Rights and Responsibilities: Report of the Mental Health Consumer Outcomes Task Force*, Australian Government Publishing Service, Canberra.

——— 1992a, *National Mental Health Plan*, Australian Government Publishing Service, Canberra.

——— 1992b, *National Mental Health Policy*, Australian Government Publishing Service, Canberra.

——— 1998, *Second National Mental Health Plan*, Mental Health Branch, Commonwealth Department of Health and Family Services, Canberra.

——— 2003, *National Mental Health Plan 2003–2008*, Australian Government Publishing Service, Canberra.

——— 2009, *Fourth National Mental Health Plan: An Agenda for Collaborative Government Action in Mental Health 2009–2014*, Commonwealth of Australia, Canberra.

Australian Health Ministers Advisory Council 2012, *A National Framework for Recovery-oriented Mental Health Services*, Commonwealth of Australia, Canberra.

Australian Housing and Urban Research Institute (AHURI) 2017, *Policy Analysis – Mental Health and Housing*, www.ahuri.edu.au/policy-analysis/mental-health-and-housing.

Australian Infant, Child, Adolescent and Family Mental Health Association (AICAFMHA) 2004, *Principles and Actions for Services and People Working with Children of Parents with a Mental Illness*, Commonwealth Department of Health and Ageing, Canberra.

Australian Institute of Health and Welfare (AIHW) 2007, *Demand for SAAP Accommodation by Homeless People 2005–06: Summary*, Australian Institute of Health and Welfare, Canberra.

——— 2013, *National Social Housing Survey: A Summary of National Results 2012*, Australian Institute of Health and Welfare, Canberra.

——— 2017–2018. *Mental Health Services in Australia, Specialised Mental Health Care Facilities*, viewed 21 July 2020, www.aihw.gov.au.

——— 2019, *Mental Health Services – in Brief 2019. Cat. no. HSE 228*, AIHW, Canberra.

Australian National Mental Health Commission 2014, *Contributing Lives Thriving Communities Report of the National Review*, Australian Government, Canberra.

Australian Parliament Senate Select Committee on Mental Health 2006, *A National Approach to Mental Health: From Crisis to Community: First Report*, Select Committee on Mental Health, Canberra.

Australian Psychological Society n.d., *Social and Emotional Wellbeing and Mental Health Services in Aboriginal Australia*, Australian Psychological Society, viewed 8 January 2014, www.sewbmh.org.au.

Ayres, L. 2000, 'Narratives of Family Caregiving: The Process of Making Meaning', *Research in Nursing and Health*, vol. 23, pp. 424–34.

Bakshi, L., Rooney, R. & O'Neil, K. 1999, *Reducing the Stigma About Mental Illness in Transcultural Settings: A Guide*, Australian Transcultural Mental Health Network, Melbourne.

Barry, K. L., Zeber, J. E., Blow, F. C. & Valenstein, M. 2003, 'Effect of Strengths Model Versus Assertive Community Treatment Model on Participant Outcomes and Utilization: Two-Year Follow-Up', *Psychiatric Rehabilitation Journal*, vol. 26, no. 3, pp. 268–77.

Barry, M. 2007, 'Building Capacity for Effective Implementation of Mental Health Promotion', *Advances in Mental Health*, vol. 6, no. 2, pp. 82–90.

Barton, D., Joubert, L., Alvarenga, M., Norrie, P., Brenchley, C., Smith, D. & Grigg, M. 2012, 'Anxiety Disorders', in *Mental Health in Australia: Collaborative Community Practice*, 3rd edn, eds G. Meadows, J. Farhall, E. Fossey, M. Grigg, F. McDermott & B. Singh, Oxford University Press, Melbourne, pp. 648–65.

Barton, D., Joubert, L., Norrie, P., Brenchley, C., Alvarenga, M., Smith, D. & Grigg, M. 2012, 'Affective Disorders', in *Mental Health in Australia: Collaborative Community Practice*, 3rd edn, eds G. Meadows, J. Farhall, E. Fossey, M. Grigg, F. McDermott & B. Singh, Oxford University Press, Melbourne, pp. 666–93.

Bauer, D., Batson, R., Hayden, W. & Counts, M. M. 2005, 'Integrating Behavioral Health Services within a Primary Care Center in a Rural Setting', *Families in Society*, vol. 86, no. 1, pp. 63–70.

Baxter, S. K. & Brumfitt, S. M. 2008, 'Professional Differences in Interprofessional Working', *Journal of Interprofessional Care*, vol. 22, no. 3, pp. 239–51.

Be You 2018, *Evidence summary*, http:beyou.edu.au.

Beatson, J., Rao, S. & Watson, C. 2010, *Borderline Personality Disorder: Towards Effective Treatment*, Australian Postgraduate Medicine, Fitzroy.

Bebbington, P. 2004, 'Recent Findings in Bipolar Affective Disorder', *Psychological Medicine*, vol. 34, no. 5, pp. 767–76.

Bennett, B., Green, S., Gilbert, S. & Bessarab, D. (eds) 2013, *Our Voices: Aboriginal and Torres Strait Islander Social Work*, Palgrave Macmillan, South Yarra.

Bennett, C., Sundram, S., Farhall, J., Fossey, E., Grigg, M. & Jeffs, S. 2012, 'Schizophrenia and Related Disorders', in *Mental Health in Australia: Collaborative Community Practice*, 3rd edn, eds G. Meadows, J. Farhall, E. Fossey, M. Grigg, F. McDermott & B. Singh, Oxford University Press, Melbourne, pp. 741–88.

Bentley, K. 2003, *Social Work Practice in Mental Health Canada*, Brooks/Cole Thomson Learning, Pacific Grove, CA.

Best, D. 2012, 'Recovery: The Definition Trap', *Of Substance*, vol. 10, no. 2, p. 16.

Betancourt, H. & López, S. R. 1993, 'The Study of Culture, Ethnicity, and Race in American Psychology', *American Psychologist*, vol. 48, no. 6, pp. 629–37.

Beyondblue 2010, *Depression in Older People*, beyondblue, viewed 28 May 2010, www.beyondblue.org.au/index.aspx?link_id=101.

Bisson, J. I., Brayne, M., Ochberg, F., M. & Everly, G. S. Jr 2007, 'Early Psychosocial Intervention Following Traumatic Events', *American Journal of Psychiatry*, vol. 164, no. 7, pp. 1016–19.

Black Dog Institute 2012, *Bipolar Disorder: Symptoms*, Black Dog Institute, Randwick, NSW, www.blackdoginstitute.org.au/docs/symptomsofbipolardisorder.pdf.

Blackman, T. & Harvey, J. 2001, 'Housing Renewal and Mental Health: A Case Study', *Journal of Mental Health*, vol. 10, no. 5, pp. 571–83.

Bland, R. 1987, 'Social Work with the Family of the Schizophrenic Patient', *Australian Social Work*, vol. 40, no. 2, pp. 25–30.

——— 1994, 'Supportive Approaches to Families in Australia: Drawing Conclusions from Practice', *New Directions for Mental Health Services*, vol. 1994, no. 62, pp. 61–9.

——— 1998, 'Understanding Grief and Guilt as Common Themes in Family Response to Mental Illness', *Australian Social Work*, vol. 51, no. 4, pp. 27–34.

——— 2002, 'Policy Reform in Australia and Family Roles: Learning from Experience', in *Family Interventions in Mental Illness: International Perspectives*, eds H. Lefley & D. Johnson, Praeger, Westport, CT, pp. 195–208.

Bland, R. 2006, *An Implementation Plan for the National Practice Standards, Unpublished Report*, prepared for the Australian Health Ministers' Advisory Council, Canberra.

Band, R. & Darlington, Y. 2002, 'The Nature and Sources of Hop: Perspectives of Family Carers of People with Serious Mental Illness', *Perspectives on Psychiatric Care*.

Bland, R. & Drake, G. 2019, 'Community and Mental Health', in *Social Work and Mental Health,* eds R. Ow & A. Poon, Springer Publications, New York.

Bland, R. & Epstein, M. 2008, 'Encouraging Principles of Consumer Participation and Partnership: The Way Forward in Mental Health Practice in Australia', in *Health Care Practice in Australia*, eds S. Taylor, M. Foster & J. Fleming, Oxford University Press, Melbourne, pp. 239–54.

Bland, R., Farhall, J., Fernbacher, S., Fossey, E., Happell, B., Kazantzis, N., King, R., Meadows, G., Minas, H., Petrik, A. M. & Willshire, D. 2012, 'Assessment: Specialised Assessment Skills', in *Mental Health in Australia: Collaborative Community Practice*, 3rd edn, eds G. Meadows, J. Farhall, E. Fossey, M. Grigg, F. McDermott & B. Singh, Oxford University Press, Melbourne, pp. 394–427.

Bland, R. & Foster, M. (2012) Families and Mental Illness: Contested Perspectives and Implications for Practice and Policy, *Australian Social Work*, vol. 65, no 4, pp. 517–34.

Bland, R. & Harrison, C. 2000, 'Developing and Evaluating a Psychoeducation Program for Caregivers of Bipolar Affective Disorder Patients: Report of a Pilot Project', *Research on Social Work Practice*, vol. 10, no. 2, pp. 209–28.

Bland R. & Pearce, R. 2006, 'Report of a Social Work and Basketball Project', National Conference of the Australian Association of Social Workers, Perth (unpublished).

Bland, R. & Tullgren, A. 2016, 'The Lived Experience of Mental Illness', in *Psychosocial Dimensions in Medicine*, eds G. Byrne & J. Fitzgerald, IP Communications, Melbourne, pp. 43–56.

Bland, R. & Wyder, M. 2017. 'Working with People Who Have Psychotic Illness: Balancing Risk and Recovery/ Risk and Mental Health' in *Beyond the Risk Paradigm in Mental Health Policy and Practice*, eds S. Stanford, E. Sharland, N. Heller & J. Warner, Palgrave, London.

Bouverie Centre 2009, *Seven Principles of Family Sensitive Practice*, Bouverie Centre, viewed 8 March 2009, www.bouverie.org.au/taxonomy/term/233.

Boyce, P., Carter, G., Penrose-Wall, J., Wilhelm, K. & Goldney, R. 2003, 'Summary Australian and New Zealand Clinical Practice Guideline for the Management of Adult Deliberate Self-Harm (2003)', *Australasian Psychiatry*, vol. 11, no. 2, pp. 150–5.

Brandish, E. K. & Baldwin, D. S. 2012, 'Anxiety Disorders', *Medicine*, vol. 40, no. 11, pp. 599–606.

Brodsky, B. S. & Stanley, B. 2013, *The Dialectical Behavior Primer: How DBT Can Inform Clinical Practice*, Wiley Blackwell, Hoboken, NJ.

Brophy, L. 2012, 'Involuntary Treatment in the Community', in *Mental Health in Australia: Collaborative Community Practice*, 3rd edn, eds G. Meadows, J. Farhall, E. Fossey, M. Grigg, F. McDermott & B. Singh, Oxford University Press, Melbourne, pp. 445–8.

Burgess, P., Pirkis, J., Coombs, T. & Rosen, A. 2011, 'Assessing the Value of Existing Recovery Measures for Routine Use in Australian Mental Health Services', *Australian and New Zealand Journal of Psychiatry*, vol. 45, no. 4, pp. 267–80.

Burgy, M. 2008, 'The Concept of Psychosis: Historical and Phenomenological Aspects', *Schizophrenia Bulletin*, vol. 34, no. 6, pp. 1200–10.

Butterworth, P. 2003, *Estimating the Prevalence of Mental Disorders among Income Support Recipients: Approach, Validity and Findings*, Policy Research Paper No. 21, Commonwealth Department of Family and Community Services, Canberra.

Butterworth, P., Burgess, P. M. & Whiteford, H. 2011, 'Examining Welfare Receipt and Mental Disorders After a Decade of Reform and Prosperity: Analysis of the 2007 National Survey of Mental Health and Wellbeing', *Australian and New Zealand Journal of Psychiatry*, vol. 45, no. 1, pp. 54–62.

Byrne, L., Wang, L., Roennfeldt, H., Chapman, M. & Darwin, L. 2019, *Queensland Framework for the Development of the Mental Health Lived Experience Workforce*. Queensland Government, Brisbane.

Cameron, J. 2013, 'Take Note! Case Notes and the AOD Sector', *Of Substance*, vol. 11, no. 1, pp. 20–1.

Campbell, J. & Davidson, G. 2012, *Post-Qualifying Mental Health Social Work Practice*, Sage, London.

Caplan, G. & Caplan, R. 2000, 'Principles of Community Psychiatry', *Community Mental Health Journal*, vol. 36, no. 1, pp. 7–24.

Carey, M., Jones, K., Meadows, G., Sanson-Fisher, R., D'Este, C., Inder, K., Yoong, S. L. & Russell, G. (2014). Accuracy of General Practitioner Unassisted Detection of Depression. *The Australian and New Zealand Journal of Psychiatry*, vol. 48, no. 6, pp. 571–8. https://doi.org/10.1177/0004867413520047.

Carpenter, J. 2002, 'Mental Health Recovery Paradigm: Implications for Social Work', *Health and Social Work*, vol. 27, no. 2, pp. 86–94.

Casey, M. F., Perera, D. N. & Clarke, D. M. 2012, 'Psychosocial Treatment Approaches to Difficult-to-Treat Depression', *Medical Journal of Australia Open*, vol. 1, no. suppl. 4, pp. 52–5.

Cawte, J. 1998, *The Last of the Lunatics*, Melbourne University Press, Carlton, Vic.

Chamberlain, C., Johnson, G. & Theobald, J. 2007, *Homelessness in Melbourne: Confronting the Challenge*, RMIT Publishing, Melbourne.

Champ, S. 1998, 'A Most Precious Thread', *Australian and New Zealand Journal of Mental Health Nursing*, vol. 7, no. 2, pp. 54–9.

Chwastiak, L. A. & Tek, C. 2009, 'The Unchanging Mortality Gap for People with Schizophrenia', *The Lancet*, vol. 374, no. 9690, pp. 590–2.

Coholic, D. 2007, 'Social Work Group Practice', in *Spirited Practices*, eds F. Gale, N. Bolzan & D. McRae-McMahon, Allen & Unwin, Sydney, pp. 142–50.

Commonwealth Department of Health and Aged Care 2000, *Promotion, Prevention and Early Intervention for Mental Health – a Monograph*, Mental Health and Special Programs Branch, Commonwealth Department of Health and Aged Care, Canberra.

Commonwealth of Australia 2006, *A National Approach to Mental Health: From Crisis to Community*. Final Report of the Senate Select Committee Inquiry into Mental Health, Commonwealth of Australia.

——— 2017, *The Fifth National Mental Health and Suicide Prevention Plan*, Commonwealth of Australia, Canberra.

Coombs, T., Nicholas, A. & Pirkis, J. 2013, 'A Review of Social Inclusion Measures', *Australian and New Zealand Journal of Psychiatry*, vol. 47, no. 10, pp. 906–19.

Coppock, V. & Dunn, B. 2010, *Understanding Social Work Practice in Mental Health*, Sage, London.

Corcoran, J. & Walsh, J. 2009, *Mental Health in Social Work: A Casebook on Diagnosis and Strengths-Based Assessment*, Pearson, Boston.

Council of Australian Governments 2006, *National Action Plan on Mental Health 2006–2011*, COAG, Canberra.

Cousins, C. 2004, 'Becoming a Social Work Supervisor: A Significant Role Transition', *Australian Social Work*, vol. 57, no. 2, pp. 175–85.

Cowling, V. (ed.) 2004, *Children of Parents with Mental Illness 2: Personal and Clinical Perspectives*, ACER Press, Camberwell, Vic.

Craig, T. & Timms, P. 2000, 'Facing up to Social Exclusion: Services for Homeless Mentally Ill People', *International Review of Psychiatry*, vol. 12, no. 3, pp. 206–11.

Crawford, P., Gilbert, P., Gilbert, J., Gale, C. & Harvey, K. 2013, 'The Language of Compassion in Acute Mental Health Care', *Qualitative Health Research*, vol. 23, no. 6, pp. 719–27.

Darlington, Y. & Feeney, J. A. 2008, 'Collaboration between Mental Health and Child Protection Services: Professionals' Perceptions of Best Practice', *Children and Youth Services Review*, vol. 30, no. 2, pp. 187–98.

Das, J., Do, Q.-T., Friedman, J., McKenzie, D. & Scott, K. 2007, 'Mental Health and Poverty in Developing Countries: Revisiting the Relationship', *Social Science & Medicine*, vol. 65, no. 3, pp. 467–80.

Davidson, J. C. 2005, 'Professional Relationship Boundaries: A Social Work Teaching Module', *Social Work Education*, vol. 24, no. 5, pp. 511–33.

Davidson, L. & Chan, K. K. S. 2014, 'Common Factors: Evidence-Based Practice and Recovery', *Psychiatric Services*, vol. 65, no. 5, pp. 675–7.

Davidson, L., O'Connell, M., Tondora, J., Lawless, M. & Evans, A. C. 2005, 'Recovery in Serious Mental Illness: A New Wine or Just a New Bottle?', *Professional Psychology: Research and Practice*, vol. 36, no. 5, pp. 480–7.

Davidson, L., O'Connell, M., Tondora, J., Styron, T. & Kangas, K. 2006a, 'The Top Ten Concerns About Recovery Encountered in Mental Health System Transformation', *Psychiatric Services*, vol. 57, no. 5, pp. 640–5.

Davidson, L., Tondora, J., Staeheli, M., O'Connell, M., Frey, J. & Chinman, M. J. 2006b, 'Recovery Guides: An Emerging Model of Community-Based Care for Adults with Psychiatric Disabilities', in *Handbook of Community-Based Clinical Practice*, eds A. Lightburn & P. Sessions, Oxford University Press, New York, pp. 476–501.

Davies, J. 2003, *A Manual of Mental Health Care in General Practice*, revised edn, Commonwealth Department of Health and Aged Care, Canberra.

Deakin Human Services Australia 1999, *Learning Together: Education and Training Partnerships in Mental Health Service. Final Report*, Commonwealth Department of Health and Aged Care, Canberra.

Dearing, E. 2008, 'Psychological Costs of Growing up Poor', *Annals of the New York Academy of Sciences*, vol. 1136, no. 1, pp. 324–32.

Deegan, P. E. 1988, 'Recovery: The Lived Experience of Rehabilitation', *Psychosocial Rehabilitation Journal*, vol. 11, no. 4, pp. 11–19.

Demazeux, S. & Singy, P. (eds) 2015, *The DSM-5 in Perspective: Philosophical Reflections on the Psychiatric Babel*, Springer, Dordrecht, Netherlands.

Department of Health and Ageing 2010, *National Mental Health Report 2010: Summary of 15 Years of Reform in Australia's Mental Health Services under the National Mental Health Strategy 1993–2008*, Commonwealth of Australia, Canberra.

——— 2013, *National Mental Health Report 2013: Tracking Progress of Mental Health Reform in Australia, 1993–2011*, Commonwealth of Australia, Canberra.

Department of Health Queensland 2020a, *Advanced Health Directives*, www.health.qld.gov.au/__data/assets/pdf_file/0036/639864/Advance-Health-Directive-Guide-and-Form.pdf.

——— 2020b, *Understanding Domestic and Family Violence*, www.health.qld.gov.au/__data/assets/pdf_file/0025/952072/1_Understanding-DFV-Booklet.pdf.

Department of Health, UK 1999, *Effective Care Co-Ordination in Mental Health Services: Modernising the Care Programme Approach – a Policy Booklet*, Department of Health, UK.

Deveson, A. 1991, *Tell Me I'm Here*, Penguin, Ringwood, UK.

Diamond, R. J. 2009, 'How to Support Recovery for People with Mental Illness', *Psychiatric Services*, vol. 60, no. 9, p. 1155.

Dingwall, K. M. & Cairney, S. 2010, 'Psychological and Cognitive Assessment of Indigenous Australians', *Australian and New Zealand Journal of Psychiatry*, vol. 44, no. 1, pp. 20–30.

Dixon, L., McFarlane, W. R., Lefley, H., Lucksted, A., Cohen, M., Falloon, I., Mueser, K., Miklowitz, D., Solomon, P. & Sondheimer, D. 2001, 'Evidence-Based Practices for Services to Families of People with Psychiatric Disabilities', *Psychiatric Services*, vol. 52, no. 7, pp. 903–10.

Dixon, L. B., Dickerson, F., Bellack, A. S., Bennett, M., Dickinson, D., Goldberg, R. W., Lehman, A., Tenhula, W. N., Calmes, C., Pasillas, R. M., Peer, J. & Kreyenbuhl, J. 2010, 'The 2009

Schizophrenia PORT Psychosocial Treatment Recommendations and Summary Statements', *Schizophrenia Bulletin*, vol. 36, no. 1, pp. 48–70.

Dixon, L. B. & Lehman, A. F. 1995, 'Family Interventions for Schizophrenia', *Schizophrenia Bulletin*, vol. 21, no. 4, pp. 631–43.

Doka, K. (ed.) 1989, *Disenfranchised Grief: Recognizing Hidden Sorrow*, Lexington Books, Lexington, MA.

Douglas, K. S., Guy, L. S. & Hart, S. D. 2009, 'Psychosis as a Risk Factor for Violence to Others: A Meta-Analysis', *Psychological Bulletin*, vol. 135, no. 5, pp. 679–706.

Drake, G. 2014, 'The Transinstitutionalisation of People Living in Licensed Boarding Houses in Sydney', *Australian Social Work*, vol. 67, no. 2, pp. 240–55.

Drake, R. E. 2005, 'The Principles of Evidence-Based Mental Health Treatment', in *Evidence-Based Mental Health Practice: A Textbook*, eds R. E. Drake, M. R. Merrens & D. W. Lynde, Norton, New York, pp. 45–65.

——— 2007, 'Dual Diagnosis', *Psychiatry*, vol. 6, no. 9, pp. 381–4.

Drake, R. E., Bond, G. R. & Essock, S. M. 2009, 'Implementing Evidence-Based Practices for People with Schizophrenia', *Schizophrenia Bulletin*, vol. 35, no. 4, pp. 704–13.

Drew, N., Adams, Y. & Walker, R. 2010, 'Issues in Mental Health Assessment with Indigenous Australians', in *Working Together: Aboriginal and Torres Strait Islander Mental Health and Wellbeing Principles and Practice*, eds N. Purdie, P. Dudgeon & R. Walker, Australian Council for Educational Research, Camberwell, Vic., pp. 191–210.

Dudley, M. 2007, 'Mental Health and Young People', in *Spirited Practices*, eds F. Gale, N. Bolzan & D. McRae-McMahon, Allen & Unwin, Sydney, pp. 59–68.

Duffy, A., Horrocks, J., Doucette, S., Keown-Stoneman, C., McCloskey, S. & Grof, P. 2014, 'The Developmental Trajectory of Bipolar Disorder', *British Journal of Psychiatry*, vol. 204, no. 2, pp. 122–8.

Dunn, S. 1999, *Creating Accepting Communities: Report of the Mind Inquiry into Social Exclusion and Mental Health Problems*, Mind Publications, London.

Durà-Vilà, G., Littlewood, R. & Leavey, G. 2013, 'Depression and the Medicalization of Sadness: Conceptualization and Recommended Help-Seeking', *International Journal of Social Psychiatry*, vol. 59, no. 2, pp. 165–75.

Dziegielewski, S. F. 2010, *DSM-IV-TR in Action*, 2nd edn, John Wiley & Sons, New York.

Edan, V., Brophy, L., Weller, P. J., Fossey, E. and Meadows, G. 2019, 'The Experience of the Use of Community Treatment Orders Following Recovery-Oriented Practice Training', *International Journal of Law and Psychiatry*, vol. 64, pp. 178–83.

Eisen, P. & Wolfenden, K. 1988, *A National Mental Health Services Policy: Report to the Consultancy to Advise Commonwealth, State and Territory Health Ministers*, Department of Community Services and Health, Canberra.

Elbogen, E. B., Bradford, D. W. & Swartz, M. S. 2013, 'A Recovery-Oriented Money Management Intervention', *Psychiatric Services*, vol. 64, no. 1, p. 99.

Engel, C. & Gursky, E. 2003, 'Management and Interprofessional Collaboration', in *Interprofessional Collaboration: From Policy to Practice in Health and Social Care*, ed. A. Leathard, Brunner-Routledge, Hove, UK, pp. 44–55.

Engel, G. L. 1977, 'The Need for a New Medical Model: A Challenge for Biomedicine', *Science*, vol. 196, no. 4286, pp. 129–36.

Epstein, M. 1995, 'One Stigma or Many', The MHS Conference, May 1995.

Epstein, M. 2004, personal communication.

Epstein, M. & Our Consumer Place 1997, *Lemon Tree Learning Project*, Victorian Mental Illness Awareness Council, Melbourne.

Epstein, M., Olsen, A. & Grey, F. 2012, 'How Communities Respond to Mental Distress: A Consumer Perspective', in *Mental Health in Australia: Collaborative Community Practice*,

3rd edn, eds G. Meadows, J. Farhall, E. Fossey, M. Grigg, F. McDermott & B. Singh, Oxford University Press, Melbourne, pp. 18–30.

Everymind 2017, *Prevention First: A Prevention and Promotion Framework for Mental Health Version 2*, Everymind, Newcastle.

Evidence-Based Medicine Working Group 1992, 'Evidence-Based Medicine: A New Approach to Teaching the Practice of Medicine', *Journal of the American Medical Association*, vol. 268, no. 17, pp. 2420–5.

Fairbairn, G. J. 1998, 'Suicide, Language, and Clinical Practice', *Philosophy, Psychiatry and Psychology*, vol. 5, no. 2, pp. 157–69.

Falloon, I., Fadden, G., Muesser, K., Gingerich, S., Rappaport, S., McGill, C. W., Graham-Hole, V. & Gair, F. 2004, *Family Work Manual*, The West Midlands Family Programme, UK, Meriden.

Farhall, J., Harvey, C., Kazantzis, N., King, R., Meadows, G., O'Hanlon, B., Petrik, A. M., Rao, S., Shawyer, F., Thomas, N. & Young, J. 2012, 'Psychological Therapies', in *Mental Health in Australia: Collaborative Community Practice*, 3rd edn, eds G. Meadows, J. Farhall, E. Fossey, M. Grigg, F. McDermott & B. Singh, Oxford University Press, Melbourne, pp. 468–501.

Fawcett, B. & Karban, K. 2005, *Contemporary Mental Health: Theory, Policy and Practice*, Routledge, London.

Fervaha, G., Agid, O., Takeuchi, H., Foussias, G. & Remington, G. 2013, 'Clinical Determinants of Life Satisfaction in Chronic Schizophrenia: Data from the Catie Study', *Schizophrenia Research*, vol. 151, no. 1–3, pp. 203–8.

Fine, M. 2007, *A Caring Society? Care and Dilemmas of Human Service in the 21st Century*, Palgrave MacMillan, Hampshire, New York.

Fitzgerald, P. B. 2011, 'The Emerging Use of Brain Stimulation Treatments for Psychiatric Disorders', *Australian and New Zealand Journal of Psychiatry*, vol. 45, no. 11, pp. 923–38.

Fossey, E., Brophy, L., Grigg, M., Hamann, J., Hamilton, B., Harvey, C., Minas, H., Thorburn, K. & Watson, S. 2012, 'Case Management', in *Mental Health in Australia: Collaborative Community Practice*, 3rd edn, eds G. Meadows, J. Farhall, E. Fossey, M. Grigg, F. McDermott & B. Singh, Oxford University Press, Melbourne, pp. 428–50.

Fox, R. 1989, 'Relationship: The Cornerstone of Clinical Supervision', *Social Casework*, vol. 70, no. 3, pp. 146–52.

Frankl, V. E. 1984, *Man's Search for Meaning*, Washington Square Press, New York.

Fraser, C., James, E. L., Anderson, K., Lloyd, D. & Judd, F. 2006, 'Intervention Programs for Children of Parents with a Mental Illness: A Critical Review', *International Journal of Mental Health Promotion*, vol. 8, no. 1, pp. 9–20.

Frazer, P., Westhuis, D., Daley, J. G. & Phillips, I. 2009, 'How Clinical Social Workers Are Using the DSM-IV: A National Study', *Social Work in Mental Health*, vol. 7, no. 4, pp. 325–39.

Fukui, S., Goscha, R., Rapp, C. A., Mabry, A., Liddy, P. & Marty, D. 2012, 'Strengths Model Case Management Fidelity Scores and Client Outcomes', *Psychiatric Services*, vol. 63, no. 7, pp. 708–10.

Furlong, M. 1997, 'How Much Care and How Much Control? Looking Critically at Case Management', *Australian Journal of Primary Health – Interchange*, vol. 3, no. 4, pp. 72–89.

——— 2001, 'Constraints on Family-Sensitive Mental Health Practices', *Journal of Family Studies*, vol. 7, no. 2, pp. 217–31.

Furlong, M. & Leggatt, M. 1996, 'Reconciling the Patient's Right to Confidentiality and the Family's Need to Know', *Australian and New Zealand Journal of Psychiatry*, vol. 30, no. 5, pp. 614–22.

Galletly, C., Castle, D., Dark, F., Humberstone, V., Jablensky, A., Kullackey, E., Kulkarni, J., McGorry, P., Nielssen, O. & Tran, N. 2016, 'Royal Australian and New Zealand College of Psychiatrists Clinical Practice Guidelines for the Management of Schizophrenia and Related Disorders', *Australian and New Zealand Journal of Psychiatry*, vol. 50, no. 5, pp. 1–117.

Galloghly, D. P., Dear, G. E. & Jablensky, A. 2013, 'Reliability of Clinical Judgements of Insight in Patients with Psychoses', *Psychiatry Research*, vol. 208, no. 3, pp. 291–2.

Gambrill, E. 2013, *Social Work Practice: A Critical Thinker's Guide*, 3rd edn, Oxford University Press, New York.

Gardner, A., Cotton, S., Filia, K. & Killackey, E. 2018, 'The Social Inclusion of Young People with Serious Mental Illness: A Narrative Review of the Literature and Suggested Future Directions', *Early Interventions in Psychiatry*, vol. 12, no. s1, p. 97.

Gardner, A., Cotton, S. M., Allott, K., Filia, K. M., Hester, R. & Killackey, E. 2019, 'Social Inclusion and Its Interrelationships with Social Cognition and Social Functioning in First-Episode Psychosis', *Early Intervention in Psychiatry*, vol. 13, no. 3, pp. 477–87.

Gerrand, V., Singh, B., Nagel, T., Ash, D., Turnbull, C., Meadows, G., Fossey, E., Grigg, M., Rosen, A., Weir, W. & Benson, A. 2012, 'Mental Health Services in Australia', in *Mental Health in Australia: Collaborative Community Practice*, 3rd edn, eds G. Meadows, J. Farhall, E. Fossey, M. Grigg, F. McDermott & B. Singh, Oxford University Press, Melbourne, pp. 69–117.

Giffin, J. 2008, 'Family Experience of Borderline Personality Disorder', *Australian and New Zealand Journal of Family Therapy*, vol. 29, no. 3, pp. 133–8.

Gilgun, J. F. 2005, 'The Four Cornerstones of Evidence-Based Practice in Social Work', *Research on Social Work Practice*, vol. 15, no. 1, pp. 52–61.

Global Consortium for the Advancement of Promotion and Prevention of Mental and Behavioural Disorders 2009, *Melbourne Charter for Promoting Mental Health and Preventing Mental and Behavioural Disorders*, VicHealth, Melbourne.

Glover, H. 2005, 'Recovery Based Service Delivery: Are We Ready to Transform the Words into a Paradigm Shift? (Guest Editorial)', *Australian e-Journal for the Advancement of Mental Health*, vol. 4, no. 3, pp. 1–4.

Goering, P. N. & Streiner, D. L. 2015, 'Putting Housing First: The Evidence and Impact', *The Canadian Journal of Psychiatry*, vol. 60, no. 11, pp. 465–6.

Goffman, E. 1961, *Asylums: Essays on the Social Situation of Mental Patients and Other Inmates*, Penguin, Harmondsworth, UK.

Goldberg, D., Kendler, K. S., Sirovatka, P. J. & Regier, D. A. (eds) 2010, *Diagnostic Issues in Depression and Generalized Anxiety Disorder*, American Psychiatric Association, Arlington, VA.

Goldstein, M. J. & Miklowitz, D. J. 1994, 'Family Intervention for Persons with Bipolar Disorder', *New Directions for Mental Health Services*, vol. 1994, no. 62, pp. 23–35.

Goodwin, G. M. 2012, 'Bipolar Disorder', *Medicine*, vol. 40, no. 11, pp. 596–8.

Granello, D. H. 2010, 'The Process of Suicide Risk Assessment: Twelve Core Principles', *Journal of Counselling and Development*, vol. 88, Summer, pp. 363–70.

Gray, B., Robinson, C. & Seddon, D. 2008, 'Confidentiality Smokescreens and Carers for People with Mental Health Problems: The Perspectives of Professionals', *Health and Social Care in the Community*, vol. 16, no.4, pp. 378–87.

Gray, S. W. & Zide, M. R. 2008, *Psychopathology: A Competency-Based Assessment Model for Social Workers*, 2nd edn, Thomson Brooks/Cole, Belmont, CA.

Grenyer, B. F. S. 2013, 'Improved Prognosis for Borderline Personality Disorder', *Medical Journal of Australia*, vol. 198, no. 9, pp. 464–5.

Haddock, G., Eisner, E., Boone, C., Davies, G., Coogan, C. & Barrowclough, C. 2014, 'An Investigation of the Implementation of NICE-Recommended CBT Interventions for People with Schizophrenia', *Journal of Mental Health*, vol. 23, no. 4, pp. 162–5.

Hamovitch, E., Choy-Brown, K. & Stanhope, M. 2018, 'Person-Centered Care and the Therapeutic Alliance', *Community Mental Health Journal*, vol. 54, no. 7, pp. 951–8.

Hanley, B. & Staley, K. 2005, *User and Care Involvement: A Good Practice Guide*, Long Term Medical Conditions Alliance, London.

Happell, B. 2008, 'Determining the Effectiveness of Mental Health Services from a Consumer Perspective: Part 2: Barriers to Recovery and Principles for Evaluation', *International Journal of Mental Health Nursing*, vol. 17, no. 2, pp. 123–30.

Harding, C. M., Brooks, G. W., Ashikaga, T., Strauss, J. S. & Breier, A. 1987, 'The Vermont Longitudinal Study of Persons with Severe Mental Illness, I: Methodology, Study Sample, and Overall Status 32 Years Later', *American Journal of Psychiatry*, vol. 144, no. 6, pp. 718–26.

Harries, M. 1999, 'Social Work', in *Learning Together: Education and Training Partnerships in Mental Health Service. Final Report*, ed Deakin Human Services Australia, Commonwealth Department of Health and Aged Care, Canberra, pp. 57–62.

Harris, A. & Boyce, P. 2013, 'Why Do We Not Use Psychosocial Interventions in the Treatment of Schizophrenia?', *Australian and New Zealand Journal of Psychiatry*, vol. 47, no. 6, pp. 501–4.

Harris, N., Williams, S. & Bradshaw, T. 2002, *Psychosocial Interventions for People with Schizophrenia: A Practical Guide for Mental Health Workers*, Palgrave, Basingstoke, UK.

Hartman, A. 1995, 'Diagrammatic Assessment of Family Relationships', *Families in Society*, vol. 76, no. 2, pp. 111–22.

Harvey, C. & O'Hanlon, B. 2013, 'Family Psycho-Education for People with Schizophrenia and Other Psychotic Disorders and Their Families', *Australian and New Zealand Journal of Psychiatry*, vol. 47, no. 6, pp. 516–20.

Harvey, S. B., Modini, M., Christensen, H. & Glozier, N. 2013, 'Severe Mental Illness and Work: What Can We Do to Maximise the Employment Opportunities for Individuals with Psychosis?', *Australian and New Zealand Journal of Psychiatry*, vol. 47, no. 5, pp. 421–4.

Hasenfeld, Y. 1987, 'Power in Social Work Practice', *Social Service Review*, vol. 61, no. 3, pp. 469–83.

Hatfield, A. B. 1978, 'The Psychological Costs of Schizophrenia to the Family', *Social Work*, vol. 23, no. 5, pp. 355–9.

——— 1987, 'The Expressed Emotion Theory: Why Families Object', *Psychiatric Services*, vol. 38, no. 4, p. 341.

——— 1991, *Coping with Mental Illness in the Family: A Family Guide*, National Alliance for the Mentally Ill, Arlington, VA.

——— 1994, 'Family Education: Theory and Practice', *New Directions for Mental Health Services*, no. 62, pp. 3–11.

Hatfield, A. B. & Lefley, H. (eds) 1987, *Families of the Mentally Ill: Coping and Adaptation*, Guilford Press, New York.

Hatfield, A. B. & Lefley, H. P. 1993, *Surviving Mental Illness: Stress, Coping, and Adaptation*, Guilford Press, New York.

Healy, B. & Brophy, L. 2002, 'Law, Psychiatry and Social Work', in *In the Shadow of the Law: The Legal Context of Social Work Practice*, ed. P. A. Swain, Federation Press, Sydney, pp. 230–43.

Healy, B., Ryan, M., Renouf, N., Wright, L., Shaw, E., Gough, I., Boutlis, N. & Sago, R. 2005, *What Factors Impact on People's Capacity to Maintain Long-Term Tenancies? Did the SAAP Experience Help Them?*, Merri Outreach Support Service and La Trobe University School of Social Work and Social Policy, Melbourne.

Hernandez, L., Robson, P. & Sampson, A. 2010, 'Towards Integrated Participation: Involving Seldom Heard Users of Social Care Services', *British Journal of Social Work*, vol. 40, no. 3, pp. 714–36.

Highet, N. J., McNair, B. G., Davenport, T. A. & Hickie, I. B. 2004, '"How Much More Can We Lose?": Carer and Family Perspectives on Living with a Person with Depression', *Medical Journal of Australia*, vol. 181, no. 7, p. S6.

Hinton, T. 2007, *Forgotten Families: Raising Children with Disabilities in Tasmania*, Anglicare Tasmania, Hobart.

Hobbs, M. & Baker, M. 2012, 'Hope for Recovery – How Clinicians May Facilitate This in Their Work', *Journal of Mental Health*, vol. 21, no. 2, pp. 144–53.

Hoenig, J. & Hamilton, M. 1969, *The Desegregation of the Mentally Ill*, Routledge & Kegan Paul, London.

Holmes, A. C. N., Hodge, M. A., Bradley, G., Bluhm, A., Hodges, J., Didio, L. & Markulev, N. 2005, 'Accommodation History and Continuity of Care in Patients with Psychosis', *Australian and New Zealand Journal of Psychiatry*, vol. 39, no. 3, pp. 175–9.

Holmes, D., Molloy, L., Beckett, P., Field, J. & Stratford, A. 2013, 'Peer Support Workers Hold the Key to Opening Up Recovery-Orientated Service in Inpatient Units', *Australasian Psychiatry*, vol. 21, no. 3, pp. 282–3.

Honey, A. 1999, 'Empowerment Versus Power: Consumer Participation in Mental Health Services', *Occupational Therapy International*, vol. 6, no. 4, pp. 257–76.

Hooley, J. 1985, 'Expressed Emotion: A Review of the Critical Literature', *Clinical Psychology Review*, vol. 5, no. 2, pp. 119–39.

Hooley, J. M., Cole, S. H. & Gironde, S. 2012, 'Borderline Personality Disorder', in *The Oxford Handbook of Personality Disorders*, ed. T. A. Widiger, Oxford University Press, Oxford, pp. 409–36.

Horsfall, J., Cleary, M., Hunt, G. E. & Walter, G. 2009, 'Psychosocial Treatments for People with Co-Occurring Severe Mental Illnesses and Substance Use Disorders (Dual Diagnosis): A Review of Empirical Evidence', *Harvard Review of Psychiatry*, vol. 17, no. 1, pp. 24–34.

Horwitz, A. V. & Wakefield, J. C. 2007, *The Loss of Sadness: How Psychiatry Transformed Normal Sorrow into Depressive Disorder*, Oxford University Press, Oxford.

Hughes, L. & Phillips, P. 2012, 'Drugs, Drink and Mental Health: The Impact and Consequences of Dual Diagnosis for Mental Health Service Delivery', in *Working in Mental Health: Practice and Policy in a Changing Environment*, eds P. Phillips, T. Sandford & C. Johnston, Routledge, London, pp. 81–9.

Human Rights and Equal Opportunity Commission (HREOC) 1993, *Human Rights and Mental Illness: Report of the National Inquiry into the Human Rights of People with Mental Illness*, 2 volumes, Australian Government Publishing Service, Canberra.

Human Rights Law Centre 2011, *Mental Health Focus Area*, viewed 1 June 2014, www.humanrightsactionplan.org.au/nhrap/focus-area/mental-health.

Huxley, P. 2008, 'Mental Illness', in *The Blackwell Companion to Social Work*, 3rd edn, ed. M. Davies, Blackwell, Oxford, pp. 55–62.

Huxley, P. & Thornicroft, G. 2003, 'Social Inclusion, Social Quality and Mental Illness', *British Journal of Psychiatry*, vol. 182, no. 4, pp. 289–90.

Huxley, P. & Vick, N. 2005, 'Promoting Social Inclusion Through National Mental Health Policy', paper presented to THEMHS Conference, Adelaide.

Huxley, P., Webber, M. & Evans, S. 2005, 'Measuring Social Inclusion', paper presented to THEMHS Conference, Adelaide.

International Physical Health in Youth (iphYs) Working Group 2013, *Healthy Active Lives (HeAL) Consensus Statement*, International Physical Health in Youth, www.iphys.org.au/media/HeAL_brochure_Feb14.pdf.

Jablensky, A., McGrath, J., Herrman, H., Castle, D., Gureje, O., Morgan, V. & Korten, A. 1999, *People Living with Psychotic Illness: An Australian Study 1997–1998*, Mental Health Branch, Commonwealth Department of Health and Aged Care, Canberra.

Jack, R. 2005, 'Strengths-Based Practice in Statutory Care and Protection Work', in *Social Work Theories in Action*, eds M. Nash, R. Minford & K. O'Donoghue, Jessica Kingsley, London, pp. 174–88.

Jacka, F. N., Reavley, N. J., Jorm, A. F., Toumbourou, J. W., Lewis, A. J. & Berk, M. 2013, 'Prevention of Common Mental Disorders: What Can We Learn from Those Who Have Gone

Before and Where Do We Go Next?', *Australian and New Zealand Journal of Psychiatry*, vol. 47, no. 10, pp. 920–9.

Jacobson, N. 2009, 'A Taxonomy of Dignity: A Grounded Theory Study', *BMC International Health and Human Rights*, vol. 9, no. 3.

Johnson, D. L. 2007, 'Models of Family Intervention', in *Families as Partners in Mental Health Care: A Guidebook for Implementing Family Work*, eds D. Froggatt, G. Fadden, D. L. Johnson, M. Leggatt & R. Shankar, World Fellowship for Schizophrenia and Allied Disorders, Toronto, pp. 10–21.

Jones, D., Macias, R. L., Gold, P. B., Barreira, P. & Fisher, W. 2008, 'When Parents with Severe Mental Illness Lose Contact with Their Children: Are Psychiatric Symptoms or Substance Use to Blame?', *Journal of Loss and Trauma*, vol. 13, no. 4, pp. 261–87.

Jorm, A. F. & Kitchener, B. A. 2011, 'Noting a Landmark Achievement: Mental Health First Aid Training Reaches 1% of Australian Adults', *Australian and New Zealand Journal of Psychiatry*, vol. 45, no. 10, pp. 808–13.

Jutel, A. & Nettleton, S. 2011, 'Towards a Sociology of Diagnosis: Reflections and Opportunities', *Social Science & Medicine*, vol. 73, no. 6, pp. 793–800.

Kabat-Zinn, J. 2003, 'Mindfulness-Based Interventions in Context: Past, Present, and Future', *Clinical Psychology: Science and Practice*, vol. 10, no. 2, pp. 144–56.

Kadushin, A. & Harkness, D. 2002, *Supervision in Social Work*, 4th edn, Columbia University Press, New York.

Kanter, J. 1989, 'Clinical Case Management: Definition, Principles, Components', *Hospital and Community Psychiatry*, vol. 40, no. 4, pp. 361–8.

Keleher, H. & Armstrong, R. 2005, *Evidence-Based Mental Health Promotion Resource*, Department of Human Services and VicHealth, Melbourne.

Kemp, V. & Henderson, A. R. 2012, 'Challenges Faced by Mental Health Peer Support Workers: Peer Support from the Peer Supporter's Point of View', *Psychiatric Rehabilitation Journal*, vol. 35, no. 4, pp. 337–40.

Kiely, K. M. & Butterworth, P. 2013, 'Social Disadvantage and Individual Vulnerability: A Longitudinal Investigation of Welfare Receipt and Mental Health in Australia', *Australian and New Zealand Journal of Psychiatry*, vol. 47, no. 7, pp. 654–66.

Kitchener, B. & Jorm, A. 2009, *Mental Health First Aid Manual*, Orygen Research Centre, Melbourne.

Koubel, G. & Yardley, C. 2012, 'Managing Risk in a Complex Society', in *Rights, Risks and Responsibilities: Interprofessional Working in Health and Social Care*, eds G. Koubel & H. Bungay, Palgrave Macmillan, London, pp. 65–82.

Krantz, J. & Gilmore, T. 1990, *Projective Identification in Organizational Consultation*, Triad Consulting Group, viewed 21 April 2002, www.triadllc.com/pubprojective.html.

Kreyenbuhl, J., Buchanan, R. W., Dickerson, F. B. & Dixon, L. B. 2010, 'The Schizophrenia Patient Outcomes Research Team (PORT): Updated Treatment Recommendations 2009', *Schizophrenia Bulletin*, vol. 36, no. 1, pp. 94–103.

Kushner, H. 1981, *When Bad Things Happen to Good People*, Anchor Books, New York.

Kyrios, M., Mouding, R. & Nedeljkovic, M. 2011, 'Anxiety Disorders: Assessment and Management in General Practice', *Australian Family Physician*, vol. 40, no. 6, pp. 370–4.

Laing, R. D. 1960, *The Divided Self: An Existential Study in Sanity and Madness*, Penguin, Harmondsworth.

Large, M. & Ryan, C. 2014, 'Suicide Risk Assessment: Myth and Reality', *International Journal of Clinical Practice*, vol. 68, no. 6, pp. 679–81.

Lawrence, D., Hancock, K. J. & Kisley, S. 2013, 'The Gap in Life Expectancy from Preventable Physical Illness in Psychiatric Patients in Western Australia; Retrospective Analysis of Population-Based Registers', *British Medical Journal*, vol. 346, pp. f2539.

Lawrence-Jones, J. 2010, 'Dual Diagnosis (Drug/Alcohol and Mental Health): Service User Experiences', *Practice: Social Work in Action*, vol. 22, no. 2, pp. 115–31.

Leamy, M., Bird, V., Le Boutillier, C., Williams, J. & Slade, M. 2011, 'Conceptual Framework for Personal Recovery in Mental Health: Systematic Review and Narrative Synthesis', *British Journal of Psychiatry*, vol. 199, no. 6, pp. 445–52.

Lee, S. J., Crowther, E., Keating, C. & Kulkarni, J. 2013, 'What Is Needed to Deliver Collaborative Care to Address Comorbidity More Effectively for Adults with a Severe Mental Illness?', *Australian and New Zealand Journal of Psychiatry*, vol. 47, no. 4, pp. 333–46.

Leff, J. & Warner, R. 2006, *Social Inclusion of People with Mental Illness*, Cambridge University Press, Cambridge.

Lefley, H. 1993, 'Involuntary Treatment: Concerns of Consumers, Families and Society', *Innovations and Research*, vol. 2, no. 1, pp. 7–9.

Leggatt, M. 2002, 'Families and Mental Health Workers: The Need for Partnership', *World Psychiatry*, vol. 1, no. 1, pp. 52–4.

——— 2007, 'Meeting the Challenges', in *Families as Partners in Mental Health Care: A Guidebook for Implementing Family Work*, eds D. Froggatt, G. Fadden, D. L. Johnson, M. Leggatt & R. Shankar, World Fellowship for Schizophrenia and Allied Disorders, Toronto, pp. 22–37.

Linehan, M. M. 1993a, Cognitive Behavior Therapy for Borderline Personality Disorder, Guilford Press, New York.

——— 1993b, Skills Training Manual for Treating Borderline Personality Disorder, Guilford Press, New York.

Linhorst, D. M. 2005, *Empowering People with Severe Mental Illness: A Practical Guide*, Oxford University Press, New York.

Little, J. 2013, 'Bipolar II and the Birth of a New Physics', *Australian and New Zealand Journal of Psychiatry*, vol. 47, no. 9, p. 882.

Lopez, S. 2008, *The Soloist*, Putnam & Sons, New York.

Luntz, J. J. 1999, 'What Is Mental Health Consultation?', *Children Australia*, vol. 24, no. 3, pp. 28–33.

——— 2000, 'Mental Health Consultation: Stages in the Consultation Process', *Children Australia*, vol. 25, no. 1, pp. 21–6.

MacDonald-Wilson, K. L., Nemec, P. B., Anthony, W. A. & Cohen, M. R. 2001, 'Assessment in Psychiatric Rehabilitation', in *Handbook of Measurement and Evaluation in Rehabilitation*, 3rd edn, ed. B. Bolton, Aspen Publications, Gaithersburg, MD, pp. 423–48.

Magliano, L., Fadden, G., Economou, M., Xavier, M., Held, T., Guarneri, M., & Maj, M. 1998, 'Social and Clinical Factors Influencing the Choice of Coping Strategies in Relatives of Patients with Schizophrenia: Results of the BIOMED 1 Study', *Social Psychiatry and Psychiatric Epidemiology*, vol. 33, no. 9, pp. 413–19.

Makregiorgos, H., Joubert, L. & Epstein, I. 2013, 'Maternal Mental Health: Pathways of Care for Women Experiencing Mental Health Issues During Pregnancy', *Social Work in Health Care*, vol. 52, no. 2–3, pp. 258–79.

Malhi, G. S., Adams, D., Lampe, L., Paton, M., O'Connor, N., Newton, L. A., Walter, G., Taylor, A., Porter, R., Mulder, R. T. & Berk, M. 2009, 'Clinical Practice Recommendations for Bipolar Disorder', *Acta Psychiatrica Scandinavica*, vol. 119, pp. 27–46.

Malhi, G. S. & Henderson, S. 2013, 'The Anxiety of Separation? Partitioning Depression and Anxiety in DSM-5', *Australian and New Zealand Journal of Psychiatry*, vol. 47, no. 11, pp. 986–8.

Manuel, J. I., Appelbaum, P. S., Le Melle, S. M., Mancini, A. D., Huz, S., Stellato, C. B. & Finnerty, M. T. 2013, 'Use of Intervention Strategies by Assertive Community Treatment Teams to Promote Patients' Engagement', *Psychiatric Services*, vol. 64, no. 6, pp. 579–85.

Marel, C., Mills, K., Kingston, R., Gournay, K., Dady, M., Kay-Lambkin, F., Baker, A. & Teeson, M. 2016, *Guidelines on the Management of Co-occurring Alcohol and other Drug and Mental*

Health Conditions in Alcohol and other Drug Treatment Settings. Australian Government Department of Health, Canberra.

Martin, G. 2007, 'Editorial', *Australian e-Journal for the Advancement of Mental Health*, vol. 6, no. 3.

Maybery, D., Reupert, A., Patrick, K., Goodyear, M. & Crase, L. 2005, *VicHealth Research Report on Children at Risk in Families Affected by Parental Mental Illness*, Victorian Health Promotion Foundation, Melbourne.

McFarlane, W. R., Dixon, L., Lukens, E. & Lucksted, A. 2003, 'Family Psychoeducation and Schizophrenia: A Review of the Literature', *Journal of Marital and Family Therapy*, vol. 29, no. 2, pp. 223–45.

McGorry, P. 2005, "Every Me and Every You": Responding to the Hidden Challenge of Mental Illness in Australia', *Australasian Psychiatry*, vol. 13, no. 1, pp. 3–15.

McGorry, P. D., Purcell, R., Hickie, I. B. & Jorm, A. F. 2007, 'Investing in Youth Mental Health is a Best Buy', *Medical Journal of Australia*, vol. 187, no. 7, pp. S5–7.

McGrath, J., Saha, S., Chant, D. & Welham, J. 2008, 'Schizophrenia: A Concise Overview of Incidence, Prevalence, and Mortality', *Epidemiologic Reviews*, vol. 30, no. 1, pp. 67–76.

McGregor, P. 1994, 'Grief: The Unrecognized Parental Response to Mental Illness in a Child', *Social Work*, vol. 39, no. 2, pp. 160–6.

McKay, R. G. & Draper, B. M. 2012, 'Is It Too Late to Prevent a Decline in Mental Health Care for Older Australians?', *Medical Journal of Australia*, vol. 197, no. 2, pp. 87–8.

McPherson, S., Evans, C. & Richardson, P. 2009, 'The Nice Depression Guidelines and the Recovery Model: Is There an Evidence Base for IAPT?', *Journal of Mental Health*, vol. 18, no. 5, pp. 405–14.

McQuaide, S. & Ehrenreich, J. H. 1997, 'Assessing Client Strengths', *Families in Society*, vol. 78, no. 2, pp. 201–12.

Mead, S., Hilton, D. & Curtis, L. 2001, 'Peer Support: A Theoretical Perspective', *Psychiatric Rehabilitation Journal*, vol. 25, no. 2, pp. 134–41.

Meadows, G. 2019, 'The Experience of the Use of Community Treatment Orders Following Recovery-Oriented Practice Training', *International Journal of Law and Psychiatry*. vol. 64, pp. 178–83.

Meadows, G., Cavill, M., Epstein, M., Fossey, E., Leggatt, M., Olsen, A., Minas, H. & Willshire, D. 2012, 'Assessment: Essential Skills', in *Mental Health in Australia: Collaborative Community Practice*, 3rd edn, eds G. Meadows, J. Farhall, E. Fossey, M. Grigg, F. McDermott & B. Singh, Oxford University Press, Melbourne, pp. 342–93.

Meagher, J. 2002, 'Guest Editorial: Beyond Partnership: Hypocrisy and Challenges in the Mental Health Consumer Movement', *Australian e-Journal for the Advancement of Mental Health*, vol. 1, no. 1.

Mechanic, D., McAlpine, D. D. & Rochefort, D. A. 2014, *Mental Health and Social Policy: Beyond Managed Care*, 6th edn, Pearson, Boston.

Medibank & Nous Group 2013, *The Case for Mental Health Reform in Australia: A Review of Expenditure and System Design*, Medibank and Nous Group.

Melville-Wiseman, J. 2012, 'Taking Relationships into Account in Mental Health Services', in *Rights, Risks and Responsibilities: Interprofessional Working in Health and Social Care*, eds G. Koubel & H. Bungay, Palgrave Macmillan, London, pp. 123–41.

Mendelson, G. & Jablensky, A. 2007, 'What Does Psychiatry Encompass?', in *Foundations of Clinical Psychiatry*, 3rd edn, eds S. Bloch & B. S. Singh, Melbourne University Press, Melbourne, pp. 69–90.

Mendes, P., Allen-Kelly, K., Charikar, K., Incerti, K. & McCurdy, S. 2012, *Social Workers and Social Action: A Report for the Lyra Taylor Fund on the AASW Campaign to Restore Medicare Rebates for Accredited Mental Health Social Workers*, https://www.academia.edu/2297234/

Social_Workers_and_Social_Action_a_report_for_the_Lyra_Taylor_Fund_on_the_AASW_campaign_to_restore_Medicare_rebates_for_accredited_mental_health_social_workers.

Mental Health Commission New Zealand 1998, *Blueprint for Mental Health Services in New Zealand*, Mental Health Commission, Wellington.

Mental Health Commission New Zealand 2007, *Te Haererenga Mo to Whakaoranga 1996–2006*, Mental Health Commission, Wellington.

Mental Health Council of Australia 2005, *Not for Service: Experiences of Injustice and Despair in Mental Health Care in Australia*, Mental Health Council of Australia, Canberra.

——— 2009, *Adversity to Advocacy Report Card*, Mental Health Council of Australia, Canberra.

——— 2009, *Adversity to Advocacy: The Lives and Hopes of Mental Health Carers*, Mental Health Council of Australia, Canberra.

——— 2011, *Consumer and Carer Experiences of Stigma from Mental Health and Other Health Professionals*, Mental Health Council of Australia, Canberra.

Menzies School of Health Research 2013, *AIMhi Care Plan Documents*, Menzies School of Health Research, viewed 8 January 2014, www.menzies.edu.au/page/Resources/AIMhi_Pictorial_Care_Plan.

Milewski-Hertlein, K. A. 2001, 'The Use of a Socially Constructed Genogram in Clinical Practice', *American Journal of Family Therapy*, vol. 29, no. 1, pp. 23–38.

Miller, C., Freeman, M. & Ross, N. 2001, *Interprofessional Practice in Health and Social Care: Challenging the Shared Learning Agenda*, Arnold, London.

Miller, J. 2002, 'Social Workers as Diagnosticians', in *Social Work Practice in Mental Health: Contemporary Roles, Tasks, and Techniques*, ed. K. J. Bentley, Brooks/Cole, Pacific Grove, CA, pp. 43–72.

Milner, J. & O'Byrne, P. 2009, *Assessment in Social Work*, 3rd edn, Palgrave Macmillan, Houndmills, Basingstoke.

MindMatters 2009, *Leading Mental Health and Wellbeing*, MindMatters, viewed 8 March 2009, www.mindmatters.edu.au.

Minister of Health 2005, *Te Tāhuhu – Improving Mental Health 2005–2015: The Second New Zealand Mental Health and Addiction Plan*, Ministry of Health, Wellington.

Minkoff, K. 2001, *Behavioral Health Recovery Management Service Planning Guidelines: Co-Occurring Psychiatric and Substance Disorders*, Behavioural Health Recovery Management Project, Bloomington, IN.

Mitchell, A. J., Vaze, A. & Rao, S. 2009, 'Clinical Diagnosis of Depression in Primary Care: A Meta-Analysis', *Lancet*, vol. 374, no. 9690, pp. 609–19.

Mondy, L. & Mondy, S. (eds) 2008, *Newpin: Courage to Change Together: Helping Families Achieve Generational Change*, UnitingCare Burnside, North Parramatta, NSW.

Morgan, V. A., Waterreus, A., Jablensky, A., Mackinnon, A., McGrath, J. J., Carr, V., Bush, R., Castle, D., Cohen, M., Harvey, C., Galletly, C., Stain, H. J., Neil, A., McGorry, P., Hocking, B., Shah, S. & Saw, S. 2011, *People Living with Psychotic Illness 2010: Report on the Second Australian National Survey*, Department of Health and Ageing, Canberra.

Moulding, R., Blashki, G., Gunn, J., Mihalopoulos, C., Pirkis, J., Naccarella, L. & Joubert, L. 2007, *Optimising the Primary Mental Health Care Workforce: How Can Effective Psychological Treatments for Common Mental Disorders Best Be Delivered in Primary Care?*, Australian Primary Health Care Research Institute, Canberra.

Mowbray, C. T. & Holter, M. C. 2002, 'Mental Health and Mental Illness: Out of the Closet?', *Social Service Review*, vol. 76, no. 1, pp. 135–79.

Mrazek, P. & Haggerty, R. (eds) 1994, *Reducing the Risks for Mental Disorders: Frontiers for Preventative Intervention Research*, National Academy Press, Washington, DC.

Mueser, K. T., Silverstein, S. M. & Farkas, M. D. 2013, 'Should the Training of Clinical Psychologists Require Competence in the Treatment and Rehabilitation of Individuals with a Serious Mental Illness?', *Psychiatric Rehabilitation Journal*, vol. 36, no. 1, pp. 54–9.

Multicultural Mental Health Australia (now known as Mental Health in Multicultural Australia) 2002, *Cultural Awareness Tool: Understanding Cultural Diversity in Mental Health*, Multicultural Mental Health Australia, Parramatta, NSW.

National Alliance on Mental Illness 2008, *Women and Depression: What You Need to Know About this Medical Illness*, NAMI, Arlington, VA.

National Health and Medical Research Council (NHMRC) 2000, *Postnatal Depression: A Systematic Review of Published Scientific Literature to 1999*, National Health and Medical Research Council, Canberra.

——— 2013, *Clinical Practice Guideline for the Management of Borderline Personality Disorder*, National Health and Medical Research Council, Melbourne.

National Institute for Health and Care Excellence (NICE) 2009, *Depression: Treatment and Management of Depression in Adults, Including Adults with a Chronic Physical Health Problem*, Quick Reference Guide, National Institute for Health and Care Excellence, London.

National Mental Health Commission 2012, *A Contributing Life: The 2012 National Report Card on Mental Health and Suicide Prevention*, National Mental Health Commission, Sydney.

——— 2013, *A Contributing Life: The 2013 National Report Card on Mental Health and Suicide Prevention*, National Mental Health Commission, Sydney.

National Mental Health Consumers and Carers Forum (NMHCCF) 2010, *Consumer and Carer Participation: Key Issues and Benefits*, nmhccf.org.au.

Nelson, G., Lord, J. & Ochocka, J. 2001, *Shifting the Paradigm in Community Mental Health*, University of Toronto Press, Toronto.

Nevo, I. & Slonim-Nevo, V. 2011, 'The Myth of Evidence-Based Practice: Towards Evidence-Informed Practice', *The British Journal of Social Work*, vol. 41, no. 6, pp. 1176–97.

New Zealand Parliament 1990, New Zealand Bill of Rights Act.

Oades, L. G. & Anderson, J. 2012, 'Recovery in Australia: Marshalling Strengths and Living Values', *International Review of Psychiatry*, vol. 24, no. 1, pp. 5–10.

O'Connor, I., Hughes, M., Turner, D., Wilson, J. & Setterlund, D. 2006, *Social Work and Social Care Practice*, Sage, London.

O'Connor, N., Warby, M., Raphael, B. & Vassallo, T. 2004, 'Changeability, Confidence, Common Sense and Corroboration: Comprehensive Suicide Risk Assessment', *Australasian Psychiatry*, vol. 12, no. 4, pp. 352–60.

Office of the High Commissioner for Human Rights 1991, *Principles for the Protection of Persons with Mental Illness and the Improvement of Mental Health Care*, Office of the United Nations Commissioner for Human Rights, viewed 7 March 2009, www.unhchr.ch/html/menu3/b/68.htm.

Office of Social Services Department of Health 2019, *Reflections Mental Health – Social Work and Mental Health in Northern Ireland*, Belfast, June.

O'Grady, C. & Skinner, W. (2012) 'Journey as Destination: A Recovery Model for Families Affected by Concurrent Disorders', *Qualitative Health Research*, vol. 22, no. 8, pp. 1047–62.

Ohaeri, J. 2003, 'The Burden of Caregiving in Families with a Mental Illness: A Review of 2002', *Current Opinion in Psychiatry*, vol. 16, no. 4, pp. 457–65.

O'Hagan, M. 2004, 'Recovery in New Zealand: Lessons for Australia?', *Australian e-Journal for the Advancement of Mental Health*, vol. 3, no. 1, pp. 1–3.

O'Hagan, M. 2012, *Legal Coercion: The Elephant in the Recovery Room*, Scottish Recovery Network, www.scottishrecovery.net/resource/legal-coercion-the-elephant-in-the-recovery-room/.

O'Hagan, M., Pearson, A. & Lindberg, W. 2002, *Consumer Participation in the Project to Counter Stigma and Discrimination Associated with Mental Illness*, New Zealand Action Research Network.

Oram, S., Trevillion, K., Feder, G. & Howard, L. M. 2013, 'Prevalence of Experiences of Domestic Violence among Psychiatric Patients: Systematic Review', *British Journal of Psychiatry*, vol. 202, no. 2, pp. 94–9.

Osborn, D. P. 2012, 'Delivering Physical Health Care in Modern Mental Health Services: What Works and Why We All Have to Bother', in *Working in Mental Health: Practice and Policy in a Changing Environment*, eds P. Phillips, T. Sandford & C. Johnston, Routledge, London, pp. 159–69.

Our Consumer Place 2013, *MadQuarry Dictionary: A Consumer's Guide to the Language of Mental Health*, Our Consumer Place, Melbourne.

Padgett, D., Gulcur, L., Tsemberis, S. 2006, "Housing First Services for People Who are Homeless with Co-Occurring Serious Mental Illness and Substance Abuse" *Research on Social Work Practice*, January.

Padgett, D. K. 2012, 'Supported Housing and the Lamppost – or Supported Housing in the Spotlight?', *Psychiatric Services*, vol. 63, no. 7, p. 720.

Park, S. & Nasrallah, H. A. 2014, 'The Varieties of Anomalous Self Experiences in Schizophrenia: Splitting of the Mind at a Crossroad', *Schizophrenia Research*, vol. 152, no. 1, pp. 1–4.

Parker, G. 2004, *Dealing with Depression: A Commonsense Guide to Mood Disorders*, 2nd edn, Allen & Unwin, Crows Nest, NSW.

——— 2005, 'Beyond Major Depression', *Psychological Medicine*, vol. 35, no. 4, pp. 467–74.

Pietrek, C., Elbert, T., Weierstall, R., Müller, O. & Rockstroh, B. 2013, 'Childhood Adversities in Relation to Psychiatric Disorders', *Psychiatry Research*, vol. 206, no. 1, pp. 103–10.

Pilgrim, D. 2009, *Key Concepts in Mental Health*, 2nd edn, Sage, London.

Pinches, A. 2014, *What the Consumer Movement Says About Recovery*, n.p., Melbourne.

Pirkis, J., Ftanou, M., Williamson, J., Machlin, A., Warr, D., Christo, J., Castan, L., Spittal, M. J., Bassilios, B. & Harris, M. 2010, *Evaluation of the Better Access to Psychiatrists, Psychologists and General Practitioners through the Medicare Benefits Schedule Initiative. Component A.: A Study of Consumers and Their Outcomes. Final Report*, Centre for Health Policy, Programs and Economics, The University of Melbourne, Melbourne.

Plath, D. 2006, 'Evidence-Based Practice: Current Issues and Future Directions', *Australian Social Work*, vol. 59, no. 1, pp. 56–72.

Poole, R. 2004, 'Medical Diagnosis of Mental Illness', in *Good Practice in Adult Mental Health*, eds T. Ryan & J. Pritchard, Jessica Kingsley, London, pp. 127–44.

Prigent, A., Simon, S., Durand-Zaleski, I., Leboyer, M. & Chevreul, K. 2014, 'Quality of Life Instruments Used in Mental Health Research: Properties and Utilization', *Psychiatry Research*, vol. 215, no. 1, pp. 1–8.

Pritchard, C. 2006, *Mental Health and Social Work,* Routledge, London and New York.

Prochaska, J. O., DiClemente, C. C. & Norcross, J. C. 1992, 'In Search of How People Change: Applications to Addictive Behaviors', *American Psychologist*, vol. 47, no. 9, pp. 1102–4.

Purdie, N., Dudgeon, P. & Walker, R. (eds) 2010, *Working Together: Aboriginal and Torres Strait Islander Mental Health and Wellbeing Principles and Practice*, Australian Institute of Educational Research, Camberwell, Vic.

Queensland Department of Health 2020, *Understanding Domestic and Family Violence*, www.health.qld.gov.au/__data/assets/pdf_file/0025/952072/1_Understanding-DFV-Booklet.pdf.

Queensland Health 2008, *Queensland Health Policy: Service Delivery for People with Dual Diagnosis (Co-Occurring Mental Health and Alcohol and Other Drug Problems)*, Queensland Government, Brisbane.

Queensland Mental Health Commission 2015, *Early Action: Queensland Mental Health Promotion, Prevention and Early Intervention Plan 2015–2017*, Queensland Government, Brisbane.

——— 2018, *Shifting minds: Queensland Mental Health, Alcohol and Other Drugs Strategic Plan 2018–2023*, Queensland Government, Brisbane.

——— 2019, *Community of Peers Project Report*, Queensland Government, Brisbane.

Ramon, S. 2005, 'Approaches to Risk in Mental Health', in *Social Perspectives in Mental Health: Developing Social Models to Understand and Work with Mental Distress*, ed. J. Tew, Jessica Kingsley, London, pp. 184–99.

Rao, S., Falconer, B., Olsen, A., Grigg, M., Olsen, S. & Grey, F. 2012, 'Personality Disorders', in *Mental Health in Australia: Collaborative Community Practice*, 3rd edn, eds G. Meadows, J. Farhall, E. Fossey, M. Grigg, F. McDermott & B. Singh, Oxford University Press, Melbourne, pp. 530–59.

Rapp, C. A. & Goscha, R. J. 2012, *The Strengths Model: A Recovery-Oriented Approach to Mental Health Services*, 3rd edn, Oxford University Press, New York.

Reavley, N. J., Cvetkovski, S., Jorm, A. F. & Lubman, D. I. 2010, 'Help-Seeking for Substance Use, Anxiety and Affective Disorders among Young People: Results from the 2007 Australian National Survey of Mental Health and Wellbeing', *Australian and New Zealand Journal of Psychiatry*, vol. 44, no. 8, pp. 729–35.

Recovery Star Outcomes Site, www.outcomesstar.org.uk/using-the-star/see-the-stars/recovery-star-4/.

Reed, A. 2013, 'Therapist Attentiveness and Negative Capability in Dialogical Family Meetings for Psychosis', *Journal of Family Therapy*, vol. 35, no. 4, pp. 427–40.

Reed, S. I. 2008, 'First-Episode Psychosis: A Literature Review', *International Journal of Mental Health Nursing*, vol. 17, no. 2, pp. 85–91.

Regehr, C. & Antle, B. 1997, 'Coercive Influences: Informed Consent in Court-Mandated Social Work Practice', *Social Work*, vol. 42, no. 3, pp. 300–6.

Regier, D. A., Narrow, W. E., Rae, D. S., Manderscheid, R. W., Locke, B. Z. & Goodwin, F. K. 1993, 'The De Facto US Mental and Addictive Disorders Service System. Epidemiologic Catchment Area Prospective 1-Year Prevalence Rates of Disorders and Services', *Archives of General Psychiatry*, vol. 50, no. 2, pp. 85–94.

Reinares, M., Sánchez-Moreno, J. & Fountoulakis, K. N. 2014, 'Psychosocial Interventions in Bipolar Disorder: What, for Whom, and When', *Journal of Affective Disorders*, vol. 156, pp. 46–55.

Renouf, N. 2020, "Critical Social Work Beyond the Dominant Approach to Mental Health Practice", in *Doing Critical Social Work*, eds R. Pease, S. Goldingay, N. Hosken & S. Niperess, Routledge, London.

Repper, J. & Carter, T. 2011, 'A Review of the Literature on Peer Support in Mental Health Services', *Journal of Mental Health*, vol. 20, no. 4, pp. 392–411.

Rickwood, D. 2004, 'Recovery in Australia: Slowly but Surely (Guest Editorial)', *Australian e-Journal for the Advancement of Mental Health*, vol. 3, no. 1.

Rickwood, D., Telford, N. R., Parker, A. G., Tanti, C. & McGorry, P. D. 2014, 'Headspace – Australia's Innovation in Youth Mental Health: Who Are the Clients and Why Are They Presenting?', *Medical Journal of Australia*, vol. 200, no. 2, pp. 1–4.

Robinson, E. & Adams, R. 2008, *Housing Stress and the Mental Health and Wellbeing of Families*, Australian Family Relationships Clearinghouse, Canberra.

Robinson, E., Rodgers, B. & Butterworth, P. 2008, *Family Relationships and Mental Illness: Impacts and Service Responses*, Australian Family Relationships Clearinghouse, Canberra.

Rogers, A. & Pilgrim, D. 2003, *Mental Health and Inequality*, Palgrave Macmillan, London.

——— 2010, *A Sociology of Mental Health and Illness*, 4th edn, Open University Press, Maidenhead, UK.

Rolheiser, R. 1998, *Seeking Spirituality*, Hodder & Stoughton, New York.

Rooney, R. 2002, 'Working with Involuntary Clients', in *Social Workers' Desk Reference*, eds A. R. Roberts & G. J. Greene, Oxford University Press, Oxford, pp. 709–13.

Roper, C. 2006, personal communication.

Rose, D. 2008, 'Service User Produced Knowledge', *Journal of Mental Health*, vol. 17, no. 5, pp. 447–51.

Rose, L., Mallinson, K., & Walton-Moss, B. 2002, 'A Grounded Theory of Families Responding to Mental Illness', *Western Journal of Nursing Research*, vol. 24, pp. 516–536.

Rose, N. 1998, 'Governing Risky Individuals: The Role of Psychiatry in New Regimes of Control', *Psychiatry, Psychology and Law*, vol. 5, no. 2, pp. 177–95.

Rosenberg, S. & Hickie, I. 2013, 'Managing Madness: Mental Health and Complexity in Public Policy', *Evidence Base*, no. 3.

Rosenberg, S. & Rosen, A. 2012, 'Can Mental Health Commissions Really Drive Reform? Towards Better Resourcing, Services, Accountability and Stakeholder Engagement', *Australasian Psychiatry*, vol. 20, no. 3, pp. 193–8.

Rosenman, S. 2013, 'The Prodromal Psychosis Debate', *Australian and New Zealand Journal of Psychiatry*, vol. 47, no. 2, pp. 191–2.

Rost, K. 2009, 'Disability from Depression: The Public Health Challenge to Primary Care', *Nordic Journal of Psychiatry*, vol. 63, no. 1, pp. 17–21.

Row, J. 2011, 'Great Expectations: A Systematic Review of the Literature on the Role of Family Carers in Severe Mental Illness, and Their Relationships and Engagement with Professionals', *Journal of Psychiatric and Mental Health Nursing*, Advanced Print. Doi: 10.1111/j.1365-2850.2011.01765.x

Royal Australian and New Zealand College of Psychiatrists (RANZCP) 2013, *Electroconvulsive Therapy (ECT)*. Position Statement No. 74, Melbourne.

Royal Australian and New Zealand College of Psychiatrists (RANZCP) & beyondblue n.d., *Australian Indigenous Mental Health*, Australian and New Zealand College of Psychiatrists, viewed 8 January 2014, http://indigenous.ranzcp.org/index.php.

Royal Australian and New Zealand College of Psychiatrists (RANZCP) Clinical Practice Guidelines Team for Depression 2004, 'Australian and New Zealand Clinical Practice Guidelines for the Treatment of Depression', *Australian and New Zealand Journal of Psychiatry*, vol. 38, no. 6, pp. 389–407.

Royal Australian and New Zealand College of Psychiatrists (RANZCP) Clinical Practice Guidelines Team for the Treatment of Schizophrenia and Related Disorders 2005, 'Royal Australian and New Zealand College of Psychiatrists Clinical Practice Guidelines for the Treatment of Schizophrenia and Related Disorders', *Australian and New Zealand Journal of Psychiatry*, vol. 39, pp. 1–30.

Ryan, C. J. & Large, M. M. 2013, 'Suicide Risk Assessment: Where Are We Now?', *Medical Journal of Australia*, vol. 198, no. 9, pp. 462–3.

Ryan, M., Merighi, J. R., Healy, B. & Renouf, N. 2004, 'Belief, Optimism and Caring: Findings from a Cross-National Study of Expertise in Mental Health Social Work', *Qualitative Social Work*, vol. 3, no. 4, pp. 411–29.

Ryan, P. & Morgan, S. 2004, *Assertive Outreach: A Strengths Approach to Policy and Practice*, Churchill Livingstone, Edinburgh.

Ryle, A. & Kerr, I. B. 2002, *Introducing Cognitive Analytic Therapy: Principles and Practice*, John Wiley & Sons, Chichester, UK.

Sainsbury Centre for Mental Health 1998, *Keys to Engagement*, Briefing 1, Sainsbury Centre for Mental Health, London.

——— 2006, *The Future of Mental Health: A Vision for 2015*, Sainsbury Centre for Mental Health, London.

——— 2009, *Implementing Recovery: A New Framework for Organisational Change*, Sainsbury Centre for Mental Health, London.

Saleebey, D. 1996, 'The Strengths Perspective in Social Work Practice: Extensions and Cautions', *Social Work*, vol. 41, no. 3, pp. 296–305.

——— 2001, 'The Diagnostic Strengths Manual?', *Social Work*, vol. 46, no. 2, pp. 183–7.

Salmon, G. & Rapport, F. 2005, 'Multi-Agency Voices: A Thematic Analysis of Multi-Agency Working Practices Within the Setting of a Child and Adolescent Mental Health Service', *Journal of Interprofessional Care*, vol. 19, no. 5, pp. 429–43.

Sanders, R. 2004, *Sibling Relationships: Theory and Issues for Practice*, Palgrave Macmillan, London.

Sands, R. 2001, *Clinical Social Work Practice in Behavioural Mental Health,* Allyn & Bacon, Boston, MA.

Sands, N., Elsom, S., Gerdtz, M. & Khaw, D. 2012, 'Mental Health-Related Risk Factors for Violence: Using the Evidence to Guide Mental Health Triage Decision Making', *Journal of Psychiatric and Mental Health Nursing*, vol. 19, no. 8, pp. 690–701.

Saunders, J., Crisp, A., Gelder, M., Rix, S., Meltzer, H., & Rowlands, O. 2003, 'Stigmatization of People with Mental Illness', *British Journal of Psychiatry*, vol. 117, pp. 4–7.

Sawyer, A.-M. 2009, 'Mental Health', in *Assessment and Report Writing in the Human Services*, ed. H. Cleak, Cengage Learning, South Melbourne, pp. 73–85.

Sayce, L. 1998, 'Stigma, Discrimination and Social Exclusion: What's in a Word?', *Journal of Mental Health*, vol. 7, no. 4, pp. 331–43.

——— 1999, 'Parenting as a Civil Right: Supporting Service Users Who Choose to Have Children', in *Child Protection and Adult Mental Health: Conflict of Interest?*, eds A. Weir & A. Douglas, Butterworth Heinemann, Oxford, pp. 28–48.

Schwartz, M., Sibert, T. & Mosher, L. 1994, 'Should it be Easier to Commit People Involuntarily to Treatment?', in *Controversial Issues in Mental Health*, eds S. Kirk & S. Einbinder, Allyn & Beacon, Boston, pp. 252–64.

Scott, D. 1993, 'Inter-Agency Collaboration: Why Is It So Difficult? Can We Do It Better?', *Children Australia*, vol. 18, no. 4, pp. 4–9.

Segal, S. P., Silverman, C. J. & Temkin, T. L. 2010, 'Self-Help and Community Mental Health Agency Outcomes: A Recovery-Focused Randomized Controlled Trial', *Psychiatric Services*, vol. 61, no. 9, pp. 905–10.

Sessions, P. & Lightburn, A. 2006, 'What is Community-Based Clinical Practice? Traditions and Transformations', in *Handbook of Community-Based Clinical Practice*, eds A. Lightburn & P. Sessions, Oxford University Press, Oxford, pp. 3–18.

Sevenhuijsen, S. 2000, 'Caring in the Third Way: The Relation between Obligation, Responsibility and Care in *Third Way* Discourse', *Critical Social Policy*, vol. 20, no. 1, pp. 5–37.

Shanks, V., Williams, J., Leamy, M., Bird, V. J., Le Boutillier, C. & Slade, M. 2013, 'Measures of Personal Recovery: A Systematic Review', *Psychiatric Services*, vol. 64, no. 10, pp. 974–80.

Shaw, E. 2004, 'The "Pointy" End of Clinical Supervision: Ethical, Legal and Performance Issues', *Psychotherapy in Australia*, vol. 10, no. 2, pp. 64–70.

Sheldon, M. 2010, 'Reviewing Psychiatric Assessment in Remote Aboriginal Communities', in *Working Together: Aboriginal and Torres Strait Islander Mental Health and Wellbeing Principles and Practice*, eds N. Purdie, P. Dudgeon & R. Walker, Australian Council for Educational Research, Camberwell, Vic., pp. 211–22.

Short, T., Thomas, S., Mullen, P. & Ogloff, J. R. P. 2013, 'Comparing Violence in Schizophrenia Patients with and without Comorbid Substance-Use Disorders to Community Controls', *Acta Psychiatrica Scandinavica*, vol. 128, no. 4, pp. 306–13.

Siegel, A. W. 2008, 'Inequality, Privacy, and Mental Health', *International Journal of Law and Psychiatry*, vol. 31, no. 2, pp. 150–7.

Siegenthaler, E., Munder, T. & Egger, M. 2012, 'Effect of Preventive Interventions in Mentally Ill Parents on the Mental Health of the Offspring: Systematic Review and Meta-Analysis', *Journal of the American Academy of Child and Adolescent Psychiatry*, vol. 51, no. 1, pp. 8–17.

Silver, E. 2006, 'Understanding the Relationship Between Mental Disorder and Violence: The Need for a Criminological Perspective', *Law and Human Behavior*, vol. 30, no. 6, pp. 685–706.

Silverman, M. M. & Berman, A. L. 2014, 'Suicide Risk Assessment and Risk Formulation Part I: A Focus on Suicide Ideation in Assessing Suicide Risk', *Suicide and Life-Threatening Behavior*, vol. 44, no. 4, pp. 420–31.

Simpson, A., Oster, C. & Muir-Cochrane, E. 2018, 'Liminality in the Occupational Identity of Mental Health Peer Support Workers: A Qualitative Study', *International Journal of Mental Health Nursing*, vol. 27, no. 2, pp. 662–71.

Sinding, C., Watt, L., Miller, P., Silliker, J., Lawson, L., Kislinsky, C., Stanzlik-Elliot, C. L., O'Neill, J., Pereira, J. & McGillicuddy, P. 2013, 'Stigmas and Silos: Social Workers' Accounts of Care for People with Serious Mental Illness and Cancer', *Social Work in Mental Health*, vol. 11, no. 3, pp. 288–309.

Singh, B. 2012, 'The Preventive Model', in *Mental Health in Australia: Collaborative Community Practice*, 3rd edn, eds G. Meadows, J. Farhall, E. Fossey, M. Grigg, F. McDermott & B. Singh, Oxford University Press, Melbourne, pp. 56–9.

Singh, B. & Kirkby, K. 2007, 'The Psychiatric Interview, Mental State Examination and Formulation', in *Foundations of Clinical Psychiatry*, 3rd edn, eds S. Bloch & B. S. Singh, Melbourne University Press, Melbourne, pp. 91–125.

Sklar, M., Groessl, E. J., O'Connell, M., Davidson, L. & Aarons, G. A. 2013, 'Instruments for Measuring Mental Health Recovery: A Systematic Review', *Clinical Psychology Review*, vol. 33, no. 8, pp. 1082–95.

Slade, M. 2009, 'The Contribution of Mental Health Services to Recovery', *Journal of Mental Health*, vol. 18, no. 5, pp. 367–71.

——— 2012, 'Everyday Solutions for Everyday Problems: How Mental Health Systems Can Support Recovery', *Psychiatric Services*, vol. 63, no. 7, pp. 702–4.

Slade, M., Amering, M., Frkas, M., O'Hagan, M., Panther, G . . . Whitely, R. 2014, 'Uses and Abuses of Recovery: Implementing Recovery-Oriented Practices in Mental Health Systems', *World Psychiatry*, 13, pp. 12–20.

Slade, T., Johnston, A., Teesson, M., Whiteford, H., Burgess, P., Pirkis, J. & Saw, S. 2009, *The Mental Health of Australians 2: Report on the 2007 National Survey of Mental Health and Wellbeing*, Department of Health and Ageing, Canberra.

Smale, G., Tuson, G., Biehal, N. & Marsh, P. 1993, *Empowerment, Assessment, Care Management and the Skilled Worker*, HMSO, London.

Social Exclusion Unit 2004, *Mental Health and Social Exclusion: Social Exclusion Unit Report*, Social Exclusion Unit, Office of the Deputy Prime Minister, London.

Social Health Reference Group 2004, *Social and Emotional Well Being Framework: A National Strategic Framework for Aboriginal and Torres Strait Islander Peoples' Mental Health and Social and Emotional Well Being 2004–09*, National Aboriginal and Torres Strait Islander Health Council and National Mental Health Working Group, Canberra.

Solomon, P., Draine, J. & Delaney, M. A. 1995, 'The Working Alliance and Consumer Case Management', *Journal of Mental Health Administration*, vol. 22, no. 2, pp. 126–34.

Somers, V. 2007, 'Schizophrenia: The Impact of Parental Illness on Children', *British Journal of Social Work*, vol. 37, no. 8, pp. 1319–34.

Sousa, L. & Rodrigues, S. 2012, 'The Collaborative Professional: Towards Empowering Vulnerable Families', *Journal of Social Work Practice*, vol. 26, no. 4, pp. 411–25.

Stafford, M., De Silva, M., Stansfeld, S. & Marmot, M. 2008, 'Neighbourhood Social Capital and Common Mental Disorder: Testing the Link in a General Population Sample', *Health & Place*, vol. 14, no. 3, pp. 394–405.

Stanford, S. N. 2011, 'Constructing Moral Responses to Risk: A Framework for Hopeful Social Work Practice', *British Journal of Social Work*, vol. 41, no. 8, pp. 1514–31.

Stout, C. E. & Hayes, R. A. (eds) 2005, *The Evidence-Based Practice: Methods, Models and Tools for Mental Health Professionals*, John Wiley & Sons, Hoboken, NJ.

Substance Abuse and Mental Health Services Administration (SAMHSA) 2003, *Illness Management and Recovery Implementation Resource Kit*, SAMHSA, http://mentalhealth.samhsa.gov/cmhs/communitysupport/toolkits/illness/userguide/default.asp.

Sutherland, K. 2020, *Social Work Psychosocial Assessment Guide*, 2edn., Social Work and Welfare Clinical Education Program: Queensland Health, Unpublished. https://msh-qld.libguides.com/SWLibguide.

Swan, P. & Raphael, B. 1995, *Ways Forward: National Aboriginal and Torres Strait Islander Mental Health Policy National Consultancy Report*, Commonwealth of Australia, Canberra.

Szmukler, G. I. & Bloch, S. 1997, 'Family Involvement in the Care of People with Psychoses: An Ethical Argument', *British Journal of Psychiatry*, vol. 171, pp. 401–5.

Tanenbaum, S. 2003, 'Evidence-Based Practice in Mental Health: Practical Weaknesses Meet Political Strengths', *Journal of Evaluation in Clinical Practice*, vol. 9, no. 2, pp. 287–301.

Taylor, E. H. 2006, 'The Weaknesses of the Strengths Model: Mental Illness as a Case in Point', *Best Practices in Mental Health*, vol. 2, no. 1, pp. 1–30.

Taylor, S. & Abramowitz, J. S. 2013, 'Dissemination of Psychosocial Treatments for Anxiety: The Importance of Taking a Broad Perspective', *Journal of Anxiety Disorders*, vol. 27, no. 8, pp. 802–4.

Terkelsen, K. 1987, 'The Evolution of Family Response to Mental Illness through Time', in *Families of the Mentally Ill: Coping and Adaptation*, eds A. B. Hatfield & H. Lefley, Guilford Press, New York.

Test, M. A. & Stein, L. I. 2000, 'Practical Guidelines for the Community Treatment of Markedly Impaired Patients', *Community Mental Health Journal*, vol. 36, no. 1, pp. 47–60.

Tew, J. & Anderson, J. 2004, 'The Mental Health Dimension in the New Social Work Degree: Starting a Debate', *Social Work Education*, vol. 23, no. 2.

Tew, J., Ramon, S., Slade, M., Bird, V., Melton, J. & Le Boutillier, C. 2012, 'Social Factors and Recovery from Mental Health Difficulties: A Review of the Evidence', *British Journal of Social Work*, vol. 42, no. 3, pp. 443–60.

Thomas, A. C., Cairney, S., Gunthorpe, W., Paradies, Y. & Sayers, S. 2010, 'Strong Souls: Development and Validation of a Culturally Appropriate Tool for Assessment of Social and Emotional Well-Being in Indigenous Youth', *Australian and New Zealand Journal of Psychiatry*, vol. 44, no. 1, pp. 40–8.

Thomas, A. C. & Staiger, P. K. 2012, 'Introducing Mental Health and Substance Use Screening into a Community-Based Health Service in Australia: Usefulness and Implications for Service Change', *Health & Social Care in the Community*, vol. 20, no. 6, pp. 635–44.

Thornicroft, G. 2011, 'European Mental Health Policy: The Key Issue Is Social Inclusion', *European Journal of Public Health*, vol. 21, no. 5, pp. 548–9.

Thyer, B. A. & Wodarski, J. S. 2007, *Social Work in Mental Health: An Evidence-Based Approach*, John Wiley & Sons, Hoboken, NJ.

Topor, A., Borg, M., Mezzina, R., Sells, D., Marin, I. & Davidson, L. 2006, 'Others: The Role of Family, Friends, and Professionals in the Recovery Process', *American Journal of Psychiatric Rehabilitation*, vol. 9, no. 1, pp. 17–37.

Treatment Protocol Project 2004, *Management of Mental Disorders Vol. 1*, 4th edn, World Health Organization Collaborating Centre for Evidence in Mental Health Policy, Sydney.

Trevillion, S. 1999, *Networking and Community Partnership*, 2nd edn, Ashgate, Aldershot, UK.

Trondsen, M. V. 2012, 'Living with a Mentally Ill Parent', *Qualitative Health Research*, vol. 22, no. 2, pp. 174–88.

Tucker, R. P., Crowley, K. J., Davidson, C. L. & Gutierrez, P. M. 2015, 'Risk Factors, Warning Signs, and Drivers of Suicide: What Are They. How do They Differ, and Why Does It Matter?', *Suicide and Life-Threatening Behavior*, vol. 45, no. 6, pp. 679–89.

Tune, D. 2019, *Department of Social Services Review of the National Disability Insurance Scheme,* Act 2013, www.dss.gov.au/sites/default/files/documents/01_2020/ndis . . .

Tutu, D. 2004, *God Has a Dream*, Rider, London.

Tyrer, P. 2009, 'Are General Practitioners Really Unable to Diagnose Depression?', *Lancet*, vol. 374, no. 9690, pp. 589–90.

United Nations (UN) 2006, *Convention on the Rights of Persons with Disabilities*, United Nations Department of Public Information, viewed 7 March 2009, www.un.org/disabilities/convention/conventionfull.shtml.

UPenn Collaborative on Community Integration 2008, *Parenting with a Mental Illness: Programs and Resources*, UPenn Collaborative on Community Integration, Philadelphia.

Vaillant, G. E. 1992, 'The Beginning of Wisdom Is Never Calling a Patient a Borderline; or, the Clinical Management of Immature Defenses in the Treatment of Individuals with Personality Disorders', *Journal of Psychotherapy Practice and Research*, vol. 1, no. 2, pp. 117–34.

Van Hook, M. P. 2003, 'Psychosocial Issues Within Primary Health Care Settings: Challenges and Opportunities for Social Work Practice', *Social Work in Health Care*, vol. 38, no. 1, pp. 63–80.

Vaughn, C. E. & Leff, J. P. 1976, 'The Measurement of Expressed Emotion in the Families of Psychiatric Patients', *British Journal of Social and Clinical Psychology*, vol. 15, no. 2, pp. 157–65.

——— 1981, 'Patterns of Emotional Response in Relatives of Schizophrenic Patients', *Schizophrenia Bulletin*, vol. 7, no. 1, pp. 43–4.

Ventura, J., Subotnik, K. L., Gretchen-Doorly, D., Casaus, L., Boucher, M., Medalia, A., . . . Nuechterlein, K. H. 2019, 'Cognitive Remediation Can Improve Negative Symptoms and Social Functioning in First-Episode Schizophrenia: A Randomized Controlled Trial. *Schizophrenia Research*, vol. 203, pp. 24–31.

VicHealth 2005, *A Plan for Action 2005–2007: Promoting Mental Health and Wellbeing*, VicHealth, Melbourne.

Victorian Community Council against Violence 2005, *Identifying and Responding to Family Violence: A Guide for Mental Health Clinicians in Victoria*, Victorian Community Council against Violence, Melbourne.

Victorian Government Department of Health 2013, *National Practice Standards for the Mental Health Workforce*, Department of Health, Melbourne.

Victorian Government Department of Human Services 1996, *Needs for Service Assessment and Review: A Collaborative Approach, Resources for Case Managers*, 2nd edn, Victorian Government Department of Human Services, Aged, Community and Mental Health Division, Melbourne.

Victorian Government Department of Human Services, Community and Mental Health Division 1998, *Individual Service Planning*, Resources for Case Managers, Victorian Government Department of Human Services, Aged, Community and Mental Health Division, Melbourne.

Wadsworth, Y. (ed.) 2001, *The Essential U & I: A One-Volume Presentation of the Findings of a Lengthy Grounded Study of Whole Systems Change Towards Staff – Consumer Collaboration for Enhancing Mental Health Services, in Ongoing Collaboration with Merinda Epstein*, Victorian Health Promotion Foundation, Melbourne.

Waghorn, G. 2013, 'Severe Mental Illness and Work', *Australian and New Zealand Journal of Psychiatry*, vol. 47, no. 5, pp. 488–9.

Wakefield, J. C. 2013, 'The DSM-5 Debate Over the Bereavement Exclusion: Psychiatric Diagnosis and the Future of Empirically Supported Treatment', *Clinical Psychology Review*, vol. 33, no. 7, pp. 825–45.

Walker, G. & Bryant, W. 2013, 'Peer Support in Adult Mental Health Services: A Metasynthesis of Qualitative Findings', *Psychiatric Rehabilitation Journal*, vol. 36, no. 1, pp. 28–34.

Walker, S. & Beckett, C. 2011, *Social Work Assessment and Intervention*, 2nd edn, Russell House, Lyme Regis, UK.

Walsh, P. E., McMillan, S. S., Stewart, V. & Wheeler, A. J. 2018, 'Understanding Paid Peer Support in Mental Health', *Disability & Society*, vol. 33, no. 4, pp. 579–97.

Wasow, M. 1995, *The Skipping Stone*, Science and Behavior Books, Palo Alto, CA.

Webber, M. 2011, *Evidence-Based Policy and Practice in Mental Health Social Work*, Post-Qualifying Social Work Practice, 2nd edn, Learning Matters, Exeter, UK.

Weeks, W. 2004, 'Creating Attractive Services Which Citizens Want to Attend', *Australian Social Work*, vol. 57, no. 4, pp. 319–30.

Weick, A., Rapp, C., Sullivan, W. P. & Kisthardt, W. 1989, 'A Strengths Perspective for Social Work Practice', *Social Work*, vol. 34, no. 4, pp. 350–4.

Weissman, H., Epstein, I. & Savage, A. 1983, *Agency-Based Social Work: Neglected Aspects of Clinical Practice*, Temple University Press, Philadelphia, PA.

Wellman, N. 2006, 'Assessing Risk', in *Working with Serious Mental Illness: A Manual for Clinical Practice*, 2nd edn, eds C. Gamble & G. Brennan, Elsevier, Edinburgh, pp. 145–63.

Wesley Mission 2007, *Living with Mental Illness*, Wesley Mission, Sydney.

Wharne, S. 2005, 'Assertive Outreach Teams: Their Roles and Functions', *Journal of Interprofessional Care*, vol. 19, no. 4, pp. 326–37.

White, S., Fook, J. & Gardner, F. (eds) 2006, *Critical Reflection in Health and Social Care*, Open University Press, Maidenhead, UK.

Whiteford, H. & McKeon, G. 2012, *System-Level Intersectoral Linkages between the Mental Health and Non-Clinical Support Sectors*, School of Population Health, University of Queensland, Brisbane.

Whitehead, A. (ed.) 2002, *The ARAFMI Story: A History of the First 25 Years of ARAFMI in Queensland*, ARAFMI, Brisbane.

Whittington, C. 2003, 'A Model of Collaboration', in *Collaboration in Social Work Practice*, eds J. Weinstein, C. Whittington & T. Leiba, Jessica Kingsley Publishers, London, pp. 39–61.

Wilkinson, C. & McAndrew, S. 2008, ' "I'm not an Outsider, I'm His Mother": A Phenomenological Enquiry into Carer Experiences of Exclusion from Acute Psychiatric Wards', *International Journal of Mental Health Nursing*, vol. 17, pp. 292–401.

Willshire, L. 1999, 'Psychiatric Services: Organizing Impossibility', *Human Relations*, vol. 52, no. 6, pp. 775–804.

Wilson, G. & Daly, M. 2007, 'Shaping the Future of Mental Health Policy and Legislation in Northern Ireland: The Impact of Service User and Professional Social Work Discourses', *British Journal of Social Work*, vol. 37, no. 3, pp. 423–39.

Woodhouse, D. & Pengelly, P. 1991, *Anxiety and the Dynamics of Collaboration*, Aberdeen University Press, Aberdeen.

Woolford, A. 2013, 'Paul Brodwin, Everyday Ethics: Voices from the Front Line of Community Psychiatry', *Social Service Review*, vol. 87, no. 4, pp. 816–20.

World Health Organization (WHO) 1986, *Ottawa Charter for Health Promotion*, World Health Organization, Geneva.

——— 1997, *The Jakarta Declaration on Leading Health Promotion into the 21st Century*, World Health Organization, Geneva.

——— 2001, *World Health Report: New Understanding; New Hope*, World Health Organization, Geneva.

Wyder, M. & Bland, R. 2014, 'The Recovery Framework as a Way of Understanding Families' Responses to Mental Illness: Balancing Different Needs and Recovery Journeys', *Australian Social Work*, vol. 67, no. 2, pp. 179–96.

Wyder, M., Bland, R. & Crompton, D. 2013, 'Personal Recovery and Involuntary Mental Health Admissions: The Importance of Control, Relationships and Hope', *Health*, vol. 5, no. 3A, pp. 574–81.

Wyder, M., Bland, R., McCann, K. & Crompton, D. 2018, 'The Family Experience of the Crisis of Involuntary Treatment in Mental Health', *Australian Social Work*. DOI: 10.1080/0312407X.2018.1454484.

Zipursky, R. B., Reilly, T. J. & Murray, R. M. 2013, 'The Myth of Schizophrenia as a Progressive Brain Disease', *Schizophrenia Bulletin*, vol. 39, no. 6, pp. 1363–72.

Zisook, S., Anzia, J., Atri, A., Baroni, A., Clayton, P., Haller, E., Lomax, J. W., Mann, J. J., Oquendo, M. A., Pato, M., Perez-Rodriguez, M. M., Prabhakar, D., Sen, S., Thrall, G. & Yaseen, Z. S. 2013, 'Teaching Evidence-Based Approaches to Suicide Risk Assessment and Prevention That Enhance Psychiatric Training', *Comprehensive Psychiatry*, vol. 54, no. 3, pp. 201–8.

Index

Note: Page numbers in *italics* indicate a figure and page numbers in **bold** indicate a table on the corresponding page.